MW01200501

The Memoirs of Ardeshir Zahedi: Volume One

The Memoirs of Ardeshir Zahedi

Volume One:
From Childhood to the
End of My Father's Premiership

as told to
Ahmad Ahrar

English translation by
Farhang Jahanpour

Ibex Publishers,
Bethesda, Maryland

The Memoirs of Ardeshir Zahedi.
Volume One: From Childhood to the End of My Father's Premiership
As told to Ahmad Ahrar
English translation by Farhang Jahanpour

Copyright © 2012 Ardeshir Zahedi

Manufactured in the United States of America

The paper used in this book meets the minimum requirements of the American National Standard for Information Services—Permanence of Paper for Printed Library Materials, ANSI Z39.48–1984

Ibex Publishers strives to create books which are as complete and free of errors as possible. Please help us with future editions by reporting any errors or suggestions for improvement to the address below, or corrections@ibexpub.com

Ibex Publishers, Inc.
Post Office Box 30087
Bethesda, Maryland 20824
Telephone: 301–718–8188
Facsimile: 301–907–8707
www.ibexpublishers.com

Library of Congress Cataloging-in-Publication Data

Zahidi, Ardashir, 1928-
[Khatirat-i Ardashir Zahidi. English]
The memoirs of Ardeshir Zahedi / as told to Ahmad Ahrar ;
[English translation by Farhang Jahanpour].
p. cm.
Includes bibliographical references and index.
ISBN 978-1-58814-073-9 (hardcover : alk. paper) 1. Zahidi, Ardashir, 1928- 2. Diplomats—Iran--Biography. 3. Iran--Politics and government—1925-1979. I. Ahrar, Ahmad. II. Title.
DS316.9.Z335A313 2011
327.550092—dc22
[B]
2010044783

For Mahnaz

Table of Contents

Foreword to the English Edition

The English translation of the first volume of my four-volume memoirs and the related documents is being published with a great deal of delay, due to some technical faults that were beyond my control. I regret this unintended delay, and I apologize to my friends and those who have shown an interest in my book for the wait.

The first volume of my memoirs covers the period from my childhood and youth to my early political life, which also coincides with some major political developments and many ups and downs in Iran's contemporary history in which I have been either directly or indirectly involved. This volume ends with my father's resignation from his post as the prime minister of Iran and his departure from the country.

To the non-Iranian reader the most important part of the first volume may be the section that deals with the documents about the end of Dr. Mohammad Mossadegh's government, His Majesty Mohammad Reza Shah Pahlavi's short absence from the country, and the reinstatement of the monarchy by my father General Fazlollah Zahedi, with the support of the majority of the Iranian people, the prominent leaders of the society, and the clerics.

The second volume of the book deals with the years when my father lived abroad, my marriage to Her Royal Highness Princess Shahnaz Pahlavi, the Shah's only daughter by the former Queen Fawzia, my father's illness, my first mission to Washington (from 1959 to 1961) during the administrations of President Dwight D. Eisenhower and President John F. Kennedy, my mission to the United Kingdom (from 1962 to 1966), my father's death, and finally my work as the Iranian foreign minister in the year 1966.

The third volume covers the period of my work at the Ministry of Foreign Affairs (from 1966 to 1972), a period that coincided with the Six-Day War between the Arabs and the Israelis, and Iran's extensive diplomatic activities in many countries of the world in order to establish peace and stability in the Middle East.

The fourth volume of the memoirs covers my second term as Iranian ambassador in the United States (from 1972 to 1979), Iran's collapse after the Islamic revolution, the Shah's illness, and my efforts to try to find a suitable place of residence for the royal family. It also deals with the Shah's worsening health situation and the stories of the hospitality and gallantry of the late President Anwar Sadat of Egypt and His Majesty the late King Hasan II of Morocco. It ends with the Shah's passing and my efforts to find a way out of the Iranian crisis.

The point worth making is that for many years, due to reasons that we cannot deal with here, incorrect assessments were made of those events that changed Iran's fate, as well as initiated a political transformation in the world, which upset the balance of power under those circumstances that existed during the Cold War. However, in recent years, historians and scholars have become more familiar with the publication of some American, French, British, and Italian secret documents that have completely changed the earlier assessments. One can say that to a large extent some realistic, better-balanced, and impartial analyses have replaced the earlier accounts that were based on political and ideological prejudices.

In writing about those events, I have tried to recount the facts based on what I had personally witnessed, making every endeavor not to be swayed by family links and sentiments or by personal bias. Whenever I have expressed my personal views I have clearly stated this, so that the reader can judge for himself. Fortunately, the official documents and unbiased accounts that are now available confirm the veracity of these notes. Therefore, I hope that the first volume of my memoirs will help shed fresh light on one of the most important political events after the Second World War.

In the introduction to the French edition of my memoirs, which was published in 2009, I referred to a number of leading personalities in Europe or in the Mediterranean area and expressed my views and my gratitude to them. Clearly, a number of prominent British figures were included in that list. As the English translation is intended to be read by people in the English-speaking world, I will once again make brief references to some of them. However, most of the names mentioned in this foreword concern American personalities, with whom I had more intimate dealings and who played a more prominent role in Iranian affairs.

At the moment, I am passing through the twilight of my life, and I do not know whether God will grant me the chance to see the publication of the subsequent volumes of the book or not. Therefore, in this foreword I wish to mention the names of all the officials and friends that I can remember, so that I have paid my debt of gratitude to them and so that my conscience will be at peace.

Apart from Switzerland, which is my present place of residence and my family's second home, most of my time spent outside Iran has been in the United States. Firstly, I received my higher education there. It was in the United States that I became familiar with the scientific environment of the Western world. I benefited from the instruction of erudite professors, and as a result, the English language has become my best foreign language and in fact my second language.

On two occasions, the first time for three years (from 1959 to 1961) and the second time for seven years (from 1972 to 1979), I served as my country's ambassador to the United States. The first time I lived there with my wife Princess Shahnaz, the oldest child of the Shah of Iran, and the second time I lived there alone.

My second mission to the United States coincided with the heyday of Iran's international power, followed by the beginning of a religious revolution that ended the three-millennia-old monarchy in Iran. Naturally, during that period, Iran's relations with the rest of the world experienced many ups and downs, which I had to deal with on the basis of my many acquaintances, various contacts, and interesting relations with American leaders and the many prominent people in the ruling establishment.

Before my second mission in America, I served for four years as the Iranian ambassador to London (from 1962 to 1966), and then from 1966 to 1972 I served as Iran's foreign minister. In the course of those missions, I got to know nearly all the leading figures in the world and established friendly relations with them. My reminiscences of meetings with those personalities have been recorded briefly in the four volumes of my memoirs. However, I believe that it is my duty to mention the names of some of the personalities who are from the English-speaking world, especially from America, in this foreword so that I have discharged my debt to them.

My Contacts with American Presidents

Unfortunately, I never had the good fortune to meet with President **Harry S. Truman**, but no Iranian can ever forget the major role that he played in the liberation of Iranian Azerbaijan and Kurdistan. With his historic message to Joseph Stalin after the end of the Second World War, when Soviet forces were refusing to leave Iran, President Truman prevented the continuous presence of the Red Army and the interference of Russian forces in my country. Also, Iran was the first country that benefited from his development and reconstruction policy, known as "Truman's Point Four Program." That program was implemented under the supervision of a joint Iranian and American committee.

During the visit of the Shah and Queen Soraya to the United States in 1954, we got the opportunity to meet and get acquainted with President Truman's daughter, Margaret Truman, and her husband, Mr. Clifton Daniel, who was one of the managers of the *New York Times*. My friendship with them continued for many years after the Iranian revolution.

My first meeting with General **Dwight D. Eisenhower**, who was U.S. president from 1953 to 1961, was during the time when I was still a student, when after the end of the Second World War he served as the president of Columbia University (from 1948 to 1953). Our first formal meeting was in the year 1954 during the Shah's official visit to the United States at President Eisenhower's invitation. I was honored to meet him and get acquainted with him again when he came on an official visit to Iran in 1958. At that time, I was the Shah's civilian adjutant, and I was given the task of acting as President Eisenhower's host during his short stay in Tehran.

I remember that the welcoming ceremonies that were arranged for President Eisenhower were very warm and magnificent, befitting the visit of such a powerful friend at the height of the Cold War. He delivered an important speech in the joint session of the Iranian parliament and the senate, and then took part in a luncheon that had been given in his honor by the Shah. I shall provide more details of that visit in the second volume of my memoirs.

As it happened, a year later (in 1959) I was appointed Iran's ambassador to Washington and went to the United States with my wife Princess Shahnaz. During our first formal meeting, when I was submitting my credentials to President Eisenhower, I came to realize that not only was he a military genius who had won the Second World War but that he was also someone who had a deep grasp of international affairs. He spoke to me in detail about the situation in Kurdistan, and subsequently some American newspapers that did not even know where Kurdistan was wrote that he had spoken about Khuzestan. This was totally wrong, and we had no discussion regarding Khuzestan.

An event that made President Eisenhower very popular with the Muslims, especially the Arabs, was his and his Foreign Secretary John Foster Dulles's opposition to the Israeli, French, and British invasion of Egypt and the Suez Canal in the year 1956, which led to Sir Anthony Eden's resignation.

Our close friendship with President Eisenhower, his gracious wife Mamie, and their family continued to the end of his life. I can say that President Eisenhower was a true friend and lover of Iran. He had a great deal of respect for the Iranian monarch, and he very well understood and sympathized with Iran's stance in international issues.[1]

---

[1] One can clearly see examples of the wisdom and understanding of that great general and politician in James Ledbetter's book, *Unwarranted Influence: Dwight D. Eisenhower and the Military-Industrial Complex*, and his article in the *New York Times* entitled "What Ike Got Right," in which he wrote about fifty years of the military-industrial complex.

President **Richard M. Nixon** previously served as vice president under President Eisenhower, and the first time that I had the honor of getting to know him was in 1953, when he came to Iran at the time when my father was prime minister. Many years later, after Presidents Kennedy and Johnson, he was elected president.

Richard Nixon had a profound understanding of international and geopolitical issues and was a friend of Iran and the Iranians. That sincere friendship continued to the end of his life, so much so that he took part in the Shah's funeral in Cairo. He bravely and strongly criticized and condemned President Carter's policies toward Iran.

My friendship with him and his gracious wife Pat (Thelma Catherine) continued to the end of their lives, and anytime that they came to Europe I was honored to act as their host in Montreux. How can I forget that when my mother was in the last days of her life due to cancer, Richard Nixon and his wife Pat came all the way from America specially to see her and to sympathize with me? That was a time when, after Iran's collapse, many former friends or pseudo-friends—both Iranian and foreigners—had turned their backs on us. I shall never forget his warm and generous friendship.

I believe that in future, history will alter its judgment about President Nixon as examples of his farsightedness and political skill are recorded. With hindsight, these will exonerate him despite his having made some mistakes. One example of his political achievements was establishing relations with Communist China, and today we can see what a wise and farsighted policy that was.

I first met **John F. Kennedy** and his wife **Jacqueline Kennedy** (the future American first lady) in 1954 at a reception in the residence of Mr. and Mrs. Charles B. Wrightsman in Palm Beach, Florida, on the occasion of the visit of the Shah and Queen Soraya to the United States. His father Joseph Kennedy and his mother Mrs. Rose Kennedy, who were among the most influential figures in America, were also present at that reception. Following that visit I maintained friendly relations with Kennedy and his brothers until they came to power and for a long time afterward. I represented Iran in Kennedy's presidential inauguration ceremony. Later on, I used to see him frequently, and I will write about those meetings in the second volume of my memoirs. They are among the major events in my diplomatic life.

I also had friendly relations with President Kennedy's chief of protocol, Angier Biddle Duke, who was a very active and energetic man and who later served as U.S. ambassador to Morocco, Spain, and Norway. The account of that friendship will be given in the second volume of the memoirs.

My friendship with the **Kennedy Family** (the father, the mother, and children) dates from my first term as Iranian ambassador in Washington in the course of a visit to Florida. Those friendly relations continued during both terms that I served as Iranian ambassador in the United States.

Most people regarded Senator Edward Kennedy as an anti-Iranian figure who criticized the Shah in his speeches, and one whose criticisms were often illogical. However, it should be pointed out that he was also open to hearing and accepting the views of his opponents. He was prepared to listen to what they had to say and to accept what seemed reasonable to him.

This attitude had developed when he and his wife Joan came to Iran in the 1970s on my personal invitation, where they were received by the Shah and also met with a large number of political and cultural figures. He took part in a meeting with a number of students of Tehran University and patiently and courteously listened to their harsh criticisms of American policies in the world and his brother's record in Vietnam, although later on he also complained about that meeting.

In the United States too, although he was a Democratic senator, he would willingly listen to the criticisms of Republicans. He always adopted an impartial and non-prejudicial stance in relation to America's national interests.

After the revolution, when he came to Switzerland as the head of a delegation, he came to see me, another example of his fair, impartial, and measured attitude. He had a very open and tolerant attitude, and most leading and influential American politicians praised him for those characteristics.

I knew President **Lyndon B. Johnson** and his wife Lady Bird from the time that he was a senator. Those friendly relations continued during the time that he served as vice president and later as president. Both President Johnson and his wife, as well as the rest of the family, were warm and hospitable people. My relations with that family continued even after the end of his presidential term, and I find it necessary to express my thanks for their kindness and friendship.

Here, I also find it necessary to make a short reference to Senator **Hubert Humphrey**, vice president under President Johnson. I got to know him when I served as Iran's ambassador in Washington, and later on when I was serving as foreign minister that friendship was renewed. Vice President Humphrey was a very kind and friendly person. The friendship between Mr. and Mrs. Humphrey and my wife Princess Shahnaz and myself continued to the end of his life, and I will never forget those mutual friendships. When he died, I made sure to attend his funeral.

Gerald Ford succeeded President Nixon. I knew him from the time when he was a congressman and later on as the minority leader of the House of Representatives. He and his wife Betty were warm and hospitable friends. They had a strong affection for Iran which they did not refrain from expressing. I do not forget the kindness and friendship they showed me.

During President Ford's term, White House counsel **Phil Buchen** was one of the legal advisers and close associates of the president. He was a powerful man who was highly respected by both the Democratic and Republican Party leaders and members. Both he and his wife **Bunny** were close friends of ours, and that friendship continued till after the revolution. Not only was he a good friend of mine, he even provided help and guidance to many Iranians who were facing problems in the United States.

I will write in detail about President **Jimmy Carter** and his policies during and after the Islamic revolution in the fourth volume of my memoirs. This short note only concerns his personal and human characteristics and those of his wife **Rosalynn Smith Carter**. My personal relations with him were very warm and friendly, and I have often experienced his goodwill from him.

As far as I remember, he was the only U.S. president who offered hospitality to the Iranian royal family not only in a formal way but also privately. He arranged a lunch for Queen Farah (the Shah's wife), and when her mother and children came to the United States, on my request Mrs. Carter arranged a visit for them at the White House.

My main aim in making these comments is to show that, in addition to political issues, one should also remember the personal compassion and kindness of the Carters, especially President Carter's concern for peace and reconciliation, to which he has devoted his life since leaving office. In 2002, Carter was awarded the Nobel Peace Prize.

In Carter's administration, National Security Advisor **Zbigniew Brzezinski** was a remarkable personality, who boldly supported Iran during his mandate, and I worked closely with him during my last years of ambassadorship. When Brzezinski was at Columbia University, he visited Iran and had a meeting with Foreign Minister Abbas Aram. Later, when secretary of state Cyrus Vance appealed to me to convince the reluctant Bhutto of Pakistan—my noble friend who was brutally killed—to participate in the CENTO conference in Tehran, Brzezinski as the head of the NSC followed up on the issue and was in contact with me almost daily. Mr. Bhutto ultimately agreed to attend the conference. I will never forget Brzezinski's and his wife Emilie Benes Brzezinski's friendship and support during those crucial days.

My friendship with that noble man, President **Ronald Reagan**, and his kind wife Nancy started in the year 1960, was renewed in 1972, and continued to the end of his life. From the moment that Ronald Reagan started his campaign as the presidential candidate of the Republican Party, he very quickly became the symbol of a kind of revival of American political life and the start of the decline of Soviet imperialism. At that time, I predicted that he would be the man of the future not only for America but for the world as a whole.

Later on, I met him in Walter Hubert Annenberg's house, Rancho Mirage, near Palm Springs, California. Walter Annenberg was a prominent figure who subsequently served as ambassador in Great Britain. During that meeting, I had long talks with Mr. Reagan and I invited him to visit Iran as my personal guest. My enemies, who were many in the government and in the court, told the Shah that his visit to Iran might cause problems with our relations with the Carter administration. In this way, they created doubts in the Shah's mind about the wisdom of inviting Mr. Reagan to Iran.

I told the Shah that I was his ambassador and that I knew America and the Americans better than others, and I believed that Mr. Reagan's visit would be in Iran's interest, and if he did not accept my view I would hand in my resignation. Finally, Mr. Reagan came to Iran and stayed in my home in Hesarak. He also met with the Shah and the Shahbanou, and he traveled from north to south and from east to west of Iran and became completely familiar with Iran and the situation in the country. Later on, we noticed how he spoke about Iran and how warmly he praised it. I will provide the details of that visit in the fourth volume of my memoirs.

Certainly, history will speak of President Reagan as one of the greatest American presidents and as the man who emerged as the winner of the Cold War against communism. After President Reagan's death, my friendly relations with Mrs. Nancy Reagan continued for many years.

My friendship with that truly noble and kind man, President **George H. W. Bush**, started in the 1960s when he served first as a congressman, then as U.S. ambassador to the United Nations, director of the Central Intelligence Agency, vice president, and, finally, president. That initial acquaintance developed into a close friendship that continued during his presidency.

President Bush and First Lady Barbara Bush showed me the greatest kindness, and even after the revolution, when many of my Iranian and foreign friends had turned their backs on me, President and Mrs. Bush continued their friendship toward me and my family. They entertained me during the time when he was vice president during the

Reagan administration, in the White House when he was president, and later on in their own home. They showed me great affection and friendship, something that I shall never forget.

Political Figures

My acquaintance with **Nelson Rockefeller** started in 1958, when at the invitation of **David Rockefeller**, the chairman and chief executive of Chase Manhattan Bank, and as part of the IEBC programs I visited the branches of that bank in New York, Chicago, and Puerto Rico.

Those friendly relations were strengthened when I, together with my wife Princess Shahnaz and our daughter Mahnaz, went to America and lived there between 1959 and 1961. During the period when Nelson Rockefeller served as vice president to President Gerald Ford, our friendship was further strengthened. When Nelson Rockefeller died, I was with the Shah. I asked him to allow me to attend the funeral accompanied by His Royal Highness the Crown Prince Reza. Although I had been duly invited to the funeral, which was also attended by the then President Carter, due to a delay in my flight I did not arrive in New York in time to attend the funeral and to express the Shah's condolences to the Rockefeller family.

During President Gerald Ford's administration, when the Shah paid an official visit to the United States, Nelson Rockefeller arranged a sumptuous reception in his honor on his own private estate, from where the Shah flew straight to Europe. Nelson Rockefeller also took part in the ceremonies in the Shah's honor at the Kennedy Center, followed by a reception at the Iranian Embassy in Washington.

Those friendly relations, which were partly due to the efforts of an honorable man, former Senator Claiborne Pell, helped to cement close relations between the Shah and Nelson Rockefeller, and those relations continued until after the Iranian revolution.

I should add that when the Shah was looking for a place to live abroad after the Iranian revolution, Nelson and David Rockefeller, as well as Henry Kissinger, made great efforts to find a suitable place for the residence of the royal family. When the Shah was in Aswan in Egypt, David Rockefeller got in touch with me from Greece and asked to visit him. We arranged for that meeting to take place, and it had a very positive effect on the morale of my dear monarch.

Senator **Jay Rockefeller**, a great person and member of the Rockefeller family, is a kind and faithful friend. During his inauguration ceremony as the governor of West Virginia, which took place during the Carter administration, I was the only foreign ambassador invited. I flew to the ceremony in a small aircraft and was warmly received by him and by Nelson Rockefeller and Senator Percy. Senator Percy asked me to go back to Washington in Mr. Rockefeller's private plane, and, as the Secretary of State Cyrus Vance was also with us on that flight from Virginia to Washington, it provided an opportunity for us to talk and to become closer.

My personal friendship with the members of the Rockefeller family still continues.

Senator **Howard Baker** was an influential Republican senator, and his first wife Joy was the daughter of a former Senate minority leader, Everett Dirksen. When Princess Fatemeh, the Shah's sister, was studying in Washington, D.C., she was a fellow student and friend of Mrs. Baker and the sisters of General Dr. Moarefi. General Moarefi was active in the purchase of weapons from the United States, especially under President Carter.

During President Reagan's administration, Howard Baker served as the White House chief of staff. He has continued his friendship and correspondence with me right to the present time.

During President Kennedy's presidency, Chief Justice **William Orville Douglas** was an associate justice of the U.S. Supreme Court. He was a very kind man and an Iranophile who had a great deal of respect and affection for the Shah. In the 1950s, he traveled to Iran, accompanied by one of the Kennedy brothers, and visited different parts of the country, including the areas inhabited by the members of the Qashqai tribe that had adopted anti-Shah policies.

The Qashqai brothers, who unfortunately were the supreme examples of the saying "being a pen in the enemy's hand," filled the minds of the visitors with many mistaken and hostile ideas, so much so that when the American visitors returned home they did not have a good impression of the Shah and the Iranian government. Chief Justice Douglas even published a book, called *Strange Lands, Friendly People*, which was very critical of Iran.

When I went to the United States on my first mission as ambassador, in various meetings and discussions with the Americans I persuaded them that what they had been told about Iran had not been correct and had been the views of some people who were hostile to the government. As the result of those discussions, not only did Chief Justice Douglas change his mind about Iran, but we also managed to establish close relations with each other.

At that time, on the initiative of Professor Arthur Upham Pope, the famous American archaeologist and historian of Iranian art, and with the help and efforts of the Iranian Embassy in Washington, a conference was organized with the participation of prominent Iranian and American scientific and cultural figures. President Kennedy sent a message to that conference that was to be read out by Chief Justice Douglas. He went to the podium but instead of reading the message said, "As this message is really addressed to the Iranian ambassador, I ask him to come and read it himself."

As the result of that kind act by that famous man, our relations grew closer. Those close relations continued even after Princess Shahnaz and I left Washington.

Another prominent American who had close and warm relations with me was the distinguished judge, Chief Justice **Warren E. Burger**. That eminent man and his wife, Mrs. Elvera Burger, were responsible for my meeting with William P. Rogers, the U.S. attorney general, in 1959 during the Eisenhower administration. My friendship with Chief Justice Warren Burger was strengthened during my two terms as ambassador to Washington and continued till after the Iranian revolution.

John Foster Dulles was the first U.S. secretary of state whom I was honored to meet. He was a powerful and rather single-minded man who had very close relations with President Eisenhower. His brother Alan Dulles served as the director of the CIA during the same period.

John Foster Dulles was a lawyer, but after the end of the First World War he took part in many diplomatic meetings and conferences. For instance, in 1919 he served as a member of the War Reparations Committee at the request of President Wilson and argued strongly against the imposition of crushing war reparations on Germany.

He was in charge of American diplomacy under President Eisenhower from 1953 until 1959. He was an experienced diplomat who had traveled widely and was the most prominent expert in international relations in the Republican Party. He was appointed secretary of state at a time when confrontation between the Free World and the communist world had reached its peak. He was in fact the symbol and the leader of resistance against Soviet expansionism, a policy that came to be known as "containment." He always used to say that communism "threatened the soul of the Western world," and he believed in what he said.

I became acquainted with him before he was appointed secretary of state, when Vice President Richard Nixon brought an official invitation from President Eisenhower to the Shah and Queen Soraya to visit America, and I went back with him to the United States. It was during that trip that I got to know John Foster Dulles for the first time. That familiarity and friendship was strengthened during my first term as Iran's ambassador in Washington, and those friendly relations continued until his death in 1959.

My memories of John Foster Dulles are of a man with a strong and steadfast mind, who was an expert in international relations and who was unbending in the face of foreign threats. In the history of American diplomacy he is often referred to as one of the most distinguished secretaries of state.

A quiet and gentle linguist by the name of **Christian Herter**, a former under secretary of state, succeeded John Foster Dulles. Herter was born in Paris and attended the École Alsacienne there (1901 to 1904) and was fluent in French. He was perhaps the most educated U.S.

secretaries of state. He was a gentle, experienced, and disciplined diplomat. After President Eisenhower's term ended he left the State Department. He inaugurated the new State Department building, and in his opening speech, he joked, saying, "This place where the State Department now stands is the same place from which the Americans drove the British forces out to the other side of the river."

Sir **Harold Caccia** was a respected and popular British diplomat who served as British ambassador in Washington from 1956 to 1961. He was sent to Washington in order to repair relations between the two allies that had been badly damaged as the result of the Suez crisis of 1956.

He was a good tennis player and a skilled and discreet diplomat. His remarks were always accompanied with long and loud laughter, and as he never explained the reasons for his famous laughs, everyone was free to interpret them anyway he liked. In any case, he definitely seemed to enjoy his own jokes.

During the presidency of John F. Kennedy, **Dean Rusk** was appointed secretary of state, a position that he held from 1961 to 1969. Even after President Kennedy's assassination, he continued in that challenging post in President Johnson's administration, making him the second-longest-serving U.S. secretary of state. He was a very wise, influential, and hardworking man.

My friendship with Mr. and Mrs. Rusk continued throughout the period when I was in America and until I went back to the United States for my second term as ambassador. When I was serving as foreign minister, we met each other as colleagues in the annual meetings of the General Assembly of the United Nations. We also collaborated to find a resolution to the Arab–Israeli conflict following the 1967 war and on the drafting of the Security Council Resolution 242.

I have a special memory about an intervention that I made with Dean Rusk on behalf of Pakistan. When I was Iran's ambassador in Great Britain, Pakistan's President Ayub Khan and his foreign minister Zulfikar Ali Bhutto were going on a visit to the United States. At that time, the relations between the United States and Pakistan had grown cold, and the Americans were especially cool toward Bhutto, because they believed that he was pro-Chinese.

I used that opportunity and passed a message to Dean Rusk through our mutual friend David Bruce, the popular and active U.S. ambassador in London. I, as a friend of Dean Rusk, sent him a message proposing that although relations between the two countries were cold, he should initiate warmer relations with Zulfikar Ali Bhutto, advice which I believe he took to heart.

My acquaintance and friendship with the wonderful **William P. Rogers** started at a reception in the house of Wiley T. Buchanan, the then-head of protocol at the White House in President Eisenhower's administration. He had given a dinner in honor of Princess Shahnaz and myself, and at that reception I met with a number of leading personalities, including William P. Rogers, who at that time was the U.S. attorney general. During President Nixon's administration he came to Iran as U.S. secretary of state to take part in the CENTO meeting.

Another person I met at that reception was **George Shultz**, who was secretary of the treasury at that time and who developed a friendly relationship with me. Later on, he became secretary of state under President Reagan. Another guest at that reception was Chief Justice Burger, who was one of the leading U.S. legal authorities, and to whom I have already referred.

One night, **William Rogers** and I had dinner together in Club 21 in New York during the session of the United Nations General Assembly. Governor Harold Stassen of Minnesota, who had been a Republican presidential candidate (and sought the post 11 times between 1948 and 2000), was also there. After the dinner, in order to make sure that I did not go back to my hotel on foot by myself, they accompanied me.

As part of the friendly chat that we had during that walk, I got the impression that Richard Nixon would be the Republican candidate in the presidential election. The same night I phoned the Shah, who was on holiday in St. Moritz at that time, and informed him of our conversation.

My friendship with William Rogers, who was a true gentleman, started there, and it continued until I resigned from my post as foreign minister and returned to Washington for my second term as Iran's ambassador. At that time, he was secretary of state and his relations with me were warm and friendly. He and his wife Adele tried to get me acquainted with the leading figures in Washington.

Rogers was one of the rising stars of the Republicans. When I met him, he was secretary of treasury. Later on, in the Reagan administration, he became secretary of state, and a devoted expert on Arab–Israeli relations.

He also became a nominee for the candidate of the Republicans for the Presidency. He was a very close friend of George H. Bush. Because of their friendship, Rogers withdrew from this race. Ultimately, he became a lawyer for George W. Bush.

When the Shah left Iran during the revolution and was staying in Morocco, and when I had also become homeless, William Rogers offered to act as my lawyer. He even offered to act as the Shah's lawyer. When members of the Carter administration asked him to dissuade the Shah from going to America, William Rogers telephoned me, informed me of that decision, and apologized that he could not come to Morocco in person to pass on the message to the Shah.

After the revolution, he and Adele came to Switzerland to see me and offered any help that they could provide. For the first time, Secretary Rogers got in touch with André de Pfyffer, a legal firm in Geneva, and asked them to represent me. Later on, through them Jean Pierre Cottier acted as my lawyer and, later still, as the Shah's lawyer. His Majesty the Shah was very pleased for what he had done for him and his family.

William Rogers and members of his noble family maintained their friendship with me right to the end of his life. When Prince Reza Pahlavi, the Crown Prince, came to America to take part in the United

States Air Force Training Program, Rogers put his house on Lake Tahoe in Nevada at the Prince's disposal for a few days.

I had the privilege to honor him with the Order of Homayoun, First Class. My only regret was that when he passed away I was not able to attend the memorial services that were held for him by my good friend **James Baker**, another U.S. secretary of state, and his lovely wife Susan, at which Baker was the main speaker. When I met him, he was serving as Secretary of Treasury in the Reagan administration. During George H.W. Bush's presidency, he was appointed Secretary of State where he concentrated on Arab-Israeli relations. In 2000, he represented George W. Bush in the disputed Florida primaries finally decided by the US Supreme Court.

I first corresponded with **Henry A. Kissinger** when he was teaching at Harvard University. I met him during His Majesty's trip to the United States during Richard Nixon's presidency, when he was assistant to the president for national security affairs, 1968 to 1975, and secretary of state, 1973 to 1977. But my friendship with Henry Kissinger and his wife Nancy began during my second ambassadorship in Washington. He had a special respect for Iran and His Majesty, especially during the crisis in my country.

After the revolution, our friendship has continued, and we meet each time they visit Switzerland. Among the many awards and decorations he has received is the Order of Homayoun, First Class. Henry owes a large part of his success to Nancy, or, as I like to call her, "the column behind the throne."

Here I would like to mention a few other U.S. secretaries, governors, and diplomats who were my friends. One of them was Governor **Harold Stassen**, who served as governor of Minnesota from 1939 to 1943. He was a presidential candidate, and in the 1970s he served as U.S. ambassador to the UN. After President Nixon's election, Stassen came to Iran for bilateral talks.

Another friend was Secretary **Elliot Lee Richardson**, who was U. S. attorney general under President Nixon and who also served as secretary of state. President Nixon once sent Secretary Richardson to

Iran for bilateral talks. The visits of the two above-mentioned figures to Iran took place at the time when I was foreign minister. I met both of them in my home in Hesarak and entertained them there.

Secretary **James Schlesinger** was a very powerful and energetic secretary of defense and was very much liked by President Nixon. He was also a good friend of Iran.

Secretary **Melvin Laird** also served as defense secretary under President Nixon, and was a good friend

I got to know Senator **Barry Goldwater** and his wife Peggy when I was studying in the United States in the year 1948, and our friendship continued to the end of his life.

In his private life, Senator Barry Goldwater was a very moral and principled figure, a devoted husband and an affectionate father, and he always shared in the joys and sorrows of his friends. After the revolution, he and Mrs. Goldwater came to Montreux and honored me with their presence in my house.

In his political life and in America's recent history, he started a movement that resulted many years later in the election of President Ronald Reagan (although there were not too many similarities between these two individuals). The aim of the movement was to force the Americans to confront the realities of the world, to fight against communism, and to revive a sense of national pride. He also tried to champion solidarity with the true friends of the United States and to get away from populism.

He was the Republican Party's nominee for president in the 1964 election. Although he did not succeed in his bid, the movement that he championed for the first time and of which he was spokesman and standard-bearer nevertheless still continues.

Senator **John Goodwin Tower** was another prominent figure whom I was honored to know. My friendship with him, his wife, and members of his family continued for many years. On quite a few occasions I had the honor of receiving Senator and Mrs. Tower in Montreux. Also at the time when he served as chief U.S. negotiator at the Strategic Arms Reduction Talks in Geneva and London, I was in touch with him through the U.S. ambassador in London, Charles H. Price. He was asked by President Reagan to investigate the Iran–Contra affair. The report of the Tower Commission was issued on 26 February 1987, and it caused a major stir in political and diplomatic circles in Washington.

Unfortunately, Senator Tower and his daughter Marian were killed along with twenty-one other people in the crash of an Atlantic Southeast Airlines flight on its landing approach at Brunswick, Georgia.

Senator **Edward William Brooke** is another American friend whom I got to know in 1973, and our friendship continues to the present day. On a number of occasions I have had the honor of meeting him and Mrs. Brooke in Montreux. He was the first African American to be elected by popular vote to the U.S. Senate and was elected as a Republican senator from Massachusetts in 1966.

In 2009, this worthy politician was awarded the Congressional Gold Medal. I was honored to be invited to the ceremonies that were organized by Senator Harry Reid, the majority leader of the Senate. Held in the Houses of Congress, they were also attended by President Barack Obama.

I have known Senator and Mrs. **Charles H. Percy** since 1972, and our friendship has continued to the present time. He is an extremely patriotic, wise, experienced, logical, and well-traveled politician. In his personal life, he is also a loving husband, a model father, and a unique friend. After the revolution, on a number of occasions I have had the honor of entertaining this likable couple in Montreux.

Once, when the late king of Jordan, His Majesty King Hussein, had a certain problem, I conveyed his message to Senator Percy. This influential man followed up the matter with complete kindness, and the problem was resolved.

Another prominent American politician with whom I had very friendly relations right to the end of his life was Senator **James William Fulbright**, the chairman of the Senate Committee on Foreign Relations. He established the Fulbright Program in 1946, which has carried out cultural and educational programs right to the present day.

Approximately 294,000 scholars have participated in the program since its inception. Fulbright was an honorable person with very firm views and beliefs. He was a single-minded man who was very anxious to help developing countries. Many Iranians, especially students who went for their higher education to the United States, received Fulbright grants. His aim was to bring the citizens of other countries there so that they could have an intimate knowledge of America, its people, and its culture.

After I left America in 1961 and was appointed Iranian ambassador to Great Britain, my friendship with that honorable man continued. That friendship lasted through the period when I was Iran's foreign minister and even till after the revolution, for the duration of his life. My close relations with the members of his family still continue.

William Averell Harriman was a prominent American politician whose name is mentioned frequently in my memoirs. He was an exceptional man who had a deep insight into international politics. After graduating from Yale University he inherited the largest fortune in America.

He served as secretary of commerce under President Truman and also was the 48th governor of New York. He was a candidate for the Democratic presidential nomination in 1952. He served President Franklin Roosevelt as special envoy to Europe during the Second World War, and he was U.S. ambassador in Moscow and U.S. ambassador in Britain. Later on, he was put in charge of the Marshall Plan for the rebuilding of Europe.

He was very fond of Iran and had a great deal of respect for the Shah. He also had very friendly relations with my family. During his visit to Iran he met with my father and later on became a close friend of mine. His third and last wife **Pamela Harriman**, the former wife of Sir Winston Churchill's son Randolph, was also very interested in and knowledgeable about politics. During the Clinton administration, she served as U.S. ambassador in France and played a big role in bringing the two countries closer together.

During the oil crisis, when President Truman wanted to reach an agreement with Dr. Mossadegh and to resolve the oil dispute, Harriman was sent to Iran, and he flew there in his own private jet. General Walters, who was a colonel at that time and who was fluent in seven languages, acted as Harriman's interpreter and adviser.

Harriman established friendly relations with Iranian leaders and officials, but unfortunately he did not succeed in resolving the oil conflict. However, many scholars who have studied the history of the Iranian oil crisis believe that if Iran had accepted Harriman's proposals and the solutions that he put forward, this could have prevented many subsequent problems and hostilities. Dr. Mossadegh's obstinacy and the shallow and simplistic understanding of international realities of many of those who surrounded him prevented the success of Harriman's proposals.

During the Second World War when Harriman was U.S. ambassador in Moscow, he came to Iran to take part in the Tehran Conference with President Roosevelt, the Soviet leader Joseph Stalin, and the British Prime Minister Sir Winston Churchill. From that time, he developed a strong affection for the Shah and for Iran. In return, the Shah was very fond of him and respected him. When American forces were to leave Iran after the end of the Second World War, Harriman tried to donate much of the military equipment that was kept in Amirabad to Iran. However, this was not done and the Americans auctioned the equipment.

During the Kennedy administration, when my father lived in Switzerland, anytime that Harriman came to Switzerland he met with my father in Geneva.

Senator **Mike Mansfield** was one of the most powerful, influential, and experienced American Democratic politicians, who at the same time was very modest and friendly. He served both in the House of Representatives and the Senate and was the longest-serving majority leader of the U.S. Senate. He also served as U.S. ambassador to Japan for more than ten years, and was instrumental in expanding U.S.–Japanese relations.

I had friendly relations with that remarkable man and learned a great deal from him. My friendship with him continued until after the revolution, and since his death I have maintained my friendly and respectful relations with his wife and daughter.

Another U.S. official with whom I had friendly relations was Senator **Stuart Symington**. He also served as the first U. S. secretary of the Air Force. During the Second World War and subsequently, he was an influential man, and his son also served for a while as head of protocol at the White House. American history refers to Senator Symington as someone who had a great influence on U.S. defense and military policies. I have fond memories of my friendship with him and his wife.

I got to know Senator **Abraham Ribicoff** during President Kennedy's administration. At that time, he was U.S. Secretary of health, education, and welfare, and later on he was elected a congressman and later still a senator. Once, when my wife and I lived in the United States, he invited us to some ceremonies in New York in which he represented the president. My friendship with that honorable man and his esteemed wife continued until after the Iranian revolution.

I got to know Senator **Birch Bayh** when I first arrived in the United States, and our friendship has continued ever since. I also have a close friendship with his son Senator **Birch Evans Bayh III**, who followed in his father's footsteps and was elected a senator.

I have known Senator and Mrs. **Frank Church**, a kind and friendly couple, since 1972. He became a candidate for the Democratic nomination in the 1976 presidential election from Ohio, which is a neighboring state to Utah where I used to study.

When he came to Geneva with his friend and colleague Senator Robert Kennedy we met again. Church was critical of Iran's foreign policy, but, nevertheless, he was a fair-minded, freedom-loving, and dignified person who was not fanatical about his views and was prepared to listen to the views of his critics and to accept them if they made sense.

I first met Senator **Samuel Augustus Nunn**, Jr. and Mrs. Nunn in 1972, and our friendly relations still continue. Nunn is an influential and active person who feels very strongly about maintaining America's reputation in the world. He is a strong advocate of world peace and still cooperates with a group for the establishment of universal peace. During his tenure in the U.S. Senate, Nunn served as chairman of the powerful U.S. Senate Committee on Armed Services and the Permanent Sub-Committee on Investigations. His legislative achievements include the landmark Department of Defense Reorganization Act, drafted with the late Senator Barry Goldwater, and the Nunn-Lugar Cooperative Threat Reduction Program. To date, the Nunn-Lugar Cooperative Threat Reduction Program has deactivated more than 5900 nuclear warheads.

Knowing Nunn has been very instructive to me, and I have learned many things from him.

I have had friendly relations with Senator **Bob Dole**, who served as the U.S. Senate majority leader from 1985 to 1987 and again in 1995 and 1996. Dole was President Gerald Ford's vice presidential running mate in the 1976 election and was also the Republican Party nominee in the presidential election in 1996, losing to the incumbent president, Bill Clinton.

I met him and his lovely wife, the former Senator **Elizabeth Dole**, on many occasions in the United States. During their trip to Switzerland, I had the pleasure of meeting them again. When in 1976 I was chosen as the man of the year by Kappa Sigma fraternity, Bob Dole hosted the reception that was organized on that occasion at the U.S. Senate and showed me great kindness and affection.

During the Reagan administration, Elizabeth became secretary of labor, and the head of the U.S. Red Cross and visited Switzerland— where we met again. Both Bob and Elizabeth have been my true and noble friends.

Senator **Jacob Koppel Javits** came to Iran during the Arab–Israeli war when I was serving as Iran's minister of foreign affairs. He was one of America's most influential politicians, and my friendship with him and his wife continued till after the Iranian revolution.

My friendship with Senator **Charles McCurdy Mathias** dates from 1972. A very wise senator, he was very interested in international affairs and was a great believer in world peace. He was a friend of Iran, and visited Iran. He brought two pine trees with him from Persepolis in Iran and presented them to the Iranian Embassy in Washington, and they were planted in front of the ambassador's residence. However, I have heard that the revolutionaries removed them after they attacked the embassy during the revolution.

During President Carter's administration, after the victory of the Iranian revolution and when the revolutionaries had occupied the Iranian Embassy in Washington, they accused me of having bribed a number of American congressmen and various newspaper owners and editors. My attorney, William Rogers, raised the issue in Congress, and after investigation it was proven that those allegations were false. After spending $23 million of taxpayers' money, they finally discovered that all those allegations had been mere lies and I was fully acquitted of all charges. Senator Charles Mathias kindly sent me a copy of that ruling, for which I was grateful.

I got to know Senator **George Stanley McGovern** and his wife in 1972 during my second term as ambassador in Washington. He was the presidential nominee for the 1972 election but lost to President Nixon.

When the Shah came on an official visit to America in 1973 on President Nixon's invitation, I also invited Senator McGovern to the official reception at the Iranian Embassy. It is interesting to note that these two presidential rivals had not seen each other since the election. The photograph showing President Nixon introducing Senator McGovern to the Shah was published in many American and European newspapers. Some observers were very surprised on seeing that picture, and they attributed the warmth between Nixon and McGovern to Iranian diplomacy.

During the Carter administration, Senator McGovern was appointed as U.S. ambassador to the UN Food and Agriculture Organization

(FAO) in Rome, and during that period and since we have maintained our friendly relations.

Diplomatic Figures

Here, I would like to mention some U.S. ambassadors to Iran who helped to strengthen the relations between the two countries, and who should not be forgotten by Iranians.

Ambassador **George Allen** was a senior and experienced U.S. diplomat who, for a time, also served as U.S. assistant secretary of state for public affairs. He served as U.S. ambassador to Iran during the critical period in Azerbaijan and the separatist governments that had been set up there and in some parts of Kurdistan by the Soviet Union. Ambassador Allen adopted a strong stance against the Russians and defended Iran's rights, and he was awarded the Order of Homayoun, First Class.

According to the records that have been declassified, even at the time when the U.S. and British governments were urging the Iranian Prime Minister Ahmad Ghavam (Ghavam os-Saltaneh) not to insist on Iranian rights in those two provinces and to reach a compromise with Ja'far Pishevari, the founder and chairman of the separatist and communist Azerbaijan People's Government, Ambassador Allen, who was a close friend of Ghavam, urged him not to give up defending Iran's rights. He even openly expressed his personal support for the Iranian position in a speech, which according to many observers violated diplomatic norms.

At that time, this was a very brave action, and it provided the Iranians with the necessary support to insist on their stance. Iranians should remember and honor his services to Iran. In 1956 Ambassador George Allen came to Karachi, accompanying John Foster Dulles. The Shah was visiting Pakistan at that time, after having visited India, and a meeting was arranged with President Iskander Mirza.

Ambassador **Louis G. Dreyfus** was another prominent diplomat who served as the U.S. minister plenipotentiary in Iran during the Second World War. He served in Iran from 1940 to 1943.

Ambassador **Henry F. Grady** was U.S. ambassador in Iran during the movement for the nationalization of the oil industry, and he supported

Iran's position against the Anglo-Iranian Oil Company. My late father had a great deal of respect for Ambassador Grady, who never wavered in his love and respect for Iran and the Iranians.

Ambassador **Loy Henderson** was another U.S. ambassador in Iran who served during the period when Dr. Mohammad Mossadegh was prime minister (1951 to 1953). After his return from Iran, he served as the director of the Office of Near Eastern Affairs at the U.S. State Department. He was an honorable, patriotic, and experienced politician. As he was married to a Russian lady and had also lived for a time in Russia, he was very familiar with Soviet politics and with Russian diplomacy.

When in 1969 the Shah and I visited the United States, Ambassador Henderson made arrangements for the Shah to meet many political and economic figures. He continued to have close contacts with the Iranian Embassy in Washington and maintained his relationship with Iran for as long as he lived. He was honored with the Order of Homayoun, First Class.

Ambassador **Armin H. Mayer** was another U.S. ambassador who was highly respected by the Iranian Ministry of Foreign Affairs. Whether at the time when he served as ambassador in Iran (1965 to 1969) or when he was in Washington, he was very active on behalf of Iran. He went back to the United States during the Arab–Israeli war of 1968 (the Six-Day War). He supported Iran's views regarding the Middle East crisis and actively represented Iran's views on the conflict. He also served as U.S. ambassador to Lebanon and Japan and eventually rose to the post of deputy assistant secretary of state for Near Eastern and South Asian affairs.

Ambassador **Edward T. Wailes**, who served in Iran from 1965 to 1969, was another experienced and capable diplomat. The Russians did not look kindly on him, because the Hungarian Revolution of 1956 began when he was serving as ambassador in Hungary under President Eisenhower. During the Russian invasion of Hungary, one of the leading Hungarian religious figures, the head of the Roman Catholic Church, Cardinal Jozef Mindszenty, took refuge at the U.S.

Embassy. He lived there for nearly 15 years, unable to leave the embassy grounds. This issue caused many problems in Soviet–American and American–Hungarian relations. However, Ambassador Wailes managed that crisis with great skill.

Ambassador **Douglas MacArthur II**, a career diplomat who held many ambassadorial positions, was named after his uncle General Douglas MacArthur, the hero of World War II. My friendship with MacArthur and his wife Laura, daughter of U.S. vice president Alben Barkley, began when he became ambassador to Iran in 1969. This coincided with the period when I was the minister of foreign affairs. I have written extensively on him in the third volume of my memoirs. He was a noble man from a noble family, and he maintained the friendship after the revolution, visiting me in Montreux.

Other Notable Individuals

In the history of Iranian–American relations there have been some great individuals in addition to politicians and diplomats whose names shall remain forever in the national memory of Iranians as Iran's friends.

These great friends of Iran include figures such as **Howard Baskerville**. Baskerville was born in North Platte, Nebraska, and was raised in the Black Hills. After graduating from Princeton University, he came to Iran as a young teacher and missionary and started teaching in Tabriz, the capital of Azerbaijan. His stay in Tabriz coincided with the start of the Constitutional Revolution, when Iranians had risen up to put an end to the age-old autocratic governments and to elect a parliament. The American consulate in Tabriz had told him not to get involved in Iran's pro-democracy revolution, but he said, "The only difference between me and these people is my birthplace, which is not a big difference." He joined the revolutionaries and tried to raise a volunteer force to defend the city. In the spring of 1909, during the clashes with the Shah's forces, he was shot and killed. He was 24. His name has gone down in Iranian history as a hero of the Constitutional Revolution.

Another remarkable American whose name will always be recorded in Iranian history is **Morgan Shuster**, who came to Iran during the Constitutional Revolution. After having put an end to the period of despotism, Iranians wanted to establish Western-oriented, secular, and democratic governments in Iran and to reorganize their finances. The Iranian parliament (Majles) invited Morgan Shuster to Iran to manage Iran's finances and to pay the debts accumulated by the Qajar monarchs to the two leading colonial powers of the time, Great Britain and Russia. The hiring of Shuster and his American team worried and angered the imperial powers, and as the result of their pressure Iran was forced to expel Shuster, who had started some major reforms. Although the Iranian parliament had approved Shuster's financial powers, under Russian and British pressure, the vice-regent of Iran expelled Shuster from Iran in December 1911. Shuster's book, *Strangling of Persia,* dedicated to "The Persian People," provides an invaluable eyewitness account of the problems of a country that had fallen prey to the imperial ambitions of Great Britain and Russia.

Dr. **Arthur Chester Millspaugh**, a former adviser at the U.S. State Department's Office of the Foreign Trade, was hired by the Iranian parliament after the Constitutional Revolution to reorganize the Iranian Ministry of Finance from 1922 to 1927 and again from 1942 to 1945. At that time, the United States was regarded as a liberator from European colonial dominance. Throughout his period of service in Iran, Millspaugh tried unsuccessfully to influence the U.S. State Department's policies toward Iran. However, as the administrator-general of finances of Iran he brought positive results by balancing the Iranian budget, and his efforts were greatly appreciated by the Iranians.

Millspaugh wrote a number of important books on Iran, including *The American Task in Persia* (New York: Arno Press, 1925) and *Americans in Persia* (Washington, D.C.: Brookings Institution, 1946).

In the field of art and scholarship a number of Americans have rendered amazing service to Iran. Professor **Arthur Upham Pope** was a leading scholar in the field of Iranian arts and architecture. He and his wife Phyllis Ackerman, who was a fellow Persian art historian, lived many years in Iran and devoted their lives to the study of different Iranian art forms. Their six-volume *Survey of Persian Art from Prehistoric Times to the Present* is still regarded as the classic work on the subject. Professor Pope was the founding director, from 1965 to 1979, of the American Institute for Persian Art and Archaeology, which was founded in New York and was transferred to the University of Shiraz.

Professor Pope was so in love with Iran that in his will and testament he wrote that he wished to be buried in Isfahan, next to the Zayandeh Rud River that flows through the city. On the orders of the late Shah a fitting mausoleum in the architectural tradition of Isfahan was built for them, and both Pope and his wife are buried there. The revolutionary government has also honored his will and testament and takes good care of the mausoleum, and each year thousands of Iranian art lovers visit their tombs and honor their memory.

Professor **Harold Albert Lamb** was another great American author and scholar who wrote many books on Iran and on other Oriental topics, including *Omar Khayyam* (1934); *Cyrus the Great* (1960); *Genghis Khan: The Emperor of All Men* (1927); *Tamerlane* (1928); *The Flame of Islam* (1930); and *The Crusades* (1931). I got to know Professor Lamb when he and the famous actor Tyrone Power were planning to make a film on Cyrus the Great. However, when Tyrone Power suddenly died, that plan had to be abandoned.

Professor **Richard N. Frye** is another eminent American scholar of ancient Iran who followed Professor Pope as the director of the Institute for Persian Art and Archaeology at Pahlavi University in Shiraz. Professor Frye is Aga Khan Professor Emeritus of Iranian Studies at Harvard University, after having been visiting professor at Pahlavi University in Shiraz from 1970 to 1976. He helped found the Center for Middle Eastern Studies at Harvard. He is a great proponent of Persian civilization, which he maintains is under-appreciated by other Muslims and by the West. His *The Heritage of Persia: The Pre-Islamic History of One of the World's Great Civilizations* (World Publishing: New York, 1963), *Persia* (1969), *The Golden Age of Persia*

(1993), *Greater Iran* (2005), and many other works are regarded as classics in the field of Old Persian studies. Like Professor Pope, Professor Frye has asked to be buried in Isfahan, and the government of the Islamic Republic of Iran has given him an old, traditional Iranian home to use for life.

Professor **Franklin S. Harris** was president of Brigham Young University from 1921 until 1945 and was president of Utah State University from 1945 to 1950, during the period when I was a student there. Later on, he became the director of President Truman's Point Four Program. The Point Four Agreement was signed during the premiership of the late Ali Razmara in 1950. This technical assistance agreement was non signatory and was led by an Iranian-US joint committee. This program was led by Dr. Harris, who worked in Iran in the early 1950s. He was received by the Shah on a number of occasions, including in 1948 in Arizona. I have provided more details about Dr. Harris in this volume.

Daryl Chase, the president of Utah State University (1955 to 1968), was a very good friend to me—and to Iran. Dr. Chase had visited Iran on several occasions in the 1960s and had had an audience with my beloved King. I first met him when he was the dean of students at Utah State University. In 1955 he became the president of the University. He was very popular, especially with the foreign students with whom he met weekly over lunch. He was instrumental in our education, taking us on study trips all over the United States. In July 1960, when I was first ambassador to the United States, President Chase and Dean Milton Merrill (Dean of the College of Business and Social Sciences, 1950-59 and U.S.U.'s first Vice President under Daryl Chase in 1955) bestowed on me a doctoral degree in Law and Humanities on behalf of the University. I subsequently had the honor of bestowing upon him the Order of the Taj, second class. Throughout the years, Daryl Chase and his wife Allison showed me kindness and attention, not just in my student days but long after. That friendship continues through their son.

Grayson L. Kirk was the president of Columbia University (1953 to 1968) who awarded an honorary law doctorate to the Shah during his official visit to the United States in 1954. He was outspoken in his praise of Iran.

Glen Olds was the president of Kent State University and later became the president of Alaska University. He served as president of Kent State University under the Johnson and Nixon administrations, and it was during the latter period that he awarded me an honorary doctorate.

Point Four Program

In view of the services that President Truman's Point Four Program has rendered to Iran, I would like to mention the names of some of the directors of that useful and constructive program.

The first director of the Point Four Program, which later became the U.S. Agency for International Development (USAID), was Dr. **Franklin S. Harris**, who served in Iran in 1950. He was followed by Dr. **John Evans**. The third director of the Point Four Program in Iran, which was then called Mission for Peace between Iran and the United States, was Mr. **William E. Warne**.

The overall director of the Point Four Program was Dr. **Henry Gland Bennett**, who was unfortunately killed in an air crash en route to Iran. His successor as director general of Point Four who succeeded Dr. Bennett was **Jonathan Brewster Bingham**, who under President Carter was elected a member of the U.S. House of Representatives. He wrote a book about the activities of Point Four entitled *Shirt-Sleeve Diplomacy: Point 4 in Action* (New York, 1954). Bingham visited Iran during Dr. Mossadegh's premiership.

Reesman Fryer was the head of Point Four's Near East programs from 195–1953. He was very fond of Iran and he also had very friendly relations with me. He came to Iran when my father was the minister of the interior and again when he was a senator, and he met with my father on a number of occasions. Fryer was a hardworking and patriotic man and was very interested in establishing friendly relations between the United States and the developing countries.

During the time that I was Iranian ambassador in Washington he had very warm and close relations with my wife Princess Shahnaz and myself.

Journalists and Media

In my childhood, whenever I visited my grandfather, Motamen ol-Molk, I browsed the copies of *National Geographic* to which he subscribed and learned about the world through its pictures. My grandfather encouraged me to spend more time on journals than on playing around. In 1942 *National Geographic* featured an extensive article on Iran when my father was the army commander in Isfahan, and they featured a photo of him on the airfield with me in the background as a teenage boy. Later, in 1960, when I was ambassador to Washington, the **Grosvenor family**, owners of *National Geographic*, gave me a large copy of the photo. My friendship with **Gilbert M. Grosvenor** has continued ever since. In 1975, staff member James Blair and photographer William Graves featured a long section on Iran in the magazine.

Time and *Life* historically were very friendly toward Iran and had Reza Shah, Queen Fawzia, and the Shah on many covers. **Henry Luce**, the American publisher, was known to friends as "Father Time." His wife **Clare Boothe Luce**, a writer and politician, became the U.S. ambassador to Italy in 1953. This coincided with the period that the Shah and Queen Soraya had to leave Iran at the end of Mossadegh's premiership, and during their three-day stay in Rome they met her. During my first mission to Washington I had lunch with Henry almost once a month, and we discussed politics of the U.S. and Iran. After Henry's death in 1967 Clare moved to Hawaii, and during Crown Prince Reza's trip to the U.S. she threw a party for him at her house in Honolulu. In 1981, President Ronald Reagan appointed Clare Luce to the President's Foreign Intelligence Advisory Board.

James Linen III succeeded Luce as the publisher of *Time*, and our acquaintance commenced during my second ambassadorship. He had special interest in Iran, and we met regularly. He was always active, and, although he was confined to a wheelchair, he did not consider his disability an obstacle to achievement. He traveled many times to Iran and met the Shah.

Walter Lippmann was a famous and influential journalist and editorialist whose articles were simultaneously published in scores of newspapers throughout America. However, few people know that Lippmann was also a great scholar and thinker, as well as a political activist. After the Great Depression in 1929, Lippmann brought together a group of leading economists from all over the world to try to find a solution to that crisis. The group put forward some proposals about the crisis of which President Roosevelt did not approve. However, after the war and especially in the 60s and 70s, those proposals became more popular, and they formed a new school in economic and political theory. Lippmann was very close to President Kennedy and went to his house as soon as he was elected and congratulated him. He also became the president of the National Press Club.

Arthur Ochs Sulzberger was the publisher of the *New York Times*, and M. R. Garson, who was the day-to-day manager and the brains behind the operation of the newspaper, cooperated with him. In the 1970s, when the Shah was on one of his official visits to the United States, Mr. and Mrs. Sulzberger and Mr. Garson were received by him in Nelson Rockefeller's house in New York, and after dinner they interviewed him.

Benjamin C. Bradlee, executive editor of the *Washington Post* from 1968 to 1991, and his wife Sally, who is the daughter of a famous U.S. general, Lt. General William Wilson Quinn, came to Iran and were received by the Shah together with Senator Goldwater. It was rumored that if Goldwater had been elected president, General Quinn would have been appointed as the chairman of the joint staff of the armed forces. General Quinn helped form the CIA, and during World War II he served as an intelligence officer in Europe, where he was responsible for gathering and coordinating information for the invasion of southern France on 15 August 1944.

Walter Annenberg was a distinguished publisher, broadcaster, diplomat, and philanthropist. During the Nixon administration he served as the U.S. ambassador in London (1969 to 1974). After the revolution, when a number of opportunists who were opposed to the monarchy attacked the house of Princess Shams, the Shah's sister, in Los Angeles, that honorable man placed his house at the disposal of the Princess and the Queen Mother. Also, when I was looking for a suitable residence for the Shah and the Shahbanou in the United States, he again placed his house at my disposal and also offered his house to them as a place of residence should they so wish.

During the lead-up to the revolution, when I had gone to Iran, Annenberg constantly phoned me and asked me how I was. He was a true and steadfast friend and was very fond of Iran.

Sir **Eldon Wylie Griffiths**, a British politician and journalist who was the managing editor of *Newsweek* from 1959 to 1961 and who has authored a number of books, has been my close friend up till the present time. He wrote a fascinating book about the Iranian revolution and its aftermath, called *Turbulent Iran: Recollections, Revelations and a Proposal for Peace* (Seven Locks Press, 2006).

John Cooley was an American journalist and the author of a number of books. He specialized in terrorism and the Middle East. He was also a contributing editor of *Christian Science Monitor* and the *Boston Globe* and a correspondent for ABC News. He came to Iran with his wife and interviewed the Shah. He was a close friend of mine. Unfortunately, he died in 2008, after suffering from cancer.

Jack and Patsy Kauffmann's family had been the owners of the *Washington Star*, and Jack managed the newspaper for a time. They were two of my good friends and great supporters of Iran.

Edward R. Murrow was a famous and influential broadcast journalist. He first came to prominence with a series of broadcasts during the Second World War, which attracted millions of listeners in the United States and Canada. He had joined CBS as director of talks and education in 1935 and remained with the network for the rest of his career. In 1960 he came to Iran and interviewed the Shah. He also made a very interesting film about Iranian–American cooperation. He presented a copy of that film to me and another copy to the Shah.

Under the Kennedy administration, Edward Murrow became the director of the United States Information Agency (USIA). He was very close to President Kennedy. He was also a member of the Kappa Sigma Fraternity. In 1964 he was awarded the Presidential Medal of Freedom. After his death from cancer, I continued my friendship with his wife and his son.

Mrs. **Fleur Fenton Cowles** and her husband were among my close friends. Fleur Cowles was a writer, editor, and artist who founded the short-lived *Flair* magazine. Her third husband, Gardner Cowles Jr. (1903 to 1982) was an heir to Cowles Media Company.

In 1953, Fleur Cowles represented President Eisenhower at the coronation of Great Britain's Queen Elizabeth II. She also interviewed the Shah and Queen Soraya, as well as my dear father.

Among her many writings is a popular book, *She Made Friends and Kept Them: An Anecdotal Memoir*, which was very amusing and gave an interesting account of those days. In the first volume of my memoirs, this book is referred to in some detail.

Among other prominent American essayists, journalists, and newspaper proprietors that I wish to refer to are the following:

Arnaud de Borchgrave who was born in Belgium to Count Baudouin de Borchgrave, head of Belgium's military intelligence for the government-in-exile during World War II, is an American journalist who specializes in international politics. In 1985 he was appointed editor-in-chief of the *Washington Times*. He is currently editor-at-large of the *Washington Times* and United Press International, as well as project director for Transnational Threats and senior adviser to the Center for Strategic and International Studies.

He interviewed the Shah and myself, and he and his lovely wife Alexandra used to come and visit me in Montreux until lately.

Mrs. **Katharine Graham** was an American publisher who wielded great influence in Washington. She also led her family's newspaper, the *Washington Post*, for more than two decades, which also coincided with the Watergate affair that eventually resulted in President Nixon's resignation. I got to know her in 1961, and during my second term as ambassador to the United States, between 1972 to 1979, my friendship with her and her family became stronger.

Walter Cronkite was one of the giants of American media, who was best known as anchorman for the CBS evening news. I got to know him in 1972.

David Brinkley was another famous American broadcaster whom I got to know, along with his wife Susan, during my stay in America. From 1956 to 1970 he co-anchored NBC's top-rated nightly news program. **William Randolph Hearst**, who owned many American newspapers and magazines and was a leading publisher, invited the Shah to his mansion during one of his official visits to the United States and arranged a sumptuous reception for him.

Mrs. **Betty Beale** was another influential U.S. journalist and publisher. My acquaintance with her started at the beginning of the 1960s. She wrote a very entertaining book called *Power at Play: A Memoir of Parties, Politicians, and the Presidents in My Bedroom*, which provides a humorous account of the political and social life of leading figures in Washington.

Barbara Walters, the queen of American media and the most important woman in the history of television journalism, is an old friend of mine. She was a frequent guest at the receptions at the Iranian Embassy in Washington. She recorded a famous interview with the Shah in 1977 about the CIA's role in Iran, the rising price of oil, and the Shah's views about the West. She was one of the few reporters who interviewed the Shah when he was receiving medical treatment at the Weill Cornell Medical Hospital in New York.

Making Friends with Artists and Cultural Figures

I attach a great deal of importance to establishing contacts and reaching mutual understanding with cultural, artistic, and academic people, namely those who influence and shape public opinion. Our embassies normally limited their contacts and their scope of activities to political and diplomatic circles and perhaps to congressional and economic figures. Of course, establishing contacts with such people was useful and necessary, but it was not sufficient.

During my work as ambassador in London for one term and two terms in the United States I tried—and fortunately succeeded—in establishing exceptional contacts with intellectual communities. The doors of the embassy were always open to such people, and those relationships received extensive coverage in the domestic and foreign media and provided good publicity for Iran.

When I was serving as Iran's foreign minister, I continued that practice as far as possible with leading intellectuals and important cultural and academic figures who visited Iran for various reasons. I know that many people criticized that practice and regarded it as a form of self-glorification and self-promotion. However, as time goes by, I realize that I was justified in attaching so much importance to that issue, because political and parliamentary figures come and go, and one should of course pay a great deal of attention to them. However, intellectuals, artists, and academics have a more permanent and influential presence in various societies, and exert a great deal of influence upon public opinion.

I must add that my friendly relations with many such figures continued after the revolution, and I have been pleased and honored to entertain many of them in my home in Montreux.

I would like to pay homage to all of them, but they are too many to mention by name. Therefore, I will only refer to some of the most prominent ones among them:

I was privileged to meet Sir **Charlie Chaplin**, who was not only a unique actor but also a very friendly and learned person. Both he and his wife Lady **Oona O'Neil** were friendly and hospitable. I still continue my friendship with his children. On the basis of my recommendation, the Shah awarded Charlie Chaplin the Order of the Taj, third degree.

I was introduced to the lovely actress **Arlene Dahl** by the gracious Shirley Lords, the renowned writer and senior editor of Vogue in London and subsequently met her both in the United States and Paris.

The talented actress and singer **Polly Bergen**, who I first met in 1963, has been a true friend and remained one after the 1979 revolution.

Gary Cooper, the famous film actor, visited Iran at the invitation of the Shah and Queen Soraya. He also met the Shah and the Queen in Sun Valley, Idaho, during their visit to the United States. I established friendly relations with him and his wife and daughter from 1953.

My friendship with Mr. and Mrs. **David Niven**, the famous British actor and his wife, started in Gstaad, Switzerland, in 1963 and continued in London. We were almost neighbors, and this proximity strengthened our friendship. When David died in 1983 I made sure to attend his funeral.

I met **James Mason** and his wife Clarissa Kaye-Mason in 1963 in London. When my young daughter Mahnaz went to Lady Eden School in London, James Mason's nephew showed her a great deal of kindness and friendship. James Mason's brother was the manager of the Kensington branch of Barclays Bank, and we were good friends. He was also very interested in Iran.

I met the famous and beautiful British actress **Audrey Hepburn** in 1963, and our friendship continued to the end of her life. She was a great philanthropist and humanitarian. Her humanitarian interests led her to join UNICEF in her later career, and she became an honorary ambassador for that organization. Unfortunately, her great devotion to her work meant that she did not take good care of her health, and she died of cancer in 1993 at the relatively young age of 63. She was buried in her private home near Morges in Switzerland.

Peter Ustinov, the famous English actor, filmmaker, writer, and dramatist, was another good friend of mine. He was a wise and well-informed intellectual. He often invited me to his house, and I was very pleased to return the honor and entertain him in my home.

I met **Ava Gardner**, who was known as the Venus of Hollywood and as one of the most beautiful actresses, in 1954. In 1968 she moved to London and died there in 1990 at a relatively young age.

I met **Grace Kelly**, who later married Prince Rainier of Monaco, in 1954.

In that year I also made the acquaintance of **Cary Grant**, who was a very warm and likable person. During the 1970s, when Crown Prince Reza was studying in America, Cary Grant showed him a great deal of kindness and affection.

Sir **Roger Moore** and Lady Moore as well as **David Niven** have always been my dear friends whom I would often see in London, Gstaad, or Southern France. The same goes for my noble friends **Kirk Douglas** and his lovely wife Anne, and also Mr. and Mrs. **Gregory Peck**. Especially after the revolution, the Pecks have been exceptionally kind and sweet with me.

I met **Barbara Streisand** in London, and we also met a few times in Washington, D.C. She is a kind friend.

I had the pleasure of knowing Dame **Margot Fonteyn**, the renowned English ballerina. She was regarded as one of the greatest classical ballet dancers of all time, and in recognition of her achievements she was made a Dame Commander of the Order of the British Empire by Her Majesty Queen Elizabeth II in 1956. Her husband Dr. Robert Arias, who was a Panamanian diplomat in London, was allegedly involved in an attempted coup against the Panamanian government.

When in 1965 I accompanied the Shah during his official visit to Russia, I met Rudolf Nureyev. Later on, with the help of Margot Fonteyn and other British and American friends we managed to help Nureyev leave Russia and come to the West.

I met **Elizabeth Taylor**, one of the greatest and most beautiful actresses, in 1972. Our friendly relations continued right to the end of her life, and occasionally we talked on the telephone to exchange news. I once invited her to visit Iran, and I have some very happy memories of that visit.

Robert Mitchum and I were introduced in 1964 and we later became friends.

I was very friendly with **John Wayne**, the legendary American film actor. He was incredibly kind, modest, and hospitable and was a true gentleman who could not do enough for his friends. For instance, when my sister was recovering from a heart operation in America, John Wayne put his large yacht at her disposal to rest and convalesce. He was a great patriot and one of President Reagan's closest friends. Although he passed away more than thirty years ago, he is still regarded as a hero by most Americans who see him as a symbol of strength, chivalry, and rugged masculinity.

Frank Sinatra, the famous singer and actor, was a faithful friend and a generous philanthropist. He was very attached to his family. My friendship with him started in 1965. When he was invited to take part in the meeting of a charitable organization in Iran, he immediately accepted the invitation and traveled in his own private aircraft and at his own expense, and he even refused to accept expenses for his stay in Iran. When, after the revolution, I was looking for a suitable residence for the Shah and his family, Frank Sinatra generously and immediately put his own house in Palm Spring (near Annenberg's mansion) at my disposal.

I met **Humphrey Bogart** and **Lauren Bacall**, that artistic couple, in 1954 during the Shah's visit to the United States.

I also met **Bob Hope** and his wife Dolores in the same year and became very friendly with them. I took part in Bob Hope's 80th birthday party, which was attended by many actors and politicians, including President Reagan. My friendly relations with Mr. and Mrs. Hope continued for many years, and I kept in touch with him until a few years before his death in 2003.

Andy Warhol, the famous American painter and filmmaker who was a leading figure in the visual art movement, was a good friend of mine. Although he is no longer with us, his memory will always remain with art lovers.

My acquaintance and friendship with the great cellist **Slava Rostropovich** started in 1965 during the Shah's visit to the Soviet Union. He had close and friendly relations with the Kennedys and with President Reagan. He gave a famous concert in front of the Berlin Wall and will always be remembered by history as a staunch advocate of human rights. He was awarded the 1974 Award of the International League of Human Rights. After the revolution he offered to put his house in Lausanne at my disposal.

I met **Herbert von Karajan** in London when I was Iran's ambassador there. When I was Iran's foreign minister I invited him and his wife to Iran, and he gave a glorious and very successful concert there. On the same occasion, he was received by the Shah.

My friendship with the great conductor **Zubin Mehta** and his wife **Nancy Mehta** dates from 1972. When after the revolution, some rioters set fire to the house of Princess Shams in Los Angeles, this humane and hospitable conductor offered to put his house at my disposal. After the revolution, when we were looking for a residence for the Shah in the United States, the Mehtas showed us a great deal of sympathy and assistance. The couple have had a strong and close friendship with me, and we have had a number of memorable meetings together in Montreux, Gstaad, Vienna, Munich, Los Angeles, and many other places.

Maestro Sir **George Solti** and **Lady Solti** were also my close friends, and I wish to honor their memory.

When in 1974 I had arranged a reception for Princess Shams and Princess Fawzia, I also invited **Beverly Sills**, the famous American operatic soprano, to that reception. Our friendship began on that occasion, and she was a warm and affectionate friend. A photograph of that reception with the participation of Ms. Sills was published on the cover of a famous U.S. magazine.

I am fortunate to be a friend of **Tobias Richter**, director of the Geneva Grand Theater, famous for his work in the theater and opera, and his wife and family. Since 2004, he has been director of the International Festival of Classical Music in Montreux–Vevey, an event which has given me great enjoyment.

Mexico

Here I would like to make mention of Mr. **José López Portillo**. During the time when I was Iran's foreign minister I developed warm relations with Mexico, and it was decided that we should expand our relations and should appoint an accredited ambassador to each other's countries. Dr. Amir Aslan Afshar was the first Iranian ambassador to be given that role. During my second term as ambassador in the United States, I also served as the accredited ambassador to Mexico.

This is how I got to know the Mexican President **Luis Echeverría Álvarez**. During my meeting with President Álvarez, he sent an invitation to the Shah for an official visit to Mexico. During the Shah's visit, the Mexicans received him most warmly. Later on, Iran also hosted President Álvarez.

In the course of my visits to Mexico I became acquainted with a prominent Mexican politician, José López Portillo, who was the Mexican oil minister. I also became a friend of the Mexican ambassador to the United States, **José Juan de Olloqui y Labastida**, who later on became the Mexican foreign minister. I also found an opportunity to take the Shah's children for a visit to Mexico.

In 1976, López Portillo was elected president of Mexico. My friendship with him meant that when I was busy trying to find a suitable residence for the royal family after the revolution, I met with President López Portillo. He allowed the royal family to live in Mexico, and de Olloqui y Labastida warmly welcomed the Shah and the Empress at the airport.

I would like to express my profound and sincere gratitude to those distinguished politicians and to Mexico for their warm hospitality and for their friendship toward Iran.

Great Britain

The relationship between Great Britain (and, prior to that, the British Empire) and the members of my family has gone through many ups and downs. In the first volume of my memoirs I have referred to the kidnapping, arrest, and detention of my father for three years and the inappropriate behavior of British forces toward him.

At that time, the British regarded my father as an impediment to their policies in Iran. In a dispatch to London, the British ambassador, Sir **Reader Bullard**, described my father as the most dangerous enemy of the British Empire in Iran. Yet my father was not Britain's enemy. He was familiar with British history and culture and respected that country. However, he was always against the inappropriate interference by Britain and by other foreign countries in Iran's domestic affairs and fought against it. He was a true patriot. This is why he played a prominent role in the movement to nationalize the oil industry, and he supported Dr. Mossadegh for as long as the nationalist movement was united and harmonious. At that time, he was given the most sensitive posts in the government.

When I was appointed Iran's ambassador to the Court of St. James, in an emphatic manner and in a most eloquent tone my father told me, "You will be the representative of Iran and Iranian interests in Britain and you will become a symbol for Iranian diplomacy. You must forget your personal feelings and grudges."

He always had a great influence on me, and he was of course right in his advice. I accepted and implemented what he told me. Therefore, I cannot forget some prominent British figures whom I have known and who became my friends, and I wish to refer to some of them here and to honor their memory.

First of all, I wish to pay homage to **Her Majesty Queen Elizabeth II** and her husband **H.R.H. Prince Philip, the Duke of Edinburgh**, as well as to **Her Majesty Queen Elizabeth the Queen Mother**, who showed more than the customary and official friendship and affection toward my wife Princess Shahnaz and me. Her Majesty the Queen Mother and His Majesty King George VI were extremely popular with the British people, who admired their courage during the Second World War as they refused to leave London or send their children to Canada, even during the Blitz. This increased people's love for the royal couple.

Her Majesty Queen Elizabeth II paid a five-day official visit to Iran in March 1961, and she and Prince Philip were warmly welcomed by the Shah and the Shahbanou and by the Iranian people. Indeed, the beautiful and historic Golestan Palace, which houses the famous Peacock Throne, was for the first time refurbished for Her Majesty's stay in Tehran. The Shah and Empress Soraya had visited Britain in February 1954 privately and went again in May 1959 on a state visit.

Lord Louis Mountbatten was a true and wonderful friend of mine. He was a man of great influence. After the abdication of the former King Edward VIII, it was Lord Mountbatten who persuaded King Edward VIII's younger brother, the subsequent King George VI, to succeed his brother, and with his wisdom and statesmanship he ended the crisis that had gripped the British royal family. I can never forget Lord Mountbatten's kindness to me, and I honor his memory. I should also add to this list **Her Royal Highness Princess Margaret**, Her Majesty the Queen's sister, and **Princess Alexandra**, both of whom I had the privilege of knowing personally.

I also had the honor of knowing Sir **Winston Churchill**. I knew that that great and experienced politician had adopted some particular stance toward my country, which I could not support. However, I cannot overlook his exceptional character and the historic role that he played during the Second World War in saving the Free World from the scourge of Nazism. What he had predicted about the Cold War came to pass, and his insight into international issues was truly remarkable.

It is also necessary to refer to some other political figures, such as Sir **Harold Macmillan**, Sir **Alec Douglas-Home**, **James Callaghan**, and my very good friends **Edward Heath**, **Michael Stewart**, and **George Brown**.

I would also like to refer to a great lawyer and distinguished character, **Lord Shawcross**, who served as the lead British prosecutor at the Nuremberg War Crimes Tribunal, as well as attorney general, and his kind and honorable wife Lady Joan. Lord Shawcross was a true and sincere friend of Iran. In appreciation of his services to Iran, he was decorated with the First Order of Homayoun, First Class, by the Shah. For a number of years, he served as the president of the Iran Society. I also wish to thank his two distinguished and honorable sons, the author and historian William Shawcross and Hume Shawcross; and his distinguished daughter Dr. Joanna Shawcross, for all the kindness and friendship that they have shown my daughter and me over many years.

Among great British figures, I should also refer to the former British Prime Minister **Clement Attlee**, whom I met at an official reception that was given for the Shah by Sir Winston Churchill. I also met **Hugh Gaitskell**, former leader of the Labour Party, during the time when I was ambassador in London. I would also like to mention Lord **Dennis Healey**, whom I regard as a very distinguished and insightful British politician.

I also wish to express my respect to some of my other close and dear British friends, including Mr. and Mrs. **Mick** and **Camilla Neville**, Lady **Philippa Chelsea**, and Lady **Jane Wallop**. I would like to express my special thanks to Lady Wallop, who showed a great deal of kindness and hospitality to my daughter Mahnaz when she lived in England.

Among the British ambassadors to Iran I became very friendly with Sir **Roger** and **Lady Stevens** and Sir **Dennis** and **Lady Wright**. Both men were great scholars, as well as diplomats. Sir Roger was the author of two important books on Iran, *The Land of the Great Sophy* (1962) and *First View of Persia* (1964), both of which provide valuable information about the history of Iran and serve as guidebooks to modern travelers to Iran.

Sir **Dennis Wright** resumed friendly relationships with Iran after the rupture during the oil nationalization movement, and he was regarded as one of the most effective British ambassadors in Iran (1963–71). He authored two fascinating books, *The English Amongst the Persians* (1977) and *The Persians Amongst the English* (1985), which provide a good account of diplomatic relations between the two countries and the fascination of the two nations for each other. He retained his affection for Iran even after returning to England, holding office as chairman of the Iran Society (1976–79) and president of the British Institute of Persian Studies (1978–79).

Sir **Peter Ramsbotham** was another good friend who served as ambassador in Iran from 1971 to 1974, prior to being appointed as British ambassador to the United States. He was in Iran during the discussions about Bahrain, which eventually led to a referendum and the establishment of Bahrain as an independent state.

Sir **Paul Gore-Booth** and Sir **B. Allen**, undersecretaries of the Ministry of Foreign Affairs; **Earl and Lady Cairne**, marshal of the Diplomatic Corps; Sir **Michael Adeane**, who later became Baron Adeane, private secretary to Her Majesty Queen Elizabeth II; Mr. and Mrs. Harmsworth; and Sir Hugh and Lady Astor were a few more politicians with whom I worked closely, and to whom I wish to pay tribute. Sir Paul Gore-Booth's son, Sir **David Gore-Booth**, also served in the Foreign Office, as well as being appointed counselor and head of Chancery at the UK Mission to the United Nations and ambassador to Saudi Arabia.

Lord **Julian Amery** was another very dear friend of mine and a good friend of Iran. During the time that he served in the Foreign Office he had a lot of dealings with the country, especially over the withdrawal of Soviet forces that had invaded Iran during the Second World War and would not want to leave as had been agreed after the war. Lord Amery married **Catherine Macmillan**, daughter of the former British Prime Minister Harold Macmillan.

I also had the pleasure of knowing Sir **Christopher Soames**, later Baron Soames, and Lady Mary, the youngest daughter of Sir Winston Churchill. He held many important posts, including governor of Southern Rhodesia just before that country gained independence as Zimbabwe, leader of the House of Lords, European commissioner for external affairs, European commissioner for trade, as well as many cabinet posts in Harold Macmillan's government.

I would like also to express my thanks to the popular British broadcaster **Richard Dimbleby**, who covered the story of a major earthquake in Iran and managed to collect and send donations to the earthquake victims. Richard Dimbleby's son, the famous broadcaster David Dimbleby, also visited Iran when I was foreign minister.

The number of British scholars and academics who have made notable contributions to Iranian studies is too large to mention by name. However, I wish to pay a special tribute to my old friend **Peter Avery**,

OBE, who devoted his entire life to Iranian studies. He was an eminent scholar and fellow of King's College, Cambridge. Peter Avery spent many years in Iran and produced works on Iranian history and politics, such as *The Age of Expansion*; *Medieval Persia*; and *Modern Iran*, but Persian literature was his love. One of his best-known works was a translation (with poet John Heath-Stubbs) of *The Rubaiyat of Omar Khayyam*, first published in 1979, as well as *The Speech of the Birds: Mantiqu't-Tair of Fariddu'd-Din Attar*, published in 1998. He continued his work on Persian literature till the end of his life. He published his *Collected Lyrics of Hafiz of Shiraz* in 2007.

I was fortunate to visit my old friend in hospital shortly before his death in 2008. During a ceremony honoring Avery in London, he said that his biggest happiness in life had been his experiences studying Persian culture and language. "I am happy to have connections with Iran and Iranians, who enjoy a culture rich of civilization, kindness, truthfulness and understanding," he said, describing Iran as "my second homeland."

In these moments as I am writing these notes, I cannot help but remember a man who was, in my view, a truly dedicated and great secretary–general of the United Nations, **Dag Hammarskjöld**, a man who believed in politics in the service of humanity as so well explained in Sir Brian Urguhart's book on him 50 years after his death in Africa. Finally, I would like to express my warmest thanks and appreciation to Dr. Parviz Amouzegar, the former president of Ferdowsi University in Mashhad and the former dean of the Faculty of Law, Economy and Management in Paris, who helped in the editing of this book; and to Dr. Farhang Jahanpour, former dean of the Faculty of Languages at the University of Isfahan, former senior research fellow at the Department of Middle Eastern Studies at Harvard, and associate fellow at the Institute of Oriental Studies at the University of Oxford, for faithfully translating my memoirs.

From the time when, either willingly or unwillingly, I entered the world of politics and was involved in political developments, many of my friends encouraged me to write my memoirs. They argued that all of us will leave this earth, but history will remain. Future generations must know what has happened in the past and what earlier generations have experienced.

A book is never the work of one individual. Ahmad Ahrar asked questions, listened, and put my words on paper. Farhang Jahanpour translated the book into English. In the United States, Robin Easson quietly and carefully re-crafted the text for the English language reader. Susanne Knopp's comments, questions and suggestions after reading and re-reading this book have helped make it more accessible to the person who does not have a background in twentieth century Iranian history. In Europe, William O'Reilly also edited the English. Martine Jackson translated the French foreword into English. In England, the late Mohammad Pourdad assisted with various aspects of the book's creation. Alexandra Aber converted the Persian to Western dates. In Switzerland, Farrokh Derakhshani patiently and diligently coordinated the book's production. I wish to acknowledge and thank them all.

— Ardeshir Zahedi
Montreux, June 2012

Foreword and Acknowledgments from the Persian Edition

From the time when, either willingly or unwillingly, I entered the world of politics and was involved in political developments, many of my friends encouraged me to write my memoirs. They argued that all of us will leave this earth, but history will remain. Future generations must know what has happened in the past and what earlier generations have experienced.

However, in the face of that convincing logic, I was confronted with two problems. First, I am not a writer, and second, I was extremely busy and the pressure of work did not provide me with the luxury of sitting and writing a book. My literary and journalistic friends, who are used to writing, helped solve these problems. The conversations that I have had with them over the years have provided the basis for writing and editing my scattered political memoirs.

Here, I would like to refer to some of the friends who have always encouraged me to write my memoirs, some of whom are no longer with us. They include the late professors Zabih Behrouz and Nasrollah Falsafi and the late journalists Ali Asghar Amirani (managing editor of *Khandaniha* weekly), Dr. Rahmat Mostafavi (managing editor of *Rowshanfekr* newspaper), Abdollah Vala (managing editor of *Tehran Mosavvar* newspaper), and the Hashemi brothers (managing editors of *Ettehad-e Melli* newspaper).

My political memoirs were published for the first time in a series of articles under the title "Five Critical Days" in the periodical *Monthly Etela'at*, which was one of the leading magazines of the era, shortly after the events of August 1953. Those articles were about the dismissal of Mossadegh and my father's coming to power. Those articles, some of which have been included in the appendices of the present volume, were prepared and written with the help of my friend Nuraddin Nuri.

In those days, when I used to sit and talk with Nuraddin Nuri in a room on the third floor of the Officers' Club, I did not have an official position and was the master of my own time. Later on, as the result of the responsibilities that I accepted and the pressure of work and shortage of time, I was deprived of such leisurely conversations, which were a source of pleasure to me and a service to the country. However, during my enforced exile from my country, once again I have found the opportunity to engage in such activities.

My literary and journalistic friends, including Pari Abaselati and her husband Hushang Mirhashem, Hassan Shahbaz, Amir Taheri, Behruz Suresrafil, and the late Parviz Naghibi and Siavosh Bashiri, following our various meetings, have recorded and published some of my political memoirs. Dr. Ezatollah Homayounfar and Nur-Mohammad Askari have published two books based on their conversations with me, under the respective titles of *General Zahedi: From Soldier to Politician* and *Shah, Mossadegh, and Zahedi.* I have also had a long conversation with Dr. Habib Ladjevardi in the context of Harvard University's Iranian Oral History Project. I wish to express my thanks and gratitude to all the above-mentioned friends.

I would also like to express my gratitude for the efforts of my dear friends and colleagues, Dr. Daryoush Homayoun, Dr. Reza Ghassemi, and Dr. Ahmad Tehrani, who have played a major role in preparing and translating some of the documents and supervising the publication of this book.

I wanted to make sure that whatever I said or remembered was based on fact and that all the relevant documents would be provided in this book. However, some of my papers and documents were left behind in Iran and fell into the hands of revolutionary organizations and foundations. Some of those documents were collected and edited by the late Nasser Qushbeigi, for which I am grateful.

The present book is published by Farhad Shirzad of Ibex Publishers. Mrs. Simin Habibian and Mrs. Maryam Ghezeli tirelessly typed the Persian. Some major work, such as organizing and coordinating the contents of the book, has been carried out by Farrokh Derakhshani. I am grateful for all their efforts.

Finally, I wish to dedicate this book, which owes its preparation, arrangement, and editing to the efforts and care of my friend Ahmad Ahrar, to my daughter Mahnaz, and those of her generation. People write history from different angles. Those who live after a particular period in the world's history are entitled to have access to more than one account and one interpretation of history, so that they can better judge the past. What has been recorded in these memoirs is what I have experienced in my life. I hope it will shed some light on some details of history of which some people may not be fully familiar.

— Ardeshir Zahedi
Montreux, Spring 2006

Zahedi's Family Background

This is the translation of the first volume of a book that provides an important and exceptional account of a crucial period in Iran's history. It will be of great interest both to Iranian and international experts and scholars.

When an old friend of mine asked me to translate the memoirs of Ardeshir Zahedi, I willingly accepted, even without having seen the book. I have been fully vindicated in my expectations of the book, and I hope that this feeling will be shared by its reader. This book is important for a number of reasons.

First of all, Ardeshir Zahedi comes from one of the oldest Iranian families, which has played a leading role in Iran's political life for many centuries. On his mother's side, Ardeshir Zahedi is the grandson of Hossein Pirnia, known as Motamen ol-Molk (1875 to 1948), who was one of the most enlightened Iranian statesmen of the Constitutional period (1905 to 1911). He was elected to every session of the Iranian parliament (the Majles), which came into being after the Constitutional Revolution, from 1906 to 1943, and served as Majles speaker for many years. He was again elected from Tehran to the 14th Majles in 1943 but declined to serve due to old age. He also served as minister of education in 1918 and minister without portfolio in 1920.

Hossein Pirnia's older brother, Hassan Pirnia, known as Moshir od-Dowleh (1871 to 1935), was a famous politician and scholar who played a leading role in drafting the text of the Fundamental Law of the Constitutional Revolution signed by the Qajar King Mozaffar ed-Din Shah in 1906. After stints as minister of foreign affairs and minister of justice, Hassan Pirnia served four times as prime minister between 1915 and 1924. Following his retirement, he published a three-volume history of pre-Islamic Iran, entitled *Tarikh-e Iran-e Bastan* (History of Ancient Iran), which is still regarded as an indispensable text on the subject. Hassan and Hossein Pirnia's father, Mirza Nasrollah Khan, was also a prime minister during the Qajar era, and many of their ancestors had played leading roles in Iranian history for many centuries.

On his father's side, the Zahedi family trace their ancestry back to a famous 13ᵗʰ-century Iranian mystic whose name the family still bears, namely Taj od-Din Ebrahim, known as Sheykh Zahed Gilani, who came from the shores of the Caspian Sea. He was the Grand Murshid or Master of the famed Zahediyeh Sufi Order of Lahijan, whose beautiful shrine in the picturesque village of Sheikhanvar near Lahijan still attracts many pilgrims. His ancestors had come from Sanjan in Khorasan province, fleeing the Seljuq invasion, and they settled in Gilan in the late 11th century.

Sheikh Zahed's most notable disciple was Sheikh Safi ed-Din Arda-bili (1252 to 1334), the eponym of the Safavid Dynasty (1501 to 1736) that formed Iran's greatest dynasty after the Arab invasion in the 7th century AD. Safi ed-Din Ardabili married Sheikh Zahed's daughter Bibi Fatemeh, and their descendants ruled as Safavid monarchs. Therefore, for the past 800 years Zahedi's ancestors have played prominent roles in Iranian history.

Secondly, Ardeshir Zahedi's father, General Fazlollah Zahedi, was one of the architects of modern Iran. He was the youngest person ever to achieve the rank of general in the Iranian army. He was one of Reza Shah's closest commanders and took part in many campaigns after Reza Shah came to power in 1921, including the campaigns in Kurdistan to put an end to the rebellion by Esma'il Khan Semitqu; in Khuzistan against Sheykh Khazal, who wanted to set up an independent principality in that province; and in Gilan province against Mirza Kuchek Khan. Therefore, he played a decisive role in the consolidation of Reza Shah's reign and the establishment of a new unified Iran, which started on the path of the secular modernization of the country, with the establishment of a new regular army, new-style schools, the founding of Iran's first modern university, a new legal system; and early phases of industrialization of the country, including the introduction of the first medium-sized factories and the construction of the trans-Iranian railway.

General Fazlollah Zahedi was also the man who led the military campaign against Dr. Mohammad Mossadegh's government in 1953, after the late Shah Mohammad Reza Pahlavi had fled the country, and thus he restored the Shah to power and so initiated a most controversial period in Iran's recent history. Opinions regarding the 1953 coup are sharply divided. Some regard it as the end of Iran's boldest experimentation with democracy and the nationalization of the Iranian oil industry, while others see it as the beginning of 25 years of relative stability and rapid modernization that propelled Iran into the center of international politics at the height of the Cold War.

The third reason for the importance of this book is that Ardeshir Zahedi himself played a most crucial role in Iran's recent history. He was the Shah's son-in-law and was very close to him right to the end of his life. He served as Iranian ambassador to Great Britain (from 1962 to 1966) and twice to the United States (from 1959 to 1961 and again from 1972 to 1979) and as Iran's minister of foreign affairs (from 1966 to 1972). As the Iranian ambassador to the United States, he established close links with practically all the leading U.S. politicians and was on personal terms with a number of U.S. presidents. His lavish receptions and his closeness to many leading American figures had made him many friends in high places, as well as some enemies who accused him of interfering in U.S. domestic policies.

Apart from the high-profile posts that he held, his closeness to the Shah made him one of the most influential persons in Iran. This close relationship continued even after Zahedi and his wife, the Shah's daughter, Princess Shahnaz, separated. He was the Shah's confidant and adviser on whose advice the Shah often acted.

The fourth reason for the importance of this book is Zahedi's close involvement in the events of 1953 and 1978–1979. Zahedi's version of the ouster of Dr. Mossadegh's government is controversial and goes against the dominant narrative that the coup had been staged solely by MI6 and the CIA. Zahedi challenges the versions given by Kermit Roosevelt and Monty Woodhouse, the main architects of the coup, and other authors who have repeated their versions of events. Kermit

Roosevelt has understandably embellished some of the details about his role in the coup, but as Ardeshir Zahedi points out in the book, his father met Roosevelt for the first time after the coup. Writing in his diary about his meeting with Kermit Roosevelt when the latter gave him a personal briefing about the coup, President Eisenhower rightly stated, "I listened to his detailed report, and it seemed more like a dime novel than historical facts." Zahedi does not deny the existence of a foreign plot to unseat Mossadegh's government, but he provides evidence from declassified U.S. archives that according to the U.S. Embassy in Tehran, Kermit Roosevelt's efforts had failed.

Zahedi maintains that the coup was really an attempt by the Iranian military and a sizable section of the Iranian elite and ordinary people who were worried about the course that events had taken during the latter part of Mossadegh's government. This version of events by someone who was intimately involved in those events is certainly worth hearing, because it might correct many erroneous assumptions about those momentous events and America's role in them. It is worth noting that General Zahedi was related to Dr. Mossadegh through his wife, and in fact he served as interior minister in Mossadegh's cabinet. He was not against the nationalization of the oil industry but feared that Iran would fall to the Soviet Union, despite Dr. Mossadegh's wishes, had the dispute with the West and domestic chaos continued for much longer.

Many Iranians rightly regard Dr. Mossadegh as one of their national heroes and admire his nationalization of the Iranian oil industry. However, the notion that he was universally popular and the Shah was universally hated at the time of the coup is one that has become part of the national mythology. I personally witnessed two contrasting feelings at the time of the failed coup on the night of 15–16 August 1953 that led to the Shah's departure from Iran, followed by the military operation on 19 August that toppled Dr. Mossadegh's government and reinstated the Shah. While the feeling among many educated, urban young people, especially the followers of the communist Tudeh Party and other left-leaning parties, was strongly pro-Mossadegh, the sentiment among many other traditional classes, especially in the countryside where still most Iranians resided, was overwhelmingly pro-Shah.

I vividly remember those events as a schoolboy. My father owned some farms and gardens in a pleasant village in Kerman province, where we spent most of our summer vacations in order to escape the extreme summer heat of the town where we lived. As there were few radios in the village during those critical days of August 1953, large numbers of villagers gathered round our radio to listen to the latest news bulletins. When on 16 August it was announced that the Shah had fled the country, and Foreign Minister Hossein Fatemi announced in an insulting tone that the Shah's palaces had been seized and sealed, many villagers openly sobbed. However, when, three days later, General Fazlollah Zahedi's voice was heard on the national radio announcing the fall of the former government and asking the Shah to return to the country, many villagers ran wildly through the village shouting, "The Shah is back!"

Ardeshir Zahedi's serious involvement in politics started with the 1953 coup, in which he played an important part on his father's side, and it ended with the 1979 Iranian revolution, which he made every effort to forestall. In September 1978, shortly before the Iranian revolution, the Shah summoned Zahedi to Tehran for consultation and to discover the views of the members of the Carter administration regarding the latest developments in Iran.

His arrival in Iran gave rise to many rumors that he might be asked to form a government and repeat what his father had done for the Shah in 1953. Zahedi was certainly popular among a number of leading clerics, chief among them Grand Ayatollah Abol-Ghassem Khoi and Grand Ayatollah Mohammad Kazem Shariatmadari, who were strongly opposed to Ayatollah Ruhollah Khomeini's radical interpretation of Islam and who gave their backing to Zahedi.

Zahedi also enjoyed the overwhelming support of military commanders, who had a strong admiration for his father and urged him to "do something." However, Zahedi, who was as always loyal to the

Shah, did not want to go over his head to form a government, and the official invitation from the Shah never came. The outcome of Zahedi's possible involvement in domestic politics at such a late stage is only a matter of speculation, to which we will never know the answer. Nevertheless, it is yet another sign of the key role that he played in Iranian politics right up to the eve of the revolution. After the revolution he was engaged in desperate efforts to find a residence for the Shah and the royal family, who had been rejected by most of their former allies and friends.

The fifth reason for the importance of this book is for the mirror that it holds up to Iranian politics prior to the Islamic revolution, as well as to the approach of Western and especially U.S. politicians toward the events in Iran. That 25-year period, when Ardeshir Zahedi was at the heart of Iranian politics, constitutes the most important period in Iran's recent history. Reza Shah's reign put an end to the medieval Qajar period and ushered in the start of modern Iran. His reformist policies were continued by his son Mohammad Reza Shah.

During the reign of the two Pahlavis, Iran was transformed from one of the poorest countries in the world to a showcase of development among the Third World countries. In 1920, Iran had a largely farm-based economy with endemic poverty and starvation. In 1979, it boasted one of the most developed economies in the Middle East, having made major strides toward industrialization. During the last 15 years of the Shah's reign, Iranians' per capita income had increased twelvefold, from $195 annually in 1963 to approximately $2,400 in 1978 before the Islamic revolution. One indication of the relative decline of the Iranian economy since the victory of the revolution is the relative value of the Iranian currency. Throughout the 1970s, the Iranian tuman was pegged to the dollar at seven tumans for one dollar. During the past decades, despite hundreds of billions of dollars in oil revenue, the value of the Iranian currency has fluctuated between 1,000 and 1,100 tumans to a dollar.

Under the late Shah, thanks to considerable outlay allocated to education, health, and social welfare, great strides were made in improving the lives of millions of Iranians. Infant mortality, malnutrition, endemic diseases, and illiteracy were greatly reduced. While rural versus urban income gaps and income inequalities persisted, indicators showed that large sections of the society had moved out of poverty to relative affluence. Elementary school enrollment during the 1970s quadrupled to more than nine million, while the number of university students—all of them receiving free education and subsidies—was over two hundred thousand.

Iranians enjoyed many social liberties, including freedom of assembly, of dress, of travel, of religion, of entertainment, and the use of alcohol. Women had been emancipated, had been given the vote, and could be elected to high office, with many female ministers, university professors, judges, and lawyers. Iranians could visit almost all European countries without a visa, and some three million Iranian tourists traveled abroad annually. However, despite all those liberties and economic benefits, Iranians felt that their political freedom was restricted. The main reason behind the Islamic revolution was to create a freer and more independent country. However, while Iranians have not achieved political freedom, they have lost nearly all the other liberties that they enjoyed under the Shah.

Most Iranians, including many of those who took part in the revolution, feel cheated and look nostalgically back to the times of the Shah. Many people believe that the Pahlavi period was certainly superior to what had preceded it and clearly much more enlightened than what has followed it. Nevertheless, it is important to carefully analyze the events of those years and examine the reasons for the emergence of the Islamic revolution. A proper assessment of those fifty-seven years can provide many lessons for the Iranians, as well as for the nations in the Middle East and North Africa that have bravely arisen against dictatorship and oppression. Learning from those events can help them avoid making the same mistakes as the Iranians did after the collapse of the former regime.

For all these reasons, the present book is worthy of careful consideration by all those who are interested in Iran's recent history. It can provide lessons for the present generation of Iranians, as well as for their counterparts in the region and for the West, in deciding how to respond to these upheavals.

This book is not written as a pretentious academic exercise but is in the form of a simple conversation, with the author narrating his memories honestly and openly, mingling the good with the bad. The English translation has closely followed the original, but as some parts of the original Persian volumes were of little interest to the Western reader, with the author's consent and permission some parts of the original have been condensed, with some chapters being deleted altogether. The transliteration method used in this translation does not follow the standard academic transliteration, but the words and the names are spelled as they normally appear in the press.

This book will no doubt give rise to a great deal of debate and controversy, but this is one of the functions of any good book. Therefore I strongly commend the present book to Iranians abroad who cannot read Persian and to non-Iranians who are interested in Iran's eventful recent history.

— Farhang Jahanpour
Oxford, Spring 2011

Chapter One
My Father's Arrest and Exile

Question: After Reza Shah's resignation and the start of the reign of Mohammad Reza Shah, your father, Fazlollah Zahedi, who was by then a brigadier general, was again given responsible military posts. What was his first posting?

Zahedi: His first posting was as the commander of the National Gendarmerie, which was still called the Security Force (*amniyyeh*). In Mohammad-Ali Foroughi's cabinet, which was the first cabinet under Reza Shah's reign, Amanollah Mirza Jahanbani was appointed minister of the interior. Jahanbani was an old friend of my father's. The two of them had worked together in the battle against Semitqu, and both of them had received the Zolfaghar Medal as the result of that battle. In 1937, General Jahanbani, who was the director general of the Department of Industries (subsequently, the Ministry of Industries and Mines), had fallen out of favor with Reza Shah, who had him arrested. When Jahanbani was released from jail, my father founded a new construction firm called Zamaneh Company and appointed Jahanbani as its director so that he would not be unemployed.

In any case, at the suggestion of Major General Jahanbani, who once again had found favor with Reza Shah as the result of changed circumstances and had been made minister of the interior, my father was appointed commander of the Security Force. He did not stay more than three months in that post, but even in that short time he changed the name of the Security Force to the Gendarmerie and chose a new uniform for the gendarmes.

At this time, the central government was very concerned about the situation in the south of the country, because the Qashqais had returned to their estates and the Bakhtiaris had started an uprising against the central government. The rebels included Haj Shahab os-Saltaneh (the great uncle of Queen Soraya), Abol-Ghassem Khan, and Morteza Gholi Khan. It was rumored that a number of German spies had gone to the tribal areas in Fars province and intended to incite an uprising there, just as they had done during the First World War.

As my father had friendly relations with the leaders of the Qashqai tribe and was well known in Fars province, people would listen to him, and so, toward the end of December 1941 he was appointed commander of the Ninth Army Division of Isfahan, replacing General Shaghaghi (Hosn al-Dowleh). The man who acted as an intermediary in talks between my father and the Bakhtiaris was called Ali Abadi. Very soon afterward, Abol-Ghassem Khan and, a short time later, Morteza Gholi Khan surrendered. The Qashqais also quieted down, but after my father's arrest they launched an attack, surrounded Semirom, and killed Colonel Shaghaghi and a large number of military personnel.

That mission lasted for one year, and in December 1942 the British arrested my father and transferred him to a detention center in Palestine.[1] A number of other Iranian political and military figures were also arrested and imprisoned by the Allies on charges of collaborating with the Germans and conspiring against the Allies.

There were a number of reasons why the British were suspicious of my father. One reason was my father's friendly relations with the leaders of the Qashqai and Bakhtiari tribes. In order to establish security in the region, my father made use of his personal ties to the Qashqai and Bakhtiari tribes. At times he would go hunting in the tribal areas with them, while at the same time he was watching the situation there. The British had received reports that during those contacts my father was planning a movement called Iran's Liberation Movement, so that if the Germans managed to smash the Russian defenses and reached the Caucasus, liberation movements in Iran, with the assistance of tribal and military forces, could rise up against the occupying forces.

Another reason for the British suspicion was the way that my father had dealt with British officers, who regarded Iran as an occupied country and behaved as though they owned the country and expected Iranian officials to obey their commands.

During the war, Iran suffered from a food shortage. The Allies had confiscated all the grain that the Axis powers had stored in Iranian villages that were under their occupation. In Tehran, most people's diet consisted of a loaf of very hard, black bread, which was called silo bread and which people called "brick bread." In fact, it very much resembled a brick.[2]

At that time, *sangak* bread (a variety of local bread) was in abundance in Isfahan, because my father had ordered that the wheat harvest from each area should be stored there and that Iranian officials should be given priority to purchase it. A British official had gone to the area to discover those stores, and the head of the Department of Finance had gone with him. When my father learned of this issue he became very angry and wanted to have the head of the Department of Finance arrested. He fled to Tehran and took his complaint to Ghavam os-Saltaneh, who was the prime minister at the time. Ghavam was basically in agreement with my father's decision, but *Khorshid-e Iran* newspaper, whose managing editor was believed to have close relations with the British and worked for them, made a great deal of fuss. In an article he claimed that General Zahedi was behaving like Nasser ed-Din Shah in Isfahan and that he thought that it was still Nasser ed-Din Shah's time. The article alleged that my father had arrested and imprisoned the heads of various departments. I should add that at the time when my father was the commander of the Ninth Army Division of Isfahan, he was promoted to the rank of major general.

Another reason for the British grudge against my father was that the government had decreed that when foreign nationals wanted to go to different parts of the country they had to inform the military or the law-enforcement personnel, so that they would not face any security problems. After occupying Iran, the British did not observe those rules. As a result, there had been some disagreement between my father and the British consul in Isfahan over that issue as well. A few British families had decided to travel to different parts of the country without informing the army command. On the way, they were attacked by some armed tribal people and killed. The British blamed my father for that incident.

There was another reason for their unhappiness. A few months before Iran's occupation by the Allies, Rashid Ali Gaylani, Iraq's prime minister, and Sheikh Amin al-Hosseini, the grand mufti of Palestine, had taken refuge in Iran after the resistance movement in Iraq had been defeated. The British demanded their extradition, but the Iranian government believed that it was contrary to the laws of hospitality to hand them over to the British. Rashid Ali and the grand mufti remained in Iran for a while as the guests of the Iranian government. They were kept in the house of Fatan os-Saltaneh Majd, Rudbar's deputy in the Iranian parliament (the Majles), which was next door to our house in Valiabad Street in Tehran. When the Allies invaded Iran, the lives of those two individuals, who were regarded as Britain's enemies, were in danger. My father secretly transferred them to my aunt's house, which was also in Valiabad Street, opposite our own house. They stayed there until arrangements were made for their escape, when they were escorted to the Iran–Turkey border and went to Turkey.

To sum up, the British regarded my father's position as the commander of the Ninth Army Division of Isfahan as a source of danger to them. At the same time, they had not forgotten the events of Khuzestan and the arrest of Sheikh Khazal. Consequently, they decided to arrest my father by launching special operations and to take him out of the country. MacLean, who had been given the mission to arrest my father and who had been sent from Benghazi for that purpose, has written the details of that arrest.[3]

At that time, my sister and I were schoolchildren. My sister Homa went to the same school as Soraya Esfandiary-Bakhtiary (later Her Royal Highness Queen Soraya). I studied at Adab school, which was only 200 meters away from their school. We ate our lunch with our father and left for school. When we returned from school one day, he had been captured. We did not see our father again until he returned to Tehran from his exile in Palestine.

Question: How long was he kept in prison?

Zahedi: About three years. At first, we had no idea where our father was kept. The British consul had told him that a military team was passing through Isfahan to go to Tehran, and the commander of that team wished to meet with him and pay his respects. My father had agreed to the meeting. The team went to the house with a few military trucks carrying armed soldiers.

The trucks stopped in front of the garden of the house where my father lived. A British officer, whom my father had been led to believe was a general, although later it became clear that he was a member of the British intelligence services, went inside the house with MacLean. My father greeted them, and they suddenly pulled out weapons and told him that he had to go with them. Later on, my father told us that he thought that if he had resisted there would have been bloodshed, and it would have been futile anyway. He also had thought about us, that as we returned from school we might have been killed too. This is why he agreed to go to the British consulate with them to see what they wanted.

From there, they took him to Arak and put him in an aircraft, flew him to Palestine, and imprisoned him in a monastery close to Tel Aviv. At that time, my father sent a postcard to Sarem od-Dowleh (Akbar Mirza Masoud), saying that he had left the country and asking Sarem od-Dowleh to take care of his children.[4]

In brief, we packed all our belongings and came to Tehran. When we arrived, there were many disturbances there. The events of 17th of Azar [December 8] and riots over the shortage of bread took place, and Ghavam os-Saltaneh's house was attacked and plundered.

Question: What did you do in Tehran?

Zahedi: I enrolled in Elmiyyeh School, behind Sepahsalar Mosque, so that my studies would not be interrupted, because it was the beginning of the academic year. The head teacher was a wonderful man called Mr. Emami. Later on, when I was appointed ambassador to London, I brought him to England and put him in charge of Iranian students in Britain. He was a very patriotic man. He was also very kind to me.

In those days we could not get a straight answer from anybody we got in touch with in order to get some information about our father. Anoushiravan Sepahbodi was minister of foreign affairs, and he was related to me through my mother. Accompanied by Dr. Hosseingholi Ghazalayagh and Fazel ol-Molk, I went to see him to ask why my father had been arrested. That poor man started to cry, and for a while both of us cried, but I did not receive any answer to my question. When we left his office, Fazel ol-Molk said, "I don't know what we learned about Fazlollah, apart from all that crying!"

One day, I went to see General William Fraser, the commander of the British forces in Iran, together with Dr. Ghazalayagh, who was my father's friend and who served many years as a Majles deputy. General Fraser's deputy, Lt. Col. Gilbert Douglas Pybus, was also there. I was young and rather rude. When I asked about my father and his fate and received an inadequate response, I started cursing. General Fraser, speaking Persian with an English accent, said, "I do not understand Persian well." I said, "At least, you understand the meaning of my swearwords!" The truth is that at that time I had no idea where my father was and whether he was still alive or whether they had killed him. This is why I lost control.

By chance, many years later, when I was Iranian ambassador in England, I arranged a reception for the Anglo-Iranian Society, and General Fraser and Colonel Pybus were among the guests. They were rather worried about how we would deal with each other, but I approached them in a very friendly manner and told them that the past is the past.

Question: In *Memoirs of Service*, Fazlollah Nureddin Kia has provided some details about the power of attorney that your father had sent from prison.

Zahedi: The story of the power of attorney is rather complicated. Unfortunately, many people who my father thought would help me to receive that power of attorney, due to certain considerations, were not even prepared to accompany me (because in order to receive the document that granted us power of attorney, we had to get in touch with British officials). However, some of the details that are written in that book on this issue are mistaken. First, at that time I was in Tehran, and I had not gone to Beirut before my father was released from prison. Second, my parents had been separated for a long time by then, and there was no point about issuing the power of attorney in my mother's name.

In any case, one night when I was walking toward our home through Shahreza Avenue, a very large man suddenly emerged from behind the trees and stood right in front of me. Valiabad Street was a beautiful street and had some very old trees, and there was a stream running at the foot of the trees. Many students used to go there and sit by the stream to study their books. I was frightened and thought the man was going to attack me, but I soon discovered that he had no evil intent and wanted only to speak with me. He was an Arab Druze. He did not know my language, and I could not understand what he was saying. Under the dim light of the streetlamps he showed me an envelope, on which I recognized my father's handwriting. Still, I was not sure what to do.

The strange man, with difficulty, made me understand that nobody should learn anything about this encounter, and that he would come the following day to receive my reply to the note that he had handed me. A few days earlier it had been rumored that my father had been killed. I was very attached to him and had decided to commit suicide. I lived in a small apartment on one side of the garden, and my sister and aunt lived on the other side. I went to my room. I had a revolver that my father had given me. I put it to my head and pulled the trigger. The trigger made a noise and I did not feel anything else. Perhaps I had lost consciousness due to fear. When I opened my eyes, I thought that I had died. I kept asking myself whether I was in paradise or in hell. I took the revolver and fired toward a black bird that was sitting in a tree. Hearing the sound of the shooting, everybody in the house rushed to my room to see what had happened. At that time, I realized the bullet had not been fired and that I was still alive. I reassured everyone that nothing was wrong and that I had just wanted to shoot at a bird.

The letter that the Arab man had brought with him was no longer than a line and a half. My father had simply informed us that he was well, which of course was the best message for us. I showed the letter only to my aunt and told her that it must remain secret. We wrote a short letter in response to his note and gave it to the Arab man. He was a leading Druze Shi'i, and later on his brother became the minister of war in Lebanon. A few Druze leaders had been detained in the monastery with my father. Through them my father had managed to write those couple of lines and to send them to us. No matter how hard we tried to reciprocate the kindness of that Arab man and at least give him a gift, he did not accept.

At the same time, Rahmat Atabaki, my aunt's son-in-law, was our consul general in Lebanon. Masoud Moazed, who was the husband of Ahmad Mirfendereski's aunt and who was one of our very able diplomats, was our ambassador in Beirut. I decided to go to Beirut to continue my studies. I asked for a passport. A long time passed, but I did not receive any response. At the same time, my sister Homa became seriously ill. We had a family doctor who had been educated in Germany. His name was Dr. Alizadeh (he may be the same person referred to in Taghizadeh's memoirs, where it says that a young man by that name had been sent to Europe to study medicine). In the past, his clinic had been opposite Qurkhaneh, but later he had moved to Shahabad Street. At that time I did not have a car. I used to go on foot from Hesarak to Tajrish, where I would a catch a bus to Tehran.

I went to Tehran to bring Dr. Alizadeh with me to visit Homa. I got off the bus at Shemiran Bend, where my aunt's servant approached me and said the master was back. I said, "Which master?" He replied, "Your father!" I told him not to speak nonsense, but he swore that it was my father. He said, "He asked for you, but I told him that you were not there and had gone to Hesarak." I was stunned. I said, "My father is in a British jail. What is he doing here?" I asked him if he was certain that it was my father he had seen. He replied that the person he saw very much resembled my father. There were no public telephones in Hesarak at that time. I rushed to Dr. Alizadeh's clinic and together we went to Mokhber al-Dowleh Square and got on a bus toward Tajrish. I told the bus driver that my sister was very ill, that I had to take the doctor to her as soon as possible and would pay him if he would take us to Hesarak, and he agreed. We moved toward Hesarak, but the road was very rough. On the way, the bus got bogged down in a stream. I did not wait any longer and ran all the way to Hesarak, where I saw my father. I kissed his hands and face and wept tears of joy. A short time later, the doctor got there.[5]

---

[1] The report of the Police Department in Isfahan. Ministry of Foreign Affairs, appendix to file number 25/2/6/5 of the prime minister's office, compiled by Anushiravan Azod.

> Dated 19 Azar 1321 [10 December 1942]
> At 1800 hours on the 16 Azar [7 December 1942] a number of British officers went to General Zahedi's house in two cars, arrested him and took him with them toward Tehran [as has been recorded in Ardeshir Zahedi's memoirs, the British took General Zahedi from Isfahan to Arak and from there to Palestine].

[2] Confidential report of the Ministry of Foreign Affairs, dated 13/10/21 [2 January 1943], has the following:

> According to the reports that have been received from London, official circles there are not very happy that the Iranian ambassador has not yet been able to meet with [Sir Winston] Churchill. Although the Shah has sent a cable to the British king and the Iranian prime minister has sent a cable to Churchill, yet the Iranian ambassador has not been able to meet with Churchill yet. The Iranian

ambassador has been authorised by the Iranian government to explain to the British government that the shortage of grains in Iran has assumed dangerous proportions. He has also been told to convey the complaints of the Iranian government regarding the fact that the British have not fulfilled their commitments, and ask them to alleviate the problems in Iran by acting on their commitments.

In the course of the talks that the Iranian ambassador has had with the British foreign secretary and the heads of some departments in the Foreign Office during the past few weeks he has informed them that the situation of food-stuffs in Iran cannot be endured any further. They should not further postpone the distribution of 30,000 tonnes of wheat that they had promised last year, and the 350 lorries that are needed for distributing the grains in different parts of the country. The shortage of food, especially in the capital, has reached a critical stage, and they believe that they will not be able to prevent starvation there.

³ Below are the details of Zahedi's arrest, as published in the periodical *People*, translated by Kaveh Dehgan. They are quoted from *The Biography of General Zahedi*, edited by Ebrahim Safai (Tehran: Elmi Publications, 1372 [1993]).

British forces had a camp in Qom and they could attack Isfahan from there in order to arrest Zahedi. However, apart from the fact that such an attack would have been against the Tripartite Agreement, it might have met with resistance by Zahedi and the army division under his command. It was also possible that Zahedi's forces could have joined up with Qashqai forces, and that his resistance would have produced many difficulties, losses and damage for Britain. Even if British diplomats were thinking of talking to the Iranian government about Zahedi's arrest, they thought that no Iranian military officer would carry out that mission, especially as Zahedi's support for the Germans was also shared by many Iranian officers.

This is why they decided to kidnap Zahedi and send him into exile. Fitzroy MacLean, a British intelligence officer, was chosen to carry out that task. MacLean, who was in Benghazi at that time, received a confidential order to immediately report to General Wilson, the commander of British forces in Iran, for carrying out a special operation. MacLean came to Iran, and after many meetings and detailed talks with General Wilson and British military and intelligence experts, the plan to kidnap Zahedi was finalized. Together with another spy, MacLean left with two trucks full of British soldiers from the British commando headquarters in Qom toward Isfahan. He was given orders that if Zahedi showed any resistance while being arrested and kidnapped he should be imme-

diately shot. In Isfahan, MacLean made his plans in consultation with John
Gault, the British consul, and carefully put the house and the garden where
Zahedi was staying under strict observation. Then, John Gault phoned Zahedi
and told him that a high-ranking British officer had come from Baghdad to
Isfahan on an important mission and wished to meet with him. He then gave
the telephone to MacLean, who repeated the same message. Zahedi agreed to
that meeting and on 16 Azar 1321 [7 December 1942] at six o'clock in the afternoon, MacLean left for Zahedi's house in the consul's car with two covered
military trucks. He put the soldiers in one truck in charge of guarding the street
that led to Zahedi's house and the soldiers in the other truck of guarding the
area in front of Zahedi's house, and gave them the necessary instructions about
how to deal with any possible clashes. At the same time, the telegraph and telephone lines between the military barracks outside the city and Zahedi's headquarters had been cut. MacLean was being accompanied by another British man
who was also a spy, but on orders from higher officers he was wearing the uniform of a general. There were three soldiers armed with machine guns inside the
car. In front of Zahedi's house, a soldier who was guarding the entrance led
McLean and the British general to the building and MacLean and the intelligence general arrived in the reception room. They were served tea, and then
Zahedi, dressed in his military uniform, entered the reception room to meet his
guests. However, as he stepped in he saw the barrel of MacLean's revolver stuck
in front of his face. MacLean in a harsh tone ordered him, "Raise your arms.
Don't move. You must come with us, and if you resist you will be shot." Zahedi
asked for the reason for that behavior. MacLean repeated his previous orders.
When Zahedi saw that resistance was useless and dangerous he surrendered. He
removed his revolver on MacLean's orders and handed it to him. MacLean took
Zahedi out of the house while still holding the revolver to his head and took
him to the car. The soldiers who were guarding the front of Zahedi's house
came forward, but Zahedi ordered them to move back. MacLean took Zahedi
out of the city to a place in the desert where a British military aircraft had been
readied for flight. He and his machine gun-toting soldiers left the car and handed Zahedi to a British officer, who had been ordered to take Zahedi to Palestine.
A few British officers who were near the aircraft took Zahedi inside, and the
aircraft left for Palestine. The same night, on returning to the city, MacLean
went to Zahedi's house and searched his bedroom and found a collection of
German automatic weapons, a map of different parts of Isfahan, some papers
and a few letters that had been written to him from the German military headquarters, and he took all of them with him to the British consulate.

After Zahedi's arrest by British officers, for a number of days the telephone and telegraph links between Isfahan and Tehran and Shiraz were cut. During the same days, the Iranian armed forces had occupied the Qashqai region and had taken charge of the main road that cut that region in half. British patrol groups controlled that important and sensitive road and prevented any movement by Qashqai forces in that region.

[4] In *Memoirs of Service* by Fazlollah Nureddin Kia, we read:

Getting to know Major Abba Eban and the story of General Zahedi, the political prisoner under the British:

One day when I was working in the [Iranian] consulate, and my room was full of people who had come for some business, the doorman in the mission came hurriedly to me and said, "A British officer wishes to see you over an urgent issue." I told him to take that officer to the consul, but he replied, "No, he only wants to see you." I was forced to send the people who were in that room to another room in the mission and to stand alone at the door of the room to receive this high-ranking officer. Visits by such individuals to the consulate were unprecedented. After a few moments, a tall British officer in military uniform appeared in the corridor in front of the room. He gave me a military salute and introduced himself. He said, "I am Major Abba Eban, from the British military intelligence." I shook his hand and we sat together on a leather sofa by the desk. There were a couple of sofas in the room. Before starting our discussion he said, "You certainly know that my country and Iran are now friends and are united against our common enemy, the bloodthirsty Nazis. Therefore, I would like to ask you that our conversation today should remain secret and should remain with us." I stared at him with surprise, and I was waiting for the rest of what he had to say. He then said some officials of his country had brought a high-ranking Iranian officer for security reasons to Palestine and had kept him in the camp for the prisoners of war. That officer (at that time he did not mention his name) wishes to give the power of attorney to his wife for a number of personal and registration issues. He also wishes to write a check in the name of his son, who is studying in Beirut, and he hopes that your office in charge of consular affairs would certify his signature at the bottom of the document. He then added, "For three months I have been secretly in contact with the chief Iranian consul in Jerusalem and I wanted to have the consulate certify these documents. Unfortunately, during that period anytime I got in touch with your consul he refused to carry out our request with some excuses that did not seem logical, and this has caused a great deal of anxiety to our prisoner of war and his family in Iran. As our request is absolutely in accordance with international law and human principles, I have come to you today to make this request personally, so that you issue orders so that the request of this prisoner of war, with which we agree one hundred percent, will be carried out. I must add that when I heard that you are a positive and educated official, instead of acting on behalf of my government through the British Embassy in Tehran, I decided to do this directly through you and through Iran's mission in Jerusalem. This will please the security officials in my country and will alleviate the hardship of the family of this prisoner of war." As I was familiar with the character of our head of mission, after a little thought I told him, "Has your prisoner of war been convicted of any wrongdoing?" He answered, "No, all our prisoners of war who are kept in Palestine are high-ranking officials of their countries, who have been brought here for political reasons, and they have not been convicted of anything so far." I replied, "As far as my knowledge of the law dictates, an Iranian prisoner of war abroad, even though he might have been sentenced to death, will be able to write a will, etc. and to have those or other documents certified by the consulate of his country. The only documents that will be recognized by Iranian authorities would be those that have been certified by the Iranian missions abroad." Abba Eban became very happy at hearing those words and seeing that the issue could be solved. He said, "They were right to tell me to talk to you who are in charge of the consular issues in this mission." I advised him not to raise that issue with the chief consul, because his English was not very good and he was not able to discuss and resolve personal and consular issues. Secondly, on the following day he should bring the documents that had been signed by that Iranian officer, which have also been confirmed by government officials in Palestine, whose signature we had at the consulate so that I could do what was necessary. I also told him that I would personally raise the matter with the head of the consulate, and I would try to get his permission, as he had already talked to the consul. Abba Eban left my room very happy.

A couple of days later, Major Eban came back to me and took a document out of his bag, containing the power of attorney that the prisoner had issued in his wife's name, as well as a check, and gave them to me. At that time, it became clear that the person who was the British government's prisoner of war was General Fazlollah Zahedi, and the check was written in the name of his son, Ardeshir Zahedi, and both signatures had been certified by British government officials. After taking a copy of the documents for filing in the archives of the consulate, General Zahedi's signature and the authorization by the government of Palestine were certified by the head of the Iranian consulate and were handed back to Eban. Meanwhile, as I had repeatedly met Zahedi in the house of my brother in Tehran and as he knew me, I asked Major Eban to convey my regards to him.

While leaving my room, Major Eban all of a sudden started to read a beautiful and relevant line of poetry by the Persian poet Sa'di, namely:

> *Children of Adam are limbs of one another*
> *As in creation they are members of one body.*

I was very surprised and asked him how he had learned Persian poetry. He said, "I will come back again, and if you let me I will spend a few minutes with you and I will explain." At eight o'clock the following day when I arrived at the consulate I saw that a British jeep had parked outside the building even before my arrival, and Major Eban was waiting there for me. After customary greetings, he handed me a letter from General Zahedi in an open envelope. It was clear that Major Eban had already read it. In that letter, Zahedi had thanked me for my help and had cursed my boss who had kept him waiting for so long for such a minor issue. He had also asked me to get in touch with Rahmat Atabaki, who was in charge of consular affairs in Beirut, and to ask him to come to Beirut with Ardeshir Zahedi and receive those signed documents. Therefore, according to Zahedi's wishes, Major Eban again handed back those documents to me in return for a receipt. He stayed a few minutes in my office to have tea and to explain to me why he could speak Persian. According to him, before serving in the British Army, he had been a graduate of Cambridge University in Oriental languages and he was quite fluent in Arabic and Persian. Taghizadeh had been his Persian teacher in London.

As I was very busy in the consulate, Eban asked if he could come one day a week to my house so that we could read together some poems of Hafez and Sa'di whose books I had in my house. I willingly accepted his request, and I entertained him a few times in my house, as he was a man of letters. I also gave him a copy of the *Gulistan* of Sa'di as a gift, which he was very pleased to have. Anytime that I saw him he would praise Iranian civilization and culture and would speak highly of the Iranian people, and spoke about the influence of Persian culture on various societies and civilizations in the world. Later on, Major Eban served as Israel's foreign minister.

[5] From prison, Zahedi had written a letter to Motamen ol-Molk, and the draft of that letter is still available in some of his personal papers. He wrote:

My dear Sir,
I believe that it would very good if my children, Ardeshir and Homa, could live under your and your dear wife's supervision, and could continue their studies. If

you agree, please arrange for a nanny who also knows a foreign language to be employed, and please house the children in your own mansion. Please tell Mostafa Zahedi to pay whatever is the cost of their upkeep and the nanny's salary from the income of the farms. Whether they spend the summers in Hesarak or in town [Tehran] will be up to you.

Respectfully, your servant

Major General Zahedi

Chapter Two
From the Battlefield to the Field of Politics

Question: What was the effect of your father's release and his return to your life?

Zahedi: Only about ten days after my father's return, I received a message saying that my visa for Lebanon was ready. As long as he was in prison in Palestine, I had been refused a visa. My father told me, "I do not like lies! As you had falsely said that you wanted to go to Lebanon to continue your studies, you must go there. As Rahmat [Atabeki] is there now, go to Beirut and continue your studies there."

In fact, before the start of the war, there had been some talk of my going to Beirut to study. I wanted to go to Germany, but my mother's cousin, Davud Khan Pirnia, urged me to go to England. As it happened, I went to Lebanon. I spent only a few months there and then returned to Tehran.

My father used to frequent some regular social circles [*dowreh*] with a number of military officers, including General Ahmad Amirahmadi, General Morteza Yazdanpanah, and General Ali Razmara (who was a major general at that time). They often met in Hesarak and had lunch together. Major General Hassan Arfa, who had succeeded Razmara toward the end of 1944 as the chairman of the joint chiefs of staff of the armed forces, had imposed early retirement on my father, Razmara, and a few other officers. This was very insulting to my father. An officer who had been arrested and exiled by foreigners, instead of being supported and honored by the people in his own country and instead of their having taken steps to free him from prison, was now being forced to take early retirement. He had been very much hurt by that decision and had developed a deep resentment toward Arfa.

Apparently, General Yazdanpanah had repeated his complaints to His Majesty Mohammad Reza Shah. His Majesty summoned my father, and on that day he took me with him. We went to the Shah's private palace. There was a room next to His Majesty's office, and I stayed there while my father went to the adjoining room and was received by His Majesty. From their conversation I heard only the following sentence that I still remember. In an angry tone, my father told His Majesty, "Don't do something that I would have to pull the pole and bring the whole tent down on top of all of us. They have insulted my honor and have undermined my reputation." His Majesty tried to calm him down and said, "This must be due to some misunderstanding that will be put right." That proved to be the case, and both my father and Razmara were recalled from retirement and reinstated in their previous posts.

In March 1946, when Ghavam os-Saltaneh became prime minister and wanted to resolve the crisis in Azerbaijan, a number of leading political and military figures were arrested. Major General Arfa was one of the arrested officers. At that time, my father was the inspector general of the armed forces. Arfa was married to an English lady who came from a distinguished family. She worried that my father was intent on settling scores with her husband and wanted to take revenge for what had been done to him in the past. She came to my father to inquire about what he intended to do. My father said, "Please rest assured that I will never confuse personal grudges with national issues."[1]

After a short time, Razmara was again appointed chairman of the joint chiefs of staff of the armed forces, and Ghavam os-Saltaneh put my father in charge of restoring security in Fars province. By then it was late 1946. In Fars province, the Qashqais, the Boyrahmadis, and the Mamassani tribes had carried out an armed rebellion. A major crisis had been created and came to be known as the "uprising in the south." Tribesmen had disarmed the barracks in Kazerun, as well as a number of Gendarmerie posts between Bushehr, Shiraz, and Isfahan. They had also laid siege to Shiraz.[2]

I came to Tehran and with my father left for Shiraz. Shiraz is a city like a bowl surrounded by mountains. In Marvdasht (a small town near Shiraz), Brigadier General Hemmat, who was a brave officer and who had been shot in one of the wars with my father, came to welcome us. When we approached Shiraz, I could hear some shooting. As soon as we managed to look around we saw that armed horsemen were rushing down the mountain and were shooting at us. The forces escorting my father and Brigadier General Hemmat were shooting back. All of a sudden, I felt that I had been shot. My face felt very hot and something I thought was a bullet fell into my hand. Commander Bahador (Bakhtiari), who had been elevated to the rank of a colonel or a brigadier general, was sitting in the front seat next to the driver. My father and I were in the back seat. He was seated on the right, and I was sitting on his left.

There was shooting from all directions, and I was shooting with a Bruno rifle that I was carrying. When all the noise subsided, we discovered that fortunately no one had been shot. When I opened my fist I noticed that the object that had fallen into my hand was part of a front tooth. I was scared of telling my father that I had been shot. My father turned to me and in an anxious tone asked me what was wrong. He saw my swollen face and my bleeding lips and mouth. However, when he inspected my mouth he was less worried and started to laugh and to mock me. What had happened was that in a state of panic I had not closed the gun's breech. It had kicked back and broken part of my front tooth, which is still half broken.

My father took some steps in Shiraz to put an end to the fighting and establish order. The government had put him in command of the forces in the south, as well as made him the governor general of Fars. He sent a message to General Amirahmadi, the war minister, and Razmara, the chairman of the joint chiefs of staff of the armed forces, saying that he was engaged in fighting there and it was not a suitable place for his son. He indicated that he wanted me to go abroad to continue my studies. Therefore, it was decided that I should go to the United States. I left for Beirut and from there I went to Egypt and then to the United States. I started my studies in the United States in 1946.

During the years when I was studying in the United States my father was once again appointed head of the National Police Force (12 November 1949). Later, the Shah chose him as an appointed senator from Hamadan, and in Hossein Ala's cabinet he was appointed minister of the interior (2 March 1951).

When there was a failed assassination attempt on the life of His Majesty on 3 February 1949, the political climate of the country changed. On the one hand, the second constituent assembly was convened, and preparations were made for convening the senate. On the other hand, General Razmara, who was the chairman of the joint chiefs of staff, had achieved a great deal of power and openly interfered in political issues. At that time, Sa'ed's government submitted a bill on the new oil contract to the Majles, but it met with the intense opposition of the minority faction in the 15th Majles. By that time, my father had completely fallen out with Razmara, and they had become quite antagonistic toward each other. Therefore, my father decided to leave the country for a while.

My sister Homa was studying in Lausanne. My father went to Geneva, and he asked me to join him there from the United States. Abdol-Hosein Hazhir, the court minister, telephoned my father in Geneva and said that he had been nominated to run for the senate, but my father said that he preferred to be the appointed senator from Hamadan. However, before the new Majles was opened, Hazhir was shot dead in front of Sepahsalar Mosque. As the result of that shooting, a large number of people were arrested. Dr. Mohammad Mossadegh was exiled to his farm in Ahmadabad. Ayatollah Kashani was exiled to Lebanon. Dr. Mozaffar Baghai, Hossein Makki, and a few others were jailed. Meanwhile, general elections for the Majles in Tehran were canceled due to public protest. As the police force had been accused of interfering in the election, Brigadier General Saffari, the head of the police, was dismissed from his post and my father replaced him.

My father accepted the job as head of the police on two conditions. The first was that the elections in Tehran would be held without interference from the government and the law-enforcement forces and that police officers would cooperate with the people in protecting the ballot boxes. The second was that the files of all those who had been arrested had to be investigated as soon as possible, and those who were not found guilty had to be released.

These conditions were contrary to Razmara's policies and views, and they intensified the differences between the chairman of the joint chiefs of staff of the armed forces and the head of the National Police Force. Razmara wished to have the police under his control, but my father was not the kind of person who would submit to that demand. The policies that my father adopted as head of the police resulted in his friendship and closeness to Dr. Mossadegh and the leaders of the National Front party, who had won a majority in the elections in Tehran. If my father had not helped them, the National Front candidates would not have been elected to the Majles and the Majles would not have passed the Oil Nationalization Law. His Majesty never forgot my father's help to the National Front at that time. At every opportunity, whether in jest or seriously, he would blame my father, saying that he had been responsible for bringing those people to power.

After the convening of the first senate and the 16th national consultative assembly (the Majles), Sa'ed's government resigned and a new government, led by Ali Mansur (Mansur ol-Molk), was formed (April 1950). In that year, the remains of His Majesty Reza Shah, the Shah's father, were transferred to Tehran from Cairo. As there were some intense disagreements between my father and General Razmara, my father resigned from his post as the head of the police and went to the senate.[3]

Mansur's government did not last for more than three months, and finally General Razmara was appointed prime minister on May 25, 1950. For a long time prior to his appointment, Razmara had the ambition of becoming prime minister. It was rumored that the person who worked hardest for his appointment as prime minister was a man called Gerald Doher, who was the political attaché of the American Embassy and apparently also the head of the CIA in Iran. Doher had an Iranian wife and knew Persian. Later on, I met him in America. He later died of testicular cancer.

In any case, Razmara's appointment as prime minister was very sudden. My father was due to come to Rome so that we could see each other there. When Mansur ol-Molk suddenly resigned and Razmara was given the decree to become prime minister, my father postponed his trip, because he wanted to vote against Razmara's appointment. He remained in Tehran until the senate debated the formation of the new government. Although my father was an appointed senator, he voted against that appointment and then came to Rome. When he arrived in Rome he was very tired. We spent some time having a holiday and traveling round Europe, and then we returned to Tehran.

---

[1] In *From the Military to Politics,* referring to those events, Dr. Ezatollah Homayounfar writes:

> The cabinet was changed. Once again Ghavam os-Saltaneh was appointed prime minister, and Mozaffar Firouz, a leftist politician, was appointed deputy prime minister. As Ghavam os-Saltaneh declared in his famous statement (written for him by Hassan Arsanjani), "the captain has chosen a different course." The new policy involved getting closer to the Russians and setting aside all the Anglophiles from positions of power. One of those policies was to dismiss Major General Arfa as the chairman of the joint staff of the armed forces and even handing him over to the military tribunal to be tried for the measures that he had taken against the members of the Tudeh Party. Zahedi was appointed as the head of the military court that was to try Arfa. This appointment was not random. The civilian authorities, maybe Ghavam os-Saltaneh himself, were aware of the antagonism between Arfa and Zahedi. They might have deliberately chosen Zahedi to be in charge of Arfa's court martial, so that it would lead to greater antagonism between these two military officers, both of whom shared a common devotion to the Shah.
> Major General Arfa writes in his memoirs: "Zahedi told me quite bluntly that Mozaffar Firouz had told him that he had to convict Arfa. Otherwise, he would take away the file from me and would give it to 'the court of the masses'. However, in the same way that Zahedi was serious, strict, uncompromising and obstinate in implementing his duties, to the same extent he had the qualities of the

Pahlavans (chevaliers) and gentlemen. He would never hurt a lion that was caged. He had repeatedly demonstrated this trait, and this is why he had numerous friends. Therefore, he held a few sessions of the court martial and allowed the proceedings to continue so that there would be a delay in investigating the case, especially as in our beloved country everything changes from one moment to the next. Due to his chivalric qualities, as well as his 'obstinacy' and pride, he was not prepared to be used as a tool for implementing Mozaffar Firouz's wishes, a person that he totally and deeply disagreed with.'

By chance, an event saved both Zahedi and Arfa from the dilemma that they were facing. The tribes in the South of the country started a rebellion, and Zahedi was given the task of putting down the rebellion. Consequently, he was relieved of his responsibility as the head of the military court. The military court was delayed and Arfa was saved, and as the result of the new policies of the government that succeeded that of Ghavam os-Saltaneh, the whole issue was forgotten."

[2] Mehdigholi Hedayat (Mokhber os-Saltaneh) writes in *Khaterat va Khatarat* [Memoirs and Dangers]:

Adopting a soft approach toward Tabriz had encouraged many potential rebels. The Qashqai leaders became the standard-bearers of democracy (it is truly ludicrous).

On Sunday 20 Shahrivar [11 September 1946] a telegram was received from Shiraz. The cable said:

"As the result of the 20-year old government that has devoted all its attention to other parts of the country, the people of Fars are in complete despair. They demand that their legitimate rights are met. The following demands are the absolute minimum requirements of all the tribes and citizens of Fars province:

1. Immediate cabinet reshuffle.

2. Changing the military commanders in sensitive posts.

3. Trying and punishing the corrupt executives who served during the dictatorial era.

4. Leaving the affairs of Fars province, both military and civilian, in the hands of the people themselves.

5. Forming national societies.

6. Reviewing the number of Majles deputies.

7. Allocating sufficient funds for improving the standards in education, health, roads and public thoroughfares.

8. Reviewing harmful laws that are at variance with or contrary to the constitution.

9. Extending the railway line from the capital to Shiraz, and paving the main roads.

[signed by] Mohammad Nasser, Malek Mansur, Mohammad-Hossein Qashqai."

When people are encouraged to utter untimely and unnecessary words, when they transgress their limits and ignore their own responsibilities, when the government also makes use of those words to gain popularity, then it is not unusual to expect such telegrams.

On 3rd Mehr 1325 [25 September 1946], Nikpey, deputy prime minister in charge of administrative affairs, Sardar Fakher, governor general of Kerman province, and a few others flew to Shiraz, and a telegram in the usual forms of words were sent to the leaders of the Qashqais.

There are many reports from Bushehr that armed bandits (insurgents) have surrounded the city. On Tuesday 9th Mehr [1 October 1946] the rebellious tribes attacked Bushehr, and all the principles of democracy, such as killing, destroying, plundering and other such principles, were fully implemented.

Kazeroun was not deprived of the principles of democracy either. The local barracks managed to resist for as long as they had weapons and ammunitions, but they were finally overrun. There was no way of sending reinforcement by road, and the reinforcement sent by air was not sufficient. Major General Zahedi, who had come to Tehran to find a solution, returned to the region on 21st Mehr [13 October 1946] hoping that he could extinguish the fire by resorting to fear or favor. Finally, a telegram was received from Mohammad Nasser, which said that "Major General Zahedi and Amir Homayun conveyed the [royal] orders regarding the acceptance of the demands of the people of Fars province. Then I ordered the fighters to disperse." The blame was put on unqualified individuals who through their false propaganda wished to portray the uprising in Fars in a different way; and a number of other contradictory remarks were made. Basically, I couldn't understand who the virtuous people in Iran really were! (*Memoirs and Dangers: A few accounts of history under six kings and a part of my own life*, by Mehdigholi Hedayat (Mokhber os-Saltaneh), p. 452).

[3] Seyyed Mehdi Farrokh (Motasem os-Saltaneh), who was appointed head of the police after General Zahedi, writes in his memoirs:

A critical issue at that time was the differences or even hostility that existed between General Razmara and Major General Zahedi. Although these two military officers had old differences, when fate placed one of these two rivals at the position of the chairman of the joint chiefs of staff and the other one as the head of the police, their differences were intensified and became more overt. The head of the police wished to carry out his duties, on the basis of law, and without anyone's interference, but Razmara wanted to have the police under his control. At that time, the police force was one of the most sensitive centers of power in the country, and running it under those special circumstances was not easy. Without doubt, a person like Zahedi was able to discharge that responsibility well. On the other hand, he had a rival in Razmara who was very active and had inexhaustible energy. Zahedi was still a military man. He would take orders and would implement them, but Razmara was trying to act like a politician. He was in a hurry to achieve fame through the press... Apart from the oil issue, which the new Prime Minister Mansur ol-Molk (who had replaced Sa'ed after the opening of the new Majles) did not touch at all, what constituted the most important issue to him inside the country was the ambitions of General Razmara, who wanted to form a government within the government. In other words, he wished to appoint the head of the police, and wanted the head of the police to receive his orders from him and not from the minister of the interior or from higher officials. During those critical days, this issue was of utmost importance to Mansur ol-Molk.

Chapter Three
The Beginning of the Storm

Question: In Dr. Mossadegh's government, your father was put in charge of the Ministry of the Interior. However, later on, some differences arose between the prime minister and the interior minister. What were the relations between your father and Dr. Mossadegh like before those differences arose, and what is the background to their relations?

Zahedi: Mossadegh was related to us through my mother, and he knew my father from long ago. At the time when my father was the head of the National Police Force he rendered the greatest service to the National Front and the election of the candidates of the National Front, including Mossadegh, from Tehran. Were it not for my father's help in stopping Razmara's interference in the election, those results would not have been possible.

When my father became minister of the interior in Ala's cabinet, his relations with Mossadegh continued as before. When Mossadegh was appointed prime minister, he asked my father to remain at the same post in his cabinet. In the course of the oil nationalization campaign, due to his nationalistic feelings and his opposition to British policies, my father was a strong supporter of Mossadegh from the start, and there were no differences between them on that issue. All the problems arose from 13 July 1951, as my father did not put up with the dismissal of the head of the police and resigned from his post.[1]

Question: What were you doing during the period when your father was cooperating with Mossadegh?

Zahedi: I was busy with my own work at the Joint Committee. We had a large number of projects under consideration. If implemented, they would have made a big difference in the development of the country and improvement of people's lives. However, at that time, we faced two fundamental economic and political problems. From an economic point of view, due to the cutting of oil revenue, the government's hands were tied and it could not pay for the economic development budgets. It even found it difficult to pay for its current expenditures. From a political point of view, first of all, we faced many limitations on our travels and activities. Anytime the officials of Point Four wished to travel, they, first of all, had to inform the Ministry of Foreign Affairs and the second department of the joint chiefs of staff of the armed forces [in charge of intelligence] and receive permission. It was at that time that I got to know Abbas Aram and General Hassan Pakravan. Abbas Aram was the head of the fourth political department of the Ministry of Foreign Affairs, and General Pakravan was in charge of the second department of the joint chiefs of staff of the armed forces.

Second, some of those who had been given responsible posts under Dr. Mossadegh had strong leftist tendencies, or did not like America and the Americans, or did not agree with some of the plans that we wished to implement. For instance, in Azerbaijan the living standard of the people was very low. In the areas near the Arax River, people died of hunger. I had employed Shapur Shafa'i, General Esma'il Khan Shafa'i's son, who was a very decent and patriotic person, in Point Four. Shapur had a doctorate from Zurich University and was fluent in German, English, and French. There was a very tall American gentleman called Horace Burns, from Harvard, who had come to Iran to be in charge of Point Four programs for northern Iran. A few times we traveled together to Azerbaijan in a number of small trucks taking large quantities of blankets, dates, and other things with us to distribute among the poor people. They were so desperate that 25 or 30 of them would sleep next to each other in a sheepfold.

We were debating with those in government, telling them that they ought to halve the amount of wheat that we received from America. We should give half of it to the farmers to use as seed, so that they could produce more wheat, and we should give the other half to people to alleviate food shortage. We had to deal with the Ministry of Agriculture on the one hand and with the Ministry of Finance on the

Fazlollah Zahedi in Cossack uniform.

Fazlollah Zahedi as a child in Hamedan (front row, far left).

From right to left: Baha os-Saltaneh, Fazlollah Zahedi, Ebrahim Qavam ol-Molk, Haj Fatan ol-Molk Jalali, Taqi Khajenouri, Amir Nosrat, General Amanollah Jahanbani, Motarjem ol-Molk (head of the Telegraph Office), Shaykh ol-Molk Owrang, Moshir os-Soltan, Nasir ol-Molk, Nazem ol-Molk, and Soltan Ali Khan Ata od-Dowleh. The two children are the sons of Nasir ol-Molk: Nasrollah Khan and Azizollah Khan.

Brigadier General Fazlollah Zahedi

General Fazlollah Zahedi, commander of the Northern Brigade.

General Zahedi in formal attire.

Colonel Doctor Moghaddam and Brigadier General Fazlollah Zahedi, commander of the Independent Rasht Brigade. When Mossadegh surrendered and was detained in the Officers' Club, Dr. Moghaddam was responsible for communications between Mossadegh and his family.

Sardar Sepah (the future Reza Shah) with military commanders: General Amir Motamen (Nakhjavan), Major General Abdollah Amir Tahmasebi, General Ali Riazi, General Mahmoud Eram, Mohammad Hossein Ayrom; and General Fazlollah Zahedi. Some individuals cannot be recognized because of the age and quality of the photograph.

A group of Iranian Cossack officers after the 1921 coup d'état. Soon after they would be combined with the Gendarmerie to form the new Iranian army. The first person on the right is Colonel Fazlollah Zahedi. Turkoman chieftains can be seen standing in the back row.

General Fazlollah Zahedi accompanying Shaykh Khazal to Tehran. Khazal was a local leader who had attempted to separate Khuzestan from Iran and establish a separate state. General Zahedi was successful in the mission of arresting Khazal and bringing him to the capital. Zahedi is the officer looking toward the camera. The Shaykh is to his direct right.

General Fazlollah Zahedi in Khuzestan with the heads of the local tribes.

From left to right: Sabz Ali, who throughout his life accompanied General Zahedi and later lived with him; Karim Zahedi (later Colonel); Captain Zargham, who made great sacrifices during the Khuzestan expedition; General Zahedi; the next two cannot be identified; and Moghavam ol-Molk Zahedi.

From left to right: unknown officer, Generals Ebrahim Zarrabi, Haj Ali Razmara, Hadi Shaghaghi, Mohammad Hossein Firouz, Amanollah Jahanbani, Abdollah Hedayat, and Fazlollah Zahedi.

General Zahedi, the head of the Independent Rasht Brigade, welcomes King Amanollah of Afghanistan to Iran.

General Zahedi, the commander of the Independent Rasht Brigade, with officers of the brigade, their families, and a number of local officials.

At a military parade in front of Reza Shah. From left to right: General Amirahmadi, General Fazlollah Zahedi (the head of the parade), and General Hajali Razmara.

In this photograph, taken in 1941, Reza Shah commends General Zahedi for well-organized maneuvers. First row, from left to right: Reza Shah, General Fazlollah Zahedi, and Crown Prince Mohammad-Reza Pahlavi. Behind them are the minister of war, General Ahmad Nakhjavan, and the chief of staff of the Army, General Azizollah Zarghami. Reza Shah would be forced to leave Iran a few months later.

Fazlollah Zahedi as a young man.

From left to right, front row: Mostafa Zahedi and Fazlollah Zahedi. Second row: Houshang Razavi; Zohd Zahedi, the wife of Hassanali Zahedi; my mother, Khadijeh Pirnia; Batul Atabeki; and an unidentified woman.

General Zahedi and General Morteza Yazdanpanah.

General Zahedi, in the new military uniform, after the Cossack uniform was discontinued.

From left to right: General Fazlollah Zahedi; Karim Hedayat who would later become Chief of Health for the army and Taghi Golestan, publisher of Golestan Magazine of Shiraz. Photograph courtesy of the noted writer and filmmaker, Ebrahim Golestan.

Photograph from the August 1943 issue of *National Geographic*. Minister of War Amanollah Mirza Jahanbani and General Zahedi, commander of Isfahan can be seen on the left. Ardeshir is the child holding a machine gun. Shortly after this photograph was taken, General Zahedi would be arrested by the British.

Isfahan (1941–42), from left to right: Gholam-Hossein Mirza Masoud (son of the Zell os-Soltan), General Yazdanpanah, and General Aslani (General Zahedi's chief of staff in Isfahan).

From left to right: General Mohammad Mohtashemi, General Ahmad Khan Nakhjavan, General Matboui, General Hadi Atabai, General Ahmad Moin, General Fazlollah Zahedi, General Ali-Asghar Naghdi, and General Afkham Ebrahimi.

At a formal event, from left to right: Hossein Zamanzadeh Shahriari (later Iranian ambassador to Belgium), Colonel Alinaghi Vaziri, General Fazlollah Zahedi, and General Esmail Shafai.

Hossein Pirnia, Motamen ol-Molk.

Ardeshir's mother, Khadijeh Pirnia, the daughter of Motamen ol-Molk.

The woman with a black chador in the center of the Zahedi family photograph is Zahra Zahedi, Fazlollah's mother and Ardeshir's grandmother.

Fazlollah Zahedi, pictured with a young Ardeshir, after having resigned from military duty and having created the private Casadema Company. Later, Reza Shah asked Fazlollah Zahedi to return to military service.

During his trip to Iran in 1932, Rabindranath Tagore visited the Bersabeh School which Ardeshir attended. Ardeshir is seen standing to the left of the Nobel laureate.

Ardeshir's kindergarten class picture at the Bersabeh School. He is in the third row from the bottom, sixth from the right in the sailor suit.

Photograph taken in 1936 during a trip to Gorgan. From left to right: Hossein Zamanzadeh Shahriar; the next two individuals are unidentified; a young Ardeshir; his younger sister Homa; General Zahedi; and Akhtar Shahriar. The person behind Fazlollah Zahedi is Sergeant Sabz Ali, who always accompanied the General into battle.

From right to left: Ardeshir (sailor suit), Homa Zahedi (young girl in front), Parviz Zahedi (boy behind Homa), and Amin Ghazinouri (boy on left front).

General Zahedi with his children, Ardeshir and Homa, circa 1940.

A young Ardeshir and Akhtar Zahedi photographed at the Agricultural College in Karaj. Homa Zahedi is in the foreground. The other two girls in the photograph cannot be identified.

A very young Ardeshir with his sister, Homa.

Near the Avaj mountains near Hamedan, 1949. From left to right: Parviz Yarafshar; Amir Khosrow Afshar and his wife Parvin Afshar (Nikpour); Akhtar Yarafshar; Banoo Afshar, and Ardeshir. The young girl in the front is the Yarafshars' daughter, Setareh.

A family trip. From left to right: Abol-Ghassem Zahedi, Ardeshir's cousin; Fakhr ol-Molouk Zahedi (Samai); Akhtar Zahedi (Yarafshar); Afsar Zahedi (Elahi); and Nosrat Zohd Naraghi (Nayebi).

other. The minister of agriculture, Zia ol-Molk Farmand, who was a very good man, agreed with us. Mahmoud Nariman was the minister of finance, and although he was an honest and capable man, nevertheless, he had some very strange ideas. He used to say that if you distribute the wheat among the people, they would fall into bad habits. I responded that we had gone and seen how people lived. Large numbers of people were dying of hunger. He replied that he came to work in rough shoes and traveled by bus. The prime minister also played games with the people around him and used one against another.

Of course, Gholam Hossein Mossadegh, Dr. Mossadegh's son, had good relations with William Warne and Henderson. He used to arrange parties around the *korsi* in his house and invited them to those parties.[2] However, due to financial shortages, on the one hand, and political games on the other, various issues would get too complicated and everything moved very slowly.

When Horace Burns came, it was decided that we would take him to Azerbaijan by air. The American Embassy had a small aircraft, and its pilot, a man called Eric Pollard, was the naval attaché of the embassy. At that time, the new airport had not yet been built. Mehrabad was a very small airport with an old building, and there was a military airport nearby, which was called South Mehrabad. We went to the airport with Warne to leave, but we were stopped and told that we did not have permission to fly, although we had already received the permission from the Ministry of Foreign Affairs and the second department of the joint chiefs of staff of the armed forces. We asked for the reason. We were told that the prime minister had said that if we went there, the Russians might be upset. We responded that we were not going on a political or military mission. We were traveling in our own country to do some development work and to help our own people. What did it have to do with the Russians? To cut it short, we were not able to fly to Azerbaijan and the plan was canceled. I should add that the assistance that was provided to Iran by Point Four was in the form of grants and was given without any commitments being made by Iran.

During that period, there was also a clash between Ahmad Shafiq, who was Egyptian (he was the husband of Her Royal Highest Princess Ashraf), and myself. At that time, Javad Bushehri (Amir Homayun) was the road and transport minister, and Ahmad Shafiq was the managing director of the National Airlines. Dr. Bennett, the overall director of Point Four in the Middle East, had gone to Egypt and was returning to Tehran. In the afternoon we went to Mehrabad to receive him. Warne, Hormoz Shahrokhshahi, myself, and a number of others were there. We waited for a long time, but there was no sign of the aircraft. They kept saying that the aircraft had been delayed. Why was it delayed? Due to stormy weather, and so on and so forth. I shouted at Ahmad Shafiq, who had just come from the air control tower, and complained about the situation. I said, "You are in contact with the aircraft. Why do you not give us a clear answer?"

Finally, we returned to the city. The following day, Amir Homayoun Bushehri informed me that the aircraft had crashed and everyone on board had been killed. The aircraft had flown close to Tehran but had crashed in the Elburz mountains, only a kilometer from Mehrabad. I immediately informed Warne. We went to the crash site. Amir Homayun came with us. The crash scene was something that I cannot describe. It was the first time in my life that I had seen a corpse. The corpses were burnt and were black like charcoal. Poor Dr. Bennett and his wife were burnt like logs in the fire and had turned to charcoal. It was very tragic. We could not identify the corpses. Eventually, some experts came and identified the corpses and covered them and took them away.[3]

Those Americans really showed self-sacrifice and left many good legacies behind them in our country. Dr. Bennett was very interested in the Karkheh Dam project, as was Dr. Mossadegh. Hossein Makki, who was the government's representative with full powers to take over from the British officials in the Anglo-Iranian Oil Company, was also interested in that project. We flew with Khalil Taleghani, the minister of agriculture, and Makki to the place where the dam was to be built.

Saham os-Soltan Bayat, the head of the management board of the oil company, showed us all the courtesies.

At that time, Khuzestan was a truly backward and deprived part of the country. Some people believed that the British did not allow that region to be developed. In any case, due to many political and economic problems, the project to build the dam was delayed until after the 28th of Mordad [19 August 1953, after Mossadegh's downfall] when David Lilienthal and Gordon R. Clapp, who had been involved in the Tennessee Valley project, came to Iran and implemented the development plan in Khuzestan. Later on, Abdor-Reza Ansari continued the work.

Question: How long did you stay with Point Four?

Zahedi: Until the time when differences and clashes emerged between my father and Mossadegh and I got involved in those arguments too.

Question: What were the reasons for the differences and clashes?

Zahedi: In July 1951 Averell Harriman, President Harry S. Truman's special envoy, was due to visit Tehran. His task was to find a solution for the oil issue. The Tudeh [Communist] Party was determined to disrupt those talks and ensure their failure. Harriman was due to arrive in Tehran on July 13, and, as I mentioned earlier, he was due to stay at the U.S. Embassy in Tehran. At that time, the U.S. Embassy was in the former German Embassy building in Ferdowsi Street, opposite the Melli Bank, which the government had put at their disposal during the war.

The operational headquarters of the Tudeh Party, called "Peace House" and the "Anti-Imperialist Group," was a few steps away from that building. On the occasion of the anniversary of the strike by the workers of the oil company in Khuzestan in 1946, the Tudeh Party had organized a demonstration. The police had informed my father that those demonstrations would not be peaceful, that the demonstrators were planning to attack and burn the American and the British embassies, and that the issue of the murder of the former American deputy consul, Major Robert Imbrie, would be repeated.[4]

You know that, as Dr. Mossadegh himself said in the military court, the members of the Tudeh Party belonged to two groups: a Russian group and a British group. The groups were unanimous in their belief that the Americans should have no place in Iran and especially that the Americans should not be able to find a solution to the oil dispute. At that time, the streets in Tehran were scenes of anti-American demonstrations that were organized by the Tudeh Party. They covered all the walls with anti-American slogans, while it was the British oil company and the British government that were the parties involved in conflict with Iran. Due to those nonstop demonstrations, the shopkeepers in Tehran were forced to close their shops several times a day. The metal grilles in front of the shops went up and down several times each day, and business had come to a standstill.

In any case, to prevent any untoward incident, my father proposed that Harriman should come to Iran as the official guest of the Iranian government and stay at the Niavaran Palace. The members of the Tudeh Party organized another demonstration for July 13, marching from Ferdowsi Street toward Istanbul and Shahabad Streets, and the plans to cause riots were carried out in a different form in Baharestan Square [in front of the Majles building]. In that place, severe clashes took place between the members of the Tudeh Party and the parties that were opposed to them, such as the Pan-Iranists, the Iran Party, and the Toilers Party. Their plan was to occupy the police station near the Majles and then to attack the Majles itself and cause mayhem there.

Only a few days earlier, Major General Hassan Baghai had been appointed as the head of the police. As minister of the interior, my father went to the police station and took personal charge of establishing order. On his responsibility, he sent a few commando groups to help police officers. The demonstrators attacked the police with stones and clubs. Shooting ensued and, unfortunately, a few people were killed.

Those around Dr. Mossadegh incited him against my father by telling him that Major General Zahedi had taken charge of all those operations in order to become prime minister. In any case, Mossadegh was very angry and insisted that the head of the police had to be charged. My father told him that the head of the police had not been guilty of anything. My father insisted that he had issued the orders for the operations on his own and that he would accept all responsibility. As a result, my father resigned from his post but postponed his resignation until the end of the talks with Harriman in Tehran. Finally, his resignation was announced on 22 July 1951.[5]

After those events, my father decided to be away from Tehran for a while. We went to the villages near Hamadan and spent some time there. Naturally, during that period the relations between the prime minister and the former interior minister had grown cold. I had a weekly luncheon round with some of my former student friends. Sometimes they came to Hesarak, and sometimes we went to the Park Hotel and had lunch together, and everybody paid for his own lunch. One day, as I was leaving to go to the lunch party, I received a telephone call saying that Warne wanted to see me. I went and had lunch with my friends. When I returned I heard that Warne had phoned a number of times and had asked me to see him as soon as possible. I went to his office and noticed that he was very angry. When he was angry he would walk back and forth in the room and would twist his tongue in his mouth. He said: "Today, the prime minister summoned me and Henderson [the U.S. ambassador], and in our discussions he said that I had to expel Ardeshir Zahedi from Point Four or he would close it down. Now, we are in a difficult situation. Legally, we cannot expel you because we have nothing against you, and we have always been very satisfied with your work."

I told him, "Don't worry! National issues are more important than anything else. There is no need for you to sack me. I will resign." He said, "No, even if you resign the issue may be dragged to the U.S. Senate, which will put us under pressure." I replied, "This is a domestic issue, and at this time, when our country is so much in need of assistance by Point Four, it would be wrong for me to cause you any headache. I will resign and will go away, and there will be no problem at all." He said, "Well, go and think about it." I replied, "From this moment, I will no longer be a member of your organization, and I am very grateful to you for your kindness." I resigned and left Point Four.[6]

After those developments, Mr. Makki, Dr. Fatemi, and Mr. Haeri-zadeh tried to mediate and bring about some reconciliation. They came to see my father in Valiabad. After they talked for a while, my father called me and said, "These gentlemen are trying to help so that you will be appointed either as the minister of agriculture or as the independent head of the Irrigation Organization." I said, "Sir, if I were no good, I would not be able to do any of those jobs, and if I were good, then why did they press so hard for me to leave Point Four? Furthermore, Abol-Hassan Behnia, who is the head of the Irrigation Organization, is one of my friends and is related to our family, and I do not want to take his place. Engineer Taleghani is the minister of agriculture, and he is much more experienced than I am, and I cannot work as well as he does in the Ministry of Agriculture." In any case, my father left it to me to decide.

A few nights later, Hormoz Khan Pirnia, who was the head of proto-col at the court and one of our close relatives, came to see me. He said, "In view of all the services that you have rendered in fighting against malaria and in providing piped water in Bandar Abbas, we have asked that you should be decorated, but the prime minister has opposed that request." I said, "I have not asked for any medals, and I do not expect anyone to show gratitude to me. Don't be worried at all, and don't say anything to my father about it." But eventually my father learned about it, and it was very difficult for him to bear. He said, "Your problem is with me. Why are you doing this to my son?"

From then on, the differences between them intensified. My father, who was in charge of the Association of Retired Officers, had meetings with other officers in the premises of the association and talked to them about the current issues of the country. The government re-garded those meetings and discussions as a form of conspiracy. On 12

October 1952, Major General Hejazi and a few others were arrested. The government issued a statement alleging that those who had been detained had been active in the interest of foreigners and had acted against the government and that Major General Zahedi had been the main instigator of those activities. In response, my father spoke in the senate and issued a statement in which he wrote, "Can one deceive the people to the end of times by hiding behind the fortress of oil and using the worn-out weapon of accusing others of being 'servants of colonialism' or 'agents of foreigners'?"[7]

In the same month, the senate opposed the bills to give amnesty to Khalil Tahmassebi and confiscate the property of Ghavam os-Saltaneh, and it decided that the resolutions of the National Consultative Assembly on those issues were contrary to the constitution. Subsequently, with government approval, the National Consultative Assembly changed the law about the election of the senate. The term of senators was reduced from four to two years, and the senate was consequently dissolved. Then the government had a free hand to arrest my father. On 24 February 1953, my father was arrested on the basis of article five of the martial law. Three days later, the events of the 9th of Esfand took place, and a number of other officers and individuals were arrested.

Toward the end of March, a number of those who had been arrested, including my father, were released on the occasion of the Iranian New Year. For a few days, my father was busy with New Year's meetings and celebrations, but later on, as he knew that he would not be left alone, he went into hiding. In April a number of officers, including Brigadier General Nasrollah Zahedi, were arrested. Officers came to arrest my father but could not find him. On May 3, he took asylum inside the National Consultative Assembly building.

During that period the government's situation had changed a lot. Ayatollah Kashani, Haerizadeh, Dr. Baghai, and Makki had deserted Mossadegh. There was deep hostility between the Shah and Mossadegh. Disputes between the supporters and opponents of the government had intensified in the Majles. Outside the Majles too, despite all the detentions and persecutions, the opposition groups continued with their activities.

At that time, I had gotten involved in the struggles. I used to meet with Majles deputies and others. In the month of Tir [June–July] it was the time to vote on changing the presidium of the Majles. Ayatollah Kashani was one of the candidates for Majles speaker, but the government did not want him to remain in that post. On 10 Tir [1 July] the majority of Majles deputies elected Dr. Moazzemi to replace Ayatollah Kashani. Moazzemi was a friend of my father's and was also related to us. He was very unhappy about the situation that had come about, but he could not support my father's continued asylum in the Majles, as Ayatollah Kashani had done. There had been some talk that on the anniversary of the Constitutional Movement, when many people were invited to the Majles building to celebrate the occasion, some would get inside the building and would kill my father.

They all got together and talked and debated, and finally they promised that if my father were to leave the Majles he would be left alone. This is why they secretly drove him out of the Majles in the car of the Majles speaker, and he went home. From there, we went to Sadegh Naraghi's house, which was close to our house. A few hours into the night we noticed that several military trucks had come to our house and officers poured inside the house to arrest my father, but of course they did not find him there. At that point, my father's covert life and secret but intense activities with the aim of toppling the government began.

During those events, I was arrested once, but the excuse that was used for my arrest was something else. Before Warne, Dr. Franklin Harris was the director of Point Four, as I have already mentioned. Dr. Harris was a very decent man. He was an American and a member of the Mormons, which is a Christian sect. I can say that he loved Iran even more than America. There was a man called Mr. Mahmudi who was in charge of our accounts and resources in Point Four. He was a very honest man. Mahmudi's house was in Gholhak, and he did not have a car. One afternoon, he wanted to go home from the office and

Dr. Harris took him in his own car. On the way back, a young boy ran in front of the car and was hit. Dr. Harris's car was a Buick and had a hook in the back, and the child's head had hit that hook. There had been no one else in the street. However, as Dr. Harris was a conscientious person he got out of the car and asked for help. Eventually, the police arrived and took Dr. Harris to the police station on Amol Street, near Shemiran bend. The child was taken to a hospital.

I was sitting with my father and Nasrollah Zahedi when Dr. Harris phoned and said that he was in the police station and described what had happened. Nasrollah Zahedi and I went to the police station, and we saw that that the old man was sitting there alone and seemed very worried. Unfortunately, the child had died in the hospital. The police coroner had said that the accident had not been the driver's fault, because the child had hit the back of the car. The child's father had accepted the coroner's account. But in any case, the file was sent to the police. The head of the police, Brigadier General Daftari, who knew that there were some differences between my father and Razmara, did not close the file but sent it to the courts, due to some personal considerations. In the judiciary, the file came under the supervision of an examining magistrate. Later on, after the military network of the Tudeh Party was uncovered, the name of that examining magistrate was found on the list of Tudeh members. He committed suicide by throwing himself from a window in the building of the Ministry of Justice.

We hired a lawyer for Dr. Harris. The lawyer was Afshar Ghasemlu, who was one of our own relatives. The magistrate released Dr. Harris on bail, until the file could be dealt with in the court to pass judgment. I put up the house of Mohammad Elahi as a surety for the bail, and Dr. Harris was freed from jail. A year and a half later, Dr. Harris left and Warne replaced him. A few months after Dr. Harris's departure the prosecutor, namely, the military government, summoned me on charges that I had made arrangements for Dr. Harris to escape justice. Gendarmerie officers came to my house, handcuffed me, and took me to the headquarters of the military governor, which was in the main police building.

During the interrogation, instead of asking me about the issues that were given as the excuse for my arrest, the colonel who was interrogating me kept asking me irrelevant questions, such as who I was, what activities I had, who my father was, and what he did. I protested the way that I was being interrogated and said that I wanted to send a cable to the United Nations, protesting against the way that I was being treated. The officer told me to write it down, but he said that he was not sure if it would be sent to the United Nations. From there they took me to the room opposite, which was the office of the head of the police. The head of the police and Mr. Sadighi, the minister of the interior, were in that room. I had already met Sadighi in the committee dealing with organizing the millennium of the birth of Abu Ali Sina, and I knew him fairly well. We had traveled together to attend the opening ceremonies of the Nemazi Hospital in Shiraz. During that trip his car had been involved in an accident. At that time, he had been serving as the minister of post and telegraph. On the basis of our earlier acquaintance, I greeted him politely, but, contrary to my expectation, he came toward me in an angry and insulting manner and ordered the officers to hold my hands. I kicked him.

Meanwhile, an officer entered the room and after giving a military salute said that they had gone to Hesarak, but they had not been able to find Zahedi (my father) there. I was standing with my back to the light and he could not see me properly, but I recognized him as a colonel who was a member of the special guards at Mossadegh's house. They took me to a room in the basement of the building and detained me there. Then an officer arrived. He had some equipment in his hands, which he put in the corner of the room. I thought it was some form of equipment for exercise. I told him that I had not gone there to exercise. However, that officer said, in a very angry and sad tone, that he would never obey the orders of his superiors about me and left the room. Later on, I learned that the honorable officer was Major Darmishian. Then, another officer and two civilians entered the room.

They took the equipment that was in the corner of the room and locked my hands in it on my back. The weight of the lock, whose name I learned later, and the pressure that it exerted on me were so extreme that it froze my breath in my chest as though my chest was about to burst. The *ghapani* hand lock, which is among the worst forms of torture, is made up of two iron locks. The torturers pull one's hands to one's back from top and bottom and lock them in that contraption, and the gadget that is in the middle is twisted in such a way that it pulls the two hands together.

Later, I explained that incident to His Majesty. However, in 1978, when it was decided that Dr. Sadighi, Dr. Amini, and Abdollah Entezam were due to go to His Majesty for talks and to form a government is a development that I shall refer to later. I told His Majesty that I had been mistaken and Sadighi had not insulted me. Of course, now all of them have gone, and everything is over and I have no grudges against anyone.

In any case, when Colonel Ghane', an honorable officer who was the prosecuting officer of the military court, investigated my case and discovered that I had not committed an offense, he ordered my release. He personally came with me to the garden of the police station, and I left through the north gate. From there, I went straight to Ayatollah Kashani's house. Later on, I discovered that one of the persons who was present in that room was Ayatollah Khomeini. Ayatollah Kashani was very kind to me, and I had high regard for him. I believed that he was an honorable and patriotic man. In all issues dealing with the nation he was very brave and very emotional. This was the time when my father had taken asylum in the Majles, and Ayatollah Kashani was still the Majles speaker. Later on, I went into hiding and the military governor set a reward for my capture.

One night I was sleeping in my own house when they came to arrest me. I climbed the northern wall with the help of our servant and jumped inside my sister's house, which was next door to ours. At that time, one of my cousins lived there with her husband, Mr. Tashakkori, who was a member of the Iran Party. From there I went to the house of Rahmat Atabaki, which was next door to their house, and from there I went to Motamen ol-Molk's house and told my grandmother what was happening. My grandmother, Madame Eshrat os-Saltaneh, phoned Madame Zia Ashraf, Dr. Mossadegh's wife, who was one of her friends and also a relation. She said, "What is going on? They have arrested my grandson because he had put down surety for someone else, and they have treated him in that despicable way. Now that the prosecutor has found him not guilty they are again trying to arrest him."

Madame Zia Ashraf said that she was talking from the inner quarters of the house. She had to go to the outer quarters and ask Dr. Mossadegh about what was happening. My grandmother said, "I will stay on the phone. Please go and come back." After a while, Madame Zia Ashraf returned and said that Mossadegh had told her that what she had heard were lies and nobody wanted to do anything to me. From there I went to the house of Dr. Abol-Ghassem Pirnia, in Pirnia Street, which had a door to Manuchehri Street. I stayed there a few nights, and then I went to Mirashrafi's house and stayed there for a while. Nosratollah Moinian and General Garzan were also hiding there, and Mirashrafi provided every hospitality for us. Sardar Fakher, Makki, Haerizadeh, and two Majles deputies both of whom were called Afshar, one from Reza'iyyeh and the other one from Tabriz, came to visit me in Mirashrafi's house. We were all working hard to ensure that Ayatollah Kashani would be elected Majles speaker.

From there, I sent a letter to *Keyhan* and to another newspaper asking why I was still being pursued, but those newspapers did not publish my letter. That coincided with the time when my father, who was hiding in Javad Hamzavi's house, left his house and took asylum in the Majles.

After my stay at Mirashrafi's house, I spent some time in the orchard of Ja'far Ja'fari in Velnjak, where he had built a small hut. I was there all by myself. I cooked my own food and walked in the garden. At that time, Parviz Khan Yarafshar came to my hiding place in Mirashrafi's house and said that Dr. Abdollah Moazzemi and Engineer Ahmad

Razavi [deputy Majles speaker] had talked to my father to persuade him to go as ambassador to Rome. Through him, I sent a message to my father that if he was worried about me I would go and hand myself in. He replied, "Be assured that I am not a dishonorable and timid person. I merely wish to test them to see how strong they are." In any case, those talks also came to nothing, and the differences became unbridgeable until they ended in the events of 25 and 28 Mordad [16 and 19 August 1953, Dr. Mossadegh's downfall].

---

[1] In an article in issue 42 of the 13th year of *Khandaniha* magazine (Tehran 7/12/31 [25 February 1952]), under the title "Major General Zahedi and the National Front," Hossein Makki writes as follows:

> The elections for the 16th Majles were held during Sa'ed's government, under the influence and control of Hazhir and Razmara. Nariman and I were in charge of supervising the ballot boxes in Sepahsalar Mosque. About one o'clock in the afternoon, when the mosque was very quiet, I had a wash and wanted to go to the room of a religious student where Nariman was waiting for me to have lunch. All of a sudden, one of the gendarmes who was on guard duty over the roof of the mosque and who was sympathetic to the nationalists, hurriedly came to me and said, "They are swapping the ballot boxes." Immediately, police and gendarme forces surrounded the mosque. Before doing anything else, I informed Dr. Mossadegh and told him that the mosque was surrounded by police and gendarme forces, and that it was possible for both Nariman and myself to be detained there. Dr. Mossadegh encouraged us to remain firm in any way we could. A day earlier, Dr. Mossadegh had sent a letter through one of his aides informing me that the government was determined to swap the ballot boxes, and that I had to protect the votes of the people to the last breath like a nationalist soldier. Before having had any opportunity to talk to Nariman about the plot to swap the ballot boxes, I ran to the steps leading to the roof of the main prayer hall. Major Rahimi, a police officer, and a number of policemen blocked my way. I started to shout, and I told two nationalist guards who were also in charge of protecting the ballot boxes to ring the bells of the mosque, and that the seminary students in the mosque should also go on the rooftops and should chant the *adan*.
>
> Earlier on, I had told the shopkeepers and the residents of the areas around Sepahsalar Mosque that if the authorities decided to swap the ballot boxes we would ring the bell of the mosque and the students would also chant *adan* on rooftops in order to inform them of what was going on. The residents of the

areas around Sepahsalar Mosque heard the bell and the chanting of the *adan* and got agitated, but what could they do? The doors of the mosque had been blocked by some military trucks and police officers had surrounded the mosque. Nariman and I got involved in scuffles with the police. There were a large number of them, and they detained me in one of the rooms in the mosque. However, as their secret had been divulged and people outside had learnt about it, they did not think that it would be appropriate to read the votes in Sepahsalar Mosque. On the excuse of mourning ceremonies for Imam Hossein, they transferred the ballot boxes to the building of the National Academy, and prevented the nationalists from entering there, and they did with the ballot boxes what they had wished to do. On the following day, the number of votes cast for Dr. Mossadegh had been reduced from the first person to the tenth person, Baghai's votes had been reduced to the eleventh person and I was transferred from the third on the list to the bottom of the list, namely the twelfth person.

Hazhir's murder forced the government to cancel the election, but they did not leave us alone and they started to prepare court cases against us. In my bill of indictment they had stated that a few days before Hazhir's assassination, ten revolvers had been distributed among a number of people in Dr. Mossadegh's house, and that one of the revolvers had been the one that had been given to Emami, with which he had assassinated Hazhir. All of us were imprisoned, and we had no way to defend ourselves.

In those days, it was announced that Major-General Zahedi had been appointed as the head of the National Police. Brigadier-General Iravani, the head of police in Tehran, came to the prison at 9 o'clock at night, and told me that Major-General Zahedi wanted us to know that the police department had played no role in our detention. He had said that he would promise us that he would act honorably towards us and that he would not allow anyone to compile phony dossiers against us. I informed my comrades of Major-General Zahedi's message. A number of people from the *bazaar* and some religious students had been arrested and they were kept in a cellar in a damp and smelly room. There were some children among them too. While interrogating them, they asked them who they had voted for. If they said that they had voted for Mossadegh and his friends they would not be forgiven and would have to endure all forms of hardship. Three or four days later when Brigadier-General Iravani had come on behalf of the police to see how we were coping, he asked us if he could help in any way. I replied that I want you to release these poor people who have not committed any crimes from this torture. From the following day, they were gradually freed. After two days, the officials of the military government decided to free us (namely, Azad, Dr. Baghai and me). They took us to the office of the head of police intelligence. General Zahedi came to that room and treated me with kindness and respect. I introduced our comrades to him and we sat on the armchairs. I told him, "If you think that by releasing us you can silence us, you are mistaken. As soon as I leave here I shall intensely resume my activities and I will fight against the establishment." In a very calm voice, General Zahedi said, "I am the head of the police and I will not compile dossiers against anyone. You are free to engage in any activity within the law." That meeting lasted about one hour. Haerizadeh and Baghai also talked for a while. Finally, Zahedi said goodbye and left, and we returned to prison. We ate lunch with our comrades and said goodbye.

After a few months, the elections for the 16th Majles started all over again. Major-General Zahedi was still the head of the National Police Force. On the advice of our friends, I met with Zahedi twice and told him that the government was determined to again block our election to the Majles. Major-General Zahedi made a moral commitment never to forsake impartiality, and promised that so long as he remained the head of the police he would prevent the changing of ballot boxes or forcing the people to vote in a particular way. The elections started. One night I was informed that the government intended to swap some of the ballot boxes in the east and the west of Tehran. We tracked Zahedi down at 11 o'clock at night in the house of Brigadier-General Malek. I informed him of what we had heard on the telephone. He asked me to go immediately to Malek's house and to exchange our views on the issue. After being informed of the situation, he ordered the head of the Police Training Department to wake all the police cadets in the middle of the night and to send them to all the constituencies in Tehran to guard the ballot boxes. He also ordered them that once they had sealed the ballot boxes they should not allow anyone to touch the boxes again. I noticed that the police cadets had arrived in all the polling booths and were carefully supervising the ballot boxes. This speedy action by Major-General Zahedi prevented the swapping of the ballot boxes in Tehran. On the following day, he also appointed some of the officers that he could trust to secretly guard the ballot boxes.

In these two cases, namely our release from prison and ensuring the health of the elections, Major-General Zahedi acted in the nation's interest, despite all the obstacles that he faced and contrary to the views of the powerful government and the foreigners, and he passed that test with distinction.

---

[2] William Warne describes it in *Mission for Peace* (p. 217):

A *corsi* consists of a brazier of charcoal embers placed under a low table which is then covered over with blankets. I was introduced to it by Dr. Gholam Mossadegh, son of the prime minister, whose wife rightly thought I would like to try one. The *corsi* almost filled the room it occupied. Cushions were placed around it. I left my shoes at the door and shoved my feet under the blankets to the heat. It was snug and cozy and most welcome to me.

Parviz Adle in *Memoirs of Los Angeles* describes another aspect of Mossadegh's relations with Point Four:

> Point Four vacated the large building belonging to Mr. Taghi Sohrabi in Shah Reza Avenue and rented a building and a house in Kakh and Heshmat od-Dowleh streets that belonged to Dr. Mosaddegh. You know that Americans pay very high rents.

[3] Below is Warne's account of the air crash and Bennett's death, in *Mission for Peace* (pp. 38–42):

> As the days wore on pessimism turned to certainty that there could be no country agreement before Dr. Bennett's arrival. He and his party had been expected for several days, but there were the unexplained delays so common in Iran. We planned a Christmas party at the Darband Hotel, where all our people would be brought together to meet the director. Some of the Point 4 wives were making a neighborly project of decorating a tree. There was still a chance that Dr. and Mrs. Bennett might arrive before Christmas, but the time was growing short. I went to the ambassador's office at five o'clock on December 22 to tell him I thought it unlikely that the plane would come that way. Through the large picture window which opened to a magnificent view of the Elburz Mountains, I watched an icy, foggy dusk settling down. The atmosphere congealed. Visibility would be entirely blotted out in a few minutes. At this moment someone handed me a note from the airport. Dr. Bennett's plane had taken off from Baghdad, Iraq, and would arrive at Mehrabad about seven o'clock. I started for the airport. Snow had begun to fall. Except for one antiquated radio beacon and a few rather pale lights around the airport and along the runway, there were then no night aerial navigation aids at Mehrabad.
>
> I stopped at the Point 4 office on Sepah Avenue to pick up Ardeshir Zahedi, my principal Iranian assistant, and we hurried on. When we confirmed that the plane was en route I telephoned for the reception party.

At a few minutes after seven Ambassador Henderson, Ardeshir and I heard a plane high overhead in the cold darkness. The flares shot from the tower seemed only to emphasize the darkness. Wet snow blew in our faces. In the next thirty-five minutes we heard the plane four times. The last time it was so low that the roar of its motors shook the windows of the airport customs building at our backs.

None of us beside the runway could see the plane in the murk, but Ardeshir thought he had seen the glow of a wing blinker.

We heard the plane no more.

After a few minutes Ardeshir climbed the wood stairs to the control tower for news. "The pilot told the tower 'I see your lights' as he came over that last time," he reported when he returned. "No word at all since then."

The ambassador shook his head and blinked snow out of his eyes. "Let's invite the committee to have tea in the airport building."

But the people were restive. I suggested that some of our friends quietly persuade members of the committee to disperse. We did not want to alarm them. Ardeshir and I remained at the airport until midnight. He had rustled me a curfew pass. No word came from Baghdad, Basra or Abadan, where alternate landings might have been made. Driving past the embassy on the way home, I was flagged down by a Marine guard. He had just learned from the airport that the plane had arrived safely at Baghdad. I went to bed relieved and happy. I had been sure we were waiting for news of disaster.

The morning of December 23, 1951 was startlingly, crystalline clear. A heavy mantle of snow covered the mountains, the hills and even the plain. At the Darband I heard a small plane circling over the foothills but paid no attention. At the office an hour later I learned that a search plane had located the wreckage of Dr. Bennett's airliner. My shock was even deeper because of my trust in the false information of the previous night. No satisfactory explanation of that telephone call was ever made.

Ardeshir, son of a prominent Iranian general who later became prime minister, somehow hurriedly obtained a jeep for the trip into the Elburz foothills. We drove through rutted snow as far as roads went, then broke trail. Soon the ground became too rough even for a jeep. At the steep edge of a canyon we began a slow trek toward the reported site of the wreck. On a hilltop we saw a shattered propeller standing like a cross. We rounded a shoulder. In the bottom of the canyon we saw the little that remained of the plane. All but the wings and tail had burned. The impact had thrown Dr. and Mrs. Bennett forward, clear of the wreckage. They had died instantly. They were still side by side, strapped in their seats. Between them lay a Bible which Mrs. Bennett must have been reading. Most of the twenty-one victims were in the burned wreckage. One of these was Benjamin Hill Hardy, chief of public affairs for the Technical Cooperation Administration, whom President Truman praised as "a convinced realist" who made "important contributions" to the Point 4 idea. James Thomas Mitchell, a staff photographer, and Albert Cyril Crilley, a foreign service assistant to Dr. Bennett, had also been on the plane.

As we drove back to town Ardeshir and I took some comfort in the fact that I had not been able to persuade Si Fryer to return. It was impossible not to talk about Dr. Bennett. Ardeshir listened with a friend's indulgent silence.

"I went to say good-by to Dr. Bennett the day before I left Washington," I said. "It was only about five weeks ago. He said that we had a hard job ahead. An easy job, I told him, would not have attracted me any more than such a task would have drawn him. He said he had absolute confidence in the success of Point 4 because it was right for the great United States to help her neighbors as our pioneer forefathers had co-operated with each other on the frontiers. He added that talk of atom bombs did not frighten him. Then he said, 'I think you are like me in that we do not scare easily.' I am sure Dr. Bennett did not scare even at the end."

Ardeshir was one to understand. A tall, handsome young man, he is among the very few I have known whom I believe to be without any sense of fear. He was not reckless beyond reason, but he would and did risk his skin fearlessly when he thought it was important and right to do so. "Right," to him, meant "in the interests of Iran."

Dr. Harris had brought Ardeshir into Point 4. This was not their first contact. On an earlier advisory mission to Iran Dr. Harris had met his father, General Fazlollah Zahedi, and his family and had persuaded Ardeshir, then only a boy, to follow him to USAC to complete his education.

Persian to the very core, Ardeshir was a generous and considerate friend. One must know something of his country's history to understand how he has been molded. His father was a distinguished military commander. He had reached army field grade at an earlier age than any other in Iran's recent history. He had stopped invading rabble in a mountain valley in 1921 and had pacified rebellious tribes in the 1930s without open warfare. He had been interned by the British during the Second World War, and his son, then just a lad, had not known his father's fate for months. Rugged and independent, the general had continued to serve his country where and when he could, though his health had been undermined by some of his experiences. He carried several bullets in him. Ardeshir and his father were deeply attached.

"When you believe in a thing deeply, Bill," Ardeshir explained, "you just have to go ahead whether it's dangerous or not."

In the United States today not many are called on to live dangerously. But peril is not unusual in Iran. Dr. Bennett would have understood Ardeshir. He had died on a gravel bank by an Iranian mountain stream for something he believed in strongly.

[4] The incident has been reported as follows:

In the beginning of Khordad 1303 [late May 1924], it had been rumored that a fountain in the centre of Tehran cured sick people. A crippled person had allegedly drank water from that fountain and had been cured, while a non-believer who was said to have been a Baha'i and who had not given any donations to the beggars near the fountain had lost his sight. In a very short time, a large number of sick, blind and crippled people rushed towards the fountain. Many of them were brought on stretchers from a long way away.

On 27 Tir 1303 [18 July 1924] Major Robert Imbrie, who had arrived in Tehran four months earlier, had gone together with one of his friends, Melvin Seymore, to visit the fountain. Seymore was in charge of digging oil wells, and perhaps had come to Iran to find work, but as he did not have appropriate papers for arriving in Iran he had been housed in the American Embassy until a decision could be made on whether he could stay or not. Before coming to Iran, the *National Geographic* had given him a camera to take some pictures of interesting places during his stay in Iran. At about 10 o'clock in the morning, those two went to Aqa Sheykh Hadi Fountain and took some pictures. People had protested, because there had been some women there, and also it is forbidden for non-Muslims to go to holy sites. Then a number of people in the crowd began to shout that those people were Baha'is and had gone there to poison the water of the fountain. As the crowd looked threatening, Imbrie and Seymore rushed back to their carriage and the driver tried very hard to leave the spot. The crowds grew bigger and bigger and some people chased the carriage and stopped it, and Imbrie and Seymore were badly beaten and were severely wounded. There were a number of soldiers in the barracks near the fountain as well as on the route but none of them took any action. Eventually, the police arrived and the two Americans were transferred to the Police Hospital, which was nearby. The crowd that now exceeded 1,000 followed a man who was wearing a turban and a robe into the hospital, and a 16-year-old youth killed Imbrie with a stone. Seymore, who was in another room, escaped death. Following that incident, the oil agreement between Iran and an American oil company called

Sinclair was cancelled on the excuse that the Americans had not invested the amount that they were meant to do. It was rumoured that the incident at the fountain had actually been organised in order to achieve that goal. After that incident, martial law was declared in Tehran and Brigadier-General Morteza Khan Yazdanpanah became the military governor of Tehran.

[5] From Fuad Rouhani *Mossadegh's Political Life in the Context of the Iranian National Front* (London: 1987).

On 17th Tir 1330 [9 July 1951] (a few days after the International Court of Justice had issued its temporary ruling on the request of the British Oil Company), President Truman wrote a letter to Dr. Mossadegh and suggested to send his personal envoy, Averell Harriman, to Tehran to mediate between the Iranian government and the British Oil Company. Dr. Mossadegh welcomed that offer, and it was announced that Harriman would arrive in Tehran on 23rd Tir [15 July 1951]. Thinking that Truman's mediation either would result in a compromise [with the British Oil Company] or would replace an American concession for a British one, the Tudeh Party decided to organise demonstrations against Harriman's mission. By chance, 23rd Tir coincided with the anniversary of the strike of the oil workers in Khuzistan in the year 1325 [1946]. The Anti-Colonialist Group affiliated to the Tudeh Party called on its supporters to take part in demonstrations, allegedly for marking the anniversary of the martyrs of 23rd Tir 1325, but in reality as a protest against Truman's mediation, and preventing the success of Harriman's mission. They made some arrangements for marches and demonstrations. On the day of Harriman's arrival, a large crowd belonging to various organisations affiliated with the Tudeh Party, whose number was estimated at 20,000, took part in the demonstrations. They started marching in the capital's streets from Ferdowsi Square towards Baharestan Square.

An American writer describes the scenes of Harriman's arrival as follows:
"Harriman thought he would receive a warm welcome by the people from the airport to the city, and that he would respond to their welcome with smiles and waving of hand. However, he faced some ugly demonstrations by members of the Tudeh Party, who were armed with clubs and who were shouting anti-American slogans."

Finally, there were severe clashes in Baharestan Square between the demonstrators and the members of the Toilers Party (which was the main target of the attack by the demonstrators), and the members of the police, which resulted in many dead and injured on both sides. Those affiliated with the Tudeh Party and other opponents of the government accused the National Front of being behind those bloody incidents. *Shoja'at* newspaper in an article titled "Forward Towards the Future" in its edition of 26 Tir [17 July 1951] wrote: "The anti-nationalist government of Dr. Mossadegh is pursuing a policy of genocide, fascism, lying, and pursuing America's colonialist policies… In order to establish a calm climate for engaging in surrender and abject talks with the representative of American colonialism, Dr. Mossadegh has found it necessary to massacre the nation."

[6] Warne, who was the director of the Point Four program in Iran from 1952 to 1955, refers to his meeting with Mossadegh in the autumn of the year 1952 (from Warne 1999, 116–117):

> This was the season of portents. General Zahedi on the floor of the Senate had voiced some disapproval of the Mossadegh policies. The prime minister, in the midst of a conference on some other subject, turned to me and said he felt that Ardeshir Zahedi should not work in Point 4.
> "He is using his position in a cooperating agency for political purposes," he said.
> "He has struck my father in his most sensitive spot," Ardeshir said when I told him what had occurred. Knowing something of the closeness between father and son, I knew this was true. It was a sad parting. Ardeshir insisted on going, but asked to be on indefinite leave without pay. "I'll still have a tie to Point 4," he said. That is the way we arranged it. Opposition to General Zahedi became implacable and firm. Soon he had to take refuge in the Senate chamber for his own safety, though in doing so, as it turned out, he imperiled the Senate itself.

[7] In his statement, my father wrote:

> How sad it is that despite all those hopes and expectations and putting up with all forms of hardships now the Iranian nation receives nothing from Mosaddegh's government except poverty, unemployment, chaos, the loss of dignity and attacks on people's lives and property. Instead of enjoying security and comfort, people have to listen to populist slogans and empty noises. It is my utmost wish that one day Mossadegh and I may be tried in front of the real court of the Iranian nation so that I can lift the veil from all the deceit and inform the oppressed people of the truth. I would like to warn them against the tragic consequences of some of these activities that are carried out either knowingly or through stupidity. Can one deceive the people to the end of times by hiding behind the fortress of oil and by using the worn-out weapon of accusing

others of being "servants of colonialism" or "agents of foreigners"? What have you done and what plans do you have to improve people's lives and to put an end to all this chaos and to improve public welfare?

Mostafa Fateh, *Fifty Years of Iranian Oil* (648)
The speech of Senator Major-General Zahedi in the senate (Wednesday, 23 Mehr 1331 [15 October 1952]).

As I am not feeling very well today, I wish to apologise to the gentlemen that I cannot read my speech in a firm voice. I swear by God the Almighty that what I have got to say is not due to hostility or opposition to the government or to some individuals, but is an expression of my love for my dear country and homeland. I have nothing to ask from anyone or any country and I am not afraid of anyone except God. Let my life, my wealth, my soul and my blood be sacrificed for the sake of my homeland! I am a son of Iran and I am greatly concerned about my motherland."

As you know, yesterday the government spokesman said that Major-General Hejazi and a few others, in collusion with Major-General Zahedi, were pursuing some evil intentions, in the interest of a foreign embassy...

I strongly deny that accusation. The Iranian nation must know that there is no truth to those allegations and they are complete lies. If Dr. Mossadegh has received that information from the same source that had allegedly prepared a dossier of murder for him four years ago, one should be very sad and surprised.

I am confident that among the honourable, high-ranking Iranian officers one cannot find a single officer who would commit treason against the interests and well-being of his country. Ultimately, it will be made clear what the sources are for such rumours and such misinformation that Dr. Mossadegh has received. Meanwhile, I believe it is necessary for me to say a few words about my past relations with His Excellency Dr. Mossadegh.

Before he became prime minister, I had met him two or three times during the period of over twenty years, and I have had no other contacts with him. However, as I found his words and the demands of his friends and colleagues to be in the interest of the country and as I found them to be patriotic and self-sacrificing individuals I tried to help them within the limits of the laws and regulations.

I carried out my decision at a time when His Excellency Dr. Mossadegh was under house arrest in Ahmadabad and was under police supervision, and his friends were either imprisoned in Tehran or were being investigated by courts. At that time, a dossier had been compiled that alleged that ten pieces of weapons had been found in Dr. Mossadegh's house, in the presence of his friends and colleagues, and that they had been distributed among ten people to kill ten individuals. Hazhir was one of those ten individuals who was assassinated. That dossier was being pursued with the admission and confession of some of the aides of those gentlemen.

At that time, I was appointed the head of the National Police Force... My military honour and sense of duty did not allow me to let such measures be taken on the basis of personal hostility. The reason why they wished to find those gentlemen guilty was so that they would not be elected to the Majles.

According to the testimony of all the honourable people in the capital, I made every effort to make sure that no changes were made in the votes cast. I safeguarded people's trust that had been entrusted to me at that time as the head of the law enforcement forces. As the result of those steps Dr. Mossadegh and his friends were elected to the Majles.

In its campaigns against Razmara, I assisted the newly formed National Front with all my being. As you know, as the result of the self-sacrifice and intense struggles of the majority of the people, Mr. Mossadegh was put in charge of the affairs of the country. He asked me to serve in his cabinet. I accepted that offer and served sincerely in his cabinet. Dr. Mossadegh's honourable friends who have witnessed my services and my self-sacrifice are the best witnesses to my services during those critical times. After a few months, due to some disagreements regarding how to run the country and ensure public security, I felt obliged to leave his government and I resigned. Even after resignation, I helped his government with the help of my friends and I voted for all the bills of his government, with the exception of the bill on martial law.

Although some of his friends had sown seeds of doubt in his mind and had made him think that I wished to take the government out of his hands in my own interest, and although they had also made some accusations against some of our friends, nevertheless, everyone knows that at that time even that thought had not crossed my mind. I believe that it is contrary to honour and dignity to act treacherously towards someone that one is serving. While being a candidate for premiership is not a crime and there is nothing wrong with it, nevertheless, I have always shown utmost respect and co-operation to Dr. Mossadegh. I believed that his government had to be strengthened so that he could bring the issue of the oil nationalisation to fruition. I believed that if the doctor could bring the oil issue to fruition it would be to the great advantage of the country. I was firm in my belief until the time when he returned from his visit to America. However, his speech in the Senate made me feel doubtful and forced me to entertain feelings of despair.

The gentlemen know that despite all that background and despite my help to the National Front and the valuable services that I rendered to my country, I spent three years in imprisonment and exile outside the country in the hands of foreigners due to my patriotism. Why did they deceive me one evening in my own home and kidnap me in a dastardly manner and keep me in jail for three years? During that period I did not see any of the officials of my own country or any of my friends. Now, on the basis of which information and reports does Dr. Mossadegh accuse me of having been engaged in some activities in the interest of a foreign embassy, or that I wished to stage a coup d'état? It is truly the source of great regret.

It would be good if the Iranian nation would investigate those documents and my documents and would distinguish between the true servant and the traitor, and would get to know its self-sacrificing soldier better.

I have been and I continue to be a sincere servant of my country. By saying all this I do not mean to praise myself. On the banks of Chalus River, with a small number of people, I defeated some insurgents who intended to move towards Tehran and I saved the capital. With my columns I defeated Semitqu in Azarbaijan who claimed independence. I defeated the Turkmens on Gorgan Plains who for more than one century had refused to obey the central government and who had engaged in banditry and rebellion, and I taught them culture and civilization instead of murder and crime. Today thousands of young educated Turkmen are working in governmental and national departments and organizations. I conquered Khuzestan, whose reports have filled not only that province but the whole world, and I disarmed the insurgents in that province and in Lorestan. I captured Sheykh Khazal, that king without a crown, and I brought him to Tehran under guards. I built hundreds of schools, hospitals, drugstores and paved roads in the country, and thousands of other services that I need not mention. So how is it possible for me to take a step against national interests? Such dastardly accusations and attacks will not be acceptable and will not forgiven by the noble Iranian nation.

If Dr. Mossadegh's government has not been able to improve the affairs of the country, if despite all that expense and all that effort it has not been able to carry out the election in a satisfactory manner, if it has failed to raise the level of income in the country, and if finally it has caused or has failed to prevent so much disunity, rebellion and insecurity in the country, why does it blame me and others for all that failure? I expected everything from this dictatorial government, such as intimidation, threats, making compromises with unqualified officials, etc, but I never believed that it would engage in compiling dossiers for people.

I ask the doctor to come to his senses and be careful not to drag our country towards bloodshed and mayhem. "There is a ditch on the path and it requires open eyes and the light of the sun."

Finally, I wish to ask the Senate to select a number of honourable individuals to investigate this matter. This is something that I seriously demand.

Mostafa Fateh, in *Fifty Years of Iranian Oil* (Payam Publications), writes:

After the above statement was issued, it was made clear that Major-General Zahedi had assumed the leadership of Dr. Mossadegh's opponents. From that day onward, anyone who was opposed to Dr. Mossadegh went to Zahedi's assistance and either openly or secretly supported him.

The reporter of *Akhbar al-Jadid* newspaper, published in Cairo, writes:

When I arrived in Tehran, all the talk was about the new prime minister who would come to power after Dr. Mossadegh. General Zahedi's name was on top of the list of those who were mentioned for that post, the same general who has taken refuge in the Iranian parliament in fear of Mossadegh's government! Before being nominated by political circles in Tehran for the post of prime minister, Zahedi had nominated himself for that post under the dome of the parliament.

Dr. Fatemi, Iran's foreign minister, in an official speech had accused General Zahedi and a number of retired officers of trying to start a revolution against the government, with the support of a foreign embassy (the British Embassy). He has announced that the government had arrested all those involved in that conspiracy, with the exception of General Zahedi who enjoys parliamentary immunity, until the Senate was dissolved and Zahedi lost his parliamentary immunity. Dr. Mossadegh immediately arrested him, but as he had no evidence to try him, he released him. Once again, Mossadegh invited him to the police station to provide some explanation. This time Zahedi took asylum in the national consultative assembly, and wrote a letter to Ayatollah Kashani, the Majles speaker. In that letter he wrote, "I wish to assure the noble representatives of the nation that I have not committed any action contrary to the interests of the government, and that I am the same self-sacrificing and sincere soldier of the country that I have always been!"

Kashani called him "the dear guest of the Majles," and Zahedi said, "As Dr. Mossadegh is scared that I might become prime minister he is causing so much nuisance for me and is making those false allegations against me."

However, in his letter to the Majles speaker, Zahedi openly pointed out, "Becoming prime minister is neither a crime nor is there anything wrong with it!" I met that prime ministerial candidate in his place of asylum. He is a simple, calm and friendly candidate for premiership. He speaks French very well and eloquently. When I met him in the national consultative assembly, Haerizadeh was also present, and one of Ayatollah Kashani's sons was also in the Majles. The minority that was in opposition to the government expected Mossadegh's government to fall that day, or expected Mossadegh to hand in his resignation... I told General Zahedi, "Everywhere in the city there is talk of the new prime minister." He asked, "Who will be the new prime minister?" I told him, "Everybody regards you as the candidate for premiership in Iran." He replied, "This is what they believe, but this is not my view." I asked him why not? He replied, "Because I believe that one of these days the situation will be made clear." I asked, "That quickly, and within the next few days?" General Zahedi replied, "In three to four days I will explain my views, my thinking and my policies to you." Four days passed, and many more four days passed, and Mossadegh remained prime minister and Zahedi continued to remain under the protection of the national consultative assembly. We have to wait and see what the future has in store!

Chapter Four
The Ninth of Esfand Incident

Question: Please tell us about 9th of Esfand [28 February 1953]. How did that event take place, and what was it all about?

Zahedi: On 6 Esfand, my father was arrested on the basis of article nine of the martial law regulations.[1] The plan was to force His Majesty to leave the country. Both His Majesty and Mossadegh have written about the details of the 9th of Esfand events in their memoirs, but their accounts are quite contradictory. In any case, it was decided that His Majesty's departure had to be kept secret, and with the exception of a few courtiers and Mossadegh's aides, no one knew anything about it.

The then head of the protocol at the court, Hormoz Khan Pirnia, had informed Ghavam os-Saltaneh of the issue. Hormoz Khan was my mother's cousin, and he informed me about the plot. In turn, I passed on the news to Dr. Baghai, Makki, and Ayatollah Kashani. Ghavam os-Saltaneh sent messages to some political, military, and religious figures and warned them that if the Shah were forced to leave the country his departure would endanger national security.

At first, it was decided that I should go overnight to Qom and inform Ayatollah Borujerdi of what was going on. A letter had been written to him and given to me to hand over to him. Then the plan was changed, and they decided to talk to Ayatollah Borujerdi by telephone. He too believed that everything had to be done to make sure that His Majesty would not leave the country, because it would not be in the country's interest and would endanger the country. Ayatollah Borujerdi asked Ayatollah Behbahani to convey his message to His Majesty. We also made certain preparations to gather in front of the palace and prevent His Majesty from leaving.

The crowd that had gathered in front of the palace on 9 Esfand [28 February 1953] was made up of several groups. One group included students and young people who had been in contact with me. Another group consisted of dissatisfied government employees. Other groups included retired military officers; the traders in the bazaar; the supporters of Ayatollah Kashani and Ayatollah Behbahani; some sportsmen, such as Lieutenant Colonel Khosravani, Dr. Rahnavardi, and Shaaban Bimokh; and others. We were assembled outside the palace and of course did not know what was going on inside. We demonstrated and chanted slogans in favor of the Shah, and we were only trying to make sure that His Majesty would not leave.

I suffer from a strange form of vertigo. I can engage in acrobatic action and jump from aircraft, I can ride horses, but there seems to be something wrong with my ears or my eyes so when I am standing on an elevated spot, I feel giddy. On that day, I was so excited that I climbed a ladder and went to the top of the front porch of His Royal Highness Abdol Reza's palace, which was situated on the opposite side of His Majesty's private palace. I shouted so much and chanted slogans so loudly from the top of the porch that I grew hoarse. I was not at all conscious of the big drop below me. Finally, His Majesty appeared on the balcony of the private palace in the early evening and announced that he had changed his mind and would not be going away.

The crowd started to move toward Dr. Mossadegh's house, which was a short distance from the private palace.[2] Suddenly, I noticed that everybody was leaving and that I had been left alone on top of the entrance porch of the palace. I could not get down by myself. I felt very self-conscious and noticed that I was becoming giddy. There was an old man there who ever since the time of Reza Shah had been a guard at the palace of Esmat and His Royal Highness Abdol Reza. I told him that I could not get down by myself and was about to fall. He said, "Close your eyes and do not move, so that I can bring you down." In any case, they brought some ropes and covered my eyes, and very slowly, step by step, they brought me down the ladder.

In the meantime, the crowd had attacked Mossadegh's house, and he had fled through the adjoining house, which belonged to him and which he had rented to Point Four, and had gone to the headquarters of the armed forces. From there, he went to the Majles. In the closed session of the Majles, which became tumultuous, many people spoke for and against the Shah's departure. Mossadegh wanted to take asylum in the Majles on the excuse that his life was in danger and that he had no security at home. However, ultimately, they persuaded him to go home.

Question: Was your father still in detention?

Zahedi: Yes, my father was still in detention. They had given him a room in the police station, which was also the headquarters of the military governor of Tehran. The head of the police intelligence unit was in contact with Agha Mostafa, the son of Ayatollah Kashani, and Mehdi Mirashrafi. We used to visit our father in the police station. Darab, who later became a Majles deputy, used to come with me, and we took some food for my father. The policeman who was keeping guard used to plunge his dirty hands in the rice and meat to make sure that there was no letter hidden in the food.

After the events of 9th of Esfand, the Majles appointed an eight-man delegation to talk to the Shah and the prime minister to persuade them to put an end to their differences. At the same time, some steps were taken to release those who had been detained. Finally, on 26 Esfand [16 March 1953] my father was released from detention and returned home.

Question: But after a short time, another warrant was issued to arrest Major General Zahedi, and he went to the Majles and took asylum there. Is that right?

Zahedi: Yes. On the basis of article five of the martial law regulations, the military governor of Tehran issued a statement and summoned my father. This is why on 14 Ordibehesht [3 May 1953], with the agreement of Ayatollah Kashani, who was the Majles speaker, my father went to the Majles and took asylum there. On the basis of the same law, they summoned me and Ali Reza Gharagozlou, the husband of my aunt, Ozra Khanom.

My father continued his asylum in the Majles. They had put build-ing number five of Baharestan [Majles complex], which earlier had served as an office for the senate, at his disposal. It was in that building that he used to entertain the people who went to see him. Toward the beginning of the month of Tir [June], there were new elections for the members of the Majles presidium. Mossadegh's supporters managed to elect Abdollah Moazzemi as Majles speaker, in the place of Ayatollah Kashani. Moazzemi was a moderate man. He was related to us and used to have a great deal of respect for my father, but the situation became quite different from the time when Ayatollah Kashani was Majles speaker.[3]

Despite all those changes, as Mossadegh had not been able to bring the entire Majles under his control, and as his opponents in the Majles would not rest, he decided to close the Majles. At first, he ordered the deputies in the majority faction to resign, so that the Majles would lose its quorum. One by one they resigned. Then they thought of holding a referendum in order to dissolve the Majles.

----

[1] The following report regarding Major General Zahedi was published in the *Keyhan* newspaper:

> About seven o'clock in the morning, a police colonel and six police detectives, all of whom were armed but were wearing civilian clothes, together with a colo-nel from the military governor's office, and a police major stopped in front of the gates of Major-General Zahedi's house, only ten feet away from his home. One of them, the police colonel in civilian clothes, walked to the door and rang the bell. Major-General Zahedi's servant opened the door and asked what he wanted. The police officer told him to inform Major-General Zahedi that someone wished to see him, and was asking permission to enter the house. The servant immediately informed the general and told him that there was someone at the door, who wished to see him. The general told the servant to show the visitor to the reception room and to offer him hospitality until he could get there. As soon as the police colonel entered the house, he was immediately fol-lowed by the six police detectives, the colonel from the military governor's office and the police major. All of them went straight to the reception room and wait-ed for Major-General Zahedi. Unaware of their intention, thinking that they wished to discuss some personal affair with him, Major-General Zahedi also

went to the reception room in civilian clothes. After entering the room, the police colonel saluted him and respectfully told him that the head of the police had asked him to go to the police station on an urgent matter. Having been taken aback by this compulsory invitation, the general asked the colonel what the head of the police wanted to see him about. Major-General Zahedi said, "I have nothing to do with the police. If they wish to know something, let them put it down in writing." The police colonel insisted that the general had to accompany them to the police station, and they could resolve there any issue that the head of the police wished to discuss with him. They also told him that as they had been commanded to take him to the police station, they would be forced to carry out their duty. When he faced the insistence of the police officers, Major-General Zahedi agreed to their demand and said that he would go to the police station in his own car. After a few minutes, he got ready and together with five police officers drove in his Buick car to the police station. The rest of the officers too followed the general's car in two police vehicles. As they were leaving the house, Major-General Zahedi's wife asked the officers if he would be back home for lunch. The officers replied that he might not be back for lunch, and in fact she should not expect him to return that night either, but that she should not be worried about him. Major-General Zahedi stopped his car in front of the gates of the police station and went straight to the office of the head of the police, Afshartus. The officers who were accompanying him went to the office of the head of the police investigation department. Major-General Zahedi was offered tea and then he was informed about the reason for his arrest. The chief investigating officer and a number of other police detectives were also present, and they asked him a number of questions, which he answered. The head of the police ordered a cell to be prepared to keep the general overnight and also to inform his family to send bedding and other necessary items for him. Police officers and the military governor said that they had no information about the reason for his arrest. Some informed sources and even some official figures even expressed doubt about the report that he had been arrested. Nevertheless, in the corridors of the police station it was rumoured that some officers had been sent to arrest a few others as well, and two or more people would be arrested before the end of the evening. For the moment, the military governor has said that his arrest had been in connection with Article Five [of martial law], so that after the initial investigation he might be formally charged. An informed source said today, "Rashidian brothers had also been taken to the office of the head of the police, and Major-General Zahedi had been questioned in connection with some of their remarks."

[2] In a confidential document from the British Embassy that has recently been declassified, there is the following account about the agreement between the Shah and Mossadegh regarding the Shah's and the Queen's trip abroad:

> Mr. Palmer of the United States Embassy called on me this afternoon, having previously telephoned to say that he had information of some importance that he wanted to give me.
>
> Emphasising that what he would say was of the greatest delicacy and on the basis of strict "need to know," he gave me the following information.
>
> Mr. Henderson has just reported that the last meeting between the Shah and Dr. Musaddiq had not really been connected with the relatively minor topics which had been advertised in the press, but that Dr. Musaddiq had, in fact, suggested that the Shah should leave Persia. The Shah had been delighted and had asked how soon he could go. He suggested leaving today for Iraq from where, after visiting some of the holy places, he would proceed to Europe. Later it had been agreed that any definite plan should be postponed until Saturday. In the meantime, the Spanish Charge d'Affaires at Tehran had been asked to inform his Government that an invitation to the Shah to visit Spain would be appreciated.
>
> Mr. Henderson had taken no action. Much as he regretted to remain a spectator in view of the support which the United States had given the Shah in the past, he felt that there was really nothing he could do, more particularly now that General Zahedi had tamely allowed himself to be arrested.
>
> Mr. Palmer said that the State Department would probably be asking for our views.
>
> I told Mr. Palmer that in my personal opinion it was an illusion to think that we could influence events in Persia. I wondered what the United States government thought about it? We had not been favoured with their views, though we had given them our estimate two days ago on the spur of the moment. At that time we thought that the worst of all possibilities would be that the Shah should go and leave Dr. Musaddiq in power. However, if you had a weak Shah and a strong Prime Minister, it would probably be inevitable that the Prime Minister would win. Mr. Palmer assented and added "particularly as there is no alternative leader." Mr. Palmer again emphasised that the matter was of great secrecy. The Spanish Charge d'Affaires did not know any of the background. He added that so far there had been no mention of abdication.
>
> Mr. Palmer subsequently telephoned me to say that he hoped he had made it clear to me that Dr. Musaddiq had not suggested that the Shah should leave permanently. What he had apparently said was that the Shah should leave until the situation became settled.

(A.D.M. Ross)
26th February, 1953

Top Secret, Inward Saving Telegram, from Washington to Foreign Office, Departmental Distribution.
Sir R. Makins
No 386 Saving confidential document of the British Foreign Office
May 7, 1953, R. May 9, 1953
Addressed to Foreign Office telegram No 386 Saving. Repeated for information Saving to B.M.E.O.
Persia
The State Department has informed us as follows:
"On May 3 in the presence of Khosrow Qashqai a discussion was held between an attaché of the United States Embassy at Tehran and Abol-Ghassem Amini, Acting Minister of Court. Amini stated that the differences between the Shah and Musaddiq, which were of benefit only to Tudeh [Party], should be settled as soon as possible, and that before advising the Shah regarding the terms of settlement he would like answers to some of his questions.
Following are the questions put by Amini and the answers which Ambassador Henderson proposed be made by the Embassy attache: [The ambassador's proposed answers had been approved by the department].
(i) Q: What is United States policy regarding Iran and in particular regarding Musaddiq?
A: The fixed policy of the United States Government is not to intervene in Iranian internal affairs by giving political support to any particular Iranian political leaders or groups. The United States Government would like to maintain friendly relations and cooperate with the Iranian Government headed by Musaddiq just as with constitutional government headed by another Iranian political leader who had indicated by public word and action a desire to maintain friendly relations with the United States. There are no assurances that the United States will extend financial or substantial economic aid to Iran since it would be difficult, because of the United States public opinion, to extend this kind of aid in view of the present status of the oil dispute.
(ii) Q: If the Shah should go abroad, would the United States Embassy assist in arranging an invitation?
A: The United States Government, while not intervening in Iranian domestic affairs, is of the opinion that the institution of the Shah is a and unifying factor and that any substantial weakening of this institution might result in events which would undermine Iranian independence. Therefore, the United States

Government would not be willing to become involved in facilitating the Shah's departure from Iran.

(iii) Q: What would be the United States position if the advisability of a change of regime should be raised (shift from the system of monarchy or replacement of Mohammad by another Shah)?

A: The United States would not favour an attempt to effect a change in regime. In view of Iran's geographic position and internal political pressures, a change of regime would be a hazardous adventure which might seriously jeopardize Iranian independence and social stability."

2. In giving us the above information the State Department explained that the initial approach was made in an atmosphere of secrecy and the attache when he accepted Khosrow Qashqai's invitation had no idea he was going to have questions of this kind put to him.

3. The United States Embassy in London is being informed by the State Department, which added that reply to Amini was probably given on May 5 or 6.

[Copy sent to the Prime Minister]

[Unsigned]

The Shah remembers the events of 9th of Esfand (Mohammad-Reza Shah, *Mission for My Country*, p. 97):

In February 1953 he suggested that I temporarily leave the country. In order to give him a free hand to try out his policies, and to have a little respite from his intrigues, I agreed. He proposed that we should keep the plan a close secret, and said he would arrange for Fatemi, his Foreign Minister, personally to issue the necessary travel documents for me, my wife, and our entourage.

Amusingly enough, Mossadegh advised against our leaving by air; with more than usual acumen he remarked that crowds of people opposed to my departure might block the airport runway and prevent the plane from taking off. He proposed that instead we should travel incognito to the frontier and thence through Iraq to Beirut. I agreed.

But somehow the people had learned the secret of our planned departure. The ensuing mass demonstrations of loyalty to the Shah were so convincing and affecting that I decided to remain for the time being. The Tudeh party, no doubt in consultation with some of Mossadegh's followers, immediately called for a united front against the monarchy, but this only seemed to rally the Persian people in support of me and of the position I symbolized.

In retrospect I realized that my decision to leave may have been a hasty one and indeed a big mistake on my part; but God had turned it into a stroke of good fortune.

9th of Esfand according to the account of Dr. Mossadegh. From *Mussadiq's Memoirs*, translated by S. H. Amin and H. Katouzian (London: Jebhe, 1988), 343–346.

One cold day in the month of Bahman 1331 [February 1953], the Court Minister Mr. Hossien Ala got into a conversation with me and said that His Imperial Majesty the Shahanshah [the king of kings] and Her Imperial Majesty Queen Soraya intended to go on a foreign trip. I told him that at the present time, when the Iranian nation is engaged in a conflict with one of the major powers of the world, this trip would not produce a good impression. It will make people think that the Shahanshah is not happy with the situation and wishes remove himself from it.

Later on, on another occasion, again we got engaged in a conversation. He told me that the reason for the journey was to carry out some checks to produce a child that would become the crown prince, because it is not clear which side the fault lies. He stressed that it was necessary for His Majesty to go on that trip. Once again, I said it would be better if Her Majesty went first, and then if it was felt necessary His Majesty could go too.

Meanwhile, the court had invited a number of Majles deputies who were supporters of the government to meet with them, and from there they came to my house, but it was not clear why they had been invited. If there was any special reason for that invitation, I do not remember it now. All I can say is that shortly after they arrived in my house, Dr. Moazzemi, who was among them, was called on the telephone by the court. When he came back after answering the telephone he whispered something in the ears of a couple of his friends, which aroused everybody's curiosity. Later on, it became clear that the topic of the telephone conversation had been about His Majesty's secret visit abroad, and that it had to remain completely secret before he had left the country. Then, we were informed that the court minister and Mr. Valatabar were also coming to discuss the matter with the Prime Minister. A short time later, they arrived and Majles deputies went to another room. The gentlemen repeated to me in strict confidence what Dr. Moazzemi had already told me. It was decided that the following day, namely Tuesday 5th Esfand [24 February 1953], I should be received in an audience with His Imperial Majesty, and hear His Majesty's orders regarding his visit.

Anytime I woke up during that night I kept thinking about the issue. I wondered that if the visit had been secret, then why did they inform me on the telephone, and also if it had to be kept secret then why before my being received by His Majesty ten other people had been informed about it.

On Tuesday 5th of Esfand I was received by His Majesty to hear his orders, and I heard His Imperial Majesty's remarks, the gist of which was as follows. He said that he was forced to go abroad and that he believed that it was in the country's interest. Once again, I expressed my views to His Majesty but my pleadings proved ineffective. Then he said, "As I do not wish to let anyone know about the trip I will not leave by aircraft. I will leave Tehran by car for Ramsar and half way on the road I will change direction and will go to Iraq through Kermanshah. The minister of the interior should be in attendance up to the border." I did not say anything further, and I left His Majesty's presence.

On Thursday, 7th Esfand [26 February 1953], the court minister talked to me about foreign currency and on Saturday, 9th Esfand, he again phoned me at eight o'clock in the morning and asked me about the passports for those who would accompany His Majesty. It was agreed that they should be ready by midday, and that I should also be received by His Majesty at 13:30 to have lunch with him, and that at 14:30 the ministers should gather there so that they could officially see His Majesty off.

After those discussions, I summoned the head of the joint chiefs of staff of the armed forces, the head of the National Police Force, and Tehran's military governor and I talked to them separately as each of them came to see me. I stressed the importance of ensuring security around the royal palace, the route that His Majesty would take, and I issued the necessary orders to make sure that nothing untoward might happen and that unidentified individuals could not get close to the royal procession. As a precaution, I also summoned the head of the District One police station and made the necessary arrangements for security on the route of His Majesty's procession and checking the nearby houses.

I was busy making these arrangements when one of the *ulema* connected with the 9th Esfand [28 February 1953] telephoned me and asked me if His Majesty was going to leave the country. If I had said no, it would have been contrary to the truth; and if I had said yes, it would have been contrary to His Majesty's orders, who did not even want to leave by air so that nobody would be informed about his departure. This is why I said that there was such a rumour. He asked me why I was not stopping it. I told him that I had expressed my disagreement with the visit and that he had to take some action too in case it might succeed.

A short while later, the court minister telephoned me and then gave the receiver to His Imperial Majesty who ordered me to go to the palace at 12.00 instead of 13:30. In obedience to His Majesty's command, I left shortly before noon and I told the minister that as soon as the passports for those accompanying His Majesty were ready they had to go to the palace in order to take part in official farewell ceremonies.

I arrived in the palace at about 12:00, and I was led to the large hall. Then His Majesty entered the room and said that the members of the presidium of the Senate had gone there in order to dissuade him from leaving. I told His Majesty that what they were proposing had been correct. It would be good if His Majesty would consider their request and would change his mind about leaving. Then he left the hall in order to talk to the members of the presidium of the Senate, and I remained in the hall with Her Majesty the Queen, until His Majesty returned. It became clear that he had not accepted the requests of that delegation and had not changed his decision to leave.

Meanwhile, an envelope was received from the telephone room with the word 'urgent' written on it. It said that the American ambassador wanted urgently to meet with me, and I showed it to His Majesty. Although I thought that His Majesty's departure would be postponed until I had my meeting with the ambassador, my request was not accepted by His Majesty. He said that his brothers had not been informed about his departure until that day, and that they had come to see him. It would be better for the ministers to come first, so that then His Majesty could go and say goodbye to his brothers. This is why a servant conveyed His Majesty's command to the ministers, and all of them were received. At first, His Majesty made some remarks about the need for that visit, and then I spoke about everybody's hopes and wishes about His Majesty's health and about his safe return. Then His Majesty left the hall and went to the entrance hall and we followed him. As we approached the entrance hall our arrival coincided with the arrival of the 9th Esfand *ulema*. They did not see us and went to a waiting room near the entrance hall.

In order to say goodbye to his brothers, His Majesty left the entrance hall and went upstairs, and we remained there not knowing what to do. We were rather uncertain about what to do because the court minister had said that the ministers had to be present when His Majesty left and should take part in some sort of a ceremony. However, I did not get the same impression from His Majesty's remarks. As the situation should have been clarified so that nothing contrary to regulations should take place I turned to Mr. Hormoz Pirnia (the head of protocol) who was with us at the entrance hall and asked him to find out what should be done. He went and saw His Majesty and when he returned he conveyed His Majesty's commands, and it became clear that he had no further orders.

As our presence in the hall was no longer necessary and as I wanted to see the American ambassador, I left the building before anyone else. I was only a few steps from the main gate when I heard loud and rowdy noises coming from outside the gate. I was surprised how, despite all my instruction to the security forces to take every precaution to ensure security, a number of demonstrators had been able to gather there, and I had not been given any report about it either. I was thinking whether I should continue on my path or whether I should return and go home through a different door when suddenly someone whom I had never seen entered through the door. He passed me and in answer to my question as to whether I could leave through another door, he said certainly! He immediately called one of the servants in the court who was standing next to His Majesty's car in front of the building and told him to bring the key to the other door (he meant the door that opened on Heshmat od-Dowleh Square near the entrance to the palace of Her Royal Highness Princess Shams Pahlavi). The servant brought the key and opened the door. Then I discovered that that person was Mr. Amirsadeghi, His Majesty's driver. He guided me to that door and sent someone to bring my car, which was in front of the court to the back door. When I wanted to get into the car I saw a number of people who were coming further down the road, but the car moved before they got there. Only two or three people had reached the car, but I managed to get from there to my house which was only 150 yards away. When I inquired about those people, I was told that they had come to request His Imperial Majesty to change his mind about his departure.

Towards the evening when the crowd moved towards my house, it became clear that if I had not been behind the door in the palace and if I had not immediately left after the car arrived the crowd would have got to me and some of them who had been already given the mission would have bumped me off.

Only a short time after I arrived in my residence, Mr. Henderson, the American ambassador, accompanied as usual by Mr. Ali Pasha Saleh, arrived. The ambassador made certain remarks, for which it would not have been necessary to arrange a meeting.

The following is Princess Soraya's recollections of the events. From *Palace of Solitude*.

On 13th February 1952, the Shah decided to leave the country for a while. He seemed very depressed and he thought that his continued presence in Iran would be regarded as a form of support for Mossadegh's policies. Going abroad, but where? We did not have any clear destination in mind. Mossadegh welcomed that decision. He opened the purse and gave us 11,000 dollars from the government's foreign currency account as expenses for the trip. He insisted that no one should learn about that trip. In order to keep the matter secret, he recommended that we should leave the country by car without any fuss and should go to Beirut so that everybody would think that we had left the country to take part in winter sports.

The night before the departure, when I was sitting on an armchair in a sad and depressed mood and was looking with regret at the different parts of the private palace that I had decorated with great care and interest according to my taste, one of the protocol officers arrived and said that a trusted person had come to see me on behalf of Ayatollah Kashani. Ayatollah Kashani had sent me a message through that person to use all my power of persuasion to dissuade the Shah from going on that trip.

I was amazed: Ayatollah Kashani, on the Shah's side! Have the clerics left Mossadegh's side and have they risen up in support of the Shah in fear of communist domination! That same evening I informed the Shah of that meeting and Kashani's message. The Shah emphatically ruled out any change in his decision. He was not someone to give in to other people's views.

The next morning, Mossadegh came to say goodbye. His behaviour was polite and combined with hypocritical kindness and affection. He was in a hurry to make us leave. As we were engaged in exchanging pleasantries, we heard a noise from the street. The demonstrators, who were climbing the walls and the gates of the palace, were shouting and chanting some slogans that we could not understand. Mossadegh said, "Hurry up, start to move!"

Gradually, the slogans became more audible. It became clear that the demonstrations were in our favour, not against us. They were Kashani's supporters who demanded that we should stay in Iran. They shouted, "Long live the king, Death to Mossadegh!"

The old lion grew pale, and a sweat appeared on his forehead. I felt sorry for him. I held his hand and told him, "Leave through this door. At the end of the corridor there is a door. From there you can easily get home without confronting the crowd."

After Mossadegh left, the Shah went on the balcony and with a loudspeaker he promised the crowd that he would stay in the country. I was crying. Women's job is to cry. Although there was no change in the situation and Mossadegh remained the head of the government, nevertheless, the Shah became more hopeful. From then on, he felt that he was not alone and that there were many

Iranians who were still faithful to him, whether among the clerics, or in the armed forces, or even in the Majles.

The ninth of Esfand according to the report of the American Ambassador Loy Henderson is reprinted in facsimile in the document section of this book on page 454.
[3] After Dr. Moazzemi was elected Majles speaker, my father sent a personal letter to him in which he wrote:

> Your Excellency Dr. Moazzemi, honourable speaker of the national consultative assembly.
>
> A few nights ago, through my host, I sent a message of congratulations to you in response to Your Excellency's kindness, and I hope it has been well received. Now that my hand is a bit better, I wish to express my respects through this letter. I hope that you will be successful in your venture. Today, two figures command a great deal of respect and esteem in the country, namely the head of the legislative branch and the head of the executive branch. If those who occupy these two posts in their dealings with one another implement their legal and moral responsibilities with complete honour and courage, the affairs of the country will improve.
>
> I do not wish to tell you about the desperate situation that the Iranian nation is in. If your researches and your findings go beyond the utterances of a group of supporters and opponents and if you think fairly and deeply about the situation, you will see that the problems that the nation is facing are a thousand times more serious than what appears on the surface.
>
> You must rest assured that I am not engaged in any personal conflict and opposition with anybody. If I am persuaded that the affairs of the country are progressing satisfactorily, I will even promise that so long as I live I will not ask for a position.
>
> Of course, your personality enables you to rely upon your conscience and your personal and family honour in all affairs, and to think of a speedy remedy for the country. Otherwise, if the situation continues as it is, then one should "weep for the living, not for the dead."
>
> Finally, I would like to use this opportunity to reiterate my respect and to wish for Your Excellency's success.

Chapter Five
The Period of Hiding

Question: On 19 July 1953, Major General Zahedi left his place of asylum in the parliament on the basis of a guarantee that the Majles speaker, Dr. Moazzemi, had given him. A month later, on 19 August 1953, the report of his appointment as prime minister was broadcast on the radio. Where was your father during that period, and where were you?

Zahedi: As I have said before, we could not trust anyone's words or any official's guarantees. At first, we took my father to the house of my aunt, Fatemeh Khanom Zahedi, Basir Homayun's wife. He spent a few days in hiding there. Then he spent a few days in the house of Javad Hamzavi, in Naderi Street, which in those days was one of the main streets in the center of Tehran. Dr. Hamzavi was the son of Agha Mir Ghafghazi, who had the title of Amir Monazzam. According to Soleiman Behbudi's memoirs, Agha Mir Ghafghazi had maintained close ties with Reza Shah ever since the time when the then Reza Khan was the minister of war. In those days, he and a few others were members of a regular circle of friends who played card games with Reza Shah for fun.

Then we moved my father from there to Reza Keynejad's house, and again a few days later we transferred him to Mostafa Moghaddam's house. Moghaddam's house was a more suitable place for my father to stay, because it was connected to various streets with many doors, and any movement there attracted less attention. When my father was the head of the Military Inspectorate, Mostafa Moghaddam was the governor of Sepah Bank, and they had clashed with each other. My father did not expect him to place his house at his disposal under those circumstances. However, Moghaddam had a chivalric and tribal character and was very hospitable. I also guess that Ayatollah Kashani had urged him to show hospitality toward my father, because for the first time Agha Mostafa Kashani, Ayatollah Kashani's son, took me there in his car to see the house and to get to know the owner.

In any case, from then on, my father stayed in Moghaddam's villa in Saltanatabad in Shemiran, which was a separate district in the north of Tehran in those days but now has become a part of the city. I spent every night in a different place, because the military government was looking for me and had set a reward of 10,000 tumans, which was a considerable sum in those days, for anyone who could hand me over.

Our contacts with His Majesty had become more difficult ever since Hossein Ala resigned as court minister, due to Mossadegh's pressure, and was replaced by Abol-Ghassem Amini, because they had placed guards everywhere and were strictly controlling all the meetings and contacts with His Majesty. When His Majesty was staying in the city, we had some meetings with him. Amirsadeghi, His Majesty's trusted driver, used to take me to a street near the palace of Her Royal Highness Shams, and from there I secretly went in through the back door to the house that had been built for Her Royal Highness Shahnaz. That road led to a small volleyball court. Then we would take a few steps down to a basement room, which I think was later turned into a private cinema, and there we met with His Majesty.

Gradually, when they removed everybody from around His Majesty and had created a situation in which he could not meet and talk with anybody, I could no longer sit in the car when His Majesty wanted to receive me. They used to hide me in the car's trunk, and by the time we reached the palace I felt half-dead. The second time when I was going to see His Majesty in that fashion, traveling from the villa of Ja'far Ja'fari in Valanjak, a mountain village north of Tehran, to Sa'dabad Palace, I was taken in a small Austin car. As I had squeezed myself in the boot of that car, I got a cramp in my foot and was in acute pain, but I could not move. It was summer and I was sweating profusely. I endured the pain and did not make a murmur until we reached Sa'dabad Palace. His Majesty was waiting for me. When Amirsadeghi opened the boot, I fell on the ground like a log. My light summer suit was drenched as though I had taken a shower. It was dripping with sweat. Fortunately, my cramp eased a bit and I could stand up.

Then, His Majesty and I walked in the garden under the trees, not knowing that they had irrigated the garden in the morning and that the ground was wet. His Majesty was wearing light moccasin slip-on shoes. As we took a few steps under the trees the shoes got stuck in the mud and came off, and that created a funny situation too.

Another time, when I went with my father to Sa'dabad Palace, His Majesty took us to the dining room and all of us sat cross-legged on the dining table, because it was the safest place. We could be confident that our conversation was not being recorded and that no one was listening to us to prepare a report on what we said.

Of course, my father was unhappy about the circumstances under which those meetings and talks were held. He used to say, "After all, I have been a minister in this country, I have been a senator, I have been an army commander, I have won back Khuzestan. I wish to meet the king of our country and to talk to him on some political issues. It is not right that I should go like a thief to the Shah's palace." Nevertheless, in view of the prevailing circumstances, His Majesty believed that it was necessary to take such precautions.

Question: Basically, what did you talk about?

Zahedi: The main topic of conversation was that the country was in danger. If nothing was done, first of all, the monarchy would be eliminated and then the country would collapse. My father used to say that Dr. Mossadegh had reached a dead end and was not able to run the country. We had some firsthand information about the desperate situation of the country: the disorder in the government, economic paralysis, empty treasury, and activities of the Tudeh Party in the armed forces and in other institutions. Some of the law-enforcement and military officials were in touch with us. Colonel Naderi, head of the Intelligence Department of the Police, and Colonel Ashrafi, the military governor under Mossadegh's government, were in contact with me and used to inform me about what was going on.[1]

Question: Did all this go on despite the fact that the military governor had set a reward for your and your father's arrest?

Zahedi: Yes. Of course, there was a great deal of danger, which was increasing day by day. It had been reported to His Majesty that those meetings were dangerous for me and that the government had plans to arrest me. Colonel Naderi was gradually playing a duplicitous game. Dr. Mossadegh had given him a Buick car, similar to the cars that were used as part of the court's escort cars, as a present, and he used to come to our meeting points in that car. One evening, we had agreed to meet in the upper parts of Saltanatabad, a place that was a public park where people would come in their cars, rather like the bridge in Tajrish, to gather, to read poetry, play music, and eat fried chicken. Although Naderi was married and had children, he came in his Buick with a beautiful woman who was his mistress. I had been informed by some sources inside the police that Naderi was keeping an eye on me and wanted to see where I lived and where I slept so that he could send someone to arrest me. Of course, there were those dangers, but had I given in to fear we would have achieved nothing. Such meetings were necessary in order to gather intelligence.

A few of us got together and drew up a plan. While Colonel Naderi was sitting in our car and we were busy talking, Hormoz Shahrokhshahi pretended to be drunk. He went to Naderi's car and drove it into a ravine in the dark. The poor colonel was about to expire. He was upset that his new car had been smashed, and he did not know what to do with that young lady and how to get rid of her. While he was deep in those thoughts, Parviz Yarafshar got in the car and started the engine. We drove away and left them struggling with their plight. We drove to my hiding place, namely, Mirashrafi's house in Saba Street in the north of Tehran.

Once again, I met with Colonel Naderi in the house of Engineer Setudeh, who was known as Engineer Mustache. This time, our friends drove him to Engineer Setudeh's house in northern Tehran, but until he arrived he did not know where he was going. We sent for takeout chicken kebabs and roast chicken. When I got home I did not feel well and realized that I was suffering from food poisoning. Some friends believed that Naderi had put something in my food. However, something could have been wrong with the food, or my stomach might have become too sensitive because I was constantly on the run and had not eaten properly. God only knows. My last meeting with Naderi was in Mordad [August], but this time it was a group meeting.

Colonel (later General) Gharani, who after the revolution was appointed chairman of the joint chiefs of staff of the armed forces, was a member of the military government. A few other officers in addition to Naderi were present in that meeting. We had arranged to meet in Tehran Zoo, which belonged to the Dowlatshahi brothers. A stream runs through the zoo, and there is a weir on it. I had arranged for a few armed men to keep watch on the other side of the weir. I had also prepared a jeep, so that if there was any danger I could flee in it.

We were busy talking when Mr. Yarafshar arrived and quietly informed me that His Majesty wanted to see me. I told him to pretend that he did not intend to return and to leave his car. I told him to go behind the trees, pretending that he wanted to pass water, and then to get into the jeep. I left shortly afterward, and we got into the jeep and drove fast to Valanjak. My father was waiting for me there. He said that he had just come from visiting His Majesty, who had said that the meeting would be dangerous and that I might be arrested at any time. Apparently, Alavi-Moghaddam had reported that some of the people who met with me could not be trusted. In any case, His Majesty had summoned me partly to warn me of the danger, but he also had something more important to tell me. Once again, I squeezed myself inside the boot of the car and was driven to Sa'dabad Palace. His Majesty reproached me, saying that I was not cautious enough and would put myself in danger, and that by so doing I worried him and my father. It was at that meeting that His Majesty said that he had decided to issue a decree appointing my father as the prime minister, this despite the fact that there was a price on my father's head.

Question: What was the accusation against him?

Zahedi: According to article five of the martial law regulations, they could have arrested anyone they wanted. The charges leveled against my father were opposing the current policies of the government and expressing concern about the current affairs of the country. In his memoirs, which were published after the revolution in Iran, Brigadier General Kamal, the head of the National Police at that time, quoted from a letter from my father in which he had protested against the stationing of guards outside his house and the controlling of all his movements. This goes back to the time when the senate had not yet been dissolved and when my father still enjoyed parliamentary immunity. The date of that letter is 9 October 1952.[2]

The senate was dissolved in November 1952. In December, martial law regulations were extended for a further two months in Tehran. This time, martial law regulations extended to the suburbs as well. The only reason for that was because previously Hesarak, a district on the slopes of the mountain north of Tehran where the Zahedi family house was situated, did not fall within the martial law zone. Therefore, they extended martial law regulations to the suburbs of the city, so that they could arrest my father and other people who lived in Shemiran.

Brigadier General Kamal has written that Foreign Minister Fatemi had said in an interview that many documents had been discovered about contacts between Major General Zahedi and the British government and the oil company. However, after Major General Zahedi had written that harsh and insulting letter to him, Kamal had asked Fatemi about those documents. He had replied, "Words are like air, they do not require any documents." Then it became clear that no documents had been discovered. In those days, like the days after the revolution, people accused everybody of whatever they liked, and there was no need for evidence or document.

I wish to swear by my honor that my father had no contacts with the British government and the oil company. His contacts with British citizens were limited to his meetings with the British chargé d'affaires, Middleton, which were carried out openly. My father was a senator and had held senior political and military positions. Middleton expressed a desire to meet him. In order to prevent any suspicion or gossip, my father insisted that the meeting had to be open and that he had to go to Hesarak. Middleton went to Hesarak in a car with a diplomatic license plate. He was accompanied by another gentleman. He sat down and talked about the situation in the country. He said, "We are anxious to resolve the oil issue, and we are interested in maintaining relations between the two countries. Various things have happened, but now that the situation has reached this point and the ambassadors from the two countries have been recalled, I would like to know your views about it and how this problem can be resolved."

My father replied, "The key to that door rests in His Majesty's hands." Middleton sarcastically said, "But that key has become rather rusty!" My father became very angry that a foreigner talked like that about his country's monarch. His veins swelled and his face became red. He said, "Had I not been in my own house, I would have gotten up and left the room." I was acting as the translator. After hearing those words, Middleton understood that he had to leave, and the conversation ended there and then. He got up, said farewell, and left. The whole meeting did not last more than 15 minutes. The officials had reported that Middleton had gone to Major General Zahedi's house, and that became the basis for Fatemi's remarks.

In any case, the fictitious stories that foreigners have put together about the coup d'état are of the same nature. His Majesty was not someone who would stage a coup d'état. Whenever anybody talked to my father about the possibility of a coup d'état, my father replied, "No, a coup d'état is not right. Any thought about a coup d'état is wrong. The government should be changed and the problems must be resolved but through legal means." In all the talks with His Majesty, the only solution that was discussed was a legal solution. My father used to say to His Majesty, "As the king, you must openly express your dissatisfaction about the situation, so that the people and the majority of Majles deputies may understand the real situation." As Mossadegh suspected this and feared that his government would fall as the result of a Majles vote, he dissolved the Majles and held a referendum. With the dissolution of the Majles, the way was open for His Majesty to resort to legal measures. On the basis of the powers that the Constitution has given to the king, he had the right to depose the prime minister and appoint another one in his place.

Question: You said that on the evening that you went to Sa'dabad Palace you learned that His Majesty had decided to depose Mossadegh and to issue a decree appointing your father as the prime minister. How and where were those decrees issued and signed? In the military tribunal, Dr. Mossadegh claimed that the decree had been written on an unmarked piece of paper and this is why he had suspected that it had been forged.[3]

Zahedi: He did not tell the truth. Both decrees were handwritten with the calligraphy of Rahim Hirad, the Shah's chief of staff. His Majesty issued both decrees in Kalardasht and sent them to Tehran via Colonel Nematollah Nasiri, who was the commander of the imperial guards. That night when I saw His Majesty in Sa'dabad Palace was the last time that I saw him (before the toppling of Mossadegh's government). I did not see him anymore until he returned from Rome. It was dark when His Majesty received me. As I was leaving he commanded, "Tell Hirad to prepare the document that I have told him. It is strictly confidential, and at the moment no one should learn anything about it." When I came downstairs, I saw Hirad for the first time in the palace entrance hall, which is surrounded by four big columns. I conveyed to him His Majesty's orders and his words of caution. That honorable man became very upset. He was absolutely trustworthy. His pride was hurt and he started to sweat. I really felt embarrassed for him.

Later on, when I got closer to His Majesty and I had the honor of being with him during various trips, I was always careful to show respect to Hirad. He was a very honorable and dignified man. He was also a very religious man. Later, I saw him one day deep in thought. I asked him what the matter was. He replied, "Now, I have become qualified to go on Hajj pilgrimage, and I should ask permission and go visit God's House."

Anyway, it was planned that His Majesty's decree should reach Tehran on Sunday, 8 August 1953, and be delivered the same day. However, Nasiri's trip was delayed. It was Friday when Nasiri finally arrived. He was wearing a pale beige civilian suit. I drove him to Mostafa Moghaddam's house. Nasiri handed my father the decree appointing him prime minister.[4] My father kissed him on the face and expressed his willingness to accept the post. As it was a holiday, it was decided that the following day, Saturday, when the cabinet held its regular session, Nasiri should hand in the Shah's decree dismissing Mossadegh at the end of the session before the ministers had gone away. At the same time, some precautionary steps were taken, as the situation was not normal.

During those two days, through some of their agents, the members of the Tudeh Party had sensed something about what was going on. They wrote in their newspapers and issued official statements announcing that there were plans for a military coup against the prime minister, and they called on the people to resist.[5] Nobody was planning a coup d'état, but one could not ignore the possible reaction by Mossadegh and those around him, or the possibility of disorder and insecurity.

Of course, Nasiri made a mistake. When he handed in the decree and got a receipt for it he should not have waited any longer. He had not gone to arrest Mossadegh. This was not the order he was given, and there was no such program. He had gone there to deliver the decree, and he should not have waited there any longer.[6]

Question: You said that Colonel Nasiri made a mistake. If the aim simply was to serve the decree on Mossadegh, then why did he go to Mossadegh's house with a number of military trucks full of armed soldiers and two or three tanks? It was the manner that the decree was served that provided an excuse to the then government to portray this as a military coup in its propaganda. It also resulted in a wave of arrests of Mossadegh's opponents and put intense pressure

on political opposition groups in Tehran and other cities. What is your view about this?

Zahedi: I have already said that Nasiri made a mistake. It was due to lack of experience or ignorance or might have been for the sake of claiming a bigger role for himself than what he was ordered to do. In the military court, the military prosecutor, Brigadier General (later General) Hossein Azemoudeh, referred to that unwise move by Nasiri, who had been summoned to the court to testify, and blamed him for it. He should not have waited at Mossadegh's house. There was no need for a military escort either. In fact, he should not have entered the house and should not have handed in his weapon to the colonel who was guarding the house.

In any case, Nasiri was killed after the revolution, and he is not able to provide any explanations for his action. I am not sure whether or not the three tanks you refer to were the three tanks that were guarding Mossadegh's house. The fact is that after that ill-fated incident, Mossadegh knew that his position at the head of the government was no longer legal (and as he had dissolved the Majles there was no legal authority that could have arbitrated between the head of state and the head of the government). He was badly shaken. Consequently, he took—or was pushed by some of his aides (or at least some of his extremist aides) toward taking—a number of steps that were contrary to the constitution.

Question: What was America's stance during those three days?

Zahedi: You should read the documents of the American Embassy. You should read official and confidential reports that after many years are now declassified and are available to all. You should read the works of impartial historians who have dealt with the events of those three days during the past few years. An impartial investigation of those documents and files shows (without the possibility of the slightest doubt and ambiguity in their interpretation) that American security and intelligence organizations recalled all their agents. The American ambassador went to see Dr. Mossadegh in order to bring about reconciliation and improve understanding between him and the government. On the whole, America and Britain thought that the effort to topple the regime, which was headed by Mossadegh and which had pushed the country to an economic and political dead end, had failed.

During those three days, it was the Iranian people, my father and his supporters, and the clerical establishment, especially the Grand Ayatollah Borujerdi, who saved the country from chaos and from communism and from becoming one of Moscow's satellites. This is something that international propaganda has never admitted until recent years, when there has been a fundamental change in outlook. If you wish, we can speak in more detail about this later.

The plan was that after His Majesty's decree deposing Mossadegh had been served on him, my father would go to the prime minister's office and start his work. In those days, the prime minister's office was in Abyaz Palace, which was a part of the Arg palace complex near the bazaar in the center of Tehran. However, Mossadegh did not leave his house and had transferred the prime minister's office to his house in Kakh Street. It was located in the north of Tehran in those days, a few steps from the winter palaces of the Shah and the royal family.

My father was forced to find another place as his headquarters. Due to his former position as the head of the Officers' Club and the central position of that club, he chose that building as his early headquarters. Brigadier General Daftari escorted my father to the Officers' Club.

Question: What was the position of Brigadier General Daftari, Dr. Mossadegh's nephew, at that time?

Zahedi: At that time, Daftari was the commander of the guards at the Customs Department, and on 25 Mordad [16 August 1953] Dr. Mossadegh appointed him as the head of the police. It was rumored that he reported the program of all our activities to Mossadegh, but as my father kept him as the head of the police I doubt that the rumor was true. I don't know, only God knows. In any case, it was decided that Daftari should come with two jeeps in front of the Military

Hospital number two, in Pahlavi Street, near the waterfall. Twice I drove there, accompanied by Brigadier General Gilanshah, but I did not see any sign of Daftari and his group.

Question: Where was your father during those hours?

Zahedi: He was in Kashanian's villa near Pasian Station in Pahlavi Street, in north Tehran. But why did we move to that place? When my father received His Majesty's decree, I was given the task of inviting a few people who had to be informed of the matter, some of whom were given certain responsibilities, and talking to them. I telephoned Major General Batmanqelich, Colonel Farzanegan, Brigadier General Taghizadeh, Messrs. Haerizadeh and Faramarzi, and two Majles deputies and asked them to come to Moghaddam's villa at seven in the morning on 16 August 1953. The meeting started at eight o'clock, and my father informed all those present of the contents of His Majesty's decree. He said, "We do not intend to stage a coup d'état, but in view of the existing situation, as it is possible that Dr. Mossadegh might disobey the decrees and it may result in some disturbances, it is essential to take some precautionary measures. I have invited you gentlemen to exchange views and to decide how and at what time we should communicate the decree to Dr. Mossadegh, and what steps should be taken to prevent any possible disturbances or rebellion."

That meeting lasted for a few hours, and it was decided that Nasiri should go to Mossadegh's house between 11:00 and 11:30 at night, when the cabinet meeting was due to end, and serve the decree. At the same time, the individuals who were due to be in charge of sensitive military and law-enforcement operations were appointed. Mr. Yarafshar wrote down their decrees as they were dictated by my father. About midday a few of those who had come to the meeting returned to the city, and a few stayed behind for lunch. At about two in the afternoon, when the lunch was nearly over, my cousin Abol-Ghassem Zahedi, accompanied by Hormoz Shahrokhshahi, entered the room in a state of panic. They told us that the officials of the military government had been informed about our place of residence, and if we did not hurry up and leave all of us would be arrested. Colonel Naderi had passed that information to them.

Under such circumstances, my father had an amazing control over his nerves. While the rest of us were in a state of panic, in complete calm he told each one of us about our duties. Meanwhile, he said, "Ardeshir! You and I will be the last persons to leave this place." This is exactly what we did. After everybody had gone, my father went to Kashanian's house in Hormoz Shahrokhshahi's car, and I drove to Aqdasiyyeh to meet with Brigadier General Zangeneh, the commander of the Military College. Later, the officers from the military government had attacked Moghaddam's villa, and they had searched everywhere, including a disused storeroom, for my father, but of course the bird had already flown the nest.

Those days I had grown a mustache as a form of disguise. The officials were looking for me. I was on the run and I could not hide anywhere. I went to Aqdasiyyeh, the summer camp of the Military College, and told the guard at the gate that I wanted to see the commander of the camp. I was taken to a tent, which served as the headquarters of the commander of the Military College. Brigadier General Zangeneh was a brave officer who had shown a great deal of courage during the fighting in Azerbaijan and who had been imprisoned for a while by the members of the separatist gang. When he saw me, he looked shocked and signs of fear appeared on his face. He did not expect at all to see me there.

I informed him about what was going on and then left to go to Shemiran to see my mother. I expected some unpleasant developments the outcomes of which were hard to predict. Therefore, it was necessary for me to see my mother and to say good-bye to her. Although I did not tell her what was going on, nevertheless, due to her instinct as a mother she knew that I might be in danger. She brought me a chain with a prayer from the Koran that I still wear round my neck.

It was 7:30 in the evening when I reached Kashanian's house. General Batmanqelich, Colonel Farzanegan, Brigadier General Taghizadeh, Brigadier General She'ri, Brigadier General Aftasi, Colonel Khajenouri, Colonel Navvabi, and Messrs. Moghaddam, Yarafshar, Abol-Ghassam Zahedi, Reza Keynejad, Sadeq Naraghi, and Hormoz Shahrokhshahi were already there and were discussing the best way to seize power. Those talks lasted till nearly eleven at night.

At that time, the telephone rang. My father picked it up and said a few words in a vague manner to the person on the other side of the line. When he put down the receiver, he said, "Nasiri has left." From the few words that I could hear on the telephone in Turkish, I realized that Major Shaghaghi, an officer in the imperial guard, was talking on the phone. Later on, he committed suicide due to his disagreements with Gharabaghi.

In that way, we too started our action. General Batmanqhelich, who was wearing military uniform and who had been appointed as the chairman of the joint chiefs of the staff of the armed forces, left for the city in a car driven by Mostafa Moghaddam. He was going to the headquarters of the joint chiefs of the staff to assume his new post. Earlier, it had been decided that Farzanegan, who had been appointed minister of post and telegraph, should go and take charge of wireless and radio. Also, Colonel Khajenouri and Colonel Navvabi were told to go to the headquarters of the Second Armored Brigade and be stationed at the only properly equipped military barracks in Tehran. Then, my father changed his mind and told them that it would look like a coup d'état, and we were not planning a coup d'état. He said, "Wait for a while, and we will all go together to the Officers' Club [the place that was chosen as the headquarters for the prime minister]. After I am stationed there, I will send the rest of you to your new appointments."

This was my father's plan, provided that Mossadegh had decided to obey the decree. Otherwise, we would be faced with a different situation, which would require different measures, and under those circumstances it would have been necessary to make use of political leaders and others. Those were very sensitive moments, and all of us were in a state of anxiety, except my father, who seemed calm and serene.

Yarafshar, Shahrokhshahi, Navvabi, and Khajenouri were told to go to the city and send a report about the situation there. My father went to the courtyard and started to pace the courtyard by himself, and Farzanegan and I stayed in the room. It was after midnight, and still we had not received any news from Tehran. My father returned to the room and said, "We'd better start to move too, because by now Nasiri and Batmanqelich must have performed their mission."

My father, Farzanegan, and I got in the car and left for the city. As martial law regulations were in force, there was no traffic in Pahlavi Street. There was also absolute silence inside the car. We drove fast to Yusofabad crossroad. At this point, we noticed a car coming from the opposite direction and driving toward Shemiran. The car passed without noticing us, but as we were carefully looking at the car and its occupants we recognized Moghaddam and Batmanqelich among the occupants. My father asked, "Why are they returning? Where are they going?" One of those in the car said, "I imagine that a problem has arisen." My father told the driver to turn round and to catch up with that car. A little distance after Vanak crossroad we managed to send signals to them with our headlights. Vanak road linked Tehran with Shemiran and today it is one of the main streets in the Iranian capital.

Mostafa Moghaddam stopped the car at the side of the road. The look on their faces showed that they did not have good news. My father asked, "What has happened?" Batmanqelich replied, "Nasiri has been arrested, and military forces have been stationed around the headquarters of the joint chiefs of staff of the armed forces. When we got there, all the lights were on, and on the basis of what we gathered, Brigadier General Riahi was still in his office."

After hearing that, we were lost for words. We exchanged worried glances. After a short while, my father broke his silence and said, "You have been too cautious. You should have gone straight to the office of the chairman of the joint chiefs of the staff of the armed forces and shown him your decrees. You should have told him that on His

Majesty's orders, Zahedi has been appointed prime minister, and he has issued my decree as the new chairman of the joint chiefs of staff of the armed forces. If he disobeyed, on the basis of your higher military rank, you should have ordered him to be arrested."

In response, Moghaddam said, "The general's words would have made sense if we had been able to go inside the building. At the moment, the soldiers have surrounded the office of the chairman of the joint chiefs of staff of the armed forces, and they shoot at anyone who approaches it. Approaching the building was neither possible nor wise." However, Batmanqelich said, "If you approve of this course of action, it is still not too late and we can carry out what you say. However, when we were confronted with the situation we thought it would be better to report to you and ask for your view."

It was not wise to stay any longer in that place. My father said, "We should now go to a secure place and think of a solution." He ordered the driver to drive on. Batmanqelich and Moghaddam drove behind us, and we went to the house of Colonel Farzanegan, the younger brother of Abbas Farzanegan. The house was nearby, close to the Amaniyyeh hills. My father asked one of his aides to go to the city and gather more information. He returned about an hour later and said that the information provided by Batmanqelich and Moghaddam had been quite accurate.

After receiving the decree, Dr. Mossadegh had kept Nasiri for a while in his house, and during that period he had instructed Brigadier General Riahi to go quickly to the headquarters of the chairman of the joint chiefs of staff of the armed forces and to put all the military and law-enforcement forces on alert. The forces guarding Mossadegh's own house had been strengthened, and Nasiri had been arrested.

At this point, we could hear the sound of the chains of tanks that were moving toward Shemiran. My father ordered all the lights in the building to be turned off, and he and Batmanqelich began to look at the Pahlavi Road through a window. They noticed that a number of tanks and military trucks were moving toward Sa'dabad Palace. Now, it was quite clear that we were facing a new situation, and that we had to set aside our earlier plan and think of a new plan.[7]

---

[1] Document reads:

> I have discussed briefly with Middleton the points raised by the Department in the suggested joint appraisal.
>
> (a) This will be covered in a separate telegram.
>
> (b) Both of us are of the opinion that it does not appear likely that any alternatives to Mossadegh could be brought into power at the present time except perhaps by a coup d'état by the military; that we do not know of any outstanding military leaders of ability who have the required strength, standing or intelligence to assure the success of a coup d'état and to govern Iran in the event that such a coup d'état should be successful; that Generals Zahedi and Hedjazi seem to be best fitted for leadership in bringing about a coup d'état; that these two Generals differ in their political views, since Zahedi sympathizes with the National Front moderates whereas Hedjazi's primary interest would probably be in setting up a strong government which would exterminate the Communists and strengthen the Shah's hand. (The US has the impression that Zahedi's character is rather weak, while the British have a somewhat more favorable impression.)
>
> (c) In order to be successful, the coup d'état would have to be carried out and executed entirely by the military in the Shah's name, but without the Shah's knowledge as the Shah probably would not have the stamina to see it through and, at a certain stage, might weaken and denounce the leaders; probably it would be necessary at least for the Commander of the army division stationed in Tehran to be a fellow conspirator and, at some point, probably the Commander of the Shah's bodyguard; if the army could attain complete control of Tehran and if the conspirators, in the Shah's name, could appoint a new Chief of Staff, it is believed that most of the Provinces, with the possible exception of Khuzistan, would recognize the new Government. Difficulty might be caused by the Qashqai tribes. (From such information as had come to us, we believe that there might be more trouble from the Qashqais than the British seem to believe.)
>
> (d) Middleton and I both agreed that neither the US nor UK Government should undertake to encourage or to support a coup d'état and that the two Embassies should avoid becoming involved in any manner.
>
> It should be borne in mind as well that a successful coup d'état would almost certainly result in the Tudeh gaining control of the National movement. The military dictatorship therefore might encounter increasing difficulties in carrying out a constructive program and in controlling the country.

[2] Major General Zahedi's letter to Brigadier General Kamal.

18th Mehr 1331 [10th October 1952]

The Head of the National Police

For the past few days, we have noticed that your officers are recording the registration numbers of the cars of those who come to see me in the city and in Shemiran. It has frequently been observed that the registration numbers of the cars of my neighbours or other people who go to Jamaran for their own business are also recorded. I do not understand what the purpose behind such actions is. If the aim is to identify the individuals who come to visit me as I am ill, you very well know that a large number of leading figures from Tehran and from the provinces who have known me for many years come to visit me. Furthermore, many members of my own family often come to see me on Fridays, which is the day that I have set aside to see the members of my family. Even if it is necessary to collect all their names, which amount to a few hundred, I am not bothered by it. However, it is contrary to human values and is interference in my personal affairs and depriving me of my freedom. Such occurrences are particularly strange under Dr. Mossadegh's government. Such activities are unexpected and are not worthy of a veteran officer such as yourself, because you must be to some extent familiar with my relations with His Excellency Dr. Mossadegh and the assistance that I have provided for him and his friends. At the same time, you should know that I am a senator. Furthermore, I have served my country for many years in order to save my homeland, in a way that has been unique among all high-ranking military officers. I have had no aim but the wellbeing of the country and of my compatriots. Meanwhile, in order to safeguard my dignity and respect, I shall not refrain from any form of protest or retribution. I hope that in the future you shall refrain from such insulting and futile behaviour that is contrary to your interests and the responsibilities that are on your shoulders.

Senator Major General Zahedi

General Kamal writes in his memoirs (Tehran: 1361 [1982]):

One evening, Foreign Minister Dr. Fatemi said that a whole sack full of documents had been discovered regarding Zahedi's contacts with the British Embassy and the [British] Oil Company. As at that time I was the head of the National Police I was forced to keep Zahedi under strict surveillance, until he wrote an insulting and threatening letter to me. Therefore, in order to respond to Zahedi, I asked Dr. Fatemi about the documents that had been discovered against Zahedi. In response, he said, "Words are like air, they do not require any documents." Then it became clear that no documents had been discovered. I do not know the reasons for the hostility between Dr. Fatemi and Major-General Zahedi.

[3] Dr. Mossadegh's testimony in the military tribunal (First Session, Sunday 17 Aban 1332 [8 November 1953]).

I had built a very strong iron gate in front of my house. It took at least one hour to open it. However, that night I ordered the gate to be opened, and that esteemed officer, the head of the Royal Guards, respectfully entered my house. When I saw the decree I suspected that it had been forged. It was clear that they had used an unmarked paper and they had written the last few sentences with a big gap so that the page would be filled. I wish the text of decree was available and I could show it to you, but on the day when they bombed my house they also destroyed that document... In any case, when I noticed all the cannons and the attacks and the way that the decree was written, I suspected that it had been forged. These two issues forced me not to accept the decree.

[4] Decree appointing Fazlollah Zahedi as prime minister.

Your Excellency Mr. Fazlollah Zahedi,
As the circumstances require that a knowledgeable and experienced person should be in charge of the affairs of the country, therefore, in view of our knowledge of your capability and suitability, on the basis of this decree you will be appointed Prime Minister. You are required to make every effort to improve the affairs of the country, to resolve the present crisis, and to raise the level of people's living standards.
22nd Mordad 1332 [13 August 1953]
Mohammad Reza Pahlavi

[5] The following statement was issued as a warning by the Iranian Tudeh Party on Thursday 23 Mordad [14 August 1953] in their newspaper *Besu-ye Ayandeh* [Towards the Future]:

Patriotic workers, farmers, artisans, intellectuals, and noble Iranian nation! Once again, the enemies of the nation, the lackeys of the Court, through an extensive conspiracy wish to trample under foot all the achievements and efforts of you noble people. This time too the court is leading the conspiracy. Their aim is to seize power through a military coup d'état, and to destroy the anti-colonialist struggle of our nation in the interest of their masters. Once again, all the achievements of your long struggle are under the clouds of a serious danger. It is your duty to be vigilant and wakeful more than ever before. As soon as you sense the danger, you must enter the stage with all your power, and you should use all your capabilities in order to neutralise the conspiracy of the enemies! Your power is limitless. So far, you have repeatedly defeated the Court and its agents. This time too you are able and you must defeat their conspiracy and scatter your enemies. The enemy is making every effort with all its capabilities. Repeated defeats have completely shaken its resolve. On the other hand, the power of the nation is immense and the nation enjoys a very high morale. The enemy is grappling with intense weakness, weak morale and disunity and division. By making use of your qualitative and quantitative superiority, and by relying upon the assistance of the masses throughout the world that support your legitimate demands, you can and you must get ready to smash the enemy.

[6] Her Royal Highness Soraya writes in *Palace of Solitude*:

President Eisenhower who was worried about the expansion of the Soviet influence decided to send Kim Roosevelt, the head of the CIA in the Middle East, to Tehran to confront that threat. At the same time, Churchill also sent a message to the Shah and encouraged him to take action against Mossadegh.

Princess Ashraf, who on her own initiative had established contacts with American agents in Switzerland, arrived in Tehran unexpectedly and told the Shah that the time had come to get rid of the "old man."

Later on, it was claimed that the operations had been led by the CIA, but that was not true. The conspiracy started in Tehran and although subsequently the Americans provided some funding for it, whatever happened was the result of our own initiative.

Her Royal Highness Soraya then explains the meeting between the Shah and Zahedi as follows:

On 2 August 1953, Major-General Zahedi met with the Shah in his office. Despite my young age and lack of experience, I also took part in the talks. Was it not a fact that I had initiated the move and had encouraged the Shah to take that decision?

Zahedi looked at me with his penetrating eyes. It was the gaze of an eagle and of a man who knew that he was loved by women. Nevertheless, he is more of a warrior than a seducer of women. Zahedi had been appointed a brigadier-general at the age of 20 and was the youngest general in the armed forces. During the reign of Reza Shah he had suppressed the uprising of the Kurds, the Turkmen and the Bakhtiaris. During the war, when he was the commander of the Army Division in Isfahan he was arrested by the Allies and was exiled to Palestine. In 1941 Mohammad Reza Shah brought him back to Iran and asked him to co-operate with General [Herbert Norman] Schwarzkopf, the American military advisor, to reform the Iranian Police Force. Mossadegh had exiled him together with 86 officers who were firm supporters of the monarchy. However, now he had secretly returned to Tehran and was the leader of Mossadegh's political opponents. He enjoyed great popularity among the army and the police. They have announced 100,000 rials reward for his arrest. He is an energetic man who truly blossoms at the time of action. The action that he wishes to take against Mossadegh puts a smile on his face and enlivens his words. In a decisive tone, he asks, "When can I start the operations?"

The Shah was hesitant. That very morning he had consulted with his weak courtiers whose indecisiveness has exasperated me. They had told him, "Don't take any action against Mossadegh, it is dangerous!"

Last night in the dim light of our bedroom, in a very hesitant voice, he asked me, "Do I really have to depose Mossadegh?" I completely lost my temper and in the emotional mood of a twenty-year old I shouted at him, "For pity's sake! You have no right to sink further in depression. You must recover the man that you were and the one that I loved. If Mossadegh remains in power he will offer Iran to Moscow!"

Here, in his office, he is still hesitant. He turns his gaze away from me and looks at Zahedi who is waiting for an answer, "All right! I will issue a decree, will depose Mossadegh and will appoint you Prime Minister."

Zahedi asks, "When will I receive that decree?" The Shah turns the pages in his diary quickly and says, "You will receive the decree on 13th August [23rd Mordad], and you should deliver it to Mossadegh as soon as possible." Zahedi gets ready for his task. During this period, he has the necessary time to form his headquarters and to plan so that before Riahi, the chairman of the joint chiefs of staff of the armed forces, can do anything, he can control the sensitive places in Tehran. The die is cast. Nothing is left except to wait and hope!

A few days later, we left with aircraft for Kalardasht. Only a few of our friends were with us. According to the official announcement, we were going on a holiday. Oh, how much I loved to have a holiday as in the past! The atmosphere in the private palace has become unbearable to me. In the middle of the night, the Shah wakes me up so that we could change our room as a precaution. Every night we go to bed, we place a revolver under our pillow. Anytime that we are sitting at the table to eat, one hand is on the trigger of the revolver. Mohammad Reza refuses to eat the food that they put in front of him, because it is possible that they might want to poison him.

[7] The secret report of the British Embassy in Baghdad is reprinted in facsimile in the document section of this book on page 405.

Chapter Six
Five Critical Days

Question: As you have explained, from shortly after midnight on 24 Mordad [15 August 1953], the situation changed. Your father, who was heading toward the Officers' Club to start his work as the new prime minister, had to return to his place of hiding. Where were you from that date till 19 August 1953, when Dr. Mossadegh's government was toppled, and what were you doing?

Zahedi: All together, there were 13 or 14 of us in Colonel Farzanegan's house. After the tanks and trucks passed the street and the noise subsided, my father sat in an armchair by the window, facing the street, and we sat round him in a semicircle. It was still dark in the room and the streetlights gave it a mild glow. My father started to speak. He said, "As Mossadegh has ignored His Majesty's decree and has engaged in rebellion, and as there is no Majles that can resist his actions, now all power is in his hands. Under these circumstances, we have no security, and if we are arrested they will show no mercy to us. So far, you gentlemen have sincerely and valiantly performed all your responsibilities as patriots, and I am truly grateful to you. However, from now on, you are no longer bound by your promises. I am not prepared to endanger your lives and the well-being of your families. Personally, I have engaged in a battle against this man, and I will not give up my struggle as long as I live. I have fought alongside the late king, and I have sworn an oath of allegiance to His Imperial Majesty, and I have his decree in my hand. However, sincerely and honorably I ask you to go back to your homes or to any safe houses before it gets light, while you still have the chance to do so."

After making those remarks, he turned to me and said, "Ardeshir! In my absence, you must take care of the Zahedi family. Furthermore, you are a young man, and your future should not be wasted. You have discharged your duty toward me and toward your country. Now you should return to Hesarak, to your home and your work. If they come to arrest you, tell them that all those issues concern your father and you know nothing about it."

I replied, "I am your son and my blood is not more precious than yours. Everything that I have done has been for you, for my king, and my country. I will continue to do so, and I will never leave you alone." He said, "I order you!" I replied, "For the first time, I will disobey your orders."

All of this conversation was carried out in an excited and emotional tone. When my father noticed that I was not going to give in, he got up and kissed me and said, "My son, this is what I thought would be best for your future, but you have to decide which path you want to follow."

In any case, with the exception of one or two of those who were present who faced special circumstances, all the rest of us decided to stay. My father then sat behind a small desk and said, "In that case, we must immediately draw up our plans and make all the necessary decisions, and we must leave this place before dawn."

One of the decisions that we made that night was to take many photographs—at that time there were no photocopying machines in Iran—of the imperial order appointing my father as prime minister, and to send them to all newspapers, magazines, and government departments. I agreed to perform that task.

Another decision was that General Hedayatollah Gilanshah should supervise and coordinate all the operations in Tehran. Colonel Abbas Farzanegan was asked to establish contacts with all our friends in law-enforcement departments. Messrs. Parviz Yarafshar, Reza Keynejad, Sadeq Naraqi, and Abol-Ghassem Zahedi were asked to act as contact points between my father and those who had been given responsibilities to perform.

It was also decided that my father, accompanied by Mostafa Moghaddam, should go to Madame Moshir-Fatemi's villa, which seemed like a secure place and was connected to two streets on two sides. As we stood up to go on our different missions, my father again made some remarks and stressed the need for vigilance and alertness.

Then he said, "His Majesty is staying in the north. It is not clear what approach the government would adopt toward him."

Finally, we all left. I remember that Colonel Khajenouri left on foot toward the city. Major General Batmanqelich, Colonel Navvabi, and I left for the city in a jeep. I was wearing a beret, and I drove the car. Batmanqelich was sitting next to me, and Navvabi was in the back seat.

On Pahlavi Street, from Amaniyyeh to Vanak crossroad, nothing was happening and all seemed quiet. However, as we got close to Vanak crossroad, we saw that soldiers and tanks had blocked the road and were controlling all traffic. We immediately turned back and went toward the Old Shemiran Road. At the same time, I hid the royal decree appointing my father as prime minister under the seat, so that if we were stopped and searched they would not see it. I was sure that if they got hold of the decree, they would get rid of it.

Anyway, from what is now Zafar Street and in those days was a minor, unpaved road over hills and uneven roads, we drove toward the Old Shemiran Road. All of a sudden, through the dust behind the car, I saw the lights of a car that was following us. Major General Batman-qelich looked back and said that the car was getting closer and we had to do something. Colonel Navvabi got hold of his weapon, so we could return the fire if the other car started shooting at us. I turned off the headlights and pressed my foot on the accelerator as much as I could. God only knows how we managed to drive that fast in the dark over bumpy roads without accident! The amusing point was that later we learned that the car that was behind us, which we thought was chasing us, was that of Colonel Farzanegan. He had recognized our car and wanted to catch up with us, but due to all the dust that we had created he had driven into a ditch and its shock absorbers had been damaged.

In any case, we managed to get into the Old Shemiran Road and turned right. A number of soldiers were stationed in front of the Wireless Building (the studios of Tehran Radio). They ordered us to stop, but I paid no attention and drove fast past them. Major General

Batmanqelich, who was wearing his military uniform because he had planned to go straight to the headquarters of the joint chiefs of staff and take charge of it, gave a military salute to the soldiers. They saluted back, and we passed them without any incident. We continued our journey until we reached Zarrabkhaneh crossroads, which is the place where three important streets north of Tehran cross. The crossroads separated Tehran from Shemiran. At that time they were quite apart from each other, but since then they have joined and become parts of the bigger Tehran. At the crossroads many tanks and military trucks had blocked the road. On both sides of the street a large number of soldiers were placed at regular intervals behind heavy machine guns, ready to shoot. There was no way to go forward or backward. We were forced to slow down the car.

Batmanqelich and I exchanged a glance, which revealed total hopelessness and resignation to our fate. From the back seat, Colonel Navvabi said quietly, "Now, we can no longer escape. We must wait to see what happens." I parked the car at the side of the street, and we waited. An officer, who was a lieutenant or a major, came forward and in a harsh tone said, "Introduce yourselves! Where are you coming from at this time of the night, and where are you going?"

I replied, "I am a driver for the military, and I am driving Major General Batmanqelich and his adjutant back to the city." The officer dutifully said, "Unfortunately, I cannot let you pass. I must ask for permission from the headquarters of the joint chiefs of staff." He then went to the other side of the street to get in touch with the headquarters of the joint chiefs of staff with the wireless. I had never experienced such a difficult time as I did in those few moments. A number of armed soldiers surrounded the car. There was no way of escape and no sign of rescue. Hopeless and confused, we waited for our fate, when something almost miraculous took place. The officer paused before reaching the other side of the street, returned toward us, and stood at attention by the car. He gave a military salute and said, "Please proceed!" Meanwhile, he signaled to the soldiers to give way.

Batmanqelich thanked him with a military salute and we drove away toward the city. Most clearly, if that officer had not changed his mind and if we had been arrested, history would have taken a different course.

It was five in the morning when we reached the city. I dropped Batmanqelich and Navvabi at their houses, and I went to Hormoz Shahrokhshahi's house in Shahreza Avenue, at the end of the Sharqi Street, near Anushiravan Dadgar Secondary School. In those days, Shahreza Avenue, in the north of Tehran, was the most important avenue in the capital. Dadgar Secondary School for girls was founded by the Zoroastrian community of Iran and was one of the best schools in Tehran.

I rang the bell, and Shahrokhshahi himself opened the door. I told him to open the garage door before anything else, so that the car was not left in the street. My main concern was safeguarding His Majesty's decree, and I was determined to keep it safe. Sadeq Naraqi, Abol-Ghassem Zahedi, Rahmat Atabaki, Taghi Bahrami, and a couple of others were already there. Despite being extremely tired due to lack of sleep and nervous exhaustion, I briefly told them about what was going on. Shahrokhshahi agreed to take a few photographs of the royal decree. Hoping that I could get some sleep, I went to his bedroom and threw myself on his bed without removing my clothes or shoes, but no matter how hard I tried, I could not sleep. I got up and went back to the sitting room.

Exactly at that time, the telephone rang. Everybody wondered who might be phoning at that time in the morning. Shahrokhshahi picked up the telephone and after a short conversation gave it to me. I immediately recognized my father's voice. After going to Madame Moshir-Fatemi's house, he had been worried about me and had made calls to a number of places until he finally managed to reach me there.

Hormoz Shahrokhshahi tried to take a few photographs of the royal decree with his own camera. However, when he took the negatives to the darkroom and developed them he noticed that the text of the decree was not very legible and that it needed more advanced equipment. It was decided that he should go to Sako photo shop in Naderi Street, whose owner was a trustworthy Armenian, and take a sufficient number of copies of the decree.

Now, all of us were waiting to hear the government's announcement on the radio. From six in the morning, Tehran Radio repeatedly broadcast that at seven o'clock there would be an important announcement. We knew that the announcement would be about the events of the previous night, but we still did not know how the government would deal with those events, and whether there would be any announcement about His Majesty's decree deposing Mossadegh as prime minister and replacing him with Zahedi.

Eventually, seven o'clock arrived and the government's statement was read. There was no reference to the royal decrees, and the issue was described as a conspiracy by the royal guards to stage a coup d'état, which had failed.[1]

In fact, that statement was the start of a coup d'état staged by Mossadegh or by the extremist people around him who carried it out in his name. They had full control of the armed forces and the police force. The studios of the national radio were under their control. Their action was contrary to the constitution, because the Shah's decree was very clear and he had deposed Mossadegh. Earlier on, they had also acted illegally by dissolving the Majles.

During the next few hours, hundreds of people were arrested in Tehran, including a number of serving or retired officers. The government and the Tudeh Party started an unusual propaganda campaign. Various slogans were broadcast on the radio. They brought down the statues of Mohammad Reza Shah and Reza Shah. In northern cities, the Tudeh Party occupied a number of municipal buildings and set up the so-called soviets. They locked and sealed royal palaces. All those activities were characteristic of a coup d'état, as the term is understood by experts. If there was a coup d'état, they were the ones who had staged it. One cannot hide historical realities, and eventually truth will be revealed.

In any case, we had to continue to implement our program and inform the people of the contents of the royal decrees as soon as possible. At 8:30 in the morning, Shahrokhshahi and Abol-Ghassem Zahedi left to take photographs of the royal decree appointing my father as prime minister. At about ten they telephoned to inform us that the photographs would be ready by about 11:30 in the morning.

I decided to go to my father and inform him of the latest developments, because we could not trust telephone communications. Yarafshar and I drove to the house of Madame Moluk os-Sadat Moshir-Fatemi in the Old Shemiran Road, a little before Qeitariyyeh. She was the daughter of Emad os-Saltaneh, who had been either the commander of Rasht or the governor general of Gilan, I can't remember which, when my father had been sent on missions to the north. Their friendship went back to those days. Everyone in the house had gone to Ramsar, and only Madame Moluk os-Sadat had been left behind. She kept awake the whole night and watched all the roads around the house to inform my father of any possible danger, so that he could leave in case anybody wished to inspect the house.

We had a long discussion and exchanged views. My father said that when the photographs of the royal decree were ready he would take part in a press conference and would personally put the royal decree at the disposal of domestic and foreign reporters. We talked quite a lot about that proposal and came to the conclusion that even if it were possible to hold a press conference under those circumstances, it would not be free of danger. We also agreed that it would not be wise for him to be seen anywhere. Therefore, it was decided that I had to give an interview to reporters from foreign news agencies on behalf of my father and inform them of what was going on.

My father dictated a short text, which Yarafshar wrote down and gave to me. Yarafshar and I returned to the city. On the way, we discussed how we could find the reporters and where we could hold the interview. I knew my old classmate in 15th Bahman School, Parviz Ra'in, who was a reporter for the Associated Press, and I trusted him. Foreign reporters used to get together in the Park Hotel, where they also worked. I decided to phone the Park Hotel from a safe place and talk to Ra'in. We went to the clinic of Dr. Sa'id Hekmat, in one of the streets near Tehran University, and phoned from there. Fortunately, Ra'in was there, and we had a short conversation in English. I told him that I wanted to put some very important information about the previous night's events at the disposal of the reporters. He said that he would inform some of his colleagues and that at half past twelve in the afternoon they would wait for us at Yusofabad Square, near the Park Hotel. I gave him the license number and other details of Yarafshar's car. I told him that the car would collect them from there and would bring them to the place for the interview.

We left Hekmat's clinic a few minutes before noon and went to Shahrokhshahi's house. In order to get back in time, he had not waited for the photographs to dry. He had brought the wet photographs and had spread them on the floor to dry. Yarafshar left to meet with the reporters. Our arrangement was that I would go ahead of them to the hills near Valanjak, overlooking Za'faraniyyeh near Sa'dabad Palace, and that Yarafshar would bring the reporters there. We had chosen that spot because it overlooked the road and we could watch out for any suspicious moves, so we could save ourselves.

I sat behind the wheel of Hormoz Shahrokhshahi's red Ford motor-car and drove toward our rendezvous. It was decided that Shahrokh-shahi would follow a short distance behind me in another wood-framed Ford, to be followed by Abol-Ghassem Zahedi and Taghi Sohrabi in Sohrabi's car, so that if anything happened they could drive away and inform my father. I had two loaded revolvers next to me, and Shahrokhshahi and Zahedi were also armed, so they could defend themselves if necessary.

Like most people, we were wearing only white shirts and trousers. In Shahreza Avenue we came across a crowd, which was moving from Pahlavi Square toward Ferdowsi Square. I stopped the car by the side of the road and put on my sunglasses. I got out of the car and walked with the crowd for a while. As I became certain that nobody would recognize me the way I looked, I returned to the car and drove toward our destination, but with care. Before reaching it, I changed my car twice.

Finally, we arrived where the interview was to be held. It was on top of a hill, which was connected with two narrow dirt tracks to Valanjak Road. From the north the tracks continued to higher hills. Sohrabi and Shahrokhshahi stayed near their cars at the side of the two dirt tracks, and I went to the top of the hill. A short time later, Yarafshar arrived. In addition to Parviz Ra'in, Yusef Mazandi, a United Press reporter, and another reporter from Reuters were accompanying him.

I translated the text of my father's message for them, and they typed their reports seated on the ground on top of the hill. The gist of the message was as follows: "According to the Iranian Constitution, the monarch has the right to appoint or dismiss the prime minister and other ministers. At the moment, as Mr. Mossadegh has dissolved both the Majles and the senate on the basis of a referendum, His Imperial Majesty, on the basis of his constitutional rights, has issued a decree dismissing Mossadegh. Therefore, from the morning of 24 Mordad, I have been the legal prime minister of the country, and the present course of action adopted by the government could be described as a rebellion violating the constitution and the constitutional regime."

I then distributed the photographs of the royal decree appointing my father as prime minister. The reporters were typing as fast as they could. When I finished my remarks, they kept asking me about where General Zahedi was, what news I had about His Imperial Majesty, how the decree was announced to my father, and what we planned to do next. I told them that what I had given them was a message from my father and that I was not in a position to answer all their questions.

They turned to Yarafshar, pointing out that they did not know where they were, and asked him to take them back immediately to the city so they could transmit their reports. Then they ran down the hill, got into Yarafshar's car, and left for the city. The reports were immediately transmitted, and on the same evening the report was published on the front page of *Ettela'at* newspaper in big letters, quoting the Associated Press. On the same afternoon, on Sunday 25 Mordad [16 August

1953], a meeting was held in the house of Seyf os-Saltaneh Afshar, in which my father took part. I have provided the details of that meeting in my article titled "Five Critical Days."[2]

The meeting in the house of Seyf os-Saltaneh (the father of Amir Khosrow Afshar, who later became Iranian ambassador in London and foreign minister) lasted for more than six hours. My father wrote two letters there. One was for Colonel Teymur Bakhtiar and another was for Colonel Amir Gholi Zargham, and it was decided that we should take those letters to those two officers in Kermanshah and Isfahan, together with the copies of the royal decree. Farzanegan was chosen to go to Kermanshah and meet with Bakhtiar, and he left the same night. I volunteered to go to Isfahan, but my father was opposed to that decision.

My father wanted to spend that night in Hesarak, because he believed that "a house that has been robbed is safe for forty days" or, as they say, "lightning doesn't hit twice." The officials had already gone to that house and had searched everywhere, and they would not expect Major General Zahedi to return and spend the night there right after they had searched it. As I was driving him to Hesarak I tried very hard to make him agree to my departure for Isfahan, but I was not able to change his mind. Nevertheless, I was determined to go.

Question: Kermit (Kim) Roosevelt writes in *Counter Coup* that he had taken Major General Zahedi to the house of Zimmerman, a member of his operational team, and had hidden him in the cellar in that house.

Zahedi: It is untrue. The books that foreigners have written about the events in Iran, whether about those that led to the events of 19 August 1953, or about those leading to February 11, 1979, are full of such baseless allegations. My father met Kim Roosevelt for the first time after 28 Mordad. At the beginning of September, a few days after the return of His Majesty to Iran, when we were playing volleyball with His Majesty in Sa'dabad Palace after lunch, Hormoz Pirnia, the head of protocol at the court, came and bowed and showed His

Majesty something. A few minutes later, His Majesty stopped the game and told me to get in touch with my father, the prime minister, and tell him to come to the court early in the evening to have tea.

My father was in a meeting with some leading politicians in the Ministry of Foreign Affairs. I passed the message to my father, and together we went to Sa'dabad Palace. His Majesty introduced Kim Roosevelt to my father in his office for the first time. We sat down together and had tea.

My American acquaintances were limited to a member of the U.S. Embassy staff, called Rocky Stone, Alex Gagarin, and Eric Pollard. I knew Eric Pollard from the time that I was working at Point Four. He was the naval attaché in the U.S. Embassy in Tehran. He had a French wife, and he was a good pilot. As we did not have an aircraft at Point Four, we made use of his plane for our visits to different parts of the country. I remember that when we had gone to Bandar Abbas in connection with a water project there, Pollard had slept under the wing of his plane. I got to know Alex Gagarin through Colonel Verba, who was a White Russian who served in the Iranian armed forces and had a rank equivalent to a colonel. He was the instructor of my father and Reza Shah in the military academy.

Gagarin was related to Colonel Verba and came from an aristocratic Russian family. Later on, we learned that when the separatist revolts were taking place in Azerbaijan he had been a military attaché. He spoke fluent Persian in addition to Russian. After returning from America, I was introduced to Alex Gagarin by Colonel Verba at a party given by Ms. Rosie Malek, the daughter of the late Malek. He was also a friend of Masoud Foroughi, a diplomat who was the son of Mohammad Ali Foroughi (Zoka ol-Molk). The latter was a prime minister during the war and is regarded by many Iranians as the man who saved Iran and the monarchy in 1941. Consequently, due to his friendship with Masoud Foroughi, Gagarin and I also became friends.

Sometimes we used to go riding together. One day when he was boasting of his skill as a rider I told him that I would prove to him that I was a better rider than he was. At that time, there was a dirt track on the two sides of Pahlavi Street, and it was a suitable place for riding. In the evenings, Major Sobhani and Major Khazai (Major General Khazai's son) would bring some horses from the military college, and we would go there and ride together. We told them to bring us some horses, and they brought some very agile and strong ones. I started to gallop and Gagarin tried to catch up with me. His horse was stronger and taller than mine. It ran with such speed that Gagarin could not control it. His glasses and hat fell off and the horse kept running. However, he was a skillful rider and eventually managed to tame the horse.

In any case, after 9 Esfand (28 February), when I was in hiding, I contacted Gagarin and Pollard. I asked them what was going on. I told them, "On the one hand, you see the situation in the country and you know what plans the communists have devised for the country. On the other hand, you support Mossadegh. On the day when the Majles is meeting to give a vote of no confidence to Mossadegh, Ambassador Henderson spends two or three hours with him and weakens the morale of his opponents." They answered, "No, this is not the case. We are obliged to have contacts with your governments and talk to them, but we have no special aim in doing so." Eventually, we agreed that I would meet with one of the political officers from the American Embassy. We agreed to meet in Darband Street, near Zahir al-Dowleh cemetery. I put on a mustache and a hat and went to the house to which I had been directed. I knocked on the door many times, but there was no answer. Later on, I learned that the person who was due to meet me had been too frightened or had been given orders not to meet me. As there was the danger that I might be arrested I returned to my hiding place, namely, Mirashrafi's house. A few days later I phoned Pollard and told him that if they did not wish to meet with us they had to tell us openly. Why did they act in a way that might result in our arrest? This was contrary to honor and honesty.

My words touched a raw nerve and hurt his military honor. Pollard asked me to phone him again in two days' time. When I phoned he said that this time somebody would definitely meet with me. We made

arrangements for another meeting at Malek Square, in the Old
Shemiran Road, which was also close to Mirashrafi's house. On the
appointed day, I went in Shahrokhshahi's car and stood at Malek
Square. I waited for a while, but no one came. The police guarding the
road recognized me, came close, and greeted me. Then he asked me to
leave so that I did not block the road. For a while, I walked up and
down some streets, but there was no sign of the car that they had
described to me. Once again, I phoned Pollard and told him that such
actions were clear indications that they were playing games with us
and acting against us. He said that the man who was supposed to meet
me was called Joe Goodwin and that he would get in touch with me.
We made another arrangement for a meeting, but later on Goodwin
phoned, saying that he would not be able to meet me and apologizing
for it.[3]

**Question: Let us return to the main developments. Finally, you
decided to go to Isfahan.**

Zahedi: Yes, when I was leaving Seyf os-Saltaneh's house, I told
General Gilanshah to stay there until I could take my father home,
and then return. I told him that I wished to discuss something with
him. As I was driving my father home I tried very hard to persuade
him to let me go to Isfahan, but he was firm in his view and did not
want me to leave Tehran at that time.

When I returned to Seyf os-Saltaneh's house, I took General Gilanshah to one side and told him that I had decided to go to Isfahan. I
also wrote a letter addressed to my father, apologizing for my action. I
left Tehran at 1:30 in the morning and traveled toward Isfahan. I had
a permit to pass checkpoints that had expired a few days earlier, but I
changed the date on it. At 3:30 in the morning I arrived in Qom and
went straight to the shrine of Her Holiness Ma'sumeh on a short
pilgrimage. It was still dark when I left Qom for Isfahan. I drove as fast
as I could and arrived outside Isfahan at eight in the morning. Police
were checking all the cars. An officer came forward and asked me if I
was traveling from Tehran, to which I said yes. He carefully checked

the front and the boot of the car and took a notebook out of his pocket and wrote down the car's registration number. He asked my name. I replied Jamshid. He asked for my surname and I said Jamshidian. He asked for the number of my identity card and I said 787. He asked for the purpose of my visit to Isfahan, and I said to visit a sick friend.

At this time, an argument broke out between one of the officers and the driver of a small truck that was transporting vegetables. The policeman turned to them and signaled me to go. It was not yet 8:30 when I arrived in town. The streets were crowded, and the situation seemed unusual. The members of the Tudeh Party had written anti-Shah slogans all over the walls, buildings, and pavements and were advocating the establishment of a democratic republic. At first, I wanted to go straight to the house of Colonel Zargham, but I noticed that some people were watching the traffic and all the movements around his house. This is why I turned my car and drove toward the house of Lotfollah Khan Zahedi, my father's cousin. He had died a few years earlier, but members of his family still lived in that large, old house.

From Lotfollah Khan's house I sent a message to Colonel Zargham through Major Zahedi, who was one of our relatives, and told him that I wished to see him. He replied that he could see me between 11:30 and 12:00 at the bottom of Soffeh Mountain, overlooking the Armenian Cemetery. Colonel Zargham was the deputy commander of the Ninth Army Division in Isfahan, which was under the command of General Mahmud Davallu. I knew him from the time when he had been appointed head of the royal guards, due to his family connections to Queen Soraya. However, under those circumstances, I could not trust anyone. The government had promised a reward for my arrest, and there was no guarantee that Colonel Zargham might not decide to arrest me.

Lotfollah Khan had an old and faithful servant from Semirom, called Mehdigholi. He was a very smart and clever person and a very good shot. I took him with me, and he sat behind a rock from where he could see us. I told him that if he saw me take my handkerchief out of my pocket and drop it on the ground, he should shoot whoever was with me, and if I was arrested he should inform Mr. Yarafshar in Tehran.

About midday Colonel Zargham arrived in a military jeep, dressed in military uniform. When I became certain that he was alone, I went forward, and he warmly shook my hand, embraced me, and asked about what was going on in Tehran. I informed him of what had happened and gave him the photograph of the royal decree. I told him that we were counting on his full support but that it was now up to him to decide what he wanted to do. I told him that if he wished, he could arrest me there and then. He became very annoyed at my remarks and threw his hat to the ground and said, "What are you talking about? I am a devoted servant of His Majesty. I regard General Zahedi as my own father, and I regard you as my brother. I am ready for any service that I can render. If necessary, I will arrest the governor general, the commander of the army division, or any other government official in the province. If necessary, I will even march at the head of the army division toward Tehran."

I told him that I would pass his message to my father and that he should wait for my father's response. I also told him that if there was any need for him to move at the head of the army toward Tehran he would receive a telegram in the name of Jamshidi, which would say, "Jamshidi needs the medicine, please send it." Also if my father decided to go to Isfahan to make it the headquarters for his operations, I would send him a telegram, with the following message: "Medicine for the illness has been sent for you to receive."

Early in the evening I left Isfahan for Tehran, and I arrived about 3:30 or 4:00 in the morning on Saturday. I went to my cousin's house. My cousin's husband, Sadeq Naraqi, lived in a house in Jamaran near our own house. In order not to wake anyone in the house, I spent the night in the car. When I woke up in the morning and asked about my father, Naraqi said that he had spent the night in Seif Afshar's house, and that he would still be there. We left Naraqi's house in a jeep and went to Seif Afshar's house in Bahar Street. The streets were so crowded and the situation was so tense that there was no proper control about what was going on. When my father saw me, he kissed my face but reprimanded me for having gone to Isfahan. He said, "Did I not tell you that I would choose the person who had to be sent to Isfahan?" I kissed his hand and said that I had apologized in writing. I explained the reason why I had done what I had and said that I had returned safe and sound and with success.

I explained the details of my trip to Isfahan and my discussions with Colonel Zargham. In the afternoon, Colonel Farzanegan, who had gone to Kermanshah, returned and reported that Colonel Bakhtiar was fully prepared to cooperate with us. We continued our discussions over lunch in Seif Afshar's house. My father said that we did not have much time left and that we had to decide quickly what we wanted to do. The main focus of the discussions was on "freeing Iran," gathering military forces, and calling on the people to engage in a national uprising and not cooperate with the government. I insisted that my father had to be stationed in Isfahan and should use it as his base of operations. Farzanegan believed that Kermanshah was more suitable. Each of us explained our reasons, and each of us insisted on our stances.

My father took Farzanegan's side, saying that Isfahan was situated in the middle of the country and the government could easily surround it and cut off its links with the rest of the country. However, Kermanshah had an ideal position for military operations, as well as a suitable geographical position, in view of its closeness to the borders and the possibility of having access to food, fuel, and other requirements.

It was decided that we should leave at dawn on Wednesday, 28 Mordad [19 August 1953], travel toward Kermanshah, and start our operations from there, but as we were busy talking the situation suddenly changed in an unbelievable manner. Certain events took place that no one had predicted and no one could have expected. From the evening of Tuesday, a number of people who had been shaken as the result of the events of those three days and who had been worried about the fate of the country, either on their own initiative or on the orders of religious sources of emulation, poured into the streets and clashed with the supporters of the Tudeh Party. We were informed that the members of the government had been completely intimidated and had lost their nerve. There had been a split among the members of the armed forces. Some of the law-enforcement forces had joined the demonstrators, and there had been clashes and shooting in the central streets of the capital.

Those developments forced us to change our plans. I spent that night in the house of Dr. Ghassem Pirnia in Niavaran and returned to the city at six in the morning. I went to see my father in Seif Afshar's house. He was having breakfast, and I joined him in that. It became clear that he had remained awake the entire night. He had received information that Mossadegh had held a meeting with his ministers and aides and that all of them had been alarmed by the critical situation in the city.[4]

At this moment, Yarafshar arrived and brought some reports about the possibility of some momentous action during the day. About lunchtime it had become certain that the city had slipped out of the government's hands and was under the control of our supporters. If the situation continued till the night and people were to return to their homes, it was not clear what would happen the next day.

Earlier on, I had driven to the city to see what was happening. I noticed that many tanks had been positioned on Pahlavi crossroads, Shah crossroads, and the streets leading to the palaces and Kakh Street in order to guard Mossadegh os-Saltaneh's house, and armed soldiers were shooting from the top of the buildings. Clashes were taking place between the forces faithful to Mossadegh and the demonstrators. Some of the military and law-enforcement forces had changed sides and joined the demonstrators, and the clashes were becoming more intense as time went by. The tanks from both sides had gradually joined the fight.

I returned and reported the situation to my father. My father consulted with his advisers, and it became clear that the time had finally arrived to gain control of the situation. Colonel Khal'atbari, who was the deputy head of the police and who had joined our group, was asked to send a tank to my father's residence. This was the tank that my father mounted; his photograph taken atop that tank became famous. As it can be seen in that photograph, a large number of military and civilian people had mounted the tank. As my father appeared in the streets on the tank, groups of people rushed toward him, mounted the tank, and surrounded my father as they chanted slogans in his support.

Nobody knew those people, and the situation was out of control. If at that time someone had decided to kill my father he could have done so, even with a knife. Fortunately, there was no nasty incident. When we passed Eshratabad we came across a blue, open-top Buick belonging to Mr. Shushtari. Colonel Khal'atbari and I sat in the front seat next to the driver. Our aim was to get to Pahlavi Wireless, the headquarters of Tehran Radio, so that my father could send a message to the nation. However, the vast crowds and heavy traffic, including private cars, military vehicles, and buses that were transporting the demonstrators, had blocked our path. I borrowed Colonel Khal'atbari's revolver, got out of the car, and shouted, "Please move aside! Major General Zahedi, the country's legal prime minister, wishes to go to the radio station to make a statement." Finally, I managed to open a path for the car until we got to Pahlavi Wireless.

The big iron gates in the main street were locked, and a number of soldiers were standing guard behind them. I moved forward with the revolver in my hand and said, "Open the gates! Major General Zahedi, the Shah's representative and the country's legal prime minister, wishes to enter." The soldiers were bewildered, not knowing what to do, but they did not seem willing to open the gates. My father got out of the tank and, surrounded by Colonel Khal'atbari and a number of others, moved forward. Suddenly, a couple of the officers guarding the station from inside shouted, "Long live the Shah! Long live Major General Zahedi!" They ordered the soldiers to open the gates. When we entered the compound, the courtyard and the buildings were full of people, and we noticed that we were surrounded by a crowd. We had not paid any attention to this issue and were solely preoccupied with protecting my father. Here too we had some difficulty moving forward due to the pressure of crowds.

It was the first time that I had seen the radio station and its equipment. There was a staircase by a glass partition to the second floor. The crowds were carrying my father on their shoulders. If somebody had dropped him from the second floor he would have died on the spot, but that moment also passed safely. We took control of the radio station. Hossein Zahedi, a member of the Post and Telegraph Ministry, managed to repair the radio transmitter that members of the Tudeh Party and supporters of the government had sabotaged. My father then made a statement on Tehran Radio as the new prime minister.

At that moment, people throughout Iran learned that Mossadegh's government had collapsed and Zahedi had seized power. In his radio message, my father specially urged the people in the provinces, as well as government officials, to maintain peace and stability. From there we moved toward the national police department near Sepah Square. We left the radio station in Ehtesham al-Dowleh Gharagozlou's car and reached Shahreza Avenue and Ferdowsi Square. The size of the crowd was such that we had to move very slowly from Ferdowsi Square to Sabt Street. We managed to drive on the other part of Sabt Street toward the national park and the northern street of the Ministry of Foreign Affairs with great difficulty, but from there it was impossible to move any further. The crowd was so dense that you could not drop a pin. My father started to walk and we followed him. Seeing my father among them, the crowd suddenly went quiet. Everybody was looking at him in a daze.

I was so excited as well as frightened that I was shaking. Being on foot and without any guards among such a large crowd of strangers created a difficult sensation. If they had decided to attack us, they could have torn us to pieces before anyone could rescue us. After walking a few steps I grabbed my father's left arm and told him to wait, because the situation was very dangerous and we could be killed. I had put my hand exactly on the scar that was the result of a bullet that he had received in one of the wars. In a manner that I had never experienced before, my father pulled his arm out of my hand and shouted, "Be quiet! Come with me." I had no option but to keep quiet. In that frightful situation my father was taking firm steps in a mood of an indescribable courage and determination. He moved toward the central police station, and we followed him. People opened a path and let him through. Nobody made the slightest noise. Soldiers and policemen were stationed all over the steps and on the stone-paved area in front of the police department and were aiming their light machine guns at us. A minor demonstration by the people or an order by one of their officers would have been sufficient for the soldiers to open fire and to slaughter all of us. God knows how those few moments passed!

Suddenly, my father stood halfway up the steps and shouted, "My dear fellow soldiers! You are here but our Shah is not among us!" I can't describe the effect that those few words had on the police officers and the forces of the military government. All of a sudden they laid down their arms, took off their hats, and shouted, "Long live the Shah! Long live Zahedi!" Police officers and soldiers stationed there lifted my father on their shoulders. They carried him inside, shouting, "Long live the Shah! Long live Zahedi!" and took him to the main office of the Police Department. My father sat behind the desk of the head of the National Police. Immediately, he wrote a few sentences on the papers with the letter headings of the police department and ordered the freeing of all political prisoners. From there, he sent a cable to His Majesty in Rome and invited him to return to the country.[5]

Due to lack of sleep and extreme fatigue my father was feeling very weak. The police doctor gave him an injection. Once again, I was worried they might want to kill him by giving him a wrong injection. It was a very sensitive time, and anything was possible.

Clashes were continuing in Kakh Street around Mossadegh os-Saltaneh's house. Yarafshar and I were given the task of going to the headquarters of the armed forces and bringing it under our control. The occupation of the headquarters of the armed forces was carried out very fast and without any clashes. I telephoned my father from the desk of the commander of the headquarters of the armed forces. A short time later, Major General Batmanqelich, who had been freed from prison, arrived and was stationed there as the chairman of the joint chiefs of staff.

Meanwhile, my father got in touch with Dr. Matindaftari, Dr. Mossadegh's nephew and son-in-law, and asked him to speak to Mossadegh, calling on him to surrender in order to prevent further bloodshed. My father sent a message to Mossadegh, saying that resistance was futile, and the longer it lasted the more people would be killed. At the same time, he promised to protect the lives of Mossadegh and his colleagues.

Unfortunately, this mediation did not produce the desired result. Brigadier General Fuladvand, who had gone to Mossadegh's house to settle the issue by peaceful means, did not receive a positive response. Eventually, at about seven in the evening Dr. Mossadegh's house fell to the demonstrators. As has been reported and written by many historians, Mossadegh fled to his neighbor's house and sent a message through Sharif-Emami that he was prepared to surrender to the new government.[6]

During the late hours in the day my father left the police department, went to the Officers' Club, and used it as the prime minister's office.

Question: For the past half-century, two different and even conflicting views have been expressed about the events of 28th of Mordad [19 August]. Some people have referred to it as a national uprising, while others have called it a British–American coup d'état in order to topple a nationalist government. What do you say in response to your opponents, especially in view of the books written by "Monty" Woodhouse and Kim Roosevelt?[7]

Zahedi: I am glad that once again you are asking this question. My answer may be useful for young people and those who had not been born at that time to be able to make a better judgment about the history of their country. To begin with, it may be useful to answer your question by asking you a question in return. Is it not an insult to the Iranian nation to claim that Kim Roosevelt came to Iran with a sack of money and managed to topple a popular government in a few days at the hands of a bunch of bought thugs?

At that time, Dr. Mossadegh was in full control of the country. He had dissolved the Majles, the senate, and the supreme court, and he made laws by decree. He had put the armed forces and the law-enforcement forces under the control of some of his trusted friends. By making use of martial law, he imprisoned all who opposed him and kept them in jail for as long as he liked. In 1952 and 1953, about 75 leading politicians were jailed. Many newspapers were banned, one after another, by the martial law authorities. Leading nationalist figures were either in jail or in exile, or they were forced to remain silent for fear of being dragged through dirt and subjected to character assassination. Even the country's king had kept away from everybody and had left Tehran in order to give the prime minister a free hand to act as he saw fit.

Now, is it possible for a prime minister who was allegedly adored by the masses, for whom they were allegedly prepared to sacrifice their lives, to be toppled by a few Americans so easily and in a few hours? Nobody asks where the people were at that time, and why nobody supported him; why nobody came out, as on 30 Tir of the previous year (21 July 1952), to support the allegedly beloved nationalist prime minister of the country. Everybody says that Major General Zahedi staged a military coup, but my father was a retired officer. The armed forces were under the command of Riahi, who was fully trusted by Mossadegh. On 28 Mordad, Mossadegh ordered the armed forces to shoot to kill at the demonstrators. On that day, about 400 of Mossadegh's opponents were killed or wounded. What kind of a military coup was this when the armed forces were firing on the crowds?

As far as I know, a military coup means changing a regime violently with the use of the armed forces. In Mordad 1332, in the absence of the parliament, the Shah made use of his constitutional right and dismissed the prime minister. It was the prime minister who violated the constitution and acted illegally and issued orders like a dictator. Instead of acting on the basis of the law, the prime minister decided to act as a rebel and to ignore the constitution. Now, the question is who was carrying out a coup—the Shah, who wanted to implement the constitution, or the deposed prime minister, who regarded himself as above the law?

The truth is that Mossadegh had reached the end of the road. He could not run the country, nor was he prepared to solve the oil problem in the best way possible for Iran in those days, an opportunity that was lost later on. People were tired of daily-increasing chaos and high prices. The economy was in a state of collapse. Some people were rising up in different parts of the country. Each day, a number of people were injured as the result of clashes in the streets of Tehran. Nearly all of Mossadegh's benefactors, who had helped him and had fought for him over many years and had made great self-sacrifices for him, were accused of treason and had left him. If I mentioned the names of all those political, military, and religious figures who had felt concerned about the situation of the country and who were accused of treason, it would take up a few pages of the book. Was everyone who was opposed to Mossadegh's method of running the government a traitor?

The most important issue was the danger of communism. Each day the Tudeh Party was becoming stronger, and it had infiltrated the armed forces and the law-enforcement forces. Later on, we discovered how close the Tudeh Party had gotten to staging a coup and seizing power. Even some of the officers close to my father had joined the Tudeh Party. Had the events of 28th of Mordad not taken place, the Tudeh Party would have easily deposed Mossadegh a short time later, in the same way that the communists had done to the Czech President Edward Benes a few years earlier. Had that happened in Iran, America and Britain would not have kept still. As they had always threatened, they would have occupied the oil-rich areas in the south and the west of the country for themselves, and Iran would have experienced the same fate as Vietnam and Korea and been partitioned.

What I am saying is not an afterthought that we have fabricated today. These were some of the issues that were raised and discussed in every gathering in those days. Everybody was worried about prospects in Iran. On 25 and 26 Mordad our people clearly saw what future awaited them. This is why they decided to make sure that Iran's independence and territorial integrity would not be jeopardized by the Tudeh Party and Dr. Fatemi.

Our young people cannot imagine the state of our people in those days, when His Majesty had left the country and the members of the Tudeh Party were roaming the streets in large numbers and were pulling down the Shah's statues. Mossadegh's foreign minister was constantly engaged in making speeches and giving interviews and was using the most insulting terms regarding the Shah of Iran, who had left the country. The newspapers that were sympathetic to the Tudeh Party and the government were also engaged in using foul terms and making all sorts of accusations. The country's fabric was disintegrating.

The reason why the people rose up as one on 28 Mordad was because they had become truly frightened of the situation. On 28 Mordad, I saw with my own eyes the vast crowds of people in the streets of Tehran who were shouting "Long live the Shah!" There was not a single person who shouted "Long live Mossadegh!" Fortunately, there are some people still alive who witnessed those days and people's demonstrations in Tehran and the provinces.

If the situation was as simple as Kim Roosevelt has claimed in his baseless and distorted book, why is it that the Americans have not been able to do anything for the past forty years against Cuba, which is only a few miles away from them? Why were they not able to change the situation in Libya? Even when it is dealing with Iraq and Afghanistan, according to its own admission, the United States has to spend billions of dollars to depose a dictator, yet it managed to topple a legal and popular government in a few hours by spending $60,000! Has not the

U.S. Congress approved $90 million to fight against the Islamic Republic? What has been achieved?

Some people accept Roosevelt's baseless claims, but nobody pays any attention to some other admissions in his book, as when he says that he had only a few accomplices but counted on the support of the armed forces and the people for the Shah. Had it not been for the support of the armed forces and the people for the Shah, that plan would not have come to fruition. When Kim Roosevelt was asked to accept responsibility for similar operations to topple the government in Guatemala he refused to accept it, because he knew that the same circumstances did not exist there.

I believe that by examining the documents in the U.S. State Department one can see most clearly how surprised the Americans were by the success of the events of 28th of Mordad. In some CIA documents that were written shortly after the events of 28th of Mordad, we read that it was an unbelievable incident. Even after the Americans had received the reports about the people's victory, they still could not believe it and thought it was just a joke. The Russians were equally surprised. It is regrettable that some people inside and outside Iran have become so attached to a few lies that no matter how many new facts are revealed, they still repeat those lies. In that case, what is the use of historical documents?[8]

I am confident that as time goes by, people will make a better judgment and all the baseless propaganda will lose its effect. No matter what some people may say, 28th of Mordad was a day that saved Iran. Our country will ultimately become a developed and prosperous country. However, if on that day a number of brave men had not risen up and confronted the danger, the country would have fallen to the communists. Had they not been able to prevent the country's partition, there would be nothing left for us to build and develop later on.

Question: Your explanations are quite clear. Nevertheless, many people still regard Kim Roosevelt's book as an authoritative source. What do you think about the claims?

Zahedi: I have referred to this issue before, but let me repeat it in greater detail. My father had never met that man before everything was over. The best proof of that is what I have already mentioned. Basically, my father did not know German that he could talk to Roosevelt and have a political discussion with him in German. The research done by recent historians has clearly identified the places where my father was hiding during those critical days. These views are not just mine, which could be interpreted as being biased. Others have confirmed what I have said.

Kim Roosevelt had heard that the British had detained and had exiled my father during the Second World War on suspicion of being friendly toward the Germans. We know that my father had no connection with the Germans. He was a patriot and was opposed to British imperialism. According to available documents, the British regarded my father as the most dangerous enemy of British policies in Iran, and historians have recently confirmed this point. However, Kim Roosevelt was not interested in those details. He imagined that as the British had accused my father of pro-German sympathy, he must have known German. Therefore, he invented the fictitious story of having had discussions with him in German. This is how false reports creep into history and distort it. However, in some cases these lies are exposed after a number of years, and history will make a correct judgment.

Earlier, I mentioned that during those critical days, I often tried to get in touch with some members of the U.S. Embassy whom I knew in the past in order to persuade them not to support Mossadegh. I wished to tell them that ultimately he would bring the communists to power in Iran (exactly as it had happened a short time earlier in Czechoslovakia in the case of Edward Benes). They did not agree to meet me, or made some appointments for a meeting but did not come. Therefore, all these stories are mere fiction.

Question: In your view, why did the Americans, or at least some of them, take credit for those actions or allege that the British had been involved? Why did they give credence to those rumors?

Zahedi: In the international political climate in those days—namely the Cold War period, when the East and the West were confronting each other and the West was trying to prevent the expansion of the Soviet bloc—preventing Iran from falling under Soviet domination was a major achievement. In fact, it resembled a miracle. The Iranians themselves were responsible for that great achievement, or miracle. The Iranian people had reached the end of their tether and were desperate for political stability, economic development, calm, and security. The clergy, led by the Grand Ayatollah Borujerdi, were rightly worried about the domination of the communists over Iran. Finally, my father, who was regarded as the leader of the opposition and the symbol of resistance, succeeded in bringing about those victories with the help of the above-mentioned groups.

However, when everything had been done and victory had been achieved, many people tried to take credit for it. It was regarded as a great bonus for the West and its policies to attribute that great success to itself, or at least to keep quiet about such allegations. As the famous saying goes, "Defeat is lonely but victory has many friends." 28th of Mordad is a victory achieved by the Iranian people.

Question: How do you interpret the stances adopted by Britain, the Soviet Union, and the global communist movement toward those events?

Zahedi: The British Embassy in Tehran and the British government did not have a favorable view of my father. They knew that General Zahedi would not be an agent for implementing the policies of foreigners. Please read the available reports and documents. After my father's success on 28 Mordad, the incitements by the British Embassy in Tehran against his government started immediately. Various researchers and historians with different affiliations have stressed this point during the past few years.

However, the case of the Soviets is even clearer. The events of 28th of Mordad were a historical defeat for the communists and for Moscow's policies. Even Soviet Ambassador Anatoly Lavrentiev, who had been given the task by the Politburo of picking the ripe fruit of Iran for Moscow, tried to commit suicide, but fortunately they managed to save him. He was so ashamed of the defeat that he had suffered—or he was also afraid of the punishment that awaited him—that he tried to take his own life. If this had happened under Stalin, he would probably have been executed. Therefore, it was in the interest of the Soviet Union and the international communist movement to describe those events as a coup d'état and an American conspiracy and to try to justify their defeat in that way.

However, the communists in Iran, due to their radical and extremist behavior during the few chaotic days that preceded the people's uprising, the crimes that they had committed earlier on, and their lack of support for Mossadegh, were also partly responsible for that defeat (which was a great victory for the Iranian nation). If you read the memoirs of the leaders of the Tudeh Party, from Anvar Khame'i to Fereidoun Keshavarz to Iraj Eskandari, any remaining doubt about how strongly they felt about the defeat that they suffered will be eliminated.

Question: You have made a number of references to the role played by the members of the clergy, especially Grand Ayatollah Borujerdi. A great deal has already been written about the role played by Ayatollah Kashani and Ayatollah Mir Seyyed Mohammad Behbahani, but there has not been a great deal written about Grand Ayatollah Borujerdi. Can you provide us with more details about his role so we can achieve a better understanding of historical facts?

Zahedi: Today's generation is not aware of the enormous influence and standing of that great man. Grand Ayatollah Borujerdi was not only the most eminent person in the Shi'a clerical hierarchy. Without wishing to underestimate the role of a few other leading clerics, most scholars and commentators are unanimous that he was the most eminent or the only source of emulation for the Shi'is and was highly respected by all.

However, a point that has not been stressed enough is that Grand Ayatollah Borujerdi was in constant touch with my father, and there was a feeling of mutual respect and affection between them. Not only was Grand Ayatollah Borujerdi an eminent cleric and a renowned and universally respected jurist, but he was also a true Iranian patriot who always thought of Iran's independence and territorial integrity. He was always concerned about the possible collapse of the government and the deterioration of law and order in Iran, and he was quite justified in his concern. A few decades later, other grand ayatollahs and sources of emulation, such as Ayatollah Shariatmadari and especially Grand Ayatollah Khoi, shared the same concern, and I will talk about them in greater detail later on.

The late Grand Ayatollah Borujerdi supported the national movement for saving Iran. On 28 Mordad, a few hours before midday, the leading figures in the bazaar phoned him and explained the situation in Tehran. They informed him that thousands of people had poured into the streets in order to put an end to chaos and to prevent the collapse of the country. They asked his view about what they should do. Borujerdi's answer was quite clear and explicit. He allowed them to close the bazaar and allowed the merchants in the bazaar to join other people in the city. As the result of his instruction, the movement that had already started was turned into an unstoppable wave of resistance.

In many recent books and articles all these points have been recorded with full documentation and evidence. If we ignore all this research, then what is the point of writing history books or publishing documents?

After the victory of the uprising on 28th of Mordad, when my father was put in charge of national affairs, a number of telegrams were exchanged between His Majesty the Shah and Grand Ayatollah Borujerdi and Ayatollah Behbahani. The Shah thanked them for their help, and with a feeling of paternal affection Grand Ayatollah Borujerdi replied, "You saved Iran and Islam." Later on, some people did not wish those documents to be published, but some historians have recently published them. Those messages are more powerful than any other evidence, and they provide the definitive answer to this question.

Question: Nevertheless, some still speak of the sums that were distributed among the people, and they believe that people were mobilized due to the distribution of those funds.

Zahedi: Was it $10,000, $60,000, or $100,000? It is strange that some people who wish to insinuate that what happened on 28th of Mordad was a coup d'état still refer to those sums as the most powerful evidence of the American or British involvement in those events. They do not understand (or they deliberately wish to mislead the people) that with such allegations they are even questioning the importance of the oil nationalization movement, which was a truly national and popular movement. They even belittle in the most shameful way their leader Dr. Mossadegh, whom they wish to honor with such allegations. Was the great movement of the Iranian people, which they claim was led by Dr. Mossadegh in those days, so weak that it could be defeated with the expenditure of $10,000 or $100,000? In the words of our poet, "Everybody moans of the misdeeds of the enemies, I moan due to the misdeeds of my friends." Or, according to a French saying, "O God save me from my friends, I can save myself from my enemies!"

These foolish friends of Dr. Mossadegh are doing him more harm than his enemies have ever done and are in fact committing treason against him. So far, America has spent over $400 billion in Iraq. According to a study carried out by a reputable scientific journal, *Lancet*, since the invasion of Iraq more than 565,000 Iraqis have been killed due to the war and associated violence. Even according to official figures provided by the Iraqi government, more than 285,000 Iraqis have been killed. On a daily basis, 3,000 Iraqis are fleeing their homeland. Yet, despite all that expenditure, all those casualties, and the presence of 150,000 foreign forces in that country, no great progress has been made in Iraq after four years. One can refer to many similar examples.

Is it not shameful and insulting when some of Mossadegh's supporters say that his government was brought down by the Americans spending a few thousand dollars? Is it possible to buy the loyalty of the Iranian people with a few thousand dollars? Is this not the greatest insult to the Iranian people and to Dr. Mossadegh himself?

Question: The events of 28th of Mordad, or, according to you, the five critical days, marked a turning point in Iranian history, which changed the fate of the country for the next quarter century. There is no doubt about that. Some people believe those changes were positive and praise them, while others believe that they were negative and criticize them. Did those events also influence the situation in the world at large? It was clearly a great defeat for the communist world and a big victory for the "Free World," as they used to say in those days. As with other great historical events, half a century later many Iranians still debate those issues and carry out research about them, and many foreign authors and scholars have written extensively about the importance of those events. Your memoirs, which look at those events from within, provide valuable documentary material for historians. Some of your assessments of those events here and there will be of great interest to historians. The documents that you have collected with a great deal of effort over many years and have appended to this book will enable the reader to make a fresh and unavoidably different assessment of some of those events. From that point of view, this chapter is of particular national and international significance and of great value to future historians. What is your own view about the most important historical revision that must be made regarding those events?

Zahedi: If one can set aside personal and political prejudices as well as one's likes and dislikes, one will be better able to make a correct assessment of those events and to provide a more accurate scientific and historical analysis.

The same is true about all major historic events and characters that have had a major influence on the course of history. There are even many differences between modern and traditional views regarding the date and the place of birth and the teachings of Jesus. Napoleon is apparently the leader about whom the largest number of books have been written. Yet what we know about him today is very different from what we knew about him in the past. Whenever we find a new document and a new historical record, our attitude changes and we view past events from a new perspective. This is the nature of historical research, and it is as the result of the combined work of all historians that we will be able to have a more accurate account of a historical event. We should try to set aside our prejudices and bias and should analyze past events from an impartial and scientific point of view.

Today, fresh documents about the events of 28th of Mordad are available in French, British, and American archives. I have collected most of them and have carefully read them, and I have quoted many of them in this book. A few years ago, in an interview I said that I had read at least a hundred books and many articles on the events of 28th of Mordad and my father's role in those events. These new books and documents have completely changed the former views regarding those events. Since then, scores of other books and articles have been published. Many more reputable and impartial Iranian historians and scholars, and even some scholars who follow different political ideologies, have tried to make a new evaluation of those events. Even in contemporary Iran, despite strict censorship, many interesting works have been published that can provide fresh material for historians.

Just during the past eighteen months, many new analytical books and articles have been published, such as the works of Jalal Matini, Houshang Nahavandi, Abbas Milani, Ali Mir-Petros, Daryoush Homayoun, Mohamad-Ali Movahed, Darioush Bayandor, and others. They have based their works on some important documents whose veracity cannot be denied. Earlier on, some historians, such as Ebrahim Safai, Askari, Homayunfar, Alamuti, and others, had published many accounts and personal memoirs regarding those events. Some very interesting accounts by the friends and colleagues of Dr. Mossadegh and the leaders of the Tudeh Party have been published during the past few years. The result of all this new research has forced us to make a different assessment of the events of 28th of Mordad and the five days that changed Iran's fate.

What happened on 28 Mordad was not a coup d'état but a popular movement. Had it not been for the resistance of the guards at Mossadegh's house, the number of casualties would not have exceeded single figures. The change of government could have taken place calmly and on the basis of the constitution. On 2Mordad, the armed forces were under the control of the government, but later they changed sides or remained impartial. My father did not have any forces under his control. Many of his supporters were imprisoned. The Iranian people provided the main impetus for changing the situation, helped by the clergy and of course the leadership and coordination provided by General Zahedi. With every passing day, my father's leadership and the role that he played during those critical days becomes clearer, and personally I am very proud of him.

During the events of 28th of Mordad, the Western world, especially the Americans, were most anxious to get out of the crisis that had come about with minimum disruption. Of course, later on, they supported the changes that had come about. However, after the failure of Colonel Nasiri and what has been wrongly described as a coup d'état by the royal guards, the foreigners adopted a very cautious stance and preferred to cooperate with Dr. Mossadegh, despite all the dangers that his government posed for them. The "American coup d'état" is a lie, and very few historians and scholars believe in it anymore. New evidence changes one's outlook, and we must accept these changes. One cannot write history by issuing a diktat or passing a resolution.

Just imagine what would have happened if a few days after 25 Mordad Iran had been changed into "a democratic, popular republic" and had become a satellite of Moscow and a communist country! What a calamity and tragedy it would have been for the Iranian nation and for the region! Where would we be now? It is said that "the past is a mirror for the future" or, according to a Senegalese proverb, "If you do not know where you are going, at least look back so that you know where you have come from."

The events of 28th of Mordad provided an experience for the Iranian nation that can serve it well in the future. It is alleged that in his will and testament Peter the Great had urged his country to try to gain access to the warm waters of the Persian Gulf. Of course, there is no such written document, but there is no doubt about the significance of the idea behind that saying. The Russians, followed by the Soviet Union, never forgot that goal. The victory of the Iranian people on 28th of Mordad prevented the realization of that dream and the Soviet control over Iran, the Persian Gulf, and the oil resources of the region, and perhaps changed the course of world history. In any case, it was an event of international significance. That region is still one of the most sensitive places in global equations.

Of course, the ending of Mossadegh's government was in the interest of the Free World and was a defeat for international communism. However, Iranians, not foreigners, were responsible for that great historic event. Today too it is important to change the course of Iran's political system, but this should be achieved at the hands of the Iranians, especially young Iranians. Look at all the countries in our neighborhood. Nothing can be achieved with the use of force and money provided by foreigners, without the will and determination of the people themselves.

Question: Let us go back again. Many historians have written that General Zahedi was against Dr. Mossadegh's trial and imprisonment after he surrendered, and that Zahedi proposed that Mossadegh should be allowed to live respectfully in his estate in Ahmadabad under supervision and should not be persecuted. It is also claimed that after the arrest and trial of Dr. Fatemi, Zahedi was against his death sentence and had demanded a pardon and commutation of his death sentence to life imprisonment. They have described those cases as some points of difference between him and Mohammad Reza Shah. What is your view about those claims?

At the Zahedi residence in Hesarak around 1942. From left to right: Soghra Zahedi; Ali-Reza Gharogozlu; Abol-Ghassem Zahedi; Nasrollah Zahedi; Dr. Gharanfoul, a Lebanese dentist; Ardeshir; Mohammad Elahi, and Javad Vakili. At this time General Zahedi was being held prisoner by the Allies.

After the occupation of Iran by the Allies in 1941, General Zahedi had been kidnapped by the British, and rumors had it that he had been executed. One day, a two-line letter arrived from the general via the British Embassy stating that he was well and asking for a photograph of his children. This photograph was taken by Sako, a well-known photographer of the time, and was sent to the general. We see a fifteen-year-old Ardeshir and a twelve-year-old Homa.

Beirut, 1946. Iranian New Year's picnic. Ardeshir; the daughter of Mr. Hakimi, the chargé d'affaires of the Iranian Embassy in Beirut; Princess Keykavussi; and Nader Hakimi can be seen in the photograph.

At the Iranian New Year's picnic in Beirut in 1946, with embassy staff. Mrs. Fahimi, Mrs. Moazed, Princess Keykavussi, and Ms. Hakimi are in the back. Ardeshir and Mrs. Batul Atabaki can be seen in the front.

The Shah and Federal Councillor Max Petitpierre, in Bern during the Shah's official visit to Switzerland in 1948.

Enrico Celio, president of Switzerland, H.I.M. Mohammad Reza Pahlavi and Max Petitpierre, Federal Councillor in Bern during the Shah's official visit to Switzerland in 1948.

Celebration of Nowruz by Iranian students in Utah. From left to right: Ardeshir, Mehdi Omana, and Fereydoun Farmanfarmaian.

Ardeshir presents a Persian carpet to Franklin Harris, the president of Utah State.

Ardeshir with the members of the Cosmopolitan Club at Utah State. He was the president of the club.

In 1944, in Beirut, Iranian students gathered to organize a protest at the Soviet Embassy against the occupation of Azerbaijan by Soviet troops. Ardeshir, who is in the back row, was the leader of the demonstration. In this photograph Masoud Moazed, the Iranian ambassador to Lebanon, Mrs. Moazed, Mrs. Fahim ol-Molk Fahimi, and Rahmat Atabeki can also be spotted.

Ardeshir graduating from Utah State in 1951. Franklin Harris, the head of the university, is presenting him with the diploma.

The Shah made his first formal visit to the United States in 1949 during the presidency of Harry Truman. In this photograph, taken in Phoenix, Arizona, he can be seen with Ardeshir, who represented the Iranian students at Utah State, and Franklin Harris, the president of the university.

Ardeshir at a hunting ground near Hamedan in 1944.

9 June, 1949. Abdollah Mansour, Abdol-Reza Ansari, Amir-Hossein Nakhai, Mansour Esfandiari and Ardeshir in Logan, Utah.

From left to right, at the opening of the Nemazee Hospital in Shiraz: Mohammad Zolfaghari, deputy speaker of the parliament; Senator Fazlollah Zahedi; Malek Mansour Qashqai; Ardeshir; Abdollah Vala, publisher of *Tehran Mosavar* magazine; Khosrow Qashqai; and Mohammad-Hossein Qashqai.

Dr. Mahmoud Hessaby (minister of education) and General Zahedi (minister of interior) had been part of Mossadegh's first cabinet. Hessaby, a physicist and polymath had met Albert Einstein at Princeton University. In Iran, he later became popularly known as the Einstein of Iran.

Ayatollah Kashani, the speaker of the parliament, at his desk. He did not participate in the sessions. This photograph was taken during a visit.

Senator Fazlollah Zahedi at the parliament building.

Fazlollah Zahedi in discussion with the head of the parliament, Ayatollah Kashani.

Prime Minister Mohammad Mossadegh's first cabinet. From left to right: Karim Sanjabi, minister of education; General Fazlollah Zahedi, minster of interior; Amir Homayoun Bushehri, minister of roads and spokesman for the government; Zia ol-Molk Farmand, minister of agriculture; Ali Heyat, minster of justice; Hossein Loghman Adham, minister of health; Mossadegh, prime minister; Bagher Kazemi, minister of foreign affairs and deputy prime minister, Mohammad-Ali Varasteh, minister of finance; and General Ali-Asghar Naghdi, minister of war.

Hormoz Pirnia, Prime Minister Fazlollah Zahedi, and Ardeshir before a meeting with William Warne, the head of Point Four in Iran and U.S. Ambassador Loy Henderson.

August 16, 1953. Mossadegh supporters pull down a statue of Reza Shah in Sepah Square in Tehran.

August 19, 1953. The population demonstrating in favor of the new government.

Shortly after the success of the national uprising, Fazlollah Zahedi is seen composing a telegraph asking the Shah to return. Colonel Khalatbari can be seen in the photograph.

A crowd occupies the offices of the national radio.

Prime Minster Zahedi at his desk. The first person on the left is Parviz Yarafshar.

Thursday, August 20, 1953 at the Officers' Club. Fazlollah Zahedi on the first day of his premiership.

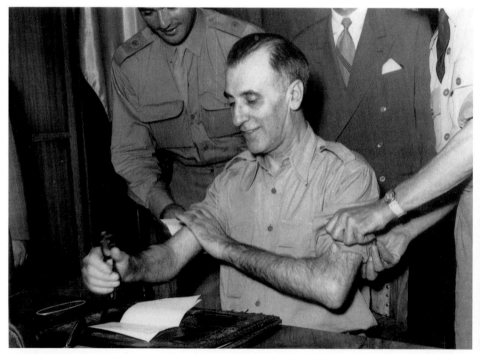

Fazlollah Zahedi, the new prime minster, at police headquarters shortly after the success of the national uprising. After being treated for exhaustion by doctors, Zahedi sent a telegraph to the Shah asking him back to his country.

The Shah and Prime Minister Zahedi greeting Queen Soraya returning to Iran in 1953.

Prime Minister Fazlollah Zahedi paying his respects to the Queen Mother at the Tehran Railway station upon her return after a long absence in 1953. From left, the Shah, the Queen Mother, Mrs. Yazdanpanah, General Zahedi, and Ardeshir.

Prime Minister Zahedi's cabinet after being presented to the Shah at the Sa'dabad Palace.

Hossein Makki and Ardeshir in discussion in parliament.

First row, from left to right: Mehdi Mirashrafi, Shams Ghanatabadi, General Zahedi, and Abol-Hossein Haerizadeh. Second row: Ahmad Bahadori and Ahmad Faramarzi. Third row: Fatollah Poursartip; Ahmad Hamidieh; Ali Abtin, chief inspector of the Senate; Ardeshir; Nadali Karimi; and Hessameddin Dowlatabadi, Deputy Prime Minister. Some staff members of the parliament can be seen in the back.

Journalist Fleur Cowles Meyer, editor in chief of *Cowles Magazine,* interviewing Prime Minister Zahedi.

Members of the Zahedi cabinet. From left to right: Jamshid Mofakham, Acting Minister of Arts; General Abdollah Hedayat, Minister of War; Seyyed Fakhreddin Shadman, Minister of Economy; Jahanshah Saleh, Minister of Health; Prime Minister Zahedi; Ali Amini Minister of the Treasury; General Abbas Garzan, Minister of Roads; Masoud Maleki, Minister of Labor; Jamaleddin Akhavi, Minister of Justice, Mousa Sarabandi, Deputy Prime Minister and Reza Jafari, Minister of Culture.

Ardeshir and his father during the first session of the 18th parliament. Chief Inspector Mehdi Ekbatani and Colonel Reza Zahedi can also be seen in the photograph.

Prime Minister Zahedi and his cabinet at the Marble Palace.

Zahedi: Both of them are correct. After the collapse of Dr. Mossadegh's government, in a statement my father respectfully called on him to hand himself in and promised him that he would be treated with respect. We knew where he was, but we did not wish to show any disrespect to him as the person who had carried out the nationalization of the oil industry with the support of all the Iranian people, with the exception of members of the Tudeh Party of course. His Majesty the Shah had supported him in that venture, and my father was minister of the interior in his cabinet and earlier had ensured that the members of the National Front were freely elected to the Majles.

When the plan was drawn up to arrest Mossadegh, my father told his aides that any person who showed any disrespect to him would be punished. Of course, his aim in making that extreme statement was to make sure that all those who were hostile to Mossadegh and who had suffered at his hands during the last days of his government would not contemplate any wrong action. Mossadegh was brought with respect to the Officers' Club. My father received him in his office and shook his hand. Mossadegh told my father, who was surrounded by a number of high-ranking military officers, including General Shahbakhti, "Now, I am a captive and you are the ruler." My father replied, "You are our highly respected guest." A short time later, they took him to a luxurious apartment in the Officers' Club, and two comfortable rooms were given to two of his associates, Dr. Sedighi and Moazzemi. Dr. Moghaddam was given the task of taking care of Mossadegh's health. He was a friend of Mossadegh and carried out his duties with care and diligence. A week later, Mossadegh was transferred from the Officers' Club to the headquarters of the armored brigade in Saltanatabad.

Everybody involved has recorded those events, including Dr. Sedighi and Dr. Mossadegh, who have provided full details of those events in their memoirs. Many people were in favor of an open trial for Mossadegh. My father was against it, as he believed that in the early stages of the nationalization of the oil industry they had all worked together. How could they try Mossadegh now? Furthermore, he believed that the trial would be a political mistake and that Mossadegh would make use of domestic and foreign media in order to defend himself and attack the Shah.

A meeting was held in the presence of His Majesty at the court, and it lasted till very late in the evening. Her Majesty Queen Soraya phoned a number of times saying that dinner was ready, but we were so rapt in discussions that we had to delay the dinner. My father did not come to that meeting because he did not wish to argue with the Shah. However, I explained his views in detail, and maybe rather too bluntly, which was due to my youth and which might have displeased the Shah a bit. Ali Heyat, the prosecutor general of the country, who had also been a minister in Mossadegh's government, was also present in that meeting, as were Dr. Mohammad Sajjadi and General Abdollah Hedayat. Finally, they reached the decision to try Dr. Mossadegh, provided that the trial would concentrate on the three days of Mossadegh's illegal government, and this decision was followed. However, my father's prediction came true, and the court and the trial proved to be a major political mistake, which ultimately harmed national interests.

Dr. Hossein Fatemi had transgressed all bounds by openly insulting His Majesty and the royal family. He used very rude and insulting terms, which would have been appropriate for louts and not for a foreign minister and a journalist. He openly advocated the ending of the monarchy and proposed a coalition with the Tudeh Party. The royal court was very angry with him, and perhaps quite rightly so. When Fatemi was sentenced to death, a number of leading figures went to my father and asked that he mediate and ask His Majesty to commute his sentence to life imprisonment. My father was in favor and tried his best. Unfortunately, it was either too late for him to act or there were other reasons why it did not succeed. In hindsight, that too was a political mistake.

His Majesty was a very kind and merciful person. He even pardoned those who took part in an assassination attempt against him. However, maybe due to pressure from some of his relatives or aides he did not commute Fatemi's death sentence. There have been many details published about those two issues, and there is no need to go into further detail here.

I hope that these detailed accounts and sometimes repetitive reminiscences may be useful for future historians and may shed some light on that part of our history.

---

[1] The government's statement that was broadcast at seven o'clock on Tehran Radio was as follows:

> From 11:30 last night a military coup d'état was staged by military officers and members of the Royal Guard. First of all, at that time, military personnel armed with machine guns and handguns arrested the minister of foreign affairs, the minister of roads, and Engineer Zirakzadeh in Shemiran. They also attacked the house of the chairman of the joint chiefs of staff of the armed forcers in order to arrest him, but as General Riahi was working in the headquarters of the joint staff they did not succeed in arresting him.
>
> At one o'clock in the morning, Colonel Nasiri, the commander of the Royal Guards, went to the prime minister's house with four military trucks, two military jeeps, and one armored vehicle, pretending that he wanted to hand over a letter to him. He intended to occupy the house, but as the guards at the prime minister's residence were watching the situation carefully, Colonel Nasiri was immediately arrested.
>
> Before arresting various individuals, the conspirators had cut the telephone lines of their houses. They had also cut the telephone line between the headquarters of the joint staff of the armed forces and the Royal Guards barracks in Bagh-e Shah. The telephone exchange in the Bazaar was also occupied by Colonel Azemoudeh and his armed companions. They also arrested the deputy chief of the joint staff of the armed forces who had gone to Bagh-e Shah to inspect the barracks there. They brought the minister of foreign affairs, the minister of roads, and Engineer Zirakzadeh from where they had been arrested in Sa'dabad to the city in four military trucks under armed guards. They took them to the headquarters of the joint staff of the armed forces, thinking that their co-conspirators had already occupied that place. However, as they became aware of their mistake, they returned them to Sa'dabad and kept them in the detention center in the Royal Guards barracks until five o'clock in the morning. At that time, when their planned coup d'état had been foiled, Brigadier-General Kiani, deputy chairman of the joint staff of the armed forces, who had been released

from detention, went to Sa'dabad and took those gentlemen back to their homes.

From that moment onward, law-enforcement forces took the initiative, and so far a number of the conspirators have been arrested. The full details of those events will be subsequently brought to the attention of the Iranian nation."

[2] From the notes by Ardeshir Zahedi, published in the *Monthly Ettela'at* in the year 1332 [1953] under the title "Five Critical Days":

The house of Mr. Mirafshar, who is one of my father's relatives and old friends, is situated in Bahar Street, which is a relatively quiet and cosy place. When we entered his house, Colonel Farzanegan was already there, and it seemed that the owner of the house had already expected our arrival, because he had chosen a quiet and tucked away room for our meeting. A few minutes later, General Gilanshah also arrived, dressed in civilian clothes. He said that the general (meaning my father) would arrive in Keynejad's car at 6:30. I asked Gilanshah, "In view of the present situation, what will we be talking about tonight?" He said that he did not know, and continued, "Through one of our contacts, the general sent me a message asking us to be here by 6:30 PM." Exactly at 6:30 my father arrived, dressed in an open-neck pale shirt, military trousers and large sunglasses. Immediately, all of us gathered together in the room that had been set aside for us. Those who had taken part in that meeting consisted of my father, Brigadier-General Gilanshah, Colonel Farzanegan, Parviz Yarafshar, Sadeq Naraqi and me. Of course, there were some other friends and relatives in Mr. Seyf Yarafshar's house, including Engineer Shahrokhshahi, Engineer Abol-Ghassem Zahedi and Habibollah Nayebi, who were mainly in charge of watching the streets surrounding the house. Also, when necessary, they took some messages from my father to some retired officers, including General Shahbakhti, and returned with some new information that they had gathered from outside. In that way, we were kept completely informed about what was going on outside and the activities of those around Mossadegh and his officials. As an example of the ability of our officials to gather information and intelligence about outside events I can refer to Major-General Batmanqelich's arrest that we learned about only 20 minutes later, which of course made us all very unhappy.

The discussions in that historic meeting lasted six hours and, in view of the decisions that were taken, that meeting was one of our most important meetings in those days. At the same time, it provided an example of my father's determination and resolve and the sincerity and faithfulness of all those who took part in that meeting. At the beginning of the meeting, we had some discussion regarding the events and the incidents of the day, the demonstrations that were held in Baharestan Square and the activities of the members of the Tudeh Party. Everybody who had some information on those issues shared them with all those who were taking part in the meeting. Then, my father said, "I think that all the gentlemen are aware of the events that have taken place since the middle of last night, and there is no need to repeat them here. Maybe this has been the divine will for those incidents to take place, so that we may face a more dangerous situation or, according to my interpretation, we are faced with a major test. These events will sort out those who will remain faithful to their oath to obey His Imperial Majesty's orders and who are prepared for self-sacrifice in the service of their country from those who will break their oaths. Those of us who are gathered here, and those who are co-operating with us from outside, have remained faithful to our oaths, and we are ready to discharge our duties towards the king and the country. I am quite aware of the efforts and sacrifices that each one of you has made since last night, and I testify that you have performed the duties that you were given with honour and dignity.

"Last night, after Nasiri was arrested, in a bigger meeting in Farzanegan's house I said that personally I would follow the path that I have chosen as far as it is in my power. I will fight to the last drop of my blood in the implementation of the orders of the head of the country and in saving my homeland from this fiasco. Even if I lose my life on this path, I will at least remain proud in the eyes of others and my descendants. Now I feel that you too valiantly wish to co-operate with me, and that there is in fact no difference between my attitude and thoughts and yours. Therefore, we must not sit still and we must not leave everything to fate. We must draw plans and must implement them with a strong morale and determined minds. We must show courage and self-sacrifice in order to achieve our goal and can claim that we have served the country to the best of our ability.

"From the start of my life as a soldier my belief has been that one can claim to have served and have taken a step in the interest of the country only when one is faced with hard, difficult and dangerous circumstances. Otherwise, under ordinary circumstances when everything is available, serving the country does not require any self-sacrifice. This is why at the start of this road with these few words I wish to dispel any feeling of despair and despondency in you. I will reassure you that if we are vigilant and calm and if we act on the basis of a wise and careful plan, we will definitely succeed. It is not worthy of us to show any fear, despair, hesitation or doubt.

"Today when I heard the statement issued by Mossadegh's agents on radio, and was informed of the afternoon's demonstrations in Baharestan Square and the nonsensical, emotive speeches made by various speakers I became hopeful of my future and the plan that we have in front of us. Do you know why? Because despite all the power and control that these groups believe that they have over national institutions, they did not dare tell the people that they had refused to obey the Shah's orders. All their comments and slogans were limited to saying that a coup d'état had been staged against them, and that they had arrested the agents and had done this and that. I expected anything of Mossadegh os-Salta-neh except that he would distort the nature of a clear and definite truth that sooner or later would be revealed.

"Had Mossadegh os-Saltaneh gone in front of the people or had he announced on the radio that the Shah had issued a decree dismissing him as prime minister and appointing Zahedi in his place and that he had refused to obey the Shah's orders I would not have complained and I might not have got myself ready to engage in battle. This is because I would have concluded that either the masses and the true people of the country had been in agreement with Mossadegh os-Saltaneh's actions or they would have been opposed to it. If they agreed with it, then I could do nothing about it, and if they were opposed to it they would have risen against that man who had declared his rebellion and rejection of the royal decree and would have dealt with him in an appropriate manner. But I see that Mossadegh and his supporters and aides did not dare tell the people that they had rebelled against the Shah's orders and wished to continue their ram-shackle government by trampling upon all the laws and regulations of the country.

"Therefore, you should be certain that at this moment the morale of Mossadegh and the members of his gang is much weaker than ours, despite the fact that we are talking together in secret in this hiding place. They are very afraid of what they have done, and all the noise that they are making and demonstrations that they are organising are for the sake of distorting the reality and deceiving the public. Therefore, our first duty is to inform the public and the national officials about the truth of the matter. Mossadegh os-Saltaneh and the few people who gather round his bedside do not constitute the government. All national organi-sations are responsible towards laws and regulations in keeping with their duties. All the efforts exerted by Mossadegh and his people are aimed at hiding the truth from those organisations and from the people."

My father spoke with such strength and enthusiasm that everybody had fixed his gaze upon his mouth and was strongly attracted to him. For me, that kind of speaking was quite new, especially as it was accompanied with certain amount of emotion and anger, because my father was naturally a very calm person and had full control over his nerves, as he is always calm and brief when he speaks.

However, that night it was quite clear that he was very upset and angry. When my father's remarks came to an end, General Gilanshah started to speak and made certain remarks in support of what my father had just said. Gilanshah's remarks were followed by those of Colonel Farzanegan and others. Each of them made certain points, but I refrain from providing their details in order to keep this short.

Then my father said, "In my view, we must first make two plans for our work. The first one is to inform the people of the Shah's decrees. Secondly, we must prepare the means for implementing those decrees by making use of the capabilities that exist in the country at the moment. As part of the first plan, this afternoon Ardeshir has given an interview to foreign reporters. Although that interview was a major step towards informing other countries about the latest developments, nevertheless, I believe that it was not enough to inform our own people, whose views I value more than anything else. As we do not have any means at our disposal for doing that, I believe that right now a number of people should be selected and each of them should be put in charge of some part of the city. Tonight, each of them should place photographs of the royal decree in the postal boxes of all ministries, state and national organisations, newspapers and magazines, and foreign embassies."

We had some discussion regarding the above proposal and, on the whole, everybody believed that it was important and effective. Immediately, five people were selected to carry out that task. They were: Messrs. Parviz Yarafshar, Engineer Hormoz Shahrokhshahi, Engineer Abol-Ghassem Zahedi, Sadeq Naraqi and Habibollah Nayebi. In view of the locations of different ministries and government departments in different parts of the capital, the city of Tehran was divided into five zones, and each of those five individuals was put in charge of one zone. At the same time, it was decided that alongside photographs of the royal decree that would be placed inside various ministries and government departments, there should also be a letter by my father, which would be in the form of a decree and warning to government officials.

My father immediately dictated that letter, and Mr. Yarafshar wrote it down. As far as I can now remember, the text of that letter was something like this: "I have been appointed prime minister on the basis of the royal decree. Therefore, hereby I warn everyone that from now on any orders issued by Dr. Mossadegh are null and void, and those who implement them would be held responsible and would be liable to prosecution." Of course, the contents of that letter were a little more detailed and more explicit than this, but it was mainly on these lines. Mr. Mirafshar immediately took that letter to his house or company and produced a large number of typed copies of that letter on paper with my father's letterhead. Meanwhile, Engineer Shahrokhshahi went home and brought a large number of the photographs of the royal decree with a large number of envelopes to Mr. Yarafshar's house. In a short time, the photographs of the royal decree and the accompanying letter were distributed among those individuals, and it was decided that at 11:00 that night they should distribute them in different parts of the city, and when the job was done to reassemble in Mr. Yarafshar's house.

Meanwhile, one of our contacts reported that a number of officials from the military governor's office had attacked Hesarak and my father's summer residence in Shemiran and had searched all the contents of the house. They had even searched the disused buildings at the bottom of the garden. A short time later, we were informed that the military governor had set up a reward of 10,000 tumans for my father's arrest. They had also prepared the following statement that were to be read out in the news services of the radio that night and the following morning:

"Following the statement No. 39, as it is necessary for the retired Major-General Zahedi to be present at the headquarters of the military governor for providing some explanations, and due to the fact that he has been informed in an announcement on the radio to hand himself in and so far he has refused to do so, therefore, hereby we inform the compatriots that if anyone who is aware of the whereabouts of the above-mentioned general can provide any information that would result in his arrest he will receive 100,000 rials reward in cash." My father carefully read the text of the statement and then started to laugh aloud. Then jokingly he said, "As we are so strapped for cash, it would be a good idea if I go and hand myself in and receive the 10,000 tumans reward. However, in view of the situation that they have created in the country, I am worried that there will not be 10,000 tumans in the government's Treasury to pay me." Then he added, "All this is the sign of these gentlemen's fear and weakness. They are afraid of what I said before, namely that the people may learn about the Shah's decree and its implementation. Therefore, without paying any attention to these issues, we must try to implement our programmes and plans as soon as possible."

Under those circumstances and the psychological state that we were experiencing, my father's joke made us laugh and to some extent lifted our spirits. At the same time, his remarks showed that those threats had not had the least effect upon his firm and determined character. However, that change of mood did not last very long and with what General Gilanshah said the situation again returned to its earlier state. He said, "In view of the arrangements that have been made and with the distribution of the photograph of your appointment as the new prime minister among various ministries, government departments, national institutions, embassies and the press, definitely by tomorrow morning a large number of people will be informed of your appointment as the new prime minister. However, in view of the path that Mossadegh and his colleagues are pursuing and in view of their control over various national departments and organisations, can one hope that the distribution of the royal decree would achieve anything and could bring us closer to our goal?"

My father replied, "As I said earlier, we have two plans ahead of us. The first one is to inform the people about the royal decree, and the second one is to prepare the means for implementing it. In my view, the implementation of the second plan is much more important and much more difficult than the first part, because no matter how much they try to hide the issue, people will eventually be informed of the royal decree. Mossadegh os-Saltaneh and his clique are also fully aware of this issue. The steps that they have taken from early this morning, including sending soldiers to Sa'adabad [Palace], locking and sealing royal palaces, or the noises that they have made and the slogans that they have chanted in the demonstrations in Baharestan Square and the fact that they have accused us of having staged a coup d'état and so on and so forth, are all due to their attempt to minimise the effect of the royal decree.

"This is because they do not dare tell the people that they had rejected the royal decree. With all the noises, insults and the hue and cry that they are making they wish to prepare the public opinion in such a way that their rejection of the royal decree would not seem important. In short, they also know that sooner or later people would be made aware of His Imperial Majesty's decree. However, our activities tonight will speed up public awareness and it will be very effective in clarifying the state of public opinion.

"As far as the implementation of the royal decree is concerned, namely seizing the reins of power and forcing this rebellious and undisciplined government to obey and accept the royal decree, I have a view which must form the basis of our discussions tonight. It is not clear on what basis the government believes that it should be in charge of the country's affairs, Therefore, I would like to have a discussion and exchange of views on the best ways to force the government to obey the royal decree. This afternoon in Moshir-Fatemi's house I was thinking how many individuals and collaborators we have in Tehran at the moment, and whether with this small number of supporters who have remained faithful to their oaths we will be able to have any activity in Tehran or not. I was thinking how we could gain control of the situation in the capital. As a result of these studies, I came to the conclusion that the chances of our success in Tehran are very weak, or would at least require a long time before they succeed. On the other hand, we have no means for implementing our plans and we have no military forces under our command. Consequently, we are forced to put up with the present situation, namely to continue this uncertain situation and live in hiding, until gradually the issue becomes clear to the people or at least those who are in charge of various departments, and this requires time.

"Nevertheless, if we feel that with the passage of time and with patience we could achieve the results that we have in mind and the country could be saved, I would be quite happy to wait. However, I am worried that any delay in carrying out our plans, and putting up with the present circumstances would only pave the way for the domination of the communists and the destruction of the foundations of the constitutional government and monarchy in this country. At the moment, the number of our active supporters is limited to the few people who have gathered here and a few who are co-operating with us from outside, whose number does not exceed ten. During yesterday and today a number of our friends have also refused to take sides and have become mere spectators, and maybe one cannot blame them too much for their attitude, because at the moment nobody's life or property is safe. The armed forces, namely the only military barracks that exist in the centre of the city, are under the government's control. They also control—at least in name—the police and the gendarmerie. If we wish to inform all those people and those organisations about the true situation we require a large number of individuals, freedom of movement, stability and a large number of helpers, and at the moment we do not have any of them. One cannot do anything effective in hiding and behind closed doors. Therefore, in view of all the problems and restrictions that we face in Tehran, I believe that our continued stay in the capital is a mistake. From a military point of view, Brigadier-General Gilanshah knows very well that exerting control over a small place, achieving power there, and preparing to extend the scope of one's control over other places would be much easier than having tenuous control over a large, tense and disparate place.

In view of the above, I came to the conclusion that it would be better for us to transfer our headquarters to one of the provinces where there is a larger concentration of military forces and where there are more appropriate facilities for military and defensive operations. In a place like that, we would have less need in the capital or in other provinces for food, fuel and other necessary equipment. From there, we can inform the people of the facts and can form a government in the name of 'free Iran', and we can inform the world about the reason for our action and about the royal decrees. We can also call on free nations for help and we can warn Mossadegh's government to put an end to its rebellion and its disobedience to the Shah's orders. With the help of military forces, we will be able to force him to obey the royal orders. Of course, these are the main principles of my suggestion, which I would like to raise with you and ask for your views. If you are in agreement with the main aspects of my suggestion, we can talk about its details and about how we can implement it. In other words, we should see which province would be more suitable for our purpose, how many military personnel, and what quantity of weapons and ammunitions would be at our disposal, which armies in which provinces would be more suitable and more trustworthy and how we can get in touch with them to co-operate with us."

My father's proposal was quite unexpected for all us. The truth is that neither I nor any of our friends who were present in that meeting had expected such a proposal so that we could have prepared ourselves to express our views about it. We thought that my father only wanted to talk to us about the current situation and which place we should use for our residence, from where we could continue our activities.

In any case, after hearing my father's proposal, Brigadier-General Gilanshah, Colonel Farzanegan, Mr. Mostafa Moghaddam, who joined the meeting a little later, and I expressed our views about his proposal. In brief, we believed that there were a number of problems regarding the implementation of that plan, to which my father had not paid sufficient attention. We believed that while we tried to leave Tehran we should carry out some major acts of sabotage, which would preoccupy Mossadegh's government and would keep him busy in trying to cope with them. We could make use of those troubles and a climate of insecurity to leave the capital and move to our new headquarters. My father agreed with that view and said, "It seems to me that you are generally in agreement with my proposal and the need to get out of Tehran and to be stationed in one of the provinces and forming a government in the name of 'free Iran'. However, you have some suggestions about how to implement that plan. We should discuss those plans and choose the one that seems the best and the easiest to implement. Therefore, in order to save time and reach a final decision we better start thinking about various provinces and choosing one of them in view of the existence of a reliable army division or brigade there."

There were different views about this issue, and we finally selected five provinces about which we had an exchange of views. Those five provinces were Azerbaijan, Gilan, Kermanshah, Khorasan and Isfahan. We had some discussion about each of those provinces and the special characteristics of each province. Those in favour of Azerbaijan believed that the number of military forces in that province was more than in other provinces and they were better equipped. At the same time, apparently a couple of the princes lived in Azarbaijan, and some of those present in that meeting believed that their presence there was a positive point.

They also argued that Azarbaijan was richer than other provinces in view of the provision of food and grains. However, my father was not in favour of that view, partly due to the large distance of Azarbaijan from the capital, and partly due to the fact that it was situated on the country's borders and our relations with one of the neighbours [the Soviet Union] were not very favourable.

My father was rather inclined towards Khorasan province, but we did not have any clear information about the number of military forces stationed in that province and the state of their weapons and ammunitions. Regarding Gilan province, it was argued that first of all it was closer to Tehran than other provinces. Secondly, as my father had been the commander of the army in that province for a long time he was very familiar with its geographical situation and had many friends there. Therefore, he was in favour of moving to that province. However, the number of forces stationed in that province was limited and they were rather weak, and we also would face some problems regarding food and fuel. Therefore, we finally concentrated our attention on two remaining provinces, Kermanshah and Isfahan.

At this time, we were asked to move to the dining room to have dinner, but our discussions had become so heated and exciting that nobody showed any interest in dinner. I even remember that the cups of tea were untouched on the table. Suddenly, we received the news that the military government had arrested Mr. Hirad, the head of the imperial bureau, in his house. All of us, especially my father, were very upset to hear that news, because the royal decree was written in Hirad's handwriting and we knew that he would be put under intense pressure. However, later we learned that this noble, sincere and faithful servant of the Shah had shown extraordinary courage and valour when faced with Mossadegh's officials. In any case, as all of us were saddened at the report of his arrest, our talks were interrupted for a few minutes.

Anyway, from the start, my father regarded Kermanshah province as being more suitable than other provinces for the mission that he had in mind. He had a number of reasons for his preference. First of all, Colonel Bakhtiar (who subsequently became a general, deputy prime minister and the head of the National Security Organisation), who was the commander of the armoured brigade in Kermanshah at that time, was a brave, patriotic and devoted servant of His Imperial Majesty. Clearly, after being informed of the royal decree he would sincerely co-operate with us. Secondly, as my father came from Hamedan, which is part of that province, and in addition to Hamedan he also had many friends and relatives apart from those who worked in his personal farms, their presence would help him achieve full control over that province in a short time. Thirdly, the oil refinery in Kermanshah, as well as access to Naft-e Shah oilfields, would provide us with all the necessary fuel and petrol for our vehicles. Fourthly, as at that time His Imperial Majesty was in Iraq, Kermanshah province, which was the closest province to Iraq, would provide us easy access to His Majesty. He could provide us with guidance and leadership and on his way to the homeland he could return through that province and would honour his sincere servants by so doing. Fifthly, if we were surrounded by government forces and were placed under siege, the wheat crops in that province would have been completely sufficient for providing the food of the people in that province. My father was particularly concerned about the last issue, namely providing people with food and necessary sustenance.

Those who were in favour of selecting Isfahan province pointed out that Colonel Amir Gholi Zargham (who later was elevated to the rank of major-general), who was the deputy commander of the Army Division in that province, was a distinguished and reliable officer. Secondly, as my father had been in charge of the Army Division in that province for many years he had a large number of friends and acquaintances there. Meanwhile, some of the leading families in that province and some of the tribal leaders in different parts of that province also were very well-disposed and friendly towards my father.

When our choice narrowed down to those two provinces, the next issue was how we could get in touch with the commanders in charge of the military forces in those provinces. After long discussions, we eventually came to the conclusion that we should immediately send one person to Kermanshah and another person to Isfahan to discuss the issue with the commanders of the Army Division in those provinces, and to inform them of the royal decree and the decisions that had been taken in Tehran.

They were asked to learn about the views of the military commanders in those provinces and immediately send us their reports through some reliable individuals. Colonel Farzanegan volunteered to go to Kermanshah to talk to Colonel Bakhtiar. He said that he would immediately leave for that province and if he were not detained he would return at the same time the following night to inform us of the result of his talks with Colonel Bakhtiar. He said that in view of his familiarity with Colonel Bakhtiar's views and loyalty he was certain that his response would most definitely be positive. Mr. Yarafshar was also prepared to carry out that mission, and other friends also warmly welcomed those plans.

However, after some discussion, my father said, "But you should bear in mind that the government has issued orders to all the towns, cities and provinces that they should immediately arrest any one of us wherever they find us. They have even sent our photographs to different local officials. Therefore, our travels will not be free of danger." He continued, "In any case, I believe that Colonel Far-

zanegan is the most suitable person to travel to Kermanshah, because he knows
Colonel Bakhtiar better than anyone else, and as the two of them are military
officers they can understand each other better." Therefore, it was definitely decided that Colonel Bakhtiar should leave for Kermanshah.

Then we started to talk about Esfahan. Again, everybody was ready to accept
that mission, but I was more insistent than others to accept that task. Brigadier-
General Gilanshah also insisted that he should go and had certain reasons for
accepting that task. I insisted on my stance, but my father was strongly against
me leaving Tehran at that time. I sensed that his feeling as a father played a big
role in coming to that decision. This is why he insisted that Farzanegan should
immediately leave for Kermanshah and we would decide about Esfahan the following day. Eventually, I submitted to his view.

[3] The classified documents of the U.S. State Department that have been released
show that the Americans were busy studying the Iranian situation at that time. They
had not yet lost hope in Mossadegh's ability to resolve the oil issue. The document,
which contains the views of the highest ranking decision-making sources in the
United States, demonstrates the American government's preoccupation with the
Iranian crisis and its various plans about how to deal with that crisis. At the same
time, this document provides an answer to the question why the officials in the
American Embassy in Tehran refrained from meeting with Ardeshir Zahedi.

The letter is reprinted in facsimile in the document section of this book on page
459-460.

In a cable, dated March 4, Henderson states that there was no evidence yet that
Mossadegh had come to any arrangements with the Tudeh Party, but he was capable
of doing so in order to retain power. Henderson added that no reconciliation
between Mossadegh and the Shah appeared possible except on terms of the latter's
capitulation.

The letter is reprinted in facsimile in the document section of this book on pages
460-468.

[4] Engineer Kazem Hasibi writes in his memoirs:

> In Dr. Mossadegh's house, Messrs. Sanjabi, Shayegan, Zirakzadeh, Fatemi, En-
> gineer Razavi, Nariman and Haqshenas had gathered together. All the talk was
> about agreeing on deciding the nature of the regime for the country and getting
> out of the present uncertainty. A number of people believed that we had to de-
> clare a republic (this view was supported by Zirakzadeh, Fatemi, Razavi). Others
> were a little less extreme because they had also listened to the views of Dr. Mos-
> sadegh himself. The few points that were agreed by all were to hold a referen-

dum, to confirm the Shah's resignation, to put an end to the Pahlavi dynasty, and to appoint a royal council.

In the meeting in the presence of Dr. Mossadegh, which took place at about 10.00, we had some long discussions on those issues. Dr. Mossadegh believed that it was sufficient to form a royal council, stressing that any member of the council who might die or might resign would be appointed on the basis of a referendum. By doing that, we would not cut off the possibility of receiving help from America and the West, who definitely would support the regime, and we would not lean towards the Soviet Union, especially as the Tudeh Party supported the establishment of a republic. With Dr. Mossadegh's explanations, eventually everybody fell into line and agreed that it would be better not to move too fast at this point...

We again came back to Dr. Mossadegh's house in order to continue the discussions. However, as the American Ambassador Henderson, who had been away from Iran for a few months, had returned to Tehran immediately after the coup d'état and was having a meeting with Dr. Mossadegh, we went to Shayegan's house. When Fatemi, who was more radical than the rest of us, joined us the talk again turned to the establishment of a republic and announcing the end of the monarchy. Dr. Mossadegh's objections were discussed, and a plan was drawn up to form the members of a royal council. Then, we moved back to Dr. Mossadegh's house and we had a meeting there till 9:50 in the evening.

[5] The text of Major-General Zahedi's cable to Rome was as follows:

His Imperial Majesty the Shahanshah!
The devoted people and the self-sacrificing armed forces are impatiently counting the minutes for the return of His Imperial Majesty. We wish to beg the dust of the feet of Your Majesty and to beg you to speed up your return and to announce the hour of your Imperial Majesty's arrival, so that the Iranian people can in person express their pure feelings at the feet of His Imperial Majesty.

The Shah's answer to that cable was as follows:

In the name of God Almighty!
I am sincerely grateful for the support of the Iranian people for me and their defense of the Constitution. I call on all the personnel of the armed forces, all the non-military officials and the entire Iranian nation to obey the orders of His Excellency Fazlollah Zahedi, who on the basis of the Constitution has been appointed by me as the head of the national and legal government of Iran. I will

speedily return to Iran and will be among my nation. May God protect Iran and the Iranian people. Mohammad Reza Pahlavi.

[6] Dr. Gholam-Hossein Sadighi, the interior minister in Dr. Mossadegh's government, who was with him on the 28th and 29th Mordad, writes in his memoirs:

> At about 6:18 we were taken from the headquarters of the military government through the main gates of the Police Department. We came down the steps. Major-General Batmanqelich, who had been appointed chairman of the joint chiefs of staff of the armed forces, was holding Dr. Mossadegh's arms. When we were about to get into the car, someone started to shout in a loud voice, chanting some slogans against us. Major-General Batmanqelich got angry and shouted, "Shut up, you son of a ...!" He stopped and we got into the car, and from the Police Department we went towards the Officers' Club through a quiet road, and entered the club. They took us to the second floor.
>
> A large number of officers and retired army and gendarmerie officers were there and some of them were standing at the entrance of the club. Brigadier-General Fuladvand and Colonel Ne'matollah Nasiri, who had been elevated to the rank of brigadier-general, were also accompanying us. When we passed through the lines of officers and arrived in an office where Major-General Zahedi and a number of others were assembled, Major-General Zahedi came forward, greeted Dr. Mossadegh and shook his hand. He was wearing a military uniform, with a light short-sleeve cream shirt and unbuttoned collar (without a tie), and light trousers, and had rather dishevelled hair. He said, "I am very sorry to see you here..."

Hesameddin Dowlatabadi writes in his memoirs:

> Dr. Mossadegh told Major-General Zahedi, "Now I am a captive and you are the ruler!" Zahedi replied, "No, you are our guest."

[7] C.M. Woodhouse, *Something Ventured* (London: Granada, 1982); Kermit Roosevelt, *Countercoup* (London: McGraw-Hill, 1979).

[8] The confidential documents in the U.S. State Department regarding the events of 25–28 Mordad from the viewpoint of U.S. foreign policy contain some very interesting points. Please note the report: "The Charge in Iran (Mattison) to thes Department of State," reprinted in the document section of this book on page 470.

The events of 28th of Mordad as reported by various newspapers, quoting *Khandaniha* magazine, one of the most reputable political publications that was published regularly from the Second World War right up to the Islamic Revolution:

> In Tehran, various groups of the supporters of the Shah were shouting "Long live the Shah" from the sides of the streets, inside lorries, taxis or private cars. Gradually, the number of people in all the roads and streets increased. All of a sudden, a group of policemen put their weapons in their pockets and joined the people shouting "Long live the Shah!"
>
> When people saw that police officers, soldiers and military officers had joined them, they got hold of their vehicles and hoisted Iran's flags on top of them. They carried large portraits of the Shah and shouted "Long live the Shah! Long live Major-General Zahedi, Iran's legal prime minister!" Their shouts shook Tehran and a large number of men and women stood on the pavements and were crying with joy.
>
> About 10:20 yesterday morning, a group of people—estimated to be 7,000— who were carrying clubs and were ready for any possible clashes moved from Istanbul Street towards Baharestan Square. Although the previous night, on behalf of the military government, radio had announced that any demonstrations would be prevented, the soldiers and the policemen did not do anything to prevent the movement of those demonstrators. On the contrary, all of them joined the crowds, shouting, "We want the Shah, death to the dictator, long live Iran, long live the armed forces!"
>
> The crowds attacked the headquarters of the Iran Party and destroyed all the furniture, frames and portraits of Mossadegh that were there. At this time, a number of the members of the Iran Party who were in the party headquarters clashed with the demonstrators, but they were severely beaten and were forced to flee. The crowd then went to the headquarters of the Pan Iranist Party, which was at the beginning of Safi Alishah Street. After destroying some of the contents, they left the party headquarters, again chanting "We want the Shah!" They tore to pieces the banners that the supporters of the Pan Iranist Party had placed on the statue of Reza Shah three days earlier. They kept chanting slogans for the Shah and against Mossadegh. The crowd then went to Nazmiyyeh Street and plundered the offices of *Bakhtar Emruz* newspaper and set it on fire.
>
> The crowd then moved towards the offices of *Shuresh* newspaper, and those offices were also looted and set on fire. They destroyed all copies of *Shuresh* newspaper that they found there. Then they moved towards the offices of *Besuye Ayandeh* and *Hajibaba* newspapers and the headquarters of Niru-ye Sevvom Party. They looted and completely destroyed the offices of *Niru-ye Sevvom*

newspaper. A number of people in those offices were injured and were forced to flee, and the party headquarters were set on fire. The crowd, whose number had now swelled to many thousands, moved towards Shahabad, assisted by the soldiers and policemen.

At this time, a few military trucks with armed policemen and soldiers were sent by Dr. Mossadegh to Tupkhaneh Square to scatter the crowd. However, shortly afterwards those policemen and soldiers also joined the crowd and began to chant slogans in favour of the Shah and against Mossadegh and Fatemi, who had referred to the Shah as a fugitive. All of them joined the demonstrators and together they moved towards Nasser Khosrow and Lalehzar Streets, and called on the shopkeepers and the bystanders to join them in the battle against Mossadegh.

As the number of demonstrators was steadily increasing, all buses volunteered to transport the demonstrators and took them to different streets. All those buses were carrying a number of portraits of the Shah on their windscreens, and also had a flag on top. Meanwhile, all cars were forced by the crowd to turn on their lights as a sign of celebration. Even those cars that did not have a portrait of the Shah to put on their windscreens put a note with the Shah's portrait instead.

At 12:30 in the afternoon when Tehran Radio normally broadcasts the summary of the news it did not mention anything about the important events that were taking place in Tehran, and it devoted its entire bulletin to foreign news. At 1:00 o'clock it fabricated a report, announcing that since 7:30 in the morning the prime minister, Dr. Mossadegh, and members of the National Front party had been meeting in his house till half an hour after lunch and had been discussing the current affairs of the country. It also broadcast a fictitious interview with Dr. Alemi about cotton, and then played music till 14:00.

People were expecting that the radio would broadcast some reports about the developments in Tehran, but the station remained quiet for half an hour, from 14:00 to 14:30. However, at 14:30 the Shah's supporters managed to occupy the radio station and reached the microphones. At this time, it was announced that Major-General Zahedi, the legal prime minister of Iran, had arrived at the Radio station, but due to the pressure of crowds could not get to the microphone. After a few minutes, the new prime minister got to the microphone and the text of the royal decree appointing Major-General Zahedi as prime minister was read out on the radio. Then Major-General Zahedi sent a message to the nation, saying that he had been appointed prime minister by His Imperial Majesty, and he announced his programme. He then left straight for the headquarters of the National Police Department. As he was not feeling well, he was given an injection to give him some energy. Then he sat behind the desk of the head of the police, a post that he had occupied in the past, and from there he started to run the government.

By six o'clock in the afternoon, all the streets in Tehran were under the control of the demonstrators, and those living on various streets joined them and together shouted "Death to Mossadegh" and "Long live the Shah!" In Baharestan Square, people were particularly excited and emotional. Mahtab photo shop had placed the portraits of the Shah, His Eminence Ayatollah Kashani, Dr. Baghai and Makki on top of the balcony and people were shouting slogans in favour of the Shah, Kashani, Baghai and Makki. At the same time, they were tearing the portraits of Mossadegh, Zirakzadeh, Sanjabi, Shayegan and Nariman.

At 6:30 in the afternoon thousands of brave people marched towards the military governor's office and other military installations and prisons and set the political prisoners free. Dr. Baghai was not prepared to leave the prison, but people persuaded him to come out. Meanwhile, Colonel Momtaz and Major Davarpanah were busy massacring the demonstrators in front of Dr. Mossadegh's residence. Consequently, Major Oskui, the brave and patriotic officer, personally took control of a tank and attacked House No. 109, defeated Colonel Momtaz and occupied that place. The report about the occupation of House No. 109, Dr. Mossadegh's residence, speedily spread throughout the city. The attitude of the people on this day was exactly the same as their attitude at 5:30 on 30th Tir 1331 [21st July 1952]. (Quoted from *Shahed* newspaper.)

Firing around Dr. Mossadegh's house started from 12:00. Every few minutes as the crowd tried to rush towards Kakh Street the soldiers fired a few shots in the air and occasionally at the people, and the crowd would momentarily withdraw. This situation continued till nearly 4:30 in the afternoon. At this time, a few other tanks came to support the demonstrators, and the crowd reached Kakh Street from the Shah crossroads. At the beginning of Kakh Street that intersects the Shah Street there is Nowsazi Building. The guards protecting Dr. Mossadegh's house had occupied and formed observation posts on the fourth floor of that building. Colonel Momtaz was in charge of protecting that area. With the very first attack by the demonstrators they were fired at with machine guns and a number of them were killed and the crowd dispersed.

Meanwhile, the tanks that were getting ready to attack Dr. Mossadegh's house began to shoot at the building and with their constant firing destroyed some parts of the upper floors of that building. These clashes lasted a long time, and a large number of soldiers and civilians and a couple of people who were on the tanks were shot. Blood began to flow on the streets, but the sound of machine gun fire did not cease. At about six o'clock the tanks fired two heavy shells and a part of the upper floors of the building was destroyed. All the neighbouring houses were also shaking due to continuous machine gun and tank fire.

Eventually, the sound of firing from those buildings stopped, and the tanks moved towards Dr. Mossadegh's house. By this time 27 tanks had surrounded Dr. Mossadegh's house and a group of people were also following those tanks and were chanting slogans. There were also a number of officers and soldiers in front and at the side of those tanks. When the tanks got close to Dr. Mossadegh's house, there was heavy machine gun fire from his house, and it became clear that there were some fortifications there too. Firing from both sides continued for a while and a number of people were wounded.

The machine guns mounted on the tanks were firing constantly and the sound of firing never stopped. At this place, the clashes were between military personnel from both sides. Both sides resisted strongly. These clashes continued until the ammunition of the soldiers guarding Dr. Mossadegh's house who were firing from the other side of the wall apparently ran out, but the tanks were still firing. When the sound of machine gun fire stopped from the other side, one of the heavy tanks drove towards the gates of Dr. Mossadegh's house, smashed it, and entered the courtyard of the house. The firing from inside Dr. Mossadegh's house still continued, and the tanks responded to their fire.

About 7:30 the firing from inside Dr. Mossadegh's house ceased, and another tank entered the courtyard. At this time the tanks started to fire in the air and the crowds pushed back, but once again they returned. The military trucks carrying soldiers and the tanks that had surrounded Dr. Mossadegh's house entered the courtyard, but they could not find anyone there. The soldiers surrendered and said that their commander at the last moment had shot himself and committed suicide. Colonel Momtaz had also been hit by a bullet and had been killed.

After disarming the guards in Dr. Mossadegh's house, people rushed to the house and started to loot all the contents. Everybody took away whatever he could. In a few minutes, the entire house was destroyed and levelled with the ground. There was nothing left in it anymore. As the tanks got into the house, a tall man was trying to get out, but he was shot at and died on the spot. The bullet had shattered his brain.

The crowds then attacked the houses around Dr. Mossadegh's house, including his son's house. There was nobody there, but all the contents of those houses also disappeared in a few minutes and the houses were levelled with the ground. People attacked the Point Four building that belonged to Dr. Mossadegh from Pahlavi Street and plundered it too. At about 8:00 o'clock the sound of shooting stopped and the crowd gradually began to turn back, but before leaving they set fire to the buildings. Today we learned that Dr. Mossadegh's house is on fire and heavy smoke rises from it.

From the early hours on Thursday people began to go to Kakh Street to see Dr. Mossadegh's house, but the law-enforcement forces prevented them from getting close to the stone gates and inside the house. At the moment, nothing but ashes, a few beams and broken masonry can be seen from Dr. Mossadegh's house, which is situated on the northern side of Heshmat od-Dowleh Square and on Kakh Street. All the contents of the house have been completely looted or destroyed and all the doors and windows too have been burnt.

In the southern part of Dr. Mossadegh's house, where there is one of the Point Four buildings, the same has happened. Dr. Mossadegh is the owner of that house, which in the past had been rented to the Iran–Soviet Union Cultural Relations Society. Till yesterday that building housed one of Point Four's offices, but today it is a complete ruin. A number of burnt out cars that belonged to Point Four can be seen inside its courtyard. There is a half-burnt out steel chest in the courtyard and it is rumoured that it had contained money.

The house across the street from Dr. Mossadegh's belongs to an engineer who had spent a very frightful night due to the sound of shooting. Some bullets had hit his house and his doors and windows. He had hidden his children in the bathroom, in corridors and inside some carpets. The poor children had cried all night till morning. That engineer says that anytime he managed to calm his children there was another loud bang from the tanks or the machine guns. A neighbour of that engineer had moved away from his house early in the morning and the engineer says that he intends to move too.

There is a large building on the cross-section of Shah and Kakh Streets, in which nearly forty families live. As that house had been used as the first fortress of the soldiers guarding Dr. Mossadegh's house, and as they were firing from the grounds and the corridors of that building, the tanks had fired back at that building and all its doors and windows had been smashed. The residents of that five-story building say that during the exchange of fire they imagined that they were on a battlefield. All of them had gathered together and had been lying low behind the walls. As soon as the shooting stopped, a large number of people had attacked the building and had plundered anything they could find, and nothing had been left behind. They were amazed how the looters had managed to take the electricity counters and wires that had been connected to the electricity.

The Registry Office No. 102 that belonged to Enayatollah Shahandeh was also situated in that building, but all its furniture and documents had also been looted. The looters had even taken out the big safe that was in that building, had broken its lock by firing at it, and about 100 title-deeds, 150 identity cards and 250,000 rials in cash, postage stamps and other documents had also been taken. Today the residents of that building are trying to leave their houses and take away whatever has been left. Some people who had lost the entire contents of their houses were jealous of those who had something left.

The house of Dr. Gholam Hossein Mossadegh, Dr. Mossadegh's son, which was situated on the southern part of the Point Four building, has been completely destroyed and set on fire. Today, when people came to see that house, they felt very sad, as they said that it was a very beautiful and nicely decorated house, but today nothing is left of it except a ruin. If someone went to Kakh Street between Sardar Sangi and Heshmat od-Dowleh Square, which has been closed to the public, he could see the blood of yesterday's martyrs on the streets and pavements and pieces of their flesh that had been scattered all over the place. The smell of death covered the entire area.

Today, the owners of the houses near Dr. Mossadegh's house have come out of their houses and were inspecting the state of the streets. Most women and children, who had been made prisoners in their houses and who had been frightened as the result of the machine gun and tank fire and were crying, felt a bit calmer today.

A report will be prepared today or tomorrow about the number of the dead and injured and will be submitted to the prime minister. Up to midnight last night, 35 people had been killed, which included one woman, six soldiers and two officers. The exact figure of the injured has not yet been prepared, but it definitely exceeds 350.

On the orders of the coroner, all the bodies of the dead have been carried to the cemetery morgue between 12.00 and 4.00 o'clock this morning. (*Khandaniha*, quoted from *Keyhan*, 31 Mordad 1332 [25 August 1953]).

Ardeshir Zahedi further discusses the events of 28 Mordad in an interview with the prominent Iranian journalist Amir Taheri:

A Review of Certain Events That Changed the Course of History
• Was replacing Dr. Mossadegh with General Zahedi an American plot?
• What factors resulted in that change of government?
• Did Mossadegh's downfall come about as the result of a military coup?
• Did the CIA encourage the Shah to dismiss Mossadegh and replace him with Zahedi?
• Why was the publication of the "confidential report" about the CIA's involvement in Iran's domestic affairs regarded as an effort to take a stance against the ruling Iranian regime?

The telephone does not stop ringing and letters and messages are continuously pouring in on the fax machine. A number of friends are ready to serve, while a number of prominent figures from all over the world keep coming and going. A smart villa in a beautiful part of Switzerland where Ardeshir Zahedi lives is full of activity, as though nobody has heard that he has had no official position for the past 21 years and is living in exile.

Zahedi was the only son-in-law of the late Shah, as well as being one of his closest advisers for nearly a quarter of a century. He occupied some high-level posts, such as ambassador in London and Washington and minister of foreign affairs. In Tehran he was very much part of the Shah's inner circle. He tried to persuade the Shah to stand and fight against the alliance of the mullahs and the communists that came into being under the leadership of Ayatollah Ruhollah Khomeini. However, the Shah was suffering from the last stages of a chronic cancer and lacked the will to fight. Consequently, he decided to go on an uncertain exile and left Iran tossed in some of the most devastating storms of history. Zahedi says: "Defeat is always bitter, but defeat without even bothering to fight is the worst form of defeat." The bitterness of that experience was so profound that Zahedi, who is 72 years old, remained silent for two decades and refused all offers of interview, and even a multimillion-dollar proposal to write his memoirs.

Zahedi quotes Emperor Marcus Aurelius's words that "the biggest pains can be endured in the biggest silences." This is why now Zahedi has decided to keep his memoirs as a legacy for future generations. He has prepared some cases of notes and documents which he has deposited in a Swiss bank, on condition that none of them will be published before his death. At the same time, he has decided to follow political developments and he has maintained his contacts with a large number of people throughout the world. Many world leaders who visit Switzerland still go to see him. Many people phone him, not only for exchanging pleasantries, but also to learn of his views regarding many issues about which he is still an authoritative source. Nevertheless, he has been careful not to express an opinion about Iranian events or developments concerning Iran.

Recently, Zahedi agreed to receive us for "an unofficial chat," which later on took the form of an interview. While his deep, dark eyes revealed a mixture of excitement and the urge to explain, Zahedi said: "I have decided to break my vow of silence. I have come to the conclusion that we live in a world where silence is not the sign of honorable rejection, but is rather regarded either as a sign of guilt or acquiescence." After breaking his vow of silence, Zahedi sent an article to the *New York Times*, which was published in that newspaper. He has also taken part in a series of radio and television interviews.

The main reason for his recent activities was a long exclusive report published by the *New York Times* in connection with the events of August 1953 in Iran. It had been claimed that the article had been prepared on the basis of a secret report by Donald Wilber, a CIA agent, who had claimed that he had played a key role in those events.

Those events led to the removal of Dr. Mohammad Mossadegh as the nationalist prime minister of Iran by the Shah and his replacement with a retired army officer, General Fazlollah Zahedi. Following the publication of Wilber's report, U.S. Secretary of State Madeleine Albright in a speech apologized for America's "interference" in Iran's domestic affairs at that time.

Zahedi says that he was very unhappy to learn of Albright's sudden statement. He adds: "This lady has not performed her duty, but has dealt with a myth that has harmed Iranian–American relations for a whole generation."

Zahedi started his political activities as a 23-year-old young man as his father's right-hand man. In 1951 General Zahedi was minister of the interior in Dr. Mossadegh's government. Dr. Mossadegh was the prime minister who initiated the plan for nationalizing the Iranian oil industry. General Zahedi and Dr. Mossadegh had family ties and felt a great deal of respect for each other. Nobody would have believed that a year later those two would be each other's implacable foes during a critical period in Iran's recent history that resembled Greek tragedies.

In an exclusive interview, Ardeshir Zahedi expressed his views about those events. Here are a few excerpts from that interview:

Question: Is it true that the United States had planned the removal of Mossadegh and the replacing of him with your father?

Zahedi: The United States might have made such a plan, but what is important is to ascertain whether Mossadegh was toppled as the result of an American conspiracy or due to other factors. What I can state most emphatically is that Mossadegh's downfall was not due to a CIA plot. Of course, victory has a thousand fathers, but defeat is an orphan. If the events of August 1953 to remove Dr. Mossadegh from power had failed, would there be many "heroes" who would try to take credit for it? There are a large number of documents, including official American, Iranian, British, and Russian documents, and the testimony of many people who were involved in those events that refute the claims regarding the CIA's involvement in those events.

Question: Can you explain?

Zahedi: What happened in August 1953 in Tehran is briefly as follows. The political scene in Iran had been divided into two camps: Mossadegh's supporters and opponents. Those who were opposed to Mossadegh were looking for a leader and they found their leader in my father, who was a retired general, a former interior minister, and a former senator. The Shah was under a great deal of pressure by many leading figures and centers of power inside the country. The Shah had clashed with Mossadegh over the control of the armed forces. People seem to have forgotten that a year earlier, in July 1952, the Shah had dismissed Mossadegh and had replaced him with Ahmad Ghavam as prime minister. At that time, the street power leaned towards Mossadegh and Ghavam, who was an old man and was not able to withstand the pressure all by himself. The Shah was forced to reinstate Mossadegh.

Therefore, contrary to the claims, the idea to dismiss Mossadegh from power was not instilled in the Shah's mind by the CIA in 1953. In March 1953, by threatening that he would leave the country, the Shah took another step in the power play with Mossadegh. Those events resulted in massive demonstrations in favour of the Shah, which for the first time in many years moved like a wave against Mossadegh.

In other words, the Shah and Mossadegh, who at the beginning of the oil nationalization movement had close cooperation with each other, in 1952 had been turned into each other's political foes. In 1953, the political tide turned completely against Mossadegh.

Question: How did the political tide turn against Mossadegh?
Zahedi: Mossadegh had brought the country to a dead end. With the stop in oil revenue, the country was suffering from poverty, unemployment, and inflation. Mossadegh closed the Majles that had been elected during his term as prime minister. He announced that he had achieved absolute power and that he would run the country on the basis of government decree. Many of his key allies, including Mozaffar Baghai, Hossein Maleki, and Abol-Hassan Haerizadeh, all of whom were among the leaders of the oil nationalization movement, had deserted him. Haerizadeh even sent a telegram to the UN Secretary General and called on him to help "save Iran from Mossadegh's dictatorship."

The most prominent religious figures in the country, including the Grand Ayatollah Hossein Borujerdi, Ayatollah Abol-Ghassem Kashani, Ayatollah Mohsen Hakim-Tabatabai, Ayatollah Mohammad Behbahani, and Grand Ayatollah Shahrestani, had turned against Mossadegh because they are worried that Mossadegh's policies would ultimately bring the communists to power.

In the spring of the year 1953 my father was seen as the main leader of the anti-Mossadegh forces. Mossadegh offered a reward for my father's arrest, despite the fact that my father was constantly appearing in public and nobody bothered to cause any trouble for him. In fact, Mossadegh even lacked the power to arrest him. Nevertheless, for a few months the Shah resisted suggestions to depose

Mossadegh and appoint my father prime minister in his place, because he knew that my father would not be a prime minister who would blindly obey all commands. He was also frightened of repeating the experience of 1952.

Question: In CIA's report it has been stated that the Americans and the British were putting pressure on the Shah to appoint your father as prime minister.

Zahedi: Yes, I know about those claims. I don't know when and how the Americans and the British talked to the Shah about that issue. However, even if they did urge the Shah to appoint my father it was due to their awareness of what was going on. In any case, my father was the main leader of the anti-Mossadegh forces. Everybody in Iran knew that if Mossadegh were removed my father would take his place. This was like betting on a winning horse, and then claiming that they had arranged for the horse to win. The British had no reason to be in favor of my father. In fact, they did not like him at all.

During the Second World War, when the British and Russian forces invaded and occupied Iran, the British regarded my father as pro-German. The British carried out a plot to arrest my father in Isfahan, where my father was the commander of the armed forces in central Iran. They arrested him and exiled him to Palestine, which was a British mandate at that time. Fitzroy MacLean, the British officer who was in charge of the operations to arrest my father, described him as the "most dangerous Iranian" for the British. This is exactly the phrase that has been used by Sir Reader Bullard about my father in his memoirs.

The British had another reason to oppose General Zahedi. In the 1920s, my father was in charge of the forces that fought against a rebellious tribal leader that the British had installed in the oil producing province of Khuzestan with the hope of separating that province from Iran and turning it into an independent sheikhdom. However, the Americans had only limited acquaintance with my father, and there was no reason for them to either like or dislike him.

Question: The CIA's report states that your father went to the American Embassy in Tehran a number of times and on different occasions talked to American officials about the conspiracy against Mossadegh.

Zahedi: The only time that my father went to the American Embassy was in 1951, when he was the interior minister, in order to take part in a reception in honor of Averell Harriman, who had come to Iran as President Dwight David Eisenhower's representative with a proposal to end the oil crisis. There is no need to say that it is quite normal for ministers and other high-ranking officials to take part in such official ceremonies, which are mainly ceremonial rather than political. General Vernon Walters has written about that meeting in his 1978 autobiography, *Silent Missions*.

I can emphatically state that my father did not know any Americans and had never talked to any American official about Iran's political situation.

An example of the views of some of Mossadegh's main allies regarding him is a telegram sent by Abol-Hassan Haerizadeh to the UN secretary general, on 18th Mordad 1332 [9 August 1953], when he was a Majles deputy. Its text is as follows:

Your Excellency the Secretary General of the United Nations,
Dr. Mosaddegh who was appointed prime minister by the vote of the Iranian Parliament has been impeached by the Iranian national consultative assembly and held accountable on charges of beating, torturing and harming the prisoners, and violating the Human Rights Charter. As he felt that he did not have a majority on his side [in parliament], and contrary to the Iranian Constitution, he has refused to come to the parliament, and instead has dissolved the parliament. He has left no freedom of action or freedom of belief for anyone. He has jailed his opponents and has suspended the free press. With the use of the police and military forces and with the help of the Tudeh Party, and by using government assets he has carried out a referendum in the most disgraceful way, and through his agents he has filled the ballot boxes in the name of the people.
By relying on that inappropriate measure, Mr. Mosaddegh intends to put a violent, dictatorial communist regime in charge of the Iranian people. Our lives are in danger. We announce to the world that Mosaddegh is a rebel who, by relying upon force, does not refrain from committing any inhumane act. Whatever he does in the future, or any referendum that he might hold, would be against the wishes of the vast majority of the Iranian people. His government is illegitimate and his action will not be binding upon the Iranian nation.
[Signed] Haerizadeh, Minority Leader of the Parliament

On 22 May, 2000, a letter from Ardeshir Zahedi regarding the events of 28 Mordad was published in the *New York Times*. Below is the exact text.

On 16 April 2000, the New York Times published a story on what was presented as a "secret report" by a CIA operative concerning the events of August 1953 in Iran. The following article is written in the interest of historical truth and attempts to put those fateful events in Iran into prospect perspective.
At that time that the future of relations between Iran and the United States is, once again, debated in public, it is Important both sides steer clear of myths that have fostered so much misunderstanding between them.

One such myth has been woven around the claim by a few CIA operatives that they hatched a plot to get rid of Prime Minister Dr. Muhammad Mussadeq in August 1953 and (propelled my father, the later General Fazollah Zahedi into power with the Shah's blessings.) That claim, first made m the early 1960's and never corroborated by and hard evidence, has over the years found a niche in the historical folklore of both nations In a recent feature the New York Times gave the claim fresh publicity, relaunching the debate over what actually happened in Iran in those remote days of the Cold War.

Victory, of course, has a thousand fathers while defeat is an orphan Had the August 1953 efforts to remove Mussadeq from office failed, there would have been no CIA <heroes> claiming the credit.

There is a mass of evidence, including US and Iranian official documents and testimonies by people who played a role m the events that give the lie to the CIA operatives' chum. Briefly, what happened in August 1953 was as follows: the Iranian political establishment was divided betweeen supporters and opponents of Mussadeq. Mussadeq's opponents looked to the Shah for a rallying poin. My father who had served as Interior Minister in Mussadeq's Cabinet has broken with him and established himself as the leader of the anti-Mussadeq faction.

The Shah was thus under pressure from many powerful circles and personalities inside Iran to dismiss Mussadeq and name my father as the new prime minister. Mussadeq recognized my father as his chief adversary at the time and did all he could to break him.

Mussadeq had been abandoned by many of his former colleagues, among them such personalities as Hussein Makin and Muzzafar Baqru, and opposed by parties that had provided the backbone of his support in 1951.

The most prominent members of the Shiite clerical establishment, including the Ayatollahs Borujedi, Hakim, Shahresetani and Kashani were solidly opposed to Mussadeq and wanted the Shah to remove him. They were all in contact with my father and supported him in their struggle against Mussadeq

A leading member of the Majlis (parliament) Hassan Haeri-Zadeh, who had been one ofMussadeq's strongest supporters until then, even cabled the United Nations' secretary general to appeal for help against Mussadeq's increasingly despotic rule

The Shah had already clashed with Mussadeq's in 1952 and forced the <doctor> to resign as prime minister. At that time, however, the politics of the street had turned against the Shah and he had been obliged to reinstate Mussadeq. In August 1953 the tide had turned against Mussadeq who had further undermined

his own position by disbanding the parliament elected under his own steward-
ship.

The rest is history, as the saying goes. Or is it?

It is quite possible that the CIA and its British counterpart were engaged in the
usual dirty tricks campaign in Tehran. Tehran had become one of the hottest
theaters of the Cold War with the Soviet Union enjoying a strong presence
through a mass Communist Party (the Tudeh), several front organizations and
at least four daily newspapers

The Communists had also infiltrated the armed forces and the police, recruiting
over 700 officers and NCOs.

What is certain is that Mussadeq's fall was not due to any dirty tricks that the
CIA might have played. Nor did the CIA have the kind of access its operatives
claim to have had to the key figures of the revolt against Mussadeq including
my father The only time my father visited the US embassy in Tehran was a
function m honor of Averell Harriman on 4th of July 1951, and in his capacity
as interior minister. Harriman had come to Tehran with a mission from President Harry Truman to persuade Mussadeq to find a way out of the crisis over
the nationalization of Iranian oil. (Cf. Vernon Walters in <Silent Missions>).

My father never had any meetings with any CIA agents. One operative has
claimed that he spoke to my father in German, ostensibly during secret meetings. The fact is that the only foreign languages my father ever spoke were Russian and Turkish, not German or English

Iranian history remembers my father as a true patriot who wore the wounds he
had won in battle like so many badges of honor. Fazollah Zahedi had fought for
virtually every inch of what he regarded as the sacred land of Iran, against a Bol-
shevik-sponsored regime along the Caspian coast to a British sponsored seces-
sionist movement in the oil rich province of Khuzestan. During the Second
World War had become a war prisoner of the British and sent into captivity and
exile in Palestine, then under British mandate. Fazollah Zahedi was always big
enough to fight his own fights, backed by his own loyal friends

To try and portray such a giant of Iran's contemporary history into a bit player
in a scenario fit for <Missionn Impossible> requires a degree of cynicism that
only frustrated egomaniacs might master.

Throughout the dramatic events that led to the fall of Mussadeq, I was at my
father's side as one of his principal political aides> Had he been involved in any
foreign intrigue I would have known, he was not.

Roy Henderson, the US ambassador to Tehran at the time, makes it abundantly
clear in his dispatches to the State Department that Mussadeq was overthrown
by a popular uprising which started from the poorest districts of the Iranian

capital. Henderson's reports have been published in a book of more than 1000 pages, translated into Persian and published in Iran.

The Iranian public, therefore, has a more balanced view of the events than its American counterpart which is fed recycled claims by former CIA operatives British and Soviet accounts at the time also make it clear that Mussadeq had fallen victim to his own hubris which antagonized his allies and forced the Iranian people into revolt.

More than 100 books, by Iraman and Amencan scholars, give the lie to the CIA operatives' selfcongratulatory account.

Barry Rubin writes "It cannot be said that the United States overthrew Mussadeq and replaced him with the Shah Overthrowing Mussadeq was like pushing an open door "

Gary Sick writes "The belief that the United States had single-handedly imposed a harsh tyrant on a reluctant populace became one of the central myths of the relationship, particularly as viewed from Iran

Amir Taheri writes "What happened was not a successful conclusion of a (CIA) conspiracy but a genuine uprising provoked by economic hardship, political fear and religious prejudice "

Richard Helms, long time CIA director, told a BBC television program that the agency did not counter rumors of in Iran because the Iranian episode looked like a success. At the time, of course, agency needed some success, especially to counter fiascoes as the Bay of Pigs

Even Donald Wilber, the CIA operative whose <secret report> has been given top billing by the NYT makes it clear that whatever he and his CIA colleagues were up to m Tehran at the time simply failed

Wilber writes: headquarters spent a day featured by depression and despair . The message sent to Tehran on the night of August 18 said that the operation has been tried and failed and that contrary operationns against Mussadeq should be discontunued."

Mussadeq was overthrown on 19 August when hundreds of thousands of Tehranis poured into the streets to demand his departure and the return of the Shah. This was not a military coup d'etat since there was no change in the constitution or any of the structures of the Iranian state. Nor was the Shah's position as head of state affected Under the constitution of 1906 the Shah had the power to name and dismiss prime ministers. He simply exercised that power by dismissing Mussadeq and nominating Zahedi in a perfectly legal and consitutional manner . Mussadeq tried to resist his dismissal but was swept away by the masses.

The army played a supportive role in the anti-Mussadeq uprising and even then only after the people had taken the initiative. At the time my father was no longer on active service, having retired from the armed forces and engaged in political activities as a senator and leader of the anti-Mussadeq coalition. Mussadeq himself held the portfolio of Defense and enjoyed the support of many key officers of the armed forces, including the Chief of Staff appointed by himself

Anyone who has studied the history of the turbulent years would also know that Mussadeq was the most pro-American senior politician Iran had produced He was the darling of the Truman Administration which raised the amount of aid to Iran, distributed through Point 4, from half a million dollars to 23 million dollars On August 18, 1953, a day before Mussadeq fell, Henderson met Mussadeq and offered him an emergency loan of 10 million dollars on behalf of the Eisenhower Administration.

Mussadeq himself never blamed the Americans for his downfall. He was intelligent enough to know why his political career led into an impasse

The anti-Mussadeq coalition did, of course, look to the United States, as the leader of the Free World, to counter any more than the soviets might have, made at the time to intervene in what was a domestic Iranian power struggle Form a geostrategic point of view, therefore, the anti-Mussadeq coalition regarded itself as part of the Free World. But does that mean that all those who fought Communism and upheld the cause of liberty throughout the Cold War were manipulated by the CIA?

Three years ago the CIA announced that almost all of its documents pertaining to the August 1953 events in Iran had been destroyed in a fire Was someone trying to cover up the CIA's most dramatic <success story>? Or did the documents burn because the good ambiance created by the Iranian myth that had been fabricated by a few individuals with a lot of imagination and very little of scruples?

Ayatollah Kashani's reflections on Mossadegh are mentioned in *A Collection of Writings, Lectures and Messages of Ayatollah Kashani*, edited by Mohammad Dehnavi (Chappakhsh Publications).

In Mordad 1332 [August 1953], the reporter of *al-Mahdi* newspaper asked the following question of Ayatollah Kashani, "Do you believe that Dr. Mossadegh is trying to establish a republican system in Iran?"
Ayatollah Kashani replied, "Four months ago, Mossadegh wanted to expel the Shah from Iran. However, I wrote a letter to the Shah and asked him not to

leave the country, and he also temporarily changed his mind about leaving the country. A week ago, Mossadegh forced the Shah to leave the country, but a day later the Shah returned with dignity and popularity."

Ayatollah Kashani then said, "Here the nation likes the Shah and a republican system is not appropriate for Iran."

Around the same period, the Voice of America also interviewed Ardeshir Zahedi about the same events.

Question: Your Excellency Mr. Ardeshir Zahedi, thank you for taking part in this interview. As a person who was completely aware of the situation in Iran during the events of 28 Mordad [19 August 1953], please tell us what the reasons were for Dr. Mohammad Mossadegh's removal as the prime minister of Iran?

Zahedi: There is a famous saying in Persian, namely "he who goes to the judge alone normally returns happy." What the *New York Times* published recently was based on a confidential report of a CIA agent regarding the events of 25–28 Mordad [16–19 August 1953], in which an attempt was made to make the role of Donald Wilber, the CIA agent, to be seen as important as possible. Nevertheless, Donald Wilber himself writes that the plan prepared by the CIA and Britain to topple Dr. Mossadegh failed. What eventually resulted in Mossadegh's removal was the uprising by the Iranian people on 28 Mordad, which started in the poorest parts of Tehran.

Before 28 Mordad, Mossadegh had reached a complete dead-end. He could not resolve the oil crisis, and he rejected every proposal that was made, lest his popularity would be damaged; while my father believed that a patriotic and honorable person would sacrifice himself for his country and not sacrifice his country for his interests. My father was opposed to communism and to any other isms. Mossadegh lost every opportunity for resolving the oil crisis in Iran's favor. By increasing the level of production in Persian Gulf littoral states, the oil companies filled the vacuum that had been created as the result of the stoppage of Iranian oil exports.

Mossadegh acted like a dictator. He closed down the senate, the consultative assembly [the parliament] and the supreme court. By relying on martial law, he jailed all his opponents and closed scores of newspapers. As a result, towards the end of his rule, no one remained with him. All the political, military, and especially the most prominent religious figures of the time—such as Ayatollah Kashani, Ayatollah Hakim and Ayatollah Shahrestani—were strongly opposed to Mossadegh, and had called on the Shah to depose him. They were in touch with my father and they supported his efforts to confront Mossadegh. This is why

Mossadegh was toppled very easily, as he had no other backers except for the guards that protected his house and the Tudeh [Communist] Party.

Question: Mr. Zahedi, in your recent writings and interviews, including what you wrote in the *New York Times*, you have claimed that the events of 28 Mordad were the result of a spontaneous uprising that started with the people's movement in the poorer areas in the south of Tehran. Could you please elaborate on this a little further?

Zahedi: In this connection, I urge you to examine the National Film Archives in Washington. These archives have scores of hours of news films about the events of 25–28 Mordad. Those films have been produced by some international organizations, such as Paramount and Vis News. They show that the real players in the events of 28 Mordad were working people. You will also see that there is no sign of the military or police, but only of many brave, valiant and patriotic Iranian people. The army and the police got involved in the developments after Mossadegh had fled and the 28 Mordad uprising had succeeded.

Also the confidential cables of Henderson, the U.S. Ambassador in Tehran, to Washington refer to people's slogans in support of the Shah and against Mossadegh. On 28 Mordad there were nearly 50 foreign reporters from all over the world in Tehran, including from the *New York Times*. Furthermore, none of the famous Iranian journalists, such as Abdol-Rahman Faramarzi, Amidi-Nuri, the Hashemi brothers, Dr. Rahmat Mostowfi, Taraghi, etc. have ever used the term coup d'état to describe the events of that day, nor have they referred to the CIA or the British. Were all of them CIA agents?

Some people have claimed that the Americans took control of Iran by spending $100,000. Since 2003, the Americans have spent more than 248 billion dollars in Iraq, and still have not got very far. More than 100 books have been written about the events in Iran, especially the book on the secret documents of the State Department from 1952–54. You can also refer to Seyyed Abol-Hassan Haerizadeh's cable to the secretary general of the United Nations, in which he referred to Mossadegh as a rebel, or you can read the letters of Mr. Lotfi, Mossadegh's minister of justice, and Dr. Alami, his minister of labor.

I must tell you that the truth of the matter is that history will not be written by a few plotters and demagogues, but by the masses. Some published documents, such as the books written by Dr. Mozaffar Baghai and Hossein Makki, show that my father brought about the release of Mossadegh and some others from prison enabling them to take part in the election in Tehran when he was elected as a Majlis deputy. Baghai, Makki and Haerizadeh were among Mossadegh's strongest supporters, but they and others gradually experienced Mossadegh's hostility.

You should remember that the Shah appointed Mossadegh as prime minister and signed the decree of his appointment. My father served as the minister of the interior in that cabinet. The Shah signed the decree of oil nationalization. Again, it should not be forgotten that my father clashed with the British even before Mossadegh did, and during the oil nationalization campaign my father was always in favor of it.

My father was the conqueror of Khuzestan and in fact he returned the oil to Iran, and the British never forgave him for that. Zahedi was the victor in the war against the Bolsheviks in Gilan. Also, he emerged victorious in the war in Azerbaijan against Semitqu, and was awarded the unique Zolfaghar Medal. He put an end to the war against the Qashqais and the Bakhtiaris without any bloodshed. During the British occupation of Iran, my father was arrested due to his patriotic feelings and was exiled to Palestine. After the parliamentary election, when a minority faction was formed, my father became a senator and later on he served as the minister of interior in Mossadegh's cabinet.

During the Tudeh Party's attack on the parliament and their occupation of the Majlis police station, Mossadegh wished to dismiss the head of the police, General Baghai, as a sign of support for the Tudeh Party, but my father refused to do so and resigned his post as the minister of the interior. After a speech that my father made in the Senate in 1330 [1951] against Mossadegh, the latter closed down the senate, declared martial law in Tehran and Shemiranat, and imprisoned my father. Later on, my father took asylum in the Majles building and took part in a sit-in there.

Finally, when Dr. Moazzemi, on behalf of Dr. Mossadegh, guaranteed my father's safety he left the Majlis in Dr. Moazzemi's car and came to our house in Hesarak. The same night, the officials of Mossadegh's military governor attacked our house in Hesarak, but fortunately they could not find my father. After that event my father remained in hiding, until Wednesday 28 Mordad when the brave people took part in demonstrations on 27 and 28 Mordad against Dr. Mossadegh and in support of the Shah, and marched from the south of Tehran to the north.

Mossadegh's military forces attacked the unarmed people and shot and killed or wounded more than 300 peaceful people of Tehran. We had in fact planned to leave Tehran for Isfahan or Kermanshah, but people rose up from Tuesday 27 Mordad, and my father said that there was no need for such an action, as the brave people had woken up.

On August 21, 1953, *Le Monde* published the following report on the fall of Mossadegh:

Paris, 20 août 1953
BULLETIN DE L'ÉTRANGER
LA FIN DE MOSSADEGH
Le 19 août à l'aube le Dr Mossadegh contrôlait la situation après l'échec du coup d'Etat militaire d'il y a trois jours. Le même jour à midi son régime s'écroulait.

Des manifestations royalistes commencées par quelques jeunes gens sont allées en s'amplifiant jusqu'à ce que l'arrivée de détachements militaires rassemblés en toute hâte par le général Zahedi eût permis de transformer la bagarre de rue en révolution.

A la stupéfaction générale ni la police ni l'armée n'ont réagi pour défendre le Dr Mossadegh. La foule, un instant indécise, a rapidement pris parti pour les plus forts, c'est-à-dire pour les royalistes.

Toute la résistance s'est limitée à quelques centaines de soldats constituant la garde personnelle du premier ministre et ayant des raisons non moins personnelles d'empêcher le renversement de ce dernier.

L'explication de ce prodigieux renversement est simple : la défection du parti Toudeh.

Jusque-là le Dr Mossadegh avait — comme toujours depuis deux ans — balayé en un clin d'œil la tentative de rébellion. Mais personne ne pouvait se faire d'illusions : cette victoire du premier ministre n'était plus due à l'unanimité des partis nationalistes groupés derrière lui, mais uniquement à l'appui lucide et délibéré du parti d'extrême gauche.

C'est ainsi que le Dr Mossadegh se trouva placé devant une cruelle alternative. La consolidation de son succès exigeait que la répression antiroyaliste fût poursuivie jusqu'au bout. Mai si le chah fugitif était déchu, la République instituée, tôt ou tard le bénéficiaire de l'opération eût été la parti Toudeh.

Celui qui mérita si longtemps le surnom de « vieux renard » crut pouvoir une fois de plus temporiser. Ajournant la décision de constituer un conseil de régence, le premier ministre entreprit de créer une opposition capable de disputer la rue à l'extrême gauche.

Cette erreur lui fut fatale. Dès 11 heures du matin hier le correspondant de l'agence France-Presse signalait que « les hésitations du gouvernement redonnaient courage à l'opposition et aux monarchistes, qui déclaraient ouvertement que le prochain coup d'Etat réussirait »...

Bientôt le bruit courut que le gouvernement préparait des mesures de rigueur contre le Toudeh. Peu après on apprenait même que les leaders du parti hitlérien « Sumka » avaient été relâchés. Cette mesure indiquait que le gouvernement n'hésitait pas pour faire échec au parti Toudeh à faire appel à des éléments factieux, mêmes fidèles au chah.

Le résultat ne se fit pas attendre : pas un seul extrémiste de gauche ne descendit dans la rue pour défendre le régime Mossadegh.

La chute de ce dernier — comme ses deux années de pouvoir — aura prouvé une fois de plus la puissance de l'organisation paracommuniste : le Toudeh soutient Mossadegh, et ce dernier triomphe de tous ses adversaires ; qui'il le lâche, et c'est l'effondrement du régime...

En réalité depuis longtemps déjà l'idéal nationaliste soutenu par le Dr Mossadegh avait été vidé de son contenu : il ne restait plus sous cette terminologie que la lutte contre l'impérialisme, c'est-à-dire le mot d'ordre par excellence du parti d'extrême gauche.

Comment les nouveaux maîtres de l'Iran parviendront-ils à lever cette hypothèque? L'armée sans doute va renforcer les mesures de répression contre le Toudeh. Oubliera-t-elle que c'est la clandestinité qui a renforcé le parti paracommuniste?

Le général Zahedi devra aussi liquider la question du pétrole. Or les grandes compagnies pétrolières — anglaises comme américaines — ont pris leur parti de l'absence du pétrole iranien ; la réouverture des puits du Khouzistan ne manquerait pas d'embarrasser les grands cartels, qui redoutent par-dessus tout la production.

Enfin, si le Dr Mossadegh a dû pendent plusieurs mois son pouvoir à l'appui des partis d'extrême gauche jusqu'au point d'être leur prisonnier, le chah, qui aujourd'hui doit son trône aux éléments militaires, religieux, voire réactionnaires, pourra-t-il échapper plus aisément à leurs exigences?

Below is the text of an article by Seyyed Mahmud Kashani, Ayatollah Kashani's son, about the events of August 1953, published in *Nimruz Weekly*, issue 827, Friday 28 Esfand 1383 [18 March 2005], published in London, quoted from *Shargh* newspaper, published in Tehran:

> **The allegation of coup d'état against Mossadegh is deceitful. Regarding the holding of a referendum and the dissolution of the Majles: did Mossadegh merely make a mistake?**
>
> When the Shah left for Rome and then decided to return to the country following Mossadegh's downfall, he sent a telegram to His Eminence Ayatollah Borujerdi. In response to that telegram Ayatollah Borujerdi wrote, "The blessed presence of His Imperial Majesty, may God bless his rule! The blessed telegram that you had sent from Rome, which contained the news of the health of His Impe-

rial Majesty, made me very happy. As you had decided to return immediately, there was some delay in my response. I hope that the felicitous arrival of His Imperial Majesty in Iran will be blissful and will correct religious ills and will enhance the glory of Islam and the well-being of Muslims." [Signed] Hossein Tabatabai-Borujerdi.

Of course, in my view, the decision of His Eminence to respond to the Shah's telegram was absolutely a correct move and was due to his sympathy for the country and the nation. Everybody knows that Grand Ayatollah Borujerdi, who was the source of emulation for all the Shi'is throughout the world, never interfered directly in political issues, but at the same time he was constantly in touch with political and religious developments in the country. In those years and before the Islamic Revolution, the monarchic system enjoyed complete legitimacy, and none of the *ulema* was interested in toppling it. Therefore, as has been the case throughout Iranian history, the *ulema* had a great influence over political issues and national security.

One should also bear in mind that Mossadegh's coalition with the Russian and British-backed Tudeh Party after the victorious uprising of 30th Tir 1331 [21 July 1952], which resulted in a massive protest by the leaders of the [National] Movement, greatly strengthened that illegal party and put it at the service of Mossadegh's programmes, which were contrary to the interests of the nation. Gradually, the main figures of the Iranian National Movement, who had been responsible for its victory, were forced out of the political arena. The Tudeh Party was turned into an unrivalled political party in the country, and each day it engaged in showmanship and demonstrated the extent of its power, which caused a great deal of concern among patriotic people and religious leaders. The show of force by that party in the religious city of Qom forced people to confront it, and the ensuing clashes resulted in the death and injury of a number of people.

In view of those developments, a prominent religious figure, such as Grand Ayatollah Borujerdi, was quite entitled to respond to the Shah's telegram, and to express his happiness at the ending of that tragic and dangerous chapter in Iran's history. In fact, it was necessary for him to do so. It is clear that, contrary to what has been claimed, Grand Ayatollah Borujerdi's attitude towards the Shah and his clear and logical stances towards the government did not weaken the clerical institution. At the same time, they strengthened the pillars of national security.

Historical events must be reported exactly as they were. Those who claim to be experts in history must not undermine the lofty position of high-ranking religious figures of the country in order to defend their own prejudices.

The dissolution of the Majles

As some people are trying to make use of any means possible to justify Mossadegh's dissolution of the Majles, which was against freedom and democracy, it should be remembered that Mossadegh's government had itself held the election for the 17th Majles. It repeatedly claimed that eighty per cent of Majles deputies were true representatives of the people. Basically, how can a prime minister who owes his position to the vote of confidence passed by the same Majles declare that Majles illegitimate and describe it as a parliament that tried to block government's efforts?

Of course, Mossadegh himself never openly accused Majles deputies of being the lackeys of the court or of accepting bribes, especially as most Majles deputies were his supporters. The Majles is the main foundation of the constitutional law and the democratic system. Therefore, there is a serious question that Mossadegh should have answered as to why he dissolved the Majles on the basis of an illegal referendum that was strongly opposed by many loyal and opposition MPs in the parliament.

Mossadegh's decision to dissolve the Majles goes back to Dey 31 [January 1952], when, making use of his legislative powers, he signed a resolution that increased the number of Majles deputies from 136 to 172. As there were only 79 MPs in the 17th Majles because the government had prevented elections from being held in 56 constituencies, the Majles was automatically dissolved. As a result, a number of MPs who were concerned about that situation submitted a bill with three urgencies, asking that the new government resolution should not apply to the 17th Majles. However, Dr. Mossadegh reacted harshly to that resolution, and his Interior Minister Dr. Sadighi was forced to announce in the Majles session on 23rd Dey 31 [13 January 1953] that "there is no intention whatsoever to dissolve or paralyse the Majles...."

However, the decision to dissolve the Majles became clear to all on 6th Tir 32 [27 June 1953]. Some of Mossadegh's colleagues, including the Majles Speaker Dr. Moazzemi, who enjoyed Mossadegh's support, emphatically asked him to change his mind.

It is instructive to read the memoirs of two of Mossadegh's aides in this connection. In an exclusive interview, Dr. Sanjabi said that he had been opposed to holding the referendum. In response to the question as to how he expressed his opposition to the holding of the referendum to Dr. Mossadegh, Dr. Sanjabi said, "I have explained it in my book. He asked my view about the referendum, arguing that the present Majles would go against us, and he explained his views about going through the method of holding a referendum. I answered, 'First of all, you have a large majority in the Majles, and you should not have any worries from that quarter. However, in the case of the referendum, your position relies upon the Majles. If there is no Majles, the Shah would have a freer hand to act sooner against your government, especially as it is customary that during the period when the Majles is not functioning the Shah will be in charge of appointing and dismissing the prime ministers, which of course is quite natural and logical.' His only answer to me was 'the Shah does not dare do that.'"

Also, in an interview with a scholar who was engaged in research on contemporary Iranian history, Dr. Gholam Hossein Sadighi said that he too had been against the referendum and the dissolution of the Majles. In response to the question as to how he had conveyed his opposition to Dr. Mossadegh, Dr. Sadighi said, "I told him, 'As you have been in charge of holding the election for this Majles, and you have also stressed that 80 per cent of Majles deputies are true representatives of the people, and as so far this Majles has also approved all your bills and has carried out your views, then from a moral point of view you should not dissolve the Majles.' I gave a second reason for my opposition to the dissolution of the Majles. I said, 'A few months ago, the question was raised in the Majles as to whether the government intended to dissolve it or not; as the interior minister, I strongly and categorically rejected that allegation. Therefore, I am not able to do this, and if you intend to dissolve the Majles you should ask someone else to do the job for you.' Dr. Mossadegh emphatically asked me not to speak of my opposition to his plan for the next two days, which fell on Thursday and Friday. He said that we would discuss the matter again, and that if we could not reach an agreement then I would be free to adopt any stance that I wished. I agreed to his request.

Yet, during those two days he ordered Majles deputies to resign, and between 30 and 40 deputies resigned, and ultimately this number exceeded 58 MPs. On the following Saturday when we had arranged to meet, Dr. Mossadegh said, 'Sir, we do not wish to dissolve the Majles. The deputies have decided to resign by themselves. The country cannot continue without the Majles, and I will ask the people to express their views whether the Majles should remain or be dissolved in a referendum.' I agreed with that suggestion and the referendum was held."

I asked Sadighi about his other reasons for his opposition to the referendum. He said, "My third and last reason was that I told Dr. Mossadegh, 'Forty-seven years have passed from 1285 [1906] to the present time (1952). If we allow the present Majles to continue to the end of its normal life, the period that the Majles has functioned will come to 34 years [there were 17 Majles sessions, and each session's term was only two years in those days]. In other words, for the remaining 14 years the Majles has been suspended. During that period, the

Shah alone has appointed the prime ministers. Therefore, after holding a referendum and dissolving the Majles, the Shah will issue a decree to remove you.' Dr. Mossadegh replied, 'The Shah does not dare do that.'"

These examples show that all of Mossadegh's friends were against the dissolution of the Majles. They went as far as warning Mossadegh about the likelihood of the Shah issuing a decree to dismiss him. Mossadegh was fully aware of the consequences of the dissolution of the Majles, and he did not deny that in case the Majles was dissolved, the Shah could dismiss him as prime minister and could appoint another person in his place. His only argument against his friends was that "the Shah does not dare do that." However, he did not think what the fate of the country, the nation, and the National Movement would be if the Shah did dare to dismiss him, to which Mossadegh had tied his fate.

Now, let us move forward to see what happened after Mossadegh dismissed the warnings of his friends—and of course later on all of them co-operated with him in that unpatriotic act—and how those who had opposed the dissolution of the Majles reacted.

Seyyed Abol-Hassan Haerizadeh, the leader of the most important opposition group in the Majles, on 7th Tir 32 [28 June 1953], a day after Mossadegh had threatened to dissolve the Majles, strongly criticised that decision. He said, "No legal power in the country has the authority to issue a decree to dissolve the Majles. Neither the Shah, nor the prime minister, nor anyone else has the authority to do this. There is only one way for dissolving the Majles, namely through the armed forces of a dictator, such as Mohammad Ali Shah, who fired cannonballs at the Majles."

In a long statement, Ayatollah Kashani also took a stance against the dissolution of the Majles. In a part of that statement he wrote, "During the past few days, it has become clear that the head of the executive has summoned Majles deputies and under the excuse of a state of emergency has threatened to suspend the Majles and the Constitution. However, I wish to inform you, the Iranian people, that the Constitutional Movement will never die. I have sworn an oath to my God that so long as I am alive I will not separate myself from you people, and that I will continue to my last breath my struggle against the foreigners, a struggle that I have been engaged in for many years. I am certain that in this battle between despotism and freedom, the Iranian nation will emerge victorious" (quoted from *Ettela'at* newspaper, 9th Tir 1332 [30 June 1953]).

Also on 7th Mordad [29 July 1953], in another long statement in protest against the holding of the referendum, Ayatollah Kashani wrote, "The stronger the foundations of the Constitution, of the nationalist government, and of the methods of parliamentary consultation and taking part in a powerful govern-

ment, the better will a weak nation be able to safeguard the pillars of its independence, self-government, national unity and territorial integrity. On the other
hand, the greater the domination of despotic rule, the weaker will be the pillars
of independence and of national unity. No powerful foreign government can
obtain something from a country that is against its national interests, but foreign governments can easily obtain it from a single individual."

Ayatollah Kashani also organised lectures in his house, which acted as the headquarters of the struggles of the Iranian National Movement and of the campaigns against Ahmad Ghavam, on 30 and 31 Tir [21 and 22 July 1953] in
order to warn the nation. However, despite the fact that those meetings were
peaceful and represented the least rights of the Iranian nation to the freedom of
expression and protesting against the dissolution of the Majles, for a number of
successive nights, mercenary groups and club-wielders associated with the government and with foreign governments attacked the people taking part in those
meetings. Finally, when a number of people had been attacked and beaten up
and one of Ayatollah Kashani's supporters was killed, he was forced to announce
in a press conference that he would stop the lectures in order to protect people's
lives. At the same time, he strongly criticised the referendum and the dissolution
of the Majles.

On 10th Mordad 32 [1 August 1953], Dr. Mozaffar Baghai and Ali Zahri, two
Majles deputies from Tehran, who had taken asylum in the Majles as they were
worried that they might be arrested by Mossadegh, in an open letter to him
wrote, "If the prime minister gives up his dangerous decision to dissolve the
Majles, we are prepared immediately to resign our membership of the Majles
and to surrender ourselves directly to your prisons" (*Ettela'at* newspaper, 10th
Mordad 32).

However, as Mossadegh had already taken the decision to dissolve the Majles
and to carry out his program he did not respond to that proposal, which would
have deprived him of another excuse for dissolving the Majles. Finally, Ayatollah Kashani, who had exhausted all options to fight against the dissolution of
the Majles and who saw that all the doors were closed on the supporters of the
Iranian National Movement, issued a statement in which he banned participation in the referendum. He described it as a "devastating plan that has been
drawn up with the help of foreigners" (*Ettela'at* newspaper, 10th Mordad 32).
Under such circumstances of suppression and dictatorship, Mossadegh carried
out his referendum on 12th Mordad (3 August 1953] in Tehran. In order to
intimidate the opponents of the dissolution of the Majles, he violated the principle that has been recognised in all democratic systems and in all electoral laws,
namely that voting should be carried out in secret. The ballot boxes for those

who wished to vote in favour of the dissolution of the Majles were placed in Sepah Square, and the ballot boxes for those who opposed it were placed in Sepahsalar Mosque (in Baharestan Square).

Le Monde newspaper, published in Paris in its edition of 4 August 1953, reported the undemocratic methods used for holding the referendum and the effective call by Ayatollah Kashani on the people not to take part in it. Of course, those who voted for the dissolution of the Majles and who also supported that decision in their newspapers were mainly the supporters of the Tudeh Party. It was under such circumstances that Dr. Mozaffar Baghai wrote a letter Dr. Sadighi on 21st Mordad [12 August 1953] and reminded him of his remarks in the Majles session on 23rd Dey 31 [13 January 1953], when he had assured the Majles that the government would under no circumstances dissolve or paralyse the Majles. In that letter, he called on him, saying that as the minister of interior who had made that promise he should refuse to publish the result of the referendum. In the same letter, he referred to the dissolution of the Majles as "Mossadegh's historic treason." These historical documents, a small part of which has been quoted here, show that the dissolution of the Majles by the prime minister was an illegal and unpatriotic move, which had been criticised by many of his close friends. They also show that Ayatollah Kashani and other Majles deputies who were opposed to the referendum fought against it with courage and self-sacrifice as much as they could. Yet Mr. Baqi writes: "Mossadegh did not dissolve the Majles with military force!" Of course, what he says is correct from a technical point of view. Mossadegh did not imitate Mohammad Ali Shah's example of making use of the Russian method of shelling the Majles by Colonel Liakhoff's forces, because our country had experienced the failure of that method. This time, the dissolution of the Majles was carried out on the basis of a method and a diplomacy that had been guided by Britain and by making use of some deceptive slogans, such as "defending freedom," "advancing national aspirations," "the Majles is not a place for disrupting the work of the government," and "asking the views of the public." This time, it was carried out by making use of government's power, putting pressure on the majority of Majles deputies and making use of their weaknesses, sending thugs and club-wielders to Ayatollah Kashani's house and to the headquarters of the Iranian National Movement, threatening opposition deputies, and making use of the organised forces of the Tudeh Party.

These methods are much more dangerous than shelling the Majles building. Mossadegh's supporters, who have praised him over the past 50 years and have described his government as a symbol of democracy and liberalism, now that the facts are being revealed, are trying somehow to justify his actions. Mr. Baqi writes, "Some of Mossadegh's friends such as … criticised the holding of the referendum by Dr. Mossadegh, but have not accused him of treachery.…"

We should add that some other people have also regarded the dissolution of the Majles as one of Mossadegh's mistakes. In the papers that Mr. Seyyed Moham-mad Khatami published in Ordibehesht 1383 [May 2004] under the title of "A letter for the future," he writes, "A number of westernised individuals under the name of Mossadegh and a number of opportunistic opponents of freedom have stolen people's genuine movement in the name of freedom…"

After all those protests and warnings by Mossadegh's friends and the strong opposition of his opponents, can the dissolution of the Majles be regarded as a mere mistake? Mistake has a clear linguistic and political meaning. How could Mossadegh, who was familiar with the history of the Iranian Constitutional Movement and the Fundamental Law, have dissolved the Majles, which was the main base of his premiership and of the Iranian National Movement, by making just a simple mistake? In my personal view, Mossadegh was completely aware of the consequences of the dissolution of the Majles, and he knew very well that one of its first consequences would be a decree by the Shah dismissing him as prime minister and replacing him with someone else. In that case, how could one explain this illegal and unpatriotic act? We should examine the course of events after the dissolution of the Majles.

The claim regarding the staging of a coup d'état

Before examining the true nature of the events of the days from 24–28 Mordad 32 [15–19 August 1953] I would like to point out that no historic event could be attributed to the actions and wishes of a particular political group and then have its file closed and sealed forever. Today, research in all scientific and social fields and different aspects of a nation's life is revolutionising learning and pro-ducing great advances in scientific and technological fields. Historical research cannot be an exception to that rule. Those who regard themselves as supporters of "pluralism" and "reform" in political, cultural and social fields cannot stick to a rigid interpretation of history and impose their views, even if they enjoy exten-sive consensus by historians, on others.

The use of the term coup d'état as a way of describing the events of Mordad, which has achieved the status of a dogma as the result of 50 years of propaganda and the publication of numerous books and articles about it and is often re-peated by many people when referring to those events, is completely incorrect. Even those who have used that term as a way of describing those events have had different interpretations of it and have accused different individuals of hav-ing been involved in it. I should add that for many years in my historical writ-ings that have been published before 1360 [1981] I have also used the term coup d'état. However, this does not mean that the Iranian nation is not entitled to carry out new research in those historic events and review and revise its views about the events that I regard as being the most complex and the most important issues in Iran's contemporary history.

Fortunately, the reassessment of the history of those events has already started in Iran and in many other countries. Only one particular political line and a special group in the United States, which we cannot deal with here, insists that the statement issued by Mossadegh's government alleging that a coup d'état had been staged on the morning of 25 Mordad 1332 (16 August 1953) has been the only correct version of events. Many scholars who are interested in those events have raised a number of important questions. One question is how did Dr. Mossadegh, who after the events of 30th Tir 1331 [21 July 1952] when he had resigned as prime minister and had retired to his house and, according to the press, had locked himself in and had cut off his contacts with the outside world, manage to regain his position as prime minister? It should be borne in mind that the Shah had issued a decree appointing Ahmad Ghavam as prime minister. The Shah had full control over the military forces and was present in the country. Then how was it that as the result of the victorious uprising of 30th Tir, led by Ayatollah Kashani and a number of Majles deputies belonging to the minority faction, Ahmad Ghavam's government collapsed and Dr. Mossadegh was restored to power? Then, how was it possible, despite his being firmly in position as prime minister and also holding the post of the minister of defence, being in control of the armed forces, the police and the gendarmerie, acquiring the legislative powers from the Majles and then dissolving it, as well as dissolving the Supreme Court, and enjoying the all-out support of the powerful Tudeh Party, for his government to collapse in an unbelievable way on a single day as the result of the events of 25 Mordad?

These are some of the questions and contradictions that have been dismissed by stating that a coup d'état had been staged against Dr. Mossadegh's government, thus trying somehow to find a justification for those events. The reason why they insist on a coup d'état is to somehow persuade the public of its reality, forcing the people to accept those claims without asking any questions.

In order to support their version of a coup d'état and to present it as a matter of consensus by all historians they have based their argument on the views expressed by a number of people. However, it is important to bear in mind that Ashraf Pahlavi [the Shah's sister] in the English text of her book not only has not referred to a coup d'état, on the contrary, on page 141 of her book she claims that she heard that term for the first time in the government statement that was broadcast by the BBC Radio [Persian Service] on the morning of 25

Mordad. She writes that she was puzzled about hearing the report about a failed coup d'état. Then she left Paris for Rome to meet with the Shah and she asked him about the coup d'état. The Shah had also stressed that the handing over of his decree to Mossadegh by Colonel Nasiri had been described by the government as a coup d'état (p. 143).

As regards Kermit Roosevelt, I must add that his book, which was published in 1978, nearly 24 years after those events, is full of incorrect material, lies and fictitious stories. However, even in his book there is no reference to what Mr. Baqi has written. Mr. Baqi claims, "Kermit Roosevelt had obtained the Shah's decree dismissing Mossadegh and appointing Zahedi as prime minister a few days before the Shah's departure from the country, and had kept it in his pocket, so that it could be used as soon as the coup d'état was staged."

What has been recorded as a historical fact is that the decrees dismissing Mossadegh and appointing Zahedi had been issued on 23rd Mordad [14 August 1952]. Colonel Nasiri had carried them from Kalardasht to Tehran and had handed them to Zahedi between 10:30 and 11:00 the same night, and had taken them to Mossadegh about the same time the following day. Furthermore, it is interesting to note that Kermit Roosevelt has called his book *Countercoup*, but those who follow a particular line of thought have changed the title of the book in its Persian translation and have published it as *Coup within Coup*. In this way, they could still continue with the notion that a coup had really taken place.

Imam Khomeini also has a completely different understanding of those events that was at variance with the views of those who wish to make the public believe that there had been a coup d'état. In a speech on 16/08/1357 [7 November 1978], Imam Khomeini said, "His other mistake was that he [Mossadegh] dissolved the Majles, and one by one he forced the Majles deputies to resign. When they resigned, the Shah found a legal justification [to dismiss Mossadegh], because as the Majles was no longer functioning it was up to the Shah to appoint the prime minister" (Sahife-ye Nur, Vol. 3, 36).

Consequently, not only is using the term coup d'état to describe those events incorrect, even those who have used that term and believe that it represents a consensus on the issue have had different interpretations of it. Therefore, how could one force everybody to give in to the claimed consensus about the formula of a coup d'état? One should feel sorry for Iranian students, whose textbooks on history have been written by individuals such as Mr. Baqi and others who think like him, who instead of reporting the truth about what really happened fill the students' minds with such erroneous ideas.

When I deny that a coup d'état was staged, it does not mean that I regard the events of 28th Mordad as a national uprising. It is clear that the claim about the staging of a coup d'état refers to the events in the early hours in the morning of 25th Mordad, and has nothing to do with what happened on 28th Mordad. The events of 28th Mordad require a thorough historical assessment and revision. Clearly, one can never accept the claims of Mossadegh's supporters, who say that a bunch of thugs, club wielders and prostitutes poured into the streets and with the help of a small amount of American dollars they managed to topple the nationalist government. The Iranian nation, which has witnessed the events after the Islamic Revolution, the eight-year war and many other plots, has realised that if a government relies upon the nation and has the determination to defend itself it can never be toppled by such ridiculous means.

Now, we should see what happened from the 11:00 hours on the evening of 24th Mordad to one o'clock in the morning on 25th Mordad, which has been described as a military coup against Mossadegh's government. One historical fact that has been kept hidden from the public is that when Colonel Nasiri called at Mossadegh's house he was kept waiting for an hour. As he was not allowed to see Mossadegh in person, he handed the Shah's decree to one of the guards in the house, and Mossadegh confirmed his receipt of the letter in his own handwriting. He wrote, "At one o'clock in the morning on 25th Mordad I was handed the sublime royal decree. [Signed] Dr. Mohammad Mossadegh." He refers respectfully to that letter as "the sublime royal decree." At the same time, he removes the title of prime minister before his name. Nevertheless, he again issues orders to arrest Colonel Nasiri, who was merely conveying the decree.

The same morning, in order to cover up his role as the one who had paved the way for the decree to be issued for his dismissal and Zahedi's appointment as prime minister, Mossadegh issued a statement, in which without making any reference to the Shah's decree he referred to a military coup d'état being staged the previous night by Colonel Nasiri. He alleged that under the cover of wanting to hand over a letter to him, Colonel Nasiri had decided to occupy his house. Consequently, the government's statement about a coup d'état was a lie and a distortion of facts. There were many motives behind concocting those lies, which we have no time to deal with here. According to the report of the correspondent of the Associated Press, government officials had claimed ignorance about the royal decree appointing Zahedi as prime minister that had been reported on 25th Mordad (*Ettela'at* newspaper, 25 Mordad, 32). Mossadegh even kept the royal decree dismissing him as prime minister hidden from his own ministers, and in the cabinet meeting that was held on the morning of 25th Mordad 1933 in his house he did not say anything about it to his ministers. Here, I would like to quote briefly the remarks of two of Mossadegh's colleagues, and there are many other such examples. Dr. Sadighi, Mossadegh's interior minister, in his interrogation about the events of 25 Mordad said, "That issue was not discussed in the cabinet meeting and no decisions were taken about it. There was absolutely no mention of the royal decree dismissing Dr. Mossadegh as prime minister. However, as to what you have asked about my personal knowledge of those events, I have already written that I had heard by the word of mouth about the royal decree in His Excellency the Prime Minister's house, which had been the reason for us gathering in his house. I asked Dr. Mossadegh about the content of the letter, and he replied, 'There was nothing.'"

Brigadier-General Riahi, the chairman of the joint staff in Mossadegh's government, in his memoirs has also referred to the events of 25 Mordad and of the previous night. He has described those issues in the following words: "At six o'clock in the morning of 26th Mordad [the correct date is 25th Mordad], after Nasiri's unsuccessful coup, I went to see Mossadegh. I told him that all foreign radio stations have broadcast reports of Nasiri's half-hearted coup, and meanwhile they have also reported that the Shah has deposed you. He said, 'No sir, that decree had been forged.' However, he did not show the text of the royal decree to me or to any of the ministers. I went to see him again at 11:00 in the morning to give him the report of the flight of the Shah and Soraya from Ramsar. I asked him, 'What will be the situation in the country now that the Shah has left?' He replied, 'We should try to make him return'."

I will not dwell on this issue here, which has to be dealt with in detail at an appropriate time. I only wish to stress a few key points that would help us to better understand the events on 25th Mordad. Why did Dr. Mossadegh describe the Shah's decree about his dismissal that he had described as "the sublime royal decree" as a coup d'état? Why did he keep it hidden from the people and even from the members of his own cabinet? Why did he not fight against that decree or at least adopt a legal and political stance against it? Why did he not ask for people's help, despite the fact that he claimed that they had dissolved the Majles with a high vote in the referendum? Finally, why did he not turn to the political parties that were supporting him to fight against the royal decree? These are some of the questions, which have to be answered as the result of more historical research and by making use of numerous documents that have come to light recently. Insisting on the claim that the events of 25th Mordad constituted a military coup is only an attempt to cover up the truth and continue with the deceptive propaganda of the past 50 years. One cannot prevent the young generation from trying to find out the truth behind those events by insisting that there is a consensus about what happened.

Fortunately, in a paper that I presented to a conference at Oxford University in 1381 [2002], I have answered some of those questions to the best of my ability, as much as one could say in one lecture. If in that lecture I did not provide any explanations as to why the military and the law-enforcement forces surrendered to Zahedi it has not been due to the fact that I did not possess necessary documents on the issue, as Mr. Baqi has claimed.

I wish to finish this article by pointing out that the Iranian nation needs to have a correct understanding of the events of the past century, especially the reasons for the successes and failures of the Iranian National Movement. Gaining a correct understanding of historical truths is necessary for evaluating the achievements of the individuals who played a major role in that important popular movement, and also for understanding the interference of Western countries in the domestic affairs of our country. The experience of the past century shows that in order to safeguard their illegitimate interests in Iran, those countries have never stopped interfering in our country and acting against our territorial integrity, independence and national security.

No doubt, many people who are interested in Iran's contemporary history often ask themselves why Iran's nationalist movement, which enjoyed the overwhelming support of the people and religious leaders, and had a Majles in which many patriotic and struggling deputies served, failed after two years and a few months. They want to know why England and America managed once again to exercise such political domination over our country that they succeeded to control our vast oil reserves and impose the oil agreement with the Consortium in Mehr 1333 [October 1954]. It is only through more extensive research and making full use of available documents that one can discover how those foreign powers could undermine our independence.

What helps the repetition of those interventions and imposes weakness and stagnation over our country is intellectual despotism that wishes to impose a certain version of truth upon the people. The formula regarding a military coup against Mossadegh's government is only a deceitful ploy to cover up the interventionist policies of foreigners in our country, which have been much more dangerous, destructive and inhumane that a military coup.

The investigation of the events of 1329 to 1332 [1950 to 53] will show that the British government's interference in our domestic affairs has been implemented through a multi-faceted conspiracy, by making use of domestic agents to topple Iran's nationalist movement. Those plots have included some of the following tactics:

• Seizing control of the executive power in the country by placing some of their affiliated individuals in key positions

• Dragging the national economy towards bankruptcy by creating a dead-end situation in the oil issue

• Expanding public dissatisfaction and weakening the forces of national resistance

• Creating differences and divisions among the people through their infiltrated agents

• The character assassination of various individuals and undermining the reputation of Ayatollah Kashani and other leaders of the national movement through a series of poisonous domestic propaganda

• Disrupting the work of the judiciary and rendering it ineffective, and closing down the Supreme Court

• Weakening the position of the Majles and eventually dissolving it

• Bringing some minor groups to power that lack any identity of their own, and giving the Tudeh Party a free hand in the political arena of the country

Without doubt, a more careful investigation of such issues and other destructive methods that have been used during the past 50 years, which have resulted in the weakening of the foundations of the Iranian National Movement in the areas of freedom, the rule of law and the loss of Iran's national assets, will be useful and will enable us to confront some of the worrying challenges that threaten our national security at the present time.

(Mr. Seyyed Mahmud Kashani wrote the above article in response to an article by Emadoddin Baqi, one of the nationalist-religious figures, in which he had criticized Ayatollah Kashani for some of the incidents that led to the downfall of Mossadegh's government. This article attracted a great deal of attention and extensive reactions when it was published in *Shargh* newspaper in Tehran.)

Chapter Seven
The Relationship between the Shah and the Prime Minister: Problems of Governance

Question: What was your official title and what were your responsibilities after the events in Mordad and your father's appointment as prime minister?

Zahedi: At the beginning, I had no official post or responsibility, and I didn't want to have any. I could help my father more easily without having an official title and position, and I was ready to do whatever needed to be done. Every day, I would go to His Majesty for half an hour or an hour, and I used to take some messages from my father to His Majesty and return with His Majesty's answers to my father, or vice versa.

For instance, one of the tasks that had to be carried out in the early days was to appoint a new court minister. At that time, there were only three eligible candidates for that post, namely Hossein Ala, Seyyed Jalal Tehrani, and Dr. Ali Akbar Siassi. Tehrani was busy pushing himself forward, but he did not have a good reputation, and my father did not believe that he was at all suitable for the post of court minister. Ala had rendered valuable services during the Azerbaijan episode, and he was also court minister during Mossadegh's time, but after the events of 9th of Esfand [28 February 1953] Mossadegh became very suspicious of him and put pressure on the Shah to dismiss him and to replace him with Abol-Ghassem Amini. In any case, Ala was again appointed as court minister.

Those comings and goings took many hours every day, especially at the time when His Majesty was in Sa'dabad. On some days it was necessary for me to travel by car two or three times from the prime minister's office to Sa'dabad.

Question: Where was the prime minister's office?

Zahedi: My father chose the Officers' Club, which he had originally built and where many years before he had worked as the chairman of the management board of the club, as his first headquarters. However, as many people complained that it had become difficult for military officers to use the club when it was being used as the prime minister's office, as they could not hold ceremonies or weddings or other meetings there, my father transferred his headquarters to the Ministry of Foreign Affairs building. He chose one of the rooms on the top floor of the Ministry of Foreign Affairs building as his office, which also had an annex composed of a bedroom and a sitting room. Later on, when I became minister of foreign affairs, I also had my office there.

At that time, Her Royal Highness Princess Ashraf, who was still living abroad and did not intend to return to Iran, complained of being short of money. It was decided that the government should buy her palace, which was next door to the Marble Palace and His Majesty's private palace. We bought that palace for three million tumans. Later on, we paid more money for the furniture, fittings, paintings, and other contents of the palace. Then, the prime minister's office was moved to that palace.

As I said before, each day, two, three, or four times, I was received by His Majesty. Each week I also took part in three or four receptions in the evenings, or I had dinner with His Majesty and Her Majesty Queen Soraya together with my sister Homa and with Mrs. Yarafshar and her husband Parviz Yarafshar. At the same time, I also took part in various committees, especially in the discussions that were held in order to bring some order to the chaotic economic and fiscal situation of the country and resolve the oil crisis.

When in the autumn of 1953 Herbert Hoover, Jr., an oil expert working for the State Department, came to Tehran, I took part in the discussions with him, of course without having any official position. The talks were led by Foreign Minister Amir Entezam, who had a very good grasp of foreign issues. Later on, a committee was formed to find a way out of the oil crisis. About the same time, Norman Paul, who was a member of the Democratic Party and later on got very close to John F. Kennedy and became undersecretary of state, came to Tehran to talk about immediate U.S. assistance in order to get the wheels of the economy turning and to help us get out of our economic problems. I took part in all those talks as well.

I should point out that when my father came to power, the treasury was empty, and the government had no funds at its disposal. It was not even able to pay the salaries of its employees. This is why my father called for immediate U.S. assistance. Norman Paul and William Warne suggested we be to given $5 million of immediate assistance and they would see what could be done later.

Something quite comical happened. As is their custom, the Americans wished to combine their assistance with propaganda and to take photographs of the ceremonies. My father felt insulted by that and became very angry. He said, "We are not beggars. We are merely asking for a loan from you, but you are behaving as though you are giving alms to us. We do not need any assistance at all." He went into a huff and rejected the $5 million loan. Less than 24 hours later, U.S. Ambassador Henderson phoned me in Hesarak and said that he wanted to see the prime minister and had a good piece of news to give him. In any case, they had decided to give $45 million of aid, instead of the $5 million. Of course, they were saying that they would pay that money directly to the prime minister so that he could spend it in any way he saw fit.

My father immediately ordered that a committee should be formed under the chairmanship of the minister of finance, Ali Amini. On the Iranian side, Ali-Asghar Nasser (governor of the Central Bank), Abdol-Hossein Nikpour, Ali Vakili, and Sadeq Naraqi were the members of that committee. Warne and I also took part in those meetings. We had a number of meetings and took a number of decisions. One of the decisions that we made in that committee was that as the government faced a shortage of foreign currency, the price of the dollar in the open market was to increase from three tumans to six tumans and two rials, so that they could give the difference to the students studying abroad, to the people going for medical treatment, and to government officials abroad.[1] All my posts and responsibilities until my father resigned from his post as prime minister were in the form that I have described above.

Of course, I should add that a few weeks after 28th of Mordad, on the occasion of a religious holiday, special ceremonies were held at Sa'dabad Palace to felicitate His Majesty. I had gone to the palace. The prime minister and other ministers were there to take part in the official ceremonies and be received by His Majesty. His Majesty summoned me. I ran upstairs to receive his orders. In the presence of the ministers and other officials present, His Majesty asked me, "What would you like to do?"

I did not understand exactly what he meant. While I was still panting due to running up the stairs, I replied, "I have not asked for anything, Your Majesty!" He replied, "No, I know you have not asked for anything. What I mean is that you must have an official position. You keep going to the Majles, you come to the palace, you take some messages and bring back some messages and you take part in some of the discussions, but the prime minister says that you are not prepared to accept an official position. You must ask for something."

I replied, "My only request for Your Majesty is to allow me to express the truth."

He said, "Well, certainly you should do that, but what post would like to have?"

I replied, "What I have just stated is the most important thing to do."

Of course, some of the ministers were pointing to me, trying to tell me that I was being impolite and that I had to ask for a post. In any case, it was decided that I should act as the special adviser to the prime minister, but without receiving any salary. A decree was written stating the above, but of course it was a mere formality, and I never made any use of it. Later on, His Majesty decided to appoint me as his civilian adjutant, but I do not know why this decision was taken, because Mr. Ala did not tell me anything about it. I don't know whether he had forgotten to tell me or did not wish to say anything about it. I had no information about it whatsoever until the 3rd Aban, when the official ceremonies were to be held in the Golestan Palace on the following day on the occasion of the anniversary of His Majesty's birthday.

As we walked with His Majesty from the Marble Palace to the private palace to have lunch with Her Majesty Queen Soraya, His Majesty joked, "Well, Mr. Civilian Adjutant! Have you got your formal uniform ready for tomorrow?"

I replied, "Your Majesty! Which uniform?"

He said, "Haven't you been informed? You are our civilian adjutant, but I know that preparing the uniform and sewing the filigree will take time. You can come in coattails or an ordinary suit. Don't worry. I just wanted you to know that from now on you are our civilian adjutant."

It came as a real surprise to me, but as soon as I left his presence I returned to the Officers' Club. I told Manuchehr Khosrowdad, Parviz Yarafshar, and Ali Abtin, "I don't know how you will do it, but I must have my formal uniform ready for tomorrow for the ceremonies at the Golestan Palace."

There was a special tailor called Abdol-Vahab Zarduz, whose shop was in Nasser Khosrow Street, near the bazaar, who could make uniforms with filigree and who also had a number of uniforms for hire. He came and measured me and in a great hurry he managed to prepare a uniform for me, maybe from an old uniform of a dead minister or a court official! However, he did not have any white trousers. There was another tailor called Hambarson who made the uniforms of court officials. He was brought to the Officers' Club, and he promised to have a pair of white trousers ready for me by the next morning. Consequently, between three in the afternoon and seven the following morning I managed to have an official uniform, and I was dressed appropriately when I took part in the official ceremonies in the Golestan Palace.

I must add that earlier on, His Majesty had decorated me with a medal, but I had never found an opportunity to wear it before that occasion. A few days after His Majesty's return to the country I had gone to submit a report. He ordered me to stay for lunch, and we played volleyball in the afternoon. When we finished our game we went to the palace to have a wash and change. His Majesty then summoned me, and I went to his private office. He gave me a box and said, "God willing, in the future your chest will be covered with many such decorations." I opened the box and saw that there was a medal in it.

I was not yet familiar with the formalities associated with receiving a medal and did not know the different medals. I thought that I should pin it to my jacket. When I went home I discovered that it was a Taj medal, third degree, and that I should wear it round my neck. During the ceremonies marking the anniversary of His Majesty's birthday, I wore that medal round my neck and went to the Golestan Palace in my new official uniform. All that was done in such a hurry that everyone was surprised. When His Majesty saw me in that uniform he smiled and made some gracious remarks.

In any case, I became His Imperial Majesty's civilian adjutant, but how gradually I managed to learn about court ceremonies and protocols is another story, which is also worth telling.

The very first time that I was introduced to His Majesty was after the Second World War, when my father returned from exile and took me with him to the private palace, and I have referred to it already. Later on, I went to the United States to continue my studies. In 1947, after the incident in Bahman [January] and the assassination attempt on His Majesty's life, His Majesty was invited by President Harry Truman to visit the United States. The very first time that His Majesty visited the United States he was received very warmly, and he traveled to different parts of America. He was also due to visit Arizona and to go from there to San Diego to visit U.S. naval bases.

I was received by His Majesty in Arizona, accompanied by Mr. Harris, who was the president of my university and later became the director of President Truman's Point Four Program in Iran. His Majesty ordered that I had to accompany him all the time that he was staying there, from that evening to the following day. I stayed in the

Camel Back Inn and had dinner with His Majesty, and he showed great kindness to me.

When I returned to Iran in 1950, I was due to work in the Joint Iran–America Commission. His Majesty, who was following my activities through my father, expressed a wish to see me. It was decided that I should go to Sa'dabad Palace. In the United States I knew nothing about official protocol. I had bent my arm on one side, and I had a photograph taken with His Majesty like that. When I sent a copy of that photograph home and my relatives saw it in Tehran they pointed out to me that it was very rude to stand like that in the presence of the Shah. This time, before I went to see His Majesty, Mostafa Zahedi, Rahmat Atabaki, and Nasrollah Khan Zahedi spent a whole day and night teaching this simple student who had returned from America the formal manners for behaving in front of His Majesty.

It was about midday when I went to Sa'dabad Palace. Hormoz Khan Pirnia, my mother's cousin and my aunt's husband, came down and took me to His Majesty in the White Palace. He asked a number of questions, which I answered, and we walked together to the car that took him to the private palace, namely, the palace that had been built exclusively for him when he was the crown prince. Later on, he gave that palace to Her Royal Highness Princess Shahnaz.

In that meeting I provided some explanation about membership in the Joint Iran–America Commission. His Majesty said, "It is a good opportunity. You can serve the country well there."

The second time that I was received by His Majesty was in the Marble Palace. At that time, I was already working in the Joint Iran–America Commission. His Majesty wanted to know what we had already done in that commission and the plans that we had for the future. On that day, I had borrowed Rahmat Atabaki's tailcoat. The sleeves and trousers were rather too short for me, and the waist was a bit too loose. I went to His Majesty in that ill-fitting tailcoat, but he liked the explanations that I provided about the work of the commission and he liked our programs. We left his office talking and went to the garden and walked under the pine trees that His Majesty Reza Shah had planted. His Majesty was walking in front and I was following him.

I had been told that when I spoke to the Shah I should not say "I" when referring to myself but "your servant" or "your slave." I had also been told that my hands should always be folded in front of me. In a hurried response to one of His Majesty's questions I said, "In my view…" I immediately realized my mistake, began to stutter, and tried to correct myself, saying, "I meant to say your slave." The Shah laughed and said, "Say what you have got to say, and leave 'your servant' and 'your slave' for later."

Then, after a few steps I became aware that I had folded my hands in my back. I tried to change my position in a hurry, and I hit His Majesty's side hard with my hand. He turned his head, and I apologized. I said, "I had been told to behave like this, and this is why I moved my hands in a hurry." He laughed for a long time and said, "Don't worry, try to feel comfortable." On that day I was very touched by His Majesty's kindness, and I realized how closely he noticed everything that was going on.

In any case, on all future occasions our discussions were about the work of the Joint Iran–America Commission and the programs of Point Four. At times, His Majesty summoned me to see him, and at other times, when there was something that I had to bring to his notice, I went through the head of protocol and His Majesty fixed a time for me to see him. The first time that I managed to have a tailcoat of my own was at the wedding ceremony of His Majesty and Queen Soraya.

I had been invited to the wedding ceremony for two reasons. The first reason was that I was a close friend of most of Her Royal Highness Soraya's cousins and relatives. When my father was the commander of the Army division in Isfahan, he had friendly relations with the leaders of the Bakhtiari tribe, such as Amir Hossein Khan Zafar Ilkhan and Amir Jang Bakhtiari. I used to play with their sons, and my sister Homa was a fellow pupil of Her Royal Highness Soraya in the girls school. The second reason was that when Her Royal Highness Soraya was studying in Zurich, her father Khalil Esfandiary and her mother Eva had also come to Zurich and were living there. They had very close contacts with Gholam-Ali Seif-Naseri. In the summer of 1949 I went to Switzerland to visit my father. I went to Zurich to get a visa for returning to America. I was walking with Seif-Naseri in Bahnhofstrasse when we came across Khalil Khan. He invited us to go to his house for tea. By chance, his daughter Princess Soraya was also there, and we renewed our acquaintance.

In any case, when we were invited to the wedding, I realized that I had to wear a proper and fitting tailcoat. I went to Lalehzar Street and bought a tailcoat from Pirayesh shop. It was the first time that I appeared in public among the high-ranking officials and personalities of the country dressed in my own tailcoat.

The wedding ceremony was held at Golestan Palace. Unfortunately, the bride was suffering from typhoid and had a high fever, but as the date of the ceremony had been fixed a long time before, she did not want to postpone the wedding. She took part in her wedding ceremony with a high temperature, after taking very strong antibiotics and different forms of medicine to keep her going for a while, but in the middle of the ceremony she felt unwell. At the end of the ceremony, there was chaos. As the palace had only one gate and proper arrangements had not been made for the departure of the guests, heavy traffic formed at the palace gate. Of course, a rumor spread very quickly throughout the city that Prime Minister Razmara had been involved in the arrangements and had deliberately caused that chaos.

Question: The marriage between Mohammad Reza Shah and Her Majesty Queen Soraya lasted for seven years. Both the Shah and Her Majesty Queen Soraya have written in their memoirs that they loved each other dearly and that the only reason for their separation was that the queen was unable to bear children. Their divorce took place during Dr. Eqbal's premiership. At that time, you were the Shah's son-in-law and were very close to the royal family. What was the situation like at that time?

Zahedi: Her Royal Highness Shahnaz and I married in September 1957 and went on our honeymoon. I was not in too much of a hurry to get back to Tehran, because I wished to keep myself away from the ill feelings that existed between the Queen Mother and the Shah's sisters and Soraya. At the same time, the Queen Mother acted like a mother to Shahnaz and me and was very kind to us. On the other hand, Her Royal Highness Soraya was a very genuine, unaffected, and likable young lady. I did not wish to get involved in their gossips and squabbles. One day His Majesty phoned me, telling me to return to Tehran for something urgent. I obeyed his order.

At that time, there were no daily flights to Tehran. Most airlines had a weekly flight. Finally, I decided to fly with KLM. Over Athens the aircraft suffered a technical problem, and one of its engines failed. The second engine caught fire near Beirut, and we managed to land at Beirut airport with some difficulty. As a result, I arrived in Tehran with some delay, and His Majesty had been very worried, especially as he had heard that the aircraft had suffered from a technical problem. When I arrived at the airport in Tehran, I noticed that a few people from the court had come to the airport. His Majesty was staying at the private palace. I went to see him there, and he received me in his bedroom. It was big, and there was a large portrait of Queen Soraya in a beautiful frame hanging on the wall.

I noticed that His Majesty kept pacing up and down the room and seemed very tired and preoccupied. Shortly, it became clear that the issue concerned the difficulties in their marital life. Her Majesty's inability to have a child had put a great deal of pressure on His Majesty, because he was anxious to have an heir who could continue the monarchy. Of course, I had certain views that I expressed, but in keeping with my youth and lack of experience those views were rather ill advised. His Majesty wanted me to consult my father about the issue and to inform him of my father's views. I said that I would obey His Majesty's command and would return to Switzerland on the first available flight. I had made some notes that I intended to talk to my father about and said that I would send a telegram back to His Majesty in code.

His Majesty said, "I prefer these issues not to be written down." I replied that I would bring back the response in person. I flew to Switzerland and informed my father of all the details. My father said, "*Divorce* is an ugly word, whether in Iran or abroad. Whether they are religious or not, people do not like that word, especially as His Majesty had divorced his first wife and there are a number of rumors about that divorce. Even at the moment the opponents are spreading many rumors about the Shah's sexual life. If there is going to be another divorce those rumors would be strengthened, and it would be harmful both to him and to the monarchy. If the issue concerns family disputes I do not wish to get involved in it, especially as I am not in a position to give advice. I also have divorced my first wife and cannot lecture others against it, so I should not say more about the harmful effects of a divorce.

"However, if the issue is about having a crown prince, that is something different. That issue would no longer be limited to family disputes. That is a national issue. In that case, one should see if there is any way of resolving that problem or not. When I was prime minister and His Majesty had gone to Europe and America, doctors there had said that the problem was not so complicated and that it could be put right with a minor operation. If there is any chance of resolving the problem through medical means, one should try to avoid divorce if at all possible. However, if there is no solution to that problem, the issue will no longer be a personal or family issue. In that case, His Majesty should not make the decision alone. A committee should be formed of national figures, which should not be limited to the prime minister, other ministers, and the heads of the Majles and the senate."

My father added, "The minor differences that arose between His Majesty and me were not of a personal nature. I always believed that His Majesty should reign, not rule, and that the government should be in charge of the executive affairs of the country. Even now, although I have retired from active duty, I still believe the same. This was due to my love for His Majesty, because I love him in the same way that I love you, and I wish only what is best for him."

My father mentioned the names of a few people who should be invited for consultation. He said, "It is important that some of the leading figures of the Bakhtiari tribe should be included in that group, people like Amir Jang As'ad and Amir Hossein Khan Zafar Ilkhan, whose sister Madame Forugh Zafar was a lady-in-waiting to the queen. She was also involved in arranging their marriage."

I returned to Tehran and informed His Majesty of my father's views. His Majesty liked most of those views and ordered me to have private conversations with a few people on that issue. I was acquainted with Amir Jang As'ad, but as there was a big age difference between us and I could have been his grandson, I telephoned Seifollah Afshar, the father of Amir Khosrow Afshar who later became foreign minister. We arranged to see Amir Jang As'ad together. We went to see him and informed him of the matter, so that when he was invited to express his views he would have some prior knowledge about it. I also talked on the phone with Amir Hossein Khan, who was a minister without portfolio in my father's cabinet. I talked to Sadr al-Ashraf, Taghizadeh, and Adl ol-Molk Dadgar, who were veteran politicians and wise and competent individuals. I also spoke with General Hedayat and General Yazdanpanah. Two of the people with whom I did not talk were the Court Minister Hossein Ala and Prime Minister Manuchehr Eqbal. I was not on friendly terms with them at that time. I asked permission from His Majesty to inform their bureau chiefs. I asked Mr. Hirad to come to Hesarak. We had dinner together, and I informed him of the matter and left it to him to inform the prime minister and the court minister in any way he saw fit.

They had a number of meetings, but I do not know exactly what they discussed in those meetings. All I know is that everything had been discussed, and the gentlemen had said whatever they thought openly and bluntly. Some of them had even advocated that His Majesty should have a concubine to have a child from. Some had talked of appointing Prince Gholam Reza as crown prince, but as his mother was from the Qajar family it was contrary to the constitution. The Shah's full brother, Prince Ali Reza, had been killed in a plane crash. The outcome of those talks was that a statement should be issued about the separation of the royal couple.[2]

In a telephone conversation, His Majesty informed Her Royal Highness Soraya of the details of the decision that had been made. At the beginning, Her Royal Highness was in St. Moritz. Later on, as the news of the separation had leaked and as there were a number of reports about it in the press, she went to stay with her parents in Cologne, and it was there that she received the divorce documents.

After the separation, the second step was who should talk to Her Royal Highness. His Majesty again consulted a few people about this issue. I suggested that the court minister should talk to her. Dr. Mohammad Ali Hedayati, a professor at the law faculty, was the court minister who had recently joined the cabinet. Fazel ol-Molk (Hamraz) had introduced Hedayati to me. He came to Geneva, I booked him a room in a hotel and met him there and we had some discussions about the issue. A couple of times he traveled between Geneva and Cologne, and both of us were in telephone contact with Tehran and informed His Majesty of the developments, until everything was settled. Her Majesty the Queen was given the title of Her Royal Highness, and His Majesty fixed a monthly salary for her so long as she remained single.[3]

---

[1] William Warne, the director of Point Four in Iran, writes in his memoirs, *Mission for Peace* (pp. 256–257):

> Ardeshir Zahedi came to me shortly after his father took office. He told me that the new prime minister was awaiting a call from me. I went with him to the general's office, in the wing of the Ministry of Foreign Affairs. Our reunion after many months was pleasant and cordial.
>
> The day was extremely hot. The whole summer had been unusually warm. I found General Zahedi in khaki shirtsleeves. His tie was hung over the back of a chair upholstered in cloth of gold. He had taken his pistol from its holster and laid it on a corner of the desk. He was hard at work when I entered the room.

General Fazlollah Zahedi and I spoke, through Ardeshir, of pleasant afternoons we had long ago spent in the Zahedi garden in Hesserick, high on the mountainside overlooking Tehran. The summer house there was always cool, even on the hottest days.

Neither of us mentioned the trials and tribulations of the months since we had seen each other there. Part of this time General Zahedi had spent under arrest, the guest of the chief of police in the latter's office. He had been for a while in sanctuary in the Majlis building. The rest of the time he had spent in hiding. In the crucial days after the Shah had issued his *firman* and before General Zahedi had been able to effectuate it Ardeshir had somehow managed to make his way into the city. It was he who had had the *firman* photostated and the copies distributed. This much, but little more, was said of that hectic time. The general was eager to discuss the future.

"That is past," he reminded Ardeshir, who might have told me more. "Let us turn to the work ahead."

General Zahedi had a hundred things in mind—agricultural advancement, improvement of transportation and roads, resumption of the Shah's land distribution, a program similar to His Majesty's for the peasants of the government-owned villages, an extension of rural education. I thought as I listened to him that in the optimism of the moment the new prime minister was underestimating the seriousness of some of the problems ahead. He was above all a soldier. And although he had served at various posts in the government he had not had much opportunity to deal with fiscal management. At that moment everyone underestimated the difficulty of Iran's financial predicament.

[2] The statement by the Royal Court was issued on 23 Esfand 1336 [14 March 1958]. The text of the statement is as follows:

> As the highest interests of the Iranian nation and the safeguarding of the future of the hereditary constitutional monarchy and avoiding any problem and uncertainty in the future require appointing an heir apparent, His Imperial Majesty raised that issue in the consultation meeting that was held on 27 Bahman 1336 [16 February 1958] at the court in the presence of His Imperial Majesty and the participation of the head of the government and the heads of the two houses of Parliament, the court ministers and Messrs. Ebrahim Hakimi (Hakim ol-Molk), As'ad Bakhtiari (Amir Jang), Mahmud Jam, Dr. Matindaftari, General Yazdanpanah, General Abdollah Hedayat, and General Amirahmadi. In view of the highest interest of the country, all those present unanimously expressed the view

that the crown prince should be in direct line from Mohammad Reza Shah Pahlavi.

As this issue was again discussed and as it was stressed in subsequent meeting that was held on 10 Esfand 1336 [1 March 1958], an envoy was sent by the Shahanshah to Queen Soraya Pahlavi, and Her Royal Highness was informed of the decision that had been reached. After returning, the above-mentioned envoy conveyed Her Royal Highness's willingness to make any self-sacrifice for the sake of the higher interests of the country and safeguarding the future of monarchy in Iran. Consequently, in the first consultation meeting that was held on 19 Esfand 1336 [10 March 1958], while expressing great pain and regret and stressing that throughout the period of marriage Her Royal Highness Soraya had not refrained from any service, kindness, and devotion towards the Iranian nation and had fully deserved her lofty status, despite all the mutual love and affection that existed between the two and in view of the fact that Her Royal Highness had expressed her willingness to accept any decision reached by His Majesty, the Shahanshah announced that he would agree with the view of the consultative committee. Therefore, contrary to his personal feelings, His Majesty has agreed to the separation in view of the highest interests of the country.

[3] In her memoirs, Her Royal Highness gives the following account of the separation:

One day in July 1957, walking alone with the Shah along the paths of the park at Sadabad, I murmured in a voice which I tried to keep assured: "Mohammed, things can't go on like this. I still have not been able to give you a child and, in the event that something were to happen to you, I would not wish to be the cause of the complications which would arise in a country left adrift without anyone to succeed."

In one's youth, one can feel heroic. Despite my sadness, as I said these words I experienced a profound loyalty towards my country and my people.

The Shah looked at me for a long while and it was as if he rediscovered in me the young woman who had brought him out of his torpor at the time he had qualms about dismissing Mossadeq.

"But what can we do?" he asked me, disconcerted by my frankness.

"You could lift the prohibition which excludes the Kajars and name one of your half-brothers as heir to the throne."

"For that, the Constitution would have to be revised by the Council of Elders. Those dignitaries would never agree to change the legislation which my father instituted."

"Why not attempt it anyway?" I said, without dropping my gaze.

I could sense he was at a loss. It was as though I were asking him to pit himself against the mighty Reza Shah, the man he had never dared confront.

"What if the Council were to reject my proposals?"

Without any hesitation, I blurted out: "Then all we can do is separate!" The words fell like the blade of a scimitar.

"There is hope. I am sure there is still hope."

Mohammed Reza looked at me and his eyes were feverish. Our life was torture. Every evening, we tried to think about other things, to make plans. They immediately appeared ridiculous. So we fell silent, each of us pretending to believe that a miracle was about to take place.

The day before, he had put a record on the gramophone and we danced in silence. Tenderly. As though we had wanted to enclose time in each other's arms.

"Oh Dounyazade," said Scheherazade to her sister: "If you are not asleep, tell me a beautiful story, one of those which used to help us while away our evenings."

Our wonderful thousand and one nights spent fighting doubt were over. Now, we were silent. What could we hope for?

He proposed to me what Shi'ite law calls the *sighe*, a temporary marriage with a woman he would reject after having a child by her.

"The legal union with this spouse will last for as long as she is pregnant. In this way, the throne will have an heir and you, you will remain always at my side."

The blood rushed out of my heart.

"How could you envisage such a thing?"

He said nothing.

"Then all we can do is separate!"

The words had gained ground in his mind. They remained engraved in mine. Like the sword of Damocles, they hung over our every conversation, our every movement. We did out utmost to remain friendly, but this had a hollow ring to it; to smile easily, but our smiles became grimaces.

One evening, more awkwardly than usual, he said to me hesitantly: "Whatever happens, if you leave Tehran, I would not want it thought that I had driven you out."

I swallowed the ball of sorrow which was rising in my throat. I affected a false indifference: "It would be better if I left for Europe where I can await the outcome of the Council of Elders' deliberations."

I no longer believed in them. Why and how would they change the country's Constitution? They did not wish to. Without a word to each other, we knew at that very moment, he and I, that it was all over.

There is nothing sadder than two people who have locked each other out in their hearts.

Chapter Eight
Accompanying the Shah on His Visit
to the United States

Question: During His Majesty's official visit to the United States, which was his first official visit after the events of 19 August 1953, you accompanied His Majesty as his civilian adjutant. What are your memories of that visit?

Zahedi: I was in charge of most of His Majesty's affairs, from the formal engagements right down to being in charge of the accounts. In December 1953, Richard Nixon, who was the U.S. vice president, paid a three-day official visit to Iran and submitted President Eisenhower's invitation to their majesties to visit the United States. His Majesty accepted the invitation, and in the official statement issued at the end of Nixon's visit it was pointed out that the date of the visit would be decided later. The official visit took place a year later and lasted for more than three months, from 4 December 1954, to 11 March, 1955. We left Tehran for Beirut and then traveled to Amsterdam and onward to Washington. On the way back, we visited Great Britain, Germany, and Iraq.

A short time before our departure His Royal Highness Prince Ali Reza was killed in an air crash. I was in the private palace together with my father. His Majesty was in mourning due to his brother's death. Over lunch we spoke about the visit. Her Majesty Soraya said, "It is good that we are going on the visit, we can have a break." In an angry tone, my father retorted, "No, no, you are not going there to have a break. You are visiting the United States on national business, and you should not regard the time that you spend there as a holiday." Clearly, His Majesty was upset at the tone of those words. I gently kicked my father's leg, but he became very angry and shouted, "Why did you kick me?" Then he turned to Her Majesty and said, "As you also need a medical checkup, of course you also need some time off [from official duties]." In this way, he tried to make up for his harsh tone, but that day all of us left the lunch in an unpleasant mood.

The way that His Majesty dealt with people in those days was different from the way that he dealt with them later. At that time, he was anxious that some people, such as Abol-Hassan Haerizadeh or Mostafa Kashani, Ayatollah Kashani's son, who had some hurt feelings regarding His Majesty, would go to visit him. We managed to persuade Haerizadeh to go for an audience with His Majesty. However, in his strong Yazdi accent, he said, "One should not go down a well with a rotten rope." When he was received by His Majesty he repeated that remark, which made His Majesty laugh.

Early in the morning of the departure for the United States, we were walking down from Hesarak accompanied by Hossein Daneshvar, Manuchehr Khosrowdad (who was a colonel at that time), Shapur Dowlatshahi, Kuch-Esfahani, and a few others. On the way, we came across a number of people wearing turbans and cloaks who were moving toward us. They had rolled up the bottom of their trousers. I had a gun in my hand, because in those days one could see partridges early in the morning and I used to carry a gun to shoot birds. Khosrodad and a policeman who was accompanying us went forward and asked what they were doing there. They replied that they had intended to go mountain climbing but had lost their way. Later on, we learned that they were members of the Feda'iyan Islam (the Devotees of Islam, a radical anti-Shah group) and that they had intended to assassinate me. We discovered this after the assassination attempt on the life of Hossein Ala, the former prime minister. At that time, a few members of the Feda'iyan Islam, including their leader Navvab Safavi, were arrested. During the interrogation, they had spoken about three attempts to kill my father and me. When Teymur Bakhtiar (the head of SAVAK) informed His Majesty of the plots, he ordered Bakhtiar to also inform him of the report.

One of those attempts was the incident to which I have just referred. In the report, it was stated that Navvab Safavi was one of the persons in that group. I did not know Navvab Safavi, and I am not sure whether or not he was in that group. In any case, Bakhtiar came to my house in Valiabad and informed me of the details of the plots. He said that as the conspirators had discovered that the situation was not appropriate for them to carry out the assassination attempt, they had left it for another time.

The second case involved my father. Every Tuesday afternoon during the time when he was prime minister, he arranged a public meeting in the Ministry of Foreign Affairs building. People could go to that meeting without making a prior appointment and talk to him about anything they wished. Then, he would order Parviz Yarafshar, Mousa Sarabandi, or Brigadier General Dadvar to investigate any complaints. One day, a member of the Devotees of Islam took part in that meeting and intended to assassinate my father, but he too had failed to carry out his mission. The third case involved the plot to assassinate my father during the funeral of His Royal Highness Prince Ali Reza. A member of the Devotees of Islam had confessed that they planned to assassinate my father as he was walking behind the coffin in Sepahsalar Mosque, but my father had looked toward them and smiled, and they imagined that he had recognized them. They had panicked and fled the scene.

At the airport, while saying good-bye, my father told me, "My son! Now that you are leaving the country, you are fully trusted by His Majesty. You have both the passes to the prime minister's office and the special pass for the court. You must not reveal any of the cables or discussions to anybody, not even to me as your father. Otherwise, you are not my son."

We embraced and said good-bye. I also said farewell to Hassan Taghizadeh and Sardar Fakher and Heyat, who had come to the airport with my father to see us off. At that time, we did not have a special royal aircraft. We hired an aircraft from KLM at about 12,000 or 14,000 dollars, which was a third or a fourth of the cost of other airlines. At that time, Holaku Rambod was the managing director and Mr. Malekian was the deputy managing director of KLM in Iran.

We flew from Tehran to Beirut. The invitation that was made to their majesties by Kamil Shamoun, the Lebanese president, was due to a special position that was enjoyed by our ambassador, Rahmat Atabaki, in Lebanon at that time. Atabaki was very close to Kamil Shamoun and had become his friend during the Shi'a–Sunni crisis in Lebanon. These close relations between the two countries had started at the time when Atabaki was our consul general in Beirut. His colleagues such as Javad Vakili, who later became the Iranian ambassador in Jordan (during the war between the Arabs and Israel), and Amir Kaviani, both of whom spoke Arabic fluently, helped him, and as a result Iran gained special influence in Lebanon. We stopped there for a few hours and had some discussions with the Lebanese authorities and then flew to Amsterdam. Although the visit to Amsterdam was an unofficial one, a dinner reception was arranged at the airport by the Dutch royal family with the participation of high-ranking Dutch officials. Then we flew to New York in the same aircraft that we had hired.

The rear part of the aircraft was reserved for their majesties, and the front part was occupied by those who were accompanying them. During the flight to New York I had taken off my shoes and was napping in the front part of the aircraft. Suddenly, an aide said that I had been summoned by His Majesty. I don't know whether His Majesty wished to jest with me and had taken one of my shoes and hidden it, or whether one of my shoes had slipped due to the movement of the aircraft. Either way, I could not find it. Consequently, I limped with one shoe toward His Majesty. He looked at me for a while and in a serious tone asked me why I looked like I did and what had happened to my other shoe. Then he laughed uproariously and changed the subject.

One day I accompanied His Majesty on a shopping trip. Nasrollah Entezam was with us. Among the items that he was looking at was a Zippo lighter made of gold. The Americans had invented that lighter for use in war, because it could be lit in wind or storm. I said that this lighter was appropriate for His Majesty. He did not say anything and we moved on. Two days later, I was received by His Majesty in his suite in the Waldorf-Astoria Hotel, and as I was leaving he gave me a small box. When I opened it I saw that it was the same lighter, but instead of the royal insignia that I had suggested it was engraved with the letters 'A.Z.'

In San Francisco His Majesty was standing on the deck of a ship, dressed in a naval uniform, and the mayor of San Francisco and Randolph Hearst, the heir to the Hearst media empire, were providing some details about the Golden Gate Bridge. I noticed that His Majesty wished to light his cigarette, but the wind was preventing him from doing so. I stepped forward and tried to light his cigarette with the lighter that he had graciously given me. The lighter emitted a big flame and burned the tip of His Majesty's nose. I felt very ashamed. During the dinner I told the famous story of the kindness of the little bear[2] as a way of apologizing. This formed a source of amusement for His Majesty and the queen, so that anytime they wished to light a cigarette, they said, "Ardeshir, where is the lighter?"

We were taken from New York to Washington in the U.S. president's special aircraft. Nasrollah Entezam was our ambassador in the United States, and Aligholi Ardalan was Iran's permanent representative at the United Nations. One evening U.S. Secretary of State John Foster Dulles gave a magnificent reception in their majesties' honor in

[2] Zahedi is referring to a story from Rumi's Masnavi. Below is a synopsis by E.H. Whinfield, page 85–86.

A kind man, seeing a serpent overcoming a bear, went to the bear's assistance, and delivered him from the serpent. The bear was so sensible of the kindness the man had done him that he followed him about wherever he went, and became his faithful slave, guarding him from everything that might annoy him. One day the man was lying asleep, and the bear, according to his custom, was sitting by him and driving off the flies. The flies became so persistent in their annoyances that the bear lost patience, and seizing the largest stone he could find, dashed it at them in order to crush them utterly; but unfortunately the flies escaped, and the stone lighted upon the sleeper's face and crushed it.

Masnaví-i Ma'naví, *The Spiritual Couplets of Mauláná Jalálu'd-din Muhammad Rúmí*, translated and abridged by E. H. Whinfield, London: 1887; 1989.

Anderson House. Later on, we had lunch with President Eisenhower at the White House. According to a previous arrangement, Mamie, the president's wife, took Her Majesty with her to visit different parts of the White House, so that His Majesty and the U.S. president could speak privately about political issues.

During the lunch at the White House I got to know Mr. Wrightsman, one of the major shareholders in American oil companies and a close friend of President Eisenhower. He invited their majesties to his house in Palm Beach and arranged a large reception. At that reception, Joseph Kennedy, President Kennedy's father, his wife, and the Kennedy brothers were introduced to their majesties.

From there we went to San Francisco and stayed in the St. Francis Hotel. On Christmas night we were invited to Randolph Hearst's castle. The castle that belongs to Hearst's famous family is situated between San Francisco and Los Angeles and is one of the most beautiful and impressive residences in that region. Each part of it belongs to a different era and has been brought from a different part of the world. As we were driving up the road toward the castle we could see different types of game grazing or lying on the lawn.

We had a rather unpleasant incident in Hearst's castle. The main dining room had been prepared and a very long dining table had been placed in its center. The program was that their majesties should take part in a cocktail party in the afternoon and exchange some gifts. We had taken a number of Persian carpets and rugs and some handmade artifacts to present to the hosts. Randolph Hearst was planning to give a silver-studded Mexican horse saddle, which was a family heirloom, to their majesties as a present. We all went to our rooms to have a short rest and to get ready for the cocktail party and dinner. The rooms of Mohammad Khatam and Hossein Mirza Jahanbani were exactly above the dining room. They had gone to their rooms to take a shower, but they had not drawn the shower curtains. As a result, water had poured onto the bathroom floors and, as the building was old, the water began to leak and poured onto the dining table.

The hosts discovered the problem when it was already too late and the water had soaked the dining room and ruined the dining table. Poor Hearst was in a state of panic, not knowing what to do. I told him that the best solution was to make the cocktail party last longer so the servants could set the table again. The servants started mopping up the water and drying the floor, setting up a new table, and changing the cutlery and crockery until the room was ready for entertainment again. Of course, the guests who were having cocktails did not know what was going on and why it was taking so long. I informed his Majesty about what had happened and he was very angry, but in any case nothing could be done. After the dinner they took us through a walkway, which resembled a tunnel, to a private cinema where we saw *White Christmas*, starring Bing Crosby and Danny Kaye.

I must add that in those years trips were simpler and less formal than in later years. We had only two security officials with us, and two people helped us with public relations affairs. One of them was Drew Dudly, the brother-in-law of a Democratic senator, and the other was a lady called Fleur Cowles, who later became Fleur Cowles Meyer, when she married her second husband, Tom Montague Meyer. Her first husband published *Cowles Magazine* and *Fortune*.

Fleur Cowles came to Iran after 28th of Mordad [19 August 1953] and interviewed my father. She also took a picture of their majesties in which they are dressed in riding clothes and sitting on the ground among trees in Kalardasht. That picture, which showed the simple and relaxed lifestyle of the king and the queen at that time, became very popular and was published many times. When Her Majesty Queen Elizabeth II was crowned in 1953, Fleur Cowles took part in the coronation ceremony on behalf of President Eisenhower, and she enjoyed a great deal of influence and high status.

A number of receptions were arranged in honor of their majesties in Los Angeles. At those receptions we were introduced to some famous Hollywood stars, including Barbara Stanwyck, Kim Novak, Greer Garson, Humphrey Bogart and his wife Lauren Bacall, who was very beautiful and had very beautiful eyes, as well as Robert Taylor and

Gary Cooper. In the reception on New Year's Eve I was dancing with Her Majesty Queen Soraya, and Bogart was dancing with Lauren Bacall. In the middle of the dance, Humphrey Bogart came to me and said, "Come and dance with a beautiful lady." He put my hands in Bacall's hands, and he started dancing with Queen Soraya. My friendship with Bogart started that night when I told him that he was my father's favorite actor in the world. Later on, we invited Gary Cooper to Iran. He was staying in the Darband Hotel but unfortunately had to cut his visit short due to illness. We later learned that he was suffering from cancer.

From Los Angeles we went to Texas. There we were the guests of an air base. The Americans insisted that the aircraft that His Majesty used should definitely have an oxygen capsule (the private Beechcraft aircraft was not equipped with one). In order to show the danger of a shortage of oxygen, someone had to go to a special room. As His Majesty had sent Khatam (the chairman of the Iranian aviation) on a special study visit, I was given the task of going into the special room. They sent me into a locked room and asked me to write down whatever I saw or felt. In that room, which resembled a simulator for training pilots, it seemed that as the aircraft flew higher over various heights the amount of oxygen was reduced so much that I could no longer hold my pen and my hand felt numb as it moved up or down. Had I stayed there a few minutes more I would certainly have been unable to breathe. Anyway, with this test they persuaded His Majesty that his aircraft should definitely have an oxygen capsule.

There I remembered that once we were flying from Tehran to the Caspian area with His Majesty's Beechcraft airplane, the same aircraft in which he flew from Kalardasht to Baghdad on 16 August, 1953, when he deposed Dr. Mossadegh. His Majesty was piloting the aircraft, and Khatam was his assistant pilot. When we were flying over the Elburz range we flew through very thick fog and did not know where we were, whether we were on the north of the Elburz or the south of it. While we were flying in this confused state, one of the engines of the aircraft froze and stopped. Khatam became rather worried and wanted to tap the engine with his hands and restart it, but he bruised his hand very badly. Fortunately, we managed to find a gap in the middle of the clouds, dived, and noticed that we were at the other side of the Kandovan tunnel. We continued to fly and, near the sea, the engine restarted, and we managed to land safely. Throughout that period I kept laughing and imagined that it was a sign of courage. Later on, I discovered that my involuntary laughter had been due to the lack of oxygen as we were flying over the top of the mountain and had nothing to do with courage. Of course, when jet aircraft were developed, all these problems were eliminated.

From Texas we flew to Florida. We spent the weekend in Palm Beach as the guest of Mr. Wrightsman, the executive manager of one of the big American oil companies. Later on, we went to Cypress Gardens where there was a festival and water skiing. Bob Hope's family arranged a reception in their majesties' honor. One of the guests at that reception was Esther Williams, the Olympic swimming champion and famous actress.

Finally, we returned to New York and for a number of days were the guests of various people and institutions. One of those receptions was given by Brazil's consul general in New York, who had served as ambassador in Iran in the past. At that reception, Grace Kelly, who later married Prince Rainier and became the Princess of Monaco, was introduced to the Iranian king and queen.

From New York we sailed to England on the Cunard liner *Queen Elizabeth*. Lord Mountbatten came to Southampton on behalf of Her Majesty Queen Elizabeth II to welcome the Shah. From Southampton we traveled by train to Queen Victoria Station in London and went straight to the Iranian Embassy. Winston Churchill had arranged a dinner reception at 10 Downing Street, and Clement Attlee was among the guests. Attlee had been defeated by Churchill in the election, and power had passed to the Conservatives. Churchill was very warm and sociable, and when those two old men joked with and teased one another in their unique British way it was very amusing.

Their majesties were staying at the Iranian Embassy, and I was given a suite in the Dorchester Hotel.

When we returned to the embassy with their majesties it became clear that both of them were still very hungry, because the dinner at the prime minister's residence had been very simple. All the refrigerators and freezers in the embassy had been locked for security reasons, and we could not find any food there. In my formal dinner dress and medals, I got in the car, went to the Dorchester Hotel, and tipped the night porter. He brought some bread, cheese, and other snacks, and I took them to the embassy. His Majesty was in his bedroom and Her Majesty joined us. We sat together and had a good late supper.

We were talking about horses. I asked His Majesty's permission to phone Amir Khosrow Afshar and tease him a bit. Amir Khosrow was the consul at the embassy. Ali Soheili, whose wife had a Russian background and was a very amusing lady, was our ambassador. Amir Khosrow was like a cousin to me, we were very close to each other. When he answered the phone I asked him some questions about horses. He was surprised that I was phoning him at two in the morning and was bothering him about horses. When he learned where I was and that I was phoning him in front of their majesties he became very upset. Later on, he often complained that I had played that trick on him!

In London, we received a cable from my father, who recommended that His Majesty should visit Germany too. The following day we visited the London Zoo, and there too something happened that was quite amusing. We were standing in front of a cage in which there was a very large snake. The director of the zoo explained that it was a boa. It could swallow rabbits and other animals of that size and crush their bones inside its stomach, but it usually posed no danger to people. Then he took the snake out of the cage and asked His Majesty if he wished to touch it. He wanted to put the snake round His Majesty's neck. I stepped forward and asked him to put it round my neck instead. Earlier on, he had said that no one should use flash photography when the snake was out of its cage, because the flash could incite it. Ali Khadem, the press photographer, had apparently not heard that warning. When they put the snake round my neck he took a flash photograph, but fortunately the snake did not react violently to it. That photograph was published shortly afterwards in *Tehran Mosavvar* newspaper.

Even though the snake did not show any violent reaction to the flash photography, it had a very unpleasant smell that lingered for 24 hours in my nose. Although I took several showers at the Dorchester when I got back to get rid of the smell, I could still detect it the following day.

Meanwhile, we received a secret cable from Ala and Ebtehaj, who insisted that His Majesty should return to Tehran as soon as possible. At that time, there were some moves against my father, and his enemies wished to insinuate to His Majesty that Zahedi wanted to stage a coup d'état. In another cable to me my father had insisted that the visit to Germany was essential and that the royal council supported his view. Their majesties were inclined to visit Germany. At that time, it was customary that whenever His Majesty left the country for a foreign visit, a royal council would be formed with the participation of the prime minister, the speaker of the parliament, and the president of the senate under the chairmanship of one of the Shah's brothers. Later on, during the premiership of Dr. Eqbal, this practice was stopped, and His Majesty said that there was no need for a royal council.

Khalil Esfandiary had spoken to me on the telephone about the invitation from Germany for their majesties' visit, and he had also sent a cable to the prime minister. However, there were two different views about the visit to Germany. My father and some other members of the royal council believed that relations with Germany were very important for Iran, while others argued that Germany was a defeated country and played no role in international politics.

Finally, it was decided that we would go ahead with the visit to Germany. We flew from London to Hamburg and then went by train from Hamburg to Cologne. We spent a day and a night in Cologne, and from there we went to Baden-Baden and then to Munich. Her Royal Highness Shahnaz came to Munich and met with her father.

This also was on the basis of my father's recommendation and insistence. He believed that it was not right for His Majesty to visit Europe and not see his only child, who was studying there.

We were due to go to Baghdad from Germany to have talks with King Faisal of Iraq and Nuri as-Sa'id Pasha about the Baghdad Pact, an idea that had been conceived in Mr. Wrightsman's house in America. In England, following the talks in America, His Majesty discussed the issue with the British prime minister and other government officials, and he wished to personally inform the Iraqi king and prime minister about the details of his talks.

At that time, we still did not have a large aircraft. When we were close to Beirut the pilot came and told me that the sky over Baghdad was very stormy and we might not be able to land there. Their majesties were asleep. I told the pilot that His Majesty was asleep and I did not wish to wake him. I advised him to continue on his path but to send a cable to the Iranian ambassador in Beirut and to the Lebanese president, Kamil Sham'un, informing them that we might not be able to land in Baghdad and might be forced to return to Beirut. I asked the pilot if he had enough fuel, and he said that he did and that we could even fly directly to Tehran. I told him that in that case he should not change the flight schedule and we would see what happened. The aircraft was a DC6. We also sent a message through the Baghdad air control tower to Qods Nakhai, our ambassador in Baghdad, to inform him that we were flying to Baghdad and would land if the weather allowed us to do so. Otherwise, we would return to Beirut. We asked him to inform the Iraqi court and government of the situation.

We continued on our journey, and fortunately there was no danger and we managed to land. In Baghdad, His Majesty King Faisal, the Crown Prince Malek Abdullah, and Prime Minister Nuri as-Sa'id had come to the airport to welcome their majesties. The plan was that we would fly by helicopter to Karbala and Najaf to visit the shrines of Imam Hossein and the Imam Ali, but as the weather was bad it was decided that we would go by car. On the way, there was a sandstorm, so that in places we could see only a yard in front of the car. Driving in those conditions was truly dangerous. I had never seen anything like that. When on our return we took a shower we noticed that our ears, noses, hair, and even our mouths were full of fine sand.

We were the dinner guests of His Majesty King Faisal. His Majesty told our ambassador to inform the palace that we were going to be a little late for the reception. When we arrived we saw that the Iraqi king, crown prince, and prime minister were standing by the stairs waiting for us. His Majesty Mohammad Reza Shah was always very polite and punctual and became angry at our delay. He reprimanded Qods Nakhai, but Nuri as-Sa'id Pasha, who spoke both Persian and Turkish, tried to resolve the problem. He said that they had been informed of the delay. Nevertheless, His Majesty King Faisal preferred to come to welcome their majesties a little earlier.

After dinner, our ambassador, Qods Nakhai, took Her Majesty back to the embassy. We went to another room, and talks regarding the Baghdad Pact started without the participation of the ambassador. This was one of the issues that intensified my father's disagreement with His Majesty.

Question: Why?

Zahedi: Because my father was basically opposed to joining the Baghdad Pact. He believed that it was not in our interest to join military pacts and that those pacts would not ensure our security, as the Sa'dabad Agreement did not prevent Iran from being occupied during the Second World War. Furthermore, joining military pacts would harm our relations with our neighbors. At that moment we did not have a conflict with the Russians, and so despite being close friends with the West, we could maintain our friendly relations with the Russians at a satisfactory level.

My father attached a great deal of importance to maintaining our friendly relations with the former Soviet Union, and the Russians welcomed that policy. Although the Russians had refused to hand back the Iranian gold that they held to Mossadegh, they returned it to Iran under my father due to the talks that were held between the two sides. At that time, it was a friendly gesture by the Russians and was of great importance to us. During my father's premiership, there were two people who were in charge of the talks with the Russians, Ali-Asghar Hekmat and Major General Esma'il Shafa'i, whom I always called "dear uncle."

Hekmat was a minister without portfolio in my father's cabinet. My father wished to appoint him as foreign minister, but he refused to accept that post because he thought that His Majesty did not have a positive view of him. There was some truth to that feeling, because His Majesty believed that by his actions, Hekmat wished to belittle him. In fact Hekmat was a very wise and patriotic man who believed in the monarchical system. Therefore, he was made a minister without portfolio. After a cabinet reshuffle, Hekmat left the cabinet. My father sent him as ambassador to India, because at that time the Russians had an active presence in India, and Hekmat could act as a go-between in the talks with the Russians there.

When I became Iranian ambassador in Washington and studied the record of secret talks between Iran and the Soviet Union, I became aware of the important role that Hekmat had played in those secret talks. I realized how this honorable and patriotic man had single-handedly confronted the Russian delegation that had come to the talks fully prepared and how he had been able to provide convincing replies to them based on historical facts. When I returned to Tehran I informed His Majesty of Hekmat's role, and he admitted that Hekmat had played a positive role. In brief, my father attached a great deal of importance to maintaining friendly relations with our northern neighbor and with all our other neighbors. I followed the same policy when I was in charge of the Ministry of Foreign Affairs.

My father believed, in addition to his principled opposition to membership of military pacts, that the talks on foreign policy of the country must be conducted with the government's knowledge and involvement and should be carried out through the Ministry of Foreign Affairs. He sent me a harsh cable when I was in Washington, telling me that it was none of my business to get involved in those talks. His view was that those talks should be carried out by the minister of foreign affairs. When I read the cable I felt very sorry for my father who so strongly took the side of the foreign minister, as the foreign minister had joined the ranks of those who were conspiring against my father.

Question: From what you say, it seems that there was some opposition to your father even inside the cabinet. Earlier on, you referred to some incitements against him. We know that at that time the differences between the Shah and the prime minister had come into the open. What were the reasons for those differences?

Zahedi: One of the reasons was that to which I have just referred, namely my father's opposition to Iran joining military pacts. However, the most fundamental difference between my father and His Majesty was that my father believed that the Shah should reign and not rule and that governments must be in charge of executive affairs. I witnessed these conversations a few times in His Majesty's presence. Her Majesty Soraya was present at some of those talks. My father told the Shah, "If you are directly involved in the talks and if you agree with them a few times, they will get into the habit of asking you for what they wish to gain. A day will come when the foreigners will make some demands that you will not be able to agree with. At that time, they will take action against you. However, if the governments are in charge, it will not matter. One government will go and another government will be appointed and the crown will remain immune to any intrigues against it."

I remember that my father often referred to the example of Moshir od-Dowleh and Mostowfi ol-Mamalek. He told His Majesty, "Those two individuals safeguarded the interests of the country during some acute crises. Depending on what the circumstances required, one of them would leave his post and the other would take his place." This was one of the fundamental differences that my father had with His Majesty right from the start. If you read the confidential documents of the American Embassy in Tehran that were published later, you will see that the American Ambassador Henderson had reported to the

U.S. secretary of state that the Shah had complained about the prime minister and had said that the ministers had been appointed without the Shah's knowledge.[1]

Another point of difference between my father and the Shah concerned the officers who had been retired under Mossadegh. His Majesty did not want them to return to active duty, but my father believed that those officers had shown great devotion in service to the country and the crown. There might be some good or bad individuals among them. We should at least bring back those who were honest officers and who did not have a blemish on their record. My father even wanted to resign from his post over this issue. I conveyed his message to His Majesty. His Majesty got upset and said, "What is all this talk of resignation for? What is the meaning of such talk?" Then he gave me a small box and said that it was for me, and he instructed me to tell my father to act in any way that he wished. I went to the prime minister's office and conveyed His Majesty's message to him. I also showed him the box. He said that it was a Taj medal, third degree. I did not know whether I had to wear it round my neck or on my chest.

The other disagreement between them was over the chairman of the Plan Organization. Abol-Ghassem Panahi was the chairman of the Plan Organization, and he had many enemies. He had very close relations with His Royal Highness Prince Abdol Reza, but the Shah was rather suspicious of his brother, because the Shah had been told that Mossadegh had decided to put him in His Majesty's place. Ernest Perron was a deadly enemy of Prince Abdol Reza and constantly tried to fan the flames of that suspicion. Panahi was aware of those developments and did not want to have any disagreements with His Majesty. He came to me a few times and asked me to give him a post in an embassy abroad, as he had a background in foreign affairs. As he was not feeling very well, he could receive medical treatment. However, my father insisted that he was very good at his work and should continue in his post.

I knew him from the time that I was a studying in the United States. We used to complain that it took weeks and months for the consulate to respond to us and deal with our problems concerning foreign currency and passports. They had even persuaded the Iranian ambassador in Washington, Ala, to reduce the amount of foreign currency that the students received (they wanted to pay us $120 instead of the $170 they used to give us). A number of other students and I decided to attack the embassy. Aram, who worked at the embassy, tried to get in touch with me, as we had sent a cable to the embassy. I met with the ambassador on behalf of the students. Before I could speak, Ala turned to me and said, "You are the grandson of Motamen ol-Molk. Now you want to attack the embassy! Don't do that." He then asked for an opportunity to resolve the matter.

That problem was eventually resolved with the help of Brigadier General Esfandiary, who later became a senator, and Ala. Later on, when Panahi became the consul general at the embassy, he paid special attention to the affairs of the students studying in the United States. Anybody who went to the consulate regarded it as his home. He used to send replies to the students by special delivery. From that time onward I was very fond of him, and I informed my father about my feelings for Panahi.

The prime minister's office used to move to Ghaytariyeh in summer, and the cabinet used to meet under a tent. Panahi wanted to go to the Darband Hotel to take part in a reception for diplomats, so he left rather early. An hour later, Colonel Zahedi, the commander of the prime minister's guard, reported that Panahi had fallen ill. A short time later, Khosrowdad reported that Panahi had suffered a heart attack during the reception and had died. The following day, His Majesty asked me who the prime minister had in mind for the post of the director of the Plan Organization. When I took my leave, Ala took me into a corner and asked me what I thought about Ebtehaj for the post. When my father heard these conversations he became very angry and said, "My friend's corpse is not yet buried. I won't do anything about his replacement until forty days after his death. Engineer Raji is

completely abreast of what is going on, and he will run the organization." His Majesty's insistence regarding the person who should be in
charge of the Plan Organization was another thing that brought the
differences between him and my father to a head.

Various intrigues gradually started. Some individuals who dreamed
of becoming prime minister constantly tried to create a rift between
the Shah and the prime minister. For a time, His Majesty did not pay
any attention to the intrigues and backbiting. Before we left for
America, I was with His Majesty, and we were playing backgammon
when the telephone rang. Sharifi, the aide, answered the phone and
came and told His Majesty that someone wanted to talk to him. The
call was from a leading national figure who was close to the court and
who was appointed prime minister later on. For a time, he and I had
some disagreements, and our friendship was on and off. As he is dead,
I do not wish to mention his name. His Majesty said, "Ask him what
he wants."

Sharifi came back and was hesitant as to whether he should say what
the man had said in front of me. Finally, he was forced to say that the
man on the telephone had said that it was not appropriate for His
Majesty to leave the country, because General Zahedi wanted to stage
a coup and would go ahead with it in His Majesty's absence. His
Majesty became angry and told Sharifi to tell him, "It is none of your
business to make such nonsensical remarks." That man did not know
that my father had been basically opposed to His Majesty going on
long trips and being away from the country for such a long time.

My father had urged me that if in my presence someone said something about him to His Majesty I should not show any reaction. One
day when I was with His Majesty and a special occasion arose I said,
"As you have allowed me to always tell the truth, I would like to say
that if one day I came and said something against my father you
should know that this could be part of a plot. You know that I am very
fond of you and have sworn an oath of allegiance to you, but I love my
father more than anyone else. I would like to ask Your Majesty never
to say anything about my father in my presence, in case I might make

an impudent remark, due to the fact that I may not be able to control myself." His Majesty made a promise, and right to the end he remained faithful to his word.

Due to what my father had told me at the airport prior to the departure for the United States, I never told him anything about the cables that we received in which certain hostile remarks were made against him. All the cables sent to His Majesty were from Court Minister Ala. When we were in New York we received a coded cable from Ala and Ebtehaj in which His Majesty had been asked to return to Iran as soon as possible because there was the possibility of a coup d'état. They had informed him that Zahedi had been engaged in plotting against His Majesty. I realized that I could not take that cable to His Majesty. Our ambassador in Washington, Nasrollah Entezam, was coming to New York. I told him that I had received such a cable, but it was not right that I would hand it to His Majesty. On the other hand, the cable concerned my father, and he had made those remarks to me on leaving Tehran. I told him that I would pretend that the cable had been given to him to decode it.

Entezam begged me not to get him involved in such issues. He said, "I am a friend of your father's and am very fond of him, and I do not even want to know anything about these developments." I said, "There is no option. You must do this for my sake and my father's sake." His Majesty resided in a suite on the 35th floor of the Waldorf-Astoria Hotel, and my suite was on the 20th floor. Entezam and I took the lift to His Majesty's suite. Jokingly, I told His Majesty, "Nasrollah has memorized the entire code book of the Ministry of Foreign Affairs but I have only recently had the honor of serving His Majesty, and my studies have been in a different field in America. Consequently, I am not very good at decoding the cables. Please allow him to go to another room and decode the message." His Majesty said, "We must be in the restaurant for dinner in 20 minutes." I said, "If he can decode the cable in that time he will be able to join us for dinner. Otherwise, he will go hungry, and it will be made clear that the rumors about his expertise at decoding the cables are not true!"

Anyway, half seriously and half jokingly, we gave the cable to Entezam and that heavy load was taken off my shoulders. We received another cable in San Francisco, which I again managed to free myself from dealing with. On the liner *Queen Elizabeth*, when we were sailing to England, we received another letter, which was full of accusations against my father and again referred to the possibility of a coup d'état by him. I told His Majesty that we had received another coded message that I could not decipher. He said, "When we get to London, give it to our Ambassador Soheili to decode." As we were traveling to London I informed Soheili of the issue in the train. He was also reluctant to get involved in it. He said, "General Zahedi made me an ambassador without any previous acquaintance with me and sent me here. My conscience would not allow me not to inform him of the issue. Therefore, please do not involve me in this issue." I told him, "I promise you that if my father were here he would ask you to do this." In London too, His Majesty told Soheili to send a cable to Tehran in response to the cable that we had received to tell them that such issues were none of their business.

Of course, His Majesty had guessed that I knew what was going on, and I did not wish to get involved. He deliberately asked me to send the replies to those cables. Later he said, "As we are returning to Iran, we must buy a present for the prime minister." He asked the views of a few people about what he should buy him. They said that for a military man the best present is a gun. He selected and purchased a very good gun that he gave as a present to my father when we returned home.

Some of these intrigues were due to the fact that some people wished to interfere in affairs and my father did not let them do so. Ala had proposed to my father that a group of consultants should be formed with the participation of Mr. Tafazzoli and a few others and that the prime minister should consult with them regarding current affairs. My father did not like that proposal, because he did not believe in such individuals and their views. Later on, they became Mr. Alam's advisers, and their meetings, which were held in Alam's house in Dezaship, had become a center for intrigue and conspiracy.[2]

As for the parliamentary elections, my father told His Majesty to let him know of anyone of whom he disapproved and that my father would take the responsibility of saying that he was opposed to that man's candidacy. As for the rest, they would act as it was done during Reza Shah's reign, namely, a number of the elders of each city would be asked their views about the local reputation of different individuals. In any place the individuals who received the backing of those elders would be put forward, and people would vote for one from among them. My father believed that he would also act in that way and that he would not be concerned about other issues.

I was with His Majesty in Ramsar. General Gharani, who at that time was the governor of Gilan, told me that His Majesty had ordered that Ne'mat Sami'i (the son-in-law of Major General Ahmad Nakhjavan and brother of Fathollah Samimi of the Ministry of Foreign Affairs) should not become a Majles deputy. I asked His Majesty the reason for his decision. His Majesty said, "During the period from 25–28 Mordad [16–19 August 1953] Sami'i had written a postcard to one of his friends saying that the Shah has left, good riddance!" The person who had received that postcard had sent it to the Shah through Qobad Zafar. His Majesty gave me the card and asked me to show it to my father.

I immediately left for Tehran. My father said, "This is something that needs a bit of study and consideration." Some people believed that the postcard had been forged. Sami'i swore on the Koran that he had not written such a postcard. Gharani also said that the person who had produced the card has been Sami'i's friend for 30 years. Why had he produced the card at that time on the eve of his own candidacy as a Majles deputy? How could one trust such a person? My father supported Gharani's views, but when he was faced with the Shah's insistence, he said, "This has nothing to do with me." Gharani also said that the issue should not become the cause of a rift between the

Shah and the prime minister. Consequently, that so-called friend of Sami'i became the Majles deputy from Rasht.

In Talesh, Holaku Rambod was a candidate for the election, and he was popular with the people. Haj Agha Reza Rafi, who had some contacts with the Shah, was opposed to Rambod, and the Shah also came under the influence of Rafi, but my father remained firm and Rambod was elected. This caused a rift between my father and Rafi.

In Golpayegan, my father had a positive view of one of the Moazzemi brothers, due to the help that Dr. Moazzemi had provided for my father during the time that he had taken asylum in the Majles. The Shah was opposed to his candidacy, and, to be honest, I was opposed to the Moazzemi candidacy too, especially as Mohammad Ali Motamed, Pirasteh's brother, was also a candidate there. This is why the Shah decided that Qobad Zafar should become a candidate. My father was upset as to why the earlier agreement had been violated. He believed that if the Shah was opposed to someone's candidacy he should have stated this from the start, rather than after Moazzemi had been promised the post. When the Moazzemi brothers saw their path blocked, they fell behind Qobad Zafar, and he was elected.

Question: Jahangir Tafazzoli has written in his memoirs that the formation of the Politburo had been his brainchild and that in addition to Alam, Amini and Entezam have also been among its members. What was the aim of forming the Politburo?

Zahedi: The aim was to weaken the government, with the Shah's support.[3] My father was opposed to the Politburo. At first, when Ebrahim Khajenouri and Mohammad Khan Akbar came to see me, they spoke about the differences between the Shah and the prime minister. They believed that something should be done to prevent misunderstanding between the court and the government. We decided that every Sunday afternoon, Khajenouri, Akbar, and Alam should go and meet the Shah, and if His Majesty had any complaints regarding the prime minister he would tell them. Then they would go to the prime minister for dinner in the evening and discuss those issues. As His Majesty could not speak openly with my father regarding the elections and the related issues, he would express his complaints to Mohammad Hossein Mirza Jahanbani, the deputy interior minister.

One evening, those three individuals came to the prime minister and said that His Majesty did not want Jahanbani to remain in his post, and they asked my father to appoint someone else in his place. Alam was present at that meeting. My father said, "From the start it was agreed that I should be in charge of the Ministry of the Interior. Mohammad Hossein Mirza Jahanbani is my representative there. If His Majesty has some complaints about the Ministry of the Interior he should tell me directly. If I remove Jahanbani, who should I put in his place? Khajenouri looked at Alam. My father asked Alam, "Are you capable of working as interior minister if I appoint you to that post?" Alam panicked and said, "No sir!" Everybody laughed, and I invited all of them to come to the table to have dinner. Later on, Alam wrote to me in a letter: "When Dr. Eqbal was about to be appointed as chancellor of Tehran University I told His Majesty the story of that night and all of us laughed a lot."[4]

Sharif Emami was another person who was involved in those intrigues. There was a reason and a background for his grudge. Sharif Emami and Kohbod were business partners. They had been involved in some influence peddling in the course of Majles elections, which had been reported to my father. Due to his intense anger, my father had ordered both of them to be shaved and exiled to Bandar Abbas. Alam came to me and said that His Majesty might get upset at this. He asked me to do something to change the general's mind. I went to the Officers' Club. My father was playing backgammon with Amirani and Kashanian. I told him that the order that he had issued could not be implemented. He asked why. I told him, "Both those individuals are bald, and they have no hair to shave." He laughed and canceled the order that he had issued.

One of the issues that had resulted in differences between His Majesty and the prime minister was that my father was not in favor of the Shah getting involved in electoral rivalries and clashes. He had ordered Brigadier Jahanbani, who was deputy minister of the interior and

worked directly under my father's supervision, to ignore any recommendations that he might receive regarding the elections, regardless of
those making those recommendations, even if they were persons of
high position. As a result, Jahanbani did not pay any attention to
recommendations and requests for favors. This clearly made many
people unhappy.

When His Majesty and I were returning to Tehran from a visit to the
south by train, my father sent a message to His Majesty, asking him to
stop on the way in Qom and have a meeting with Ayatollah Borujerdi.
He had also made arrangements for that meeting. The reason for this
decision by my father was to make up for Ayatollah Borujerdi's
displeasure regarding the latest elections in Qom. Ayatollah Borujerdi
was in favor of the election of Abolfazl Towliat. The court also wished
to implement the views of Ayatollah Borujerdi. However, Emadoddin
Sezavar, who was Towliat's rival, had a better chance of being elected.

Alam, who at that time was in charge of Pahlavi Properties, sent me a
message on His Majesty's behalf to do something to help Towliat to
get elected. Early in the morning I got in the car and left for Qom,
together with Kazem Khan Sheybani, who was a Majles candidate
from Kashan. My intention was to go to Qom and meet with Ayatollah Borujerdi and see what kind of help he expected from us. When
we got to Kushk-e Nosrat, near Qom, we saw that the head of the
police and the head of the Gendarmerie were waiting for us there. I
thought that they had come to welcome us. They treated us in a very
friendly manner and brought watermelon and melon for us to eat.
After we finished eating, we wanted to resume the journey, but they
told us very politely that we had to return to Tehran. We learned that
my father had been informed of the aim of our journey and had issued
orders for us to return to Tehran. There was nothing we could do, and
we returned. For a few days, my father was rather angry with me
because of my interference in this issue.

The elections were held, and Towliat was not elected. This upset
Ayatollah Borujerdi. My father wished to make amends for that hurt.
As a result, he had made arrangements for a meeting between the Shah

and the Source of Emulation in the holy shrine of Ma'sumeh in Qom. He had already spoken to His Majesty, telling him that if there had been any talk of the elections he should put all the blame on my father's shoulders.

Question: Regarding the visit to the south of the country that you are referring to: did it take place after the visit to Europe and America?

Zahedi: Yes. We returned to Tehran a week before Nowruz, the Iranian New Year. My father intended to go to the north of the country immediately after the official New Year ceremonies, and I was due to go with him. During the New Year ceremonies that were held at Golestan Palace, His Majesty said that I would accompany him during the visit to the south. His Majesty intended to go to Khuzestan in order to inspect oil installations and the construction work on Karkheh Dam. We left on 8 Farvardin, and that trip lasted five days. On the way back, His Majesty received a letter from Alam. After reading it, he tore it to pieces and threw it in the fire. I was playing backgammon with His Majesty. Jokingly, he said that there had been a coup d'état in Tehran. Mohsen Khan Gharagozlu, who was Ala's brother-in-law and the head of the ceremonies at the court, also had the honor of being with His Majesty. We wanted to play games with Gharagozlu. His Majesty ordered the royal train to be stopped and ordered us to tell Mohsen Khan that Nasiri has sent a report saying that there had been a coup d'état in Tehran and Ala had also been arrested, to see how he would react.

Ebtehaj, Amini, Alam, and a few others who often acted as grandees selecting the leading government figures had chosen Hossein Ala as a candidate for the premiership. Personally, Ala was not interested in becoming prime minister, and he preferred to remain as court minister. Furthermore, he was not in robust health. The interesting thing was that my father's opponents used to say that he was ill and did not have the stamina to run affairs, but their own candidate was more sickly. This is why immediately after being appointed prime minister,

Ala appointed Entezam as deputy prime minister and left for Paris to receive medical treatment.

In any case, we returned to Tehran. My father welcomed His Majesty at the station. After His Majesty left, I got in the car with my father, and he gave me a brief account of what was happening. He told me that he had decided to resign from his post as prime minister, because he was opposed to what was going on. It was at that point that I realized that Amini and Abdollah Entezam had been actively involved in the intrigues. This came as a shock to me, because I knew how strongly my father always defended his ministers.

Question: When did the relations between Amini and General Zahedi start, and why was Amini chosen as minister of finance?

Zahedi: Before answering your question, I must go back a bit and speak about our family relations. My father had some special personal traits. First of all, he would never leave any person's kindness unanswered. He was extremely faithful to anyone who had helped him. His second characteristic was that he attached a great deal of importance to his family and was very zealous and serious about family relations. This is why he was anxious that I should be close to my mother's family. A year before I returned to Iran, I came from the United States to Europe and I was my father's guest. My father took me to Paris to meet with Madame Monir Azam and Ghavam os-Saltaneh and other members of the Qajar family who lived in Paris.

Consequently, when I returned to Iran, my father had asked Madame Eshrat os-Saltaneh, my grandmother, and my mother to introduce me to every member of my extended family. One of the people I met was Madame Fakhr al-Dowleh, who was a very dear and honorable lady. When my grandmother, to whom my father was very strongly attached, died, Madame Fakhr al-Dowleh and Madame Eshrat os-Saltaneh came to her funeral. Madame Fakhr al-Dowleh had made the final arrangements for the funeral, and this had affected my father. When my grandmother was alive Madame Fakhr al-Dowleh visited her often, and these visits were often repeated during the New Year celebrations.

Ali Amini was interested in politics and used to come to visit my father. When my father was serving as interior minister under Mossadegh os-Saltaneh, despite the fact that His Majesty did not have a favorable view of Abol-Ghassem Amini, my father presented him to His Majesty as the governor general of Isfahan. After my father resigned from Mossadegh os-Saltaneh's cabinet, Ali Amini remained in the cabinet. On one feast day on the Id al-Ghadir, Madame Fakhr al-Dowleh invited my father and me to her house in Elahiyyeh for lunch. When we were there, Ali Amini, who was dressed formally, came to see his mother (I do not know whether it was by chance or was planned). On that day, Madame Fakhr al-Dowleh asked my father that if the situation changed in the future he should not forget about Ali. My father replied, "If in future you have any orders and you cannot get hold of me, Ardeshir will always be at your service."

After that meeting, from time to time some messages were exchanged between my father and Madame Fakhr al-Dowleh. On 29 Mordad [20 August 1953], the individuals who were selected to work in the cabinet were brought to the Officers' Club by Messrs. Parvaresh, Yarafshar, Sarabandi, and (I think) Amidi-Nuri to meet with the prime minister. I remember that Amir Nosrat Eskandari, who was a good friend of my father's, also came and was appointed as governor general of Isfahan. They sent a car to bring Dr. Hossein Pirnia, but he had gone to Na'in. That day, very early in the morning Madame Fakhr al-Dowleh had telephoned and wanted to talk to me. As soon as I was given the message by Major Manuchehr Khosrowdad and Yarafshar I phoned her back. She told me, "Dear Ardeshir, tell your father not to forget Ali."

I informed my father of the conversation at the earliest opportunity. Ali Amini was also called to the Officers' Club, and, as you know, he was appointed minister of finance. His Majesty was not very pleased about that appointment, as well as the ministerial posts that were given to Mohammad Hossein Mirza Jahanbani and Ali Asghar Hekmat, and on different occasions when I was received by His Majesty he would make some caustic remarks about them. I must also say honestly that I was influenced by others, and at times I informed my father about what others said about his ministers. It may be appropriate to refer to just one case here. Later on, certain developments took place and Amini was involved in some intrigues, and the fact that he did not come to the airport to see my father off after he had resigned resulted in a grudge between them. Finally, with the mediation of Abdol-Hossein Nikpour, Ahmad Vahabzadeh, and Ali-Asghar Milanchi, they brought Ali to see my father in Switzerland, and my father said that they should forget what had happened in the past.

When after my first ambassadorial post in the United States I was returning to Iran I went to Nowshahr. There, His Majesty made me make friends with Amini again, and we returned to Tehran together. At the airport, Foreign Minister Qods Nakhai had come to welcome us. There, Amini did me a favor and said that all of us should go to my house and the three of us went to Valiabad. In the midst of conversation Amini referred to the letters that we had exchanged. He said that once when he was received by His Majesty they had spoken about my letter, and His Majesty had said that Amini should not joke with me as I was a serious person and did not like frivolity. Later on, Qods Nakhai confirmed that conversation between His Majesty and Amini.

The case that I was going to speak about concerned the period when my father was still prime minister and Amini was minister of finance. One day my father and I were traveling from Mehrabad Airport to Tehran. At that time, the new airport was not yet built, and the Karaj Road was very narrow. I was sitting next to my father in his car. I told him that His Majesty was unhappy about the fact that he had brought Major General Hedayat and Amini to the cabinet. He suddenly became very angry, told me off, and said, "I will not allow you or anyone else to criticize my ministers." I became very upset and told Ebrahim Khan to stop the car. Ebrahim Khan was my father's trusted driver at the Ministry of the Interior, and when he became prime minister he brought his driver with him to the prime minister's office.

Ebrahim Khan stopped by the side of the road. I got out of the car and started walking toward the town. I remember that I was coming from some official functions and wore formal clothes. The escort cars that were following my father's car stopped for me, and everybody was amazed to see me in that state. My father's car drove slowly for a while and finally it stopped near me. My father lowered the window and called to me to get in. I got in, but I was still in a huff. My father said, "My dear son! I wanted to appoint Dr. Pirnia as the minister of finance, but it was due to your recommendation and insistence that I gave the post to Dr. Amini, while most of my friends were opposed to his appointment and kept saying that he was not trustworthy. However, now that he is a cabinet minister, it is my duty to defend him."

As regards Entezam, I have already said that my father was angry because His Majesty had become involved in political talks in the absence of the minister of foreign affairs and my father felt that he should have asked for the foreign minister's views. This is why, when I learned about all the intrigues that were carried out behind the scenes, my blood boiled. The following day I went to the court. As I entered the office of Mohammad Khan Akbar, who was the master of ceremonies, I saw that Entezam, Amini, and Ebtehaj were sitting there. I couldn't contain myself and said that a bullet fired at such individuals would be wasted. I got up and went to the entrance hall, where on 21st Farvardin there had been an assassination attempt on His Majesty's life. When they noticed how tense the situation was, they sent a message and asked His Majesty to receive them at a later date. His Majesty agreed, and those three got up and left the palace.

That was the day when my father had already written his letter of resignation and had sent it to His Majesty, but he was continuing with his work at the prime minister's office, waiting for His Majesty's response. His Majesty sent a letter inviting my father to lunch at the palace. My father excused himself, saying that he was tired and suffering from a sore arm (in one of his trips he had slipped and broken his arm). Finally, we mediated and he had lunch with His Majesty. Empress Soraya also came. After lunch, as His Majesty was saying farewell, he held my father's hand firmly in his two hands and warmly pressed it, and there is a memorial photograph of that farewell.

His Majesty had sent a message to my father through Alam, saying that he knew that my father had no money abroad, and that now that he was leaving the country he needed some money. There were about 500,000 tumans in His Majesty's properties' office and he could have that sum, but my father replied that there was no need for that. He telephoned Mostafa Tajaddod, the governor of the Bank of Commerce. He gave the property that we had in Ferdowsi Avenue as collateral, and the bank gave him about two million tumans. He settled abroad with that money.[5]

Question: How did the rumor about the possibility of a coup d'état start?

Zahedi: In his cable Ala had written that Batmanqelich had said that Zahedi intended to stage a coup. Personally, I do not believe that Batmanqelich would have said such a thing, but God only knows! The night before my father resigned he told me that if he had intended to stage a coup and get rid of the Shah he would have done that on 28th of Mordad. He said, "But I did not do that, because apart from the fact that I love Mohammad Reza Shah like my own son, in view of Iran's geopolitical situation, I believe that the existence of the Shah and the monarchy is necessary for the preservation of the country's territorial integrity. Between 28th of Mordad and His Majesty's return, many leading political figures of the country, such as Hassan Taghizadeh, Adl ol-Molk Dadgar, and Nasr ol-Molk Hedayat, urged me not to hurry in bringing the Shah back to the country. They advised that he should stay abroad for a while and the government should hold the reins of power until the situation settled down, but I did not accept their views. I said that this is a trust that I should return to its owner as soon as possible."

On Thursday morning, 17 Farvardin [April 6], my father chaired the last session of the cabinet and announced his decision to resign. While saying farewell to the ministers, he told them, "After seeking permission from His Majesty, I am going to Europe for medical treatment. All of us are and have been sincere servants of the homeland. I wish all of you luck in the service of the country, and I hope that all of you will remain sincere and faithful to His Majesty."

Amini and Entezam were in that meeting, but they did not go to the airport. Later on, Entezam had said that Amini had prevented him from going, saying that in view of the situation that had come about it would not be in their interest to go to the airport to see off the prime minister. After my father's resignation, when he was living in Switzerland, Entezam kept up a correspondence with him and was trying to overcome earlier differences. Later on, Entezam came to Paris and met my father, and my father kissed him on the cheek. He also told me that I had to forget the past. When he was serving as foreign minister in Ala's government I arranged for him to have lunch with His Majesty in Babolsar. I also talked to His Majesty and the prime minister about appointing him as the managing director of the oil company.

In any case, the same evening my father left for Europe, and there was an official farewell ceremony at the airport. I was very upset and was weeping uncontrollably. I was so sad that I had decided to leave the country together with my father and to remain abroad with him and never to return again, but my father consoled me and said that I had to stay and must remain alongside His Majesty.

When I returned from the airport, His Majesty phoned me ordering me to have dinner with him. I tried to make many excuses, but he did not accept them. That evening when I went to the palace, Her Royal Highness the Queen, as well as His Majesty, showed me great kindness. At the dinner table His Majesty asked me why I was crying. He said, "It was your father's wish to leave his post, and we shall think of an appropriate position for him, and you can go and see your father any time you like."

The day when my father resigned, Hossein Ala was given the decree to be the next prime minister. He introduced his cabinet to His Majesty on Saturday, and the following day he went to Paris to receive

From right to left: Abdol-Hossein Haerizadeh, Hossein Makki, Mozafar Baghai, Nadali Karimi, General Zahedi, and Afshar Sadeghi

At the Ministry of Foreign Affairs. On the left: Minister of Health Jahanshah Saleh and Minister of Agriculture Ahmad-Hossein Adle. Standing is Abol-Ghassem Panahi, the head of the planning organization. On the other side of the table is Minister of Justice Seyyed Jamaleddin Akhavi and General Abbas Farzanegan, acting minister of communications.

Prime Minister Zahedi on a pilgrimage to the shrine of Reza, the eighth Imam in Mashad. Governor Mohammad Mehran of Khorasan can be seen beside him.

Amir-Hossein Bushehri in discussion with Prime Minister Zahedi. Abdol-Hossein Meftah and General Mohammad-Hossein Jahanbani can also be seen in the photograph.

Meeting between Seyyed Hossein Taqiza-deh, the head of the Senate, and Prime Minister Fazlollah Zahedi.

Ardeshir and Prime Minister Fazlollah Zahedi during a formal event.

At the Officers' Club. From right to left: General Zarrabi, Senator Matin-Daftari, General Fazlollah Zahedi, Ali Heyat, and Moshir Fatemi.

Norman Paul; Loy Henderson, U.S. ambassador to Iran; Prime Minister Zahedi; and William Warne. Henderson had brought a message from President Eisenhower to Prime Minister Zahedi.

Prime Minister Zahedi; William Warne, head of the Iran-U.S. Joint Committee; and Ardeshir.

After resigning from the premiership, Fazlollah Zahedi is photographed bidding farewell to the Shah. He left soon after for Switzerland to take the post of Iranian representative to the United Nations in Geneva.

Ardeshir next to Fazlollah Zahedi, on his father's last day as prime minister.

Fazlollah Zahedi talking to his son before Ardeshir accompanied the Shah on his trip to the United States.

Ali-Asghar Amirani, the editor in chief of the influential *Khandaniha* magazine, is photographed visiting Ardeshir at the Zahedi residence in Hesarak. Amirani would be executed by the Islamic regime after the 1979 revolution.

General Zahedi and Mashadi Asghar Baghbanchi in the greenhouse at the Zahedi house in Hesarak.

The Shah, Ardeshir, and Hossein Jahanbani playing backgammon aboard the *Queen Elizabeth* on the return trip from the United States.

His Majesty and General Zahedi in conversation in 1953. Prince Ali-Reza can be seen in the background.

December 1953, at the Marble Palace. From left to right, front row: Ardeshir; Hossein Ala, minister of court; and Amir Azam Azodi, chief of protocol for the court. Second row: Holaku Rambod; Esfandiar Diba, Equerry to the Monarch and uncle to the future Queen, Farah; Mohammad Akbar, protocol officer and Equerry to the Monarch; Mohsen Gharogozlu, protocol office; and Amir Asadollah Alam, Equerry to the Monarch and the head of the Pahlavi Foundation.

The Shah visits Prime Minister Fazlollah Zahedi at the Officers' Club in 1953. Prince Gholam-Reza Pahlavi; Prince Abdol-Reza Pahlavi; General Ali Parvaresh, the head of the Officers' Club; General Abdollah Hedayat; General Gilanshah; and Ilkhan Zafar Bakhtiar can also be seen in the photograph.

The Shah visits Prime Minister Fazlollah Zahedi at the Officers' Club in 1953. Present were Foreign Minister Abdollah Entezam; Minister of Court Hossein Ala; Prince Gholam-Reza Pahlavi; Prince Abdol-Reza Pahlavi; Acting Minister of Communications Farzanegan; Parliament Deputy Mirashrafi and General Ali Parvaresh, the head of the Officers' Club.

From left to right: The Shah, Prince Abdol-Reza, General Zahedi, Ahmad Hossein Adle, and Ali Amini.

From left to right: Nowrouzi, assistant to the Queen Mother; Ardeshir; General Ali Gholi Golpeyra; General Morteza Yazdanpanah; the Shah; General Fazlollah Zahedi; and General Farhad Dadsetan.

Richard Nixon and Prime Minister Fazlollah Zahedi during the American vice president's visit to Iran in 1953.

Richard Nixon; General Ali Parvaresh, the head of the Officers' Club; and Prime Minister Fazlollah Zahedi; can be seen at a reception in honor of the visiting U.S. vice president at the Iranian Foreign Ministry.

At the same reception, from left to right: General Batmanqelich, Mrs. Patricia Nixon, Vice President Richard Nixon, and Prime Minister Fazlollah Zahedi.

On the first anniversary of the 1953 national uprising. From left to right: Gholam-Hossein Ebtehaj, the Mayor of Tehran; General Nader Batmanqelij; Ardeshir; General Abbas Farzanegan and Prime Minister Zahedi.

The first anniversary of the 1953 national uprising. From left to right: Reza Jafari; Ali Amini; General Abbas Garzan; Seyyed Fakhreddin Shadman; Minister at Large Amir Hossein Ilkhan; Prime Minister Zahedi; General Alavi Moghaddam, Head of the National Police Force; Minister of Agriculture Ahmad Hossein Adle; Ardeshir; Minister of Labor Masoud Maleki; Minister of Justice Akhavi; and Head of the National Railroads Ezatollah Hedayat.

From left to right: Ali Amini; Nasrollah Entezam; John H. Loudon, head of Royal Dutch Shell; unkown person; Herbert Hoover, Jr., special envoy of President Eisenhower for talks on the creation of the consortium; and Prime Minister Zahedi.

From left to right: Ardeshir, General Abbas Farzanegan, Prime Minister Zahedi, General Batmanqelij, and General Gilanshah. On the second row: Soleyman Behboudi, Chief of Protocol of the Court; General Taqizadeh; Mostafa Moghaddam; and Mr. Hirad, the Shah's Chief of Staff. On the third row: Esfandiar Bozorgmehr, Head of the Department of Publicity and Publication; Colonel Nasiri; Colonel Mohammad Khatami; and Colonel Khajenouri.

Friends and supporters of Fazlollah Zahedi see him off at Mehrabad Airport. From left, General Garzan, Besharat, Massoud Maleki, General Hedayat, and General Teymur Bakhtiar.

Friends and supporters of Fazlollah Zahedi see him off at the airport. Former premier, Muhammad Sa'ed Maraghei and Parviz Adle can be seen amongst the crowd on the tarmac.

Former Prime Minister Fazlollah Zahedi bids farewell and departs for Switzerland.

medical treatment. Alam, who was appointed as interior minister, insisted that I should be appointed as acting interior minister, so that he could go to the court as court minister to replace Ala. I told him that I had no familiarity with the work of the Interior Ministry. Furthermore, Mirza Ahmad Khan Fereidouni, who was a capable individual and had spent a lifetime in that ministry, was deputy minister of the interior and was more qualified to hold that post. In previous days, when Fereidouni used to come to our house, he would put me on his knee. It was difficult for someone like him to answer to someone like me.

Fortunately, as Ala wished to keep the post of the court minister secure for himself and also wanted to ensure that the position of his brother-in-law Mohsen Khan Gharagozlou was secure, he showed no interest in changing the minister of the interior, and the issue came to an end.

---

[1] See the English text of the letter, item No 353, with the headline "The Ambassador in Iran (Henderson) to the Department of State," pp. 530–533.

[2] In his memoirs, which were published after his death, Jahangir Tafazzoli writes:

> Towards the middle of the term of the government of General Zahedi, I proposed to the Shah that if he found it appropriate he should set up a politburo whose members would study and discuss His Majesty's orders and views to see what was the best and the quickest way of implementing them. I felt that the Shah very much liked the term politburo, which had Stalinist connotations and reminded one of his extraordinary power. He ordered me to make a list of the individuals whom I regarded suitable for membership in that politburo.
>
> Three days later when I was received by His Majesty I presented the names of the individuals whom I regarded to be useful for the Shah and who could provide the opportunity for the wise and considered implementation of the Shah's views. On a piece of paper I had written the names of Dr. Ali Amini, Abdollah Entezam, Amir Asadollah Alam, General Abdollah Hedayat, Brigadier-General Nasiri, the commander of the Royal Guards, and Brigadier-General Teymur Bakhtiar, the military governor of Tehran. The Shah asked, "Why have you not written your own name?" I replied, "My scope of operation is much narrower than that of those gentlemen." The Shah insisted, "Not only should you be in

the politburo, but you should act as its secretary and you should directly tell me your views."

The Shah crossed out the names of General Hedayat and Brigadier-General Nasiri from that list. However, the reason why he appointed me as the secretary of the politburo and responsible for conveying its reports to him was that General Zahedi still had a great deal of influence in the Majles. In other words, he had personally selected the majority of Majles deputies and he had a much greater influence in the armed forces than other officers. He did not wish the ministers in his cabinet or even the military governor that he had appointed to have separate contacts with the Shah.

That group (the politburo) met once a week in the house of one of the members, but most often we met in the houses of Dr. Amini and Amir Asadollah Alam.

Abdollah Entezam lived in Amini's house in Elahiyyeh and to a large extent he was regarded by both the Shah and Zahedi as a protégé of Dr. Ali Amini. During the Second World War and many years later, Abdollah Entezam lived in Europe and was not a personal friend of the Shah and had no contact with him. The politburo involved itself in some important issues that were in keeping with the views of the Shah, or policies that the Shah wished to implement, such as the downfall of Zahedi's government, the formation of Ala's government or Iran's membership in the Baghdad Pact.

When Ala became prime minister, he did not know any of his ministers. He only added the name of Ali Motamedi to the list that had been prepared by the politburo and approved by the Shah. Bakhtiar, Alam and Entezam did not know as well as Amini the individuals who would both have the qualifications needed in a minister and who also enjoyed the Shah's trust. The list was mainly prepared by Amini and to some extent by me.

[3] Abol-Hassan Ebtehaj writes in his memoirs:

Documents show that after I was put in charge of the Plan Organisation and differences arose between Zahedi and me, Zahedi met with Tamaddon ol-Molk Sajjadi, the representative of the British Embassy in Tehran. While expressing dissatisfaction regarding me and criticising me he had said that I was not a trustworthy person, and that there had been some documents in the National Bank that confirmed his suspicions. Zahedi had added that as he did not wish that there would be a great deal of publicity regarding the issue he would not reveal the documents. At the end, he had said that despite all those issues he still wished to co-operate with me.

This was the first time that someone had accused me of not being trustworthy. Throughout my long career, everybody—including my opponents, who were numerous—had confirmed my honesty and trustworthiness. What is certain is that, on the one hand, Zahedi asked the Shah to dismiss me; and, on the other hand, the Shah was looking for an opportunity to dismiss Zahedi. When Zahedi submitted his letter of resignation to the Shah, he had told the Shah, "Between Ebtehaj and me, you must choose one of us." The Shah had replied, "We need Ebtehaj who has outstanding capabilities, and we will not dismiss him." The Shah had asked Zahedi to revise his decision.

At that time, the foreigners generally and the British in particular had a negative view of the situation in Iran and its future. The British Ambassador Roger Stevens believed that the Shah was weak and indecisive, and he also believed that Zahedi was not suitable as prime minister. He believed that Zahedi was most probably busy filling his own pockets and the pockets of his friends. After Zahedi was removed, the British Foreign Office believed that Iran needed a strong and capable prime minister. One of the persons who was consulted by the Foreign Office on this issue was Ms. Anne Lambton. Lambton had said that the Shah was a useless individual, because neither was he capable of ruling, nor would he allow anyone else to rule. Regarding me, she had said that I was not capable of filling that post either, and that the only person who would be able to resolve the national issues and could save Iran was Seyyed Ziaeddin Tabatabai. Regarding Zahedi, it should be said that he was a very powerful prime minister. Although Majles deputies still carried some weight, Zahedi never paid any attention to them, and as he also had the military behind him everybody was afraid of him. His portraits could be seen next to that of the Shah in all the streets, and he had been basically known as the country's most powerful man. The Shah was naturally not very pleased that Zahedi enjoyed so much power, and was looking for an opportunity to dismiss him. Maybe the differences between Zahedi and me, especially when the engineers from Comsax had not allowed him to enter the port area in Khorramshahr, provided one of the excuses for dismissing him. Unfortunately, the differences between Zahedi and me resulted in the breakdown of all our contacts and I never saw him again.

[4] The quarterly *Contemporary Iranian History* published the following letter by the Oppressed Foundation (Bonyad-e Mostaz'afan) after Ardeshir Zahedi's property had been confiscated in Tehran. The letter was published in issue 7 of Autumn 1377 [1998], with the following introduction:

In Dey 1333 [January 1955] when the period of Dr. Ali Akbar Siassi's term as
the president of Tehran University was coming to an end … in a meeting of the
University Council on 13 Dey [3 January] a number of deans of faculties and
professors were voting to select the new president. After the votes, according to
the new law, three people were chosen and their names were put forward. One
of them, namely Dr. Manuchehr Eqbal, was approved by the Ministry of Education and was eventually appointed as the president of Tehran University by a
decree issued by the Shah on 16 Dey [6 January].

However, behind the scenes, there were some political games being played. The
Shah was strongly in favour of that appointment, but his powerful Prime Minister, Zahedi, was opposed to Eqbal's appointment and in fact for a long time
previously they were not on speaking terms with each other. Meanwhile, Asadollah Alam thought of something and settled the issue by using Ardeshir Zahedi as the middleman. The gist of Asadollah Alam's important letter to Ardeshir Zahedi is as follows:

"27/9/1333 [18 December 1954]… A very important point that I wish to write
to you about is that in the elections for the president of Tehran University, most
people believe that His Majesty is in favor of the selection of Dr. Eqbal. When
His Imperial Majesty was leaving, he did not say anything to me or to your father [Prime Minister Zahedi]. He only ordered me to tell the Prime Minister
that now that he had made friends with Sajjadi again, why didn't he also make
up with Dr. Eqbal? As it happens, when I talked to your dad, I noticed that he
was not at all opposed to that view. This is why I asked him that one evening
when he invites [illegible] and the senators to a reception he should also invite
Dr. Eqbal. In advance, I also urged Dr. Eqbal to go to that reception and to
show due respect to the Prime Minister. He also did as he was asked and, as the
result of the mediation by Tafazzoli and me, at the reception his behaviour towards the Prime Minister was not bad at all.

Two days later, Dr. Eqbal sent me a message saying that he was a candidate for
the presidency of the university and that he would like to know the Prime Minister's view about it. He pointed out that as he had now renewed his friendship
with the Prime Minister he would not like to do something without winning his
approval in advance. I also talked to your father about it. He said, 'When I have
made up with someone I would no longer act in an unfriendly and insincere
manner towards him. My only problem is that if I now help Dr. Eqbal to be
appointed university president all my friends would be hurt and they are right
to feel let down.' At the same time, your father complained that he had heard
that His Majesty had issued some orders to [Reza] Ja'fari [the minister of educa-
tion]. He was surprised that His Majesty had not issued those orders to him, as

he was the head of the government and His Majesty's sincere servant. I told him that maybe His Majesty had some reason for talking to Ja'fari before talking to him. Ja'fari might have asked His Majesty's views about the president of Tehran University, and in response maybe His Majesty had expressed a liking for Dr. Eqbal. Later on, he might have forgotten to speak to you. Then I informed your father about my own appointment as minister of the interior and the extreme affection and consideration that His Imperial Majesty had showed regarding that issue. As the result of all that talk, on the whole, your father felt much better about the issue…

Finally, we came to the conclusion that you should put the matter to His Majesty, so that if he has any views or orders you should directly send me a cable. In that case, your father will not be put in a difficult situation. In other words, when our friends know that the royal decree has been issued on the subject, they would no longer blame your father for that decision. I personally guess that His Majesty has a favourable view of Dr. Eqbal. Otherwise, he would not have ordered me to tell your father to make friends with Dr. Eqbal. Nevertheless, His Imperial Majesty is so considerate that he did not wish to issue an order before winning your dad's approval for Dr. Eqbal. Therefore, as a brother, I would like to urge you that you should not ask His Majesty's views on the issue in such a way that he might say no, and that there is no need for you to get involved in the issue. Your dad's approval has already been obtained and the issue has also been discussed in the cabinet. Therefore, it will in no way harm your father either. Although His Imperial Majesty is well disposed towards Dr. Eqbal, nevertheless, he would be pleased if you and your father also express approval for Dr. Eqbal's appointment (in other words, it means that you express your pleasure at obeying His Imperial Majesty's orders)."

[5] In *Palace of Solitude,* Princess Soraya relates:

I greatly liked Shahnaz who, two years later, with her ravishing looks, was to marry Ardeshir Zahedi, the son of the man who had overthrown Mossadeq and enabled the Shah to regain his throne. General Zahedi, the national hero.
I will always remember that lunch we had with him at Echtessassi. That same morning, the Shah had been walking up and down the drawing room. I guessed immediately that he had something serious to tell me. Shyly, I asked him: "What's the matter, Mohammed?" He planted himself in front of me and replied, ill-at-ease: "Zahedi is getting in the way a little too much, I will have to get rid of him."

I was appalled. How could he have decided to dismiss the man he owed everything to, his constant friend, his faithful prime minister?

Pretending to ignore my indignation, he shut himself up in silence.

A servant came to announce the general's arrival.

Mohammed Reza received him warmly. As if nothing were the matter. Suddenly, in the middle of the meal, he said: "General, I thank you for everything you have done for me and for Iran but I think that the responsibilities of your position have become too onerous for you. You ought to take a rest for a little while in Switzerland ... I advise you to leave as soon as possible."

Zahedi looked pale, crumpled. The Shah was smiling at him as at a very old friend to whom nothing can be refused. "I will arrange for you to be created Ambassador Extraordinaire to Geneva ... with an extremely fine house and a very handsome salary ... Will you have a little coffee?"

So it was that General Fazlollah Zahedi retired to Switzerland for ever. Later we saw him again in Montreux.

In fact, the Shah was afraid of General Zahedi's huge popularity. What if one day he tried to topple him from the Iranian throne to have himself proclaimed the Shah of Shahs, the sort of thing Nasser had done with Farouk in Egypt? Persecution mania.

In his biography of General Zahedi, *From a Soldier to a Politician*, Dr. Ezatollah Homayunfar writes:

Despite all the concern that people had regarding speaking openly about the Shah, Zahedi's resignation did not go without reaction in the Majles and in the press. In the Majles, Shushtari said, "Any deputy who has accepted the task of representing the people must say what is his legal duty to say... I am not engaging in flattery... Now, I see that some newspapers write that I am against [Ala's premiership]... Gentlemen, I know very well what I should do. Whether General Zahedi is the prime minister or not, whether he is in Iran or abroad, I and a large number of other people are fond of him (a number of Majles deputies said 'that is correct'). One day, when I was with Sardar Fakher, we were talking about all the services that the government had rendered. He said that I had gone into excess in my praise. I replied, 'I have seen two actions from General Zahedi, and I believe that every Iranian must respect him for those actions. When he was the head of the police under the late Reza Shah, Zahedi did not compile dossiers for anyone. When a dossier was formed treasonously for some people in Khorasan [for Asadi, the deputy custodian of the Holy Shrine during Bohlul's uprising], that dossier was sent to General Zahedi for review. One day, he closed the door and said that certain gentlemen had compiled that dossier and that he would not be a party to that treason, and he found them not guilty. When that dossier was brought to the notice of the late Reza Shah, His Majesty became very angry, but General Zahedi said, 'I swear by your throne and crown that this file is false.' Later on, when Reza Shah discovered the truth of that assertion, he wrote in his own hand under another file, 'Make sure that this file will not turn out to be false like the file of Khorasan.'"

Ebrahim Emami, Jamal Emami's brother, writes in *The Truth* (London: 1995):

Towards the end of his government, one day General Zahedi had complained to Jamal Emami about the Shah. He told him, "I do not know what has happened that these days he [the Shah] has changed his attitude. He constantly objects to certain policies of the government and puts obstacles on the path of the government's work." Jamal Emami had said, "I will ask for a meeting with the Shah within the next few days to see what the issue is." After having made an appointment, Jamal Emami met the Shah in the Marble Palace. He said that the Shah was walking by the pool in the Marble Palace and had a walking stick in his hand. After bowing down, I said that I have come to ask a question from Your Majesty. The Shah said, "What is the matter?" Jamal Emami said, "I have come to ask Your Majesty if General Zahedi has done something wrong." The Shah said, "What do you mean?" Jamal Emami asked, "Has General Zahedi done something against the monarchy?" The Shah said, "No, never!"

Jamal Emami told His Majesty, "I feel relieved, because when General Zahedi was appointed by the Shah as Prime Minister he came to see me in Shemiran and I made a promise to help him in any way I could, but only with one condition. I asked him to promise and to swear an oath that when he came to power he would not do anything against the monarchy. Now that His Majesty says that General Zahedi has not done anything against the monarchy, I would like to ask Your Majesty what is the reason for your displeasure regarding him?" The Shah replied, "I wish to hold the walking stick in my own hands."

Jamal Emami writes that he was rather shocked at that answer and without any delay he said, "If, God forbid, the stick fell from Your Majesty's hands, what will happen to the monarchy and to the country?"

The Shah calmly replied: "You should rest assured that the stick will never fall from my hand." The late Jamal Emami writes, "I noticed that there was no point in continuing the conversation. I said goodbye and left the Shah, and described the conversation exactly as it had happened to General Zahedi. Meanwhile, I told him, 'It is in your interest to go and resign from your post.'

He agreed with my suggestion and went and resigned. Later on, he was appointed as Iran's extraordinary ambassador in Switzerland."

After General Zahedi's departure, backbiting and intrigues continued, especially in the Senate. At that time, Jamal Emami was a senator. He sent a message to the Shah through one of his confidantes that if the nonsensical talk were not stopped he would respond to all those intrigues in his speech in the Senate on the following Wednesday. I remember that three people were sent by the Shah to persuade Jamal Emami not to make a speech against the Shah. The first person was the Friday Imam of Tehran, the second person was General Bakhtiar, and the third person was General Hedayat. Jamal Emami told those three people, "I do not wish to explain General Zahedi's services to this country one by one for you, because you have all witnessed them. I only want to briefly say that the services that he has rendered to the country have been unique in our recent history, and I am sure that all of you also bear witness to it. Is it worthy for this man [the Shah] to engage in all that demagoguery instead of showing respect and appreciating the services of that man? You have come to ask me not to respond to all that injustice and unfairness. We have seen his behaviour towards Ghavam os-Saltaneh after he saved Azarbaijan and now this is how he behaves towards General Zahedi. I am sure that in the future, each one of you will become the target of the same treatment. People have elected me to defend their rights, and it is my duty to defend the rights of every single person in this country against bullying. Now you have come to my house asking me not to discharge my duty. You must be certain that I shall not refrain from performing my duty. I ask you not to pressure me. The way that this man is proceeding he will reject every one of you. One cannot even praise his father in front of him. He thinks that he has done everything for the country and that all others are slaves who have been working under his guidance. On Wednesday, I shall lift the veil on some of these issues."

The following Wednesday, Jamal Emami made a long speech in the Senate, in which he strongly attacked the Shah and those who had obeyed his instructions in the Senate. After that talk, the relations between the Shah and Jamal Emami deteriorated and that feeling of hurt continued for a long time.

During General Zahedi's premiership, *Khandaniha* magazine published a brief biography of him written by the managing editor of the magazine, Amirani, which provides a good account of the character and moral and spiritual qualities of General Zahedi (*Khandaniha*, 10 Shahrivar 1332 [1 September 1953]). The text is as follows:

The Number One Man of Iran's Armed Forces:
Get to Know General Zahedi

Without any doubt, one of the most interesting issues today for every Iranian and for all those who follow Iran's current affairs is to learn about the hero who emerged from his place of hiding and who single-handedly and only by relying upon his faith and with the support of the Iranian people managed to defeat Mossadegh, who seemed invincible. People ask each other in wonder how this amazing man managed to bring Mossadegh to his knees in such an abject manner within a few hours. Mossadegh closed down the Senate purely because it dared to oppose him, dismissed the Majles as soon as it tried to interpolate him, forced the patriotic king of the country into exile, deprived the British government of its most vital asset in Iran, played games for three years with strong and powerful America. Yet such a man was removed so easily by this heroic man in a matter of hours.

This is why *Khandaniha* magazine has asked me, who has intimately known General Zahedi for the past 25 years, to provide a portrait of this extraordinary character. In order not to give in to my emotions, I have only briefly written about a few issues that could be supported by facts and documents, and have referred only to the main headlines of his character.

One: The most important characteristic of Iran's present Prime Minister is his courage combined with wisdom. You should judge his character for yourself from the following incidents:

1. When Reza Shah was still known as Reza Khan Mirpanj, and in 1296 [1917] was busy putting down the Jangali Rebellion, he summoned Colonel Zahedi to Rasht due to many extraordinary acts of bravery that he had witnessed by him in Hamedan. With amazing courage, he managed to put the forces of the famous Khalu Qorban to flight in a short time. About the same time, a column led by Ehsanollah Khan moved from Tanokabon towards Tehran. The chief of the armed forces, Sardar Sepah [Reza Khan], again called on Zahedi to stop the attacks by Ehsanollah Khan. Despite inadequate equipment and few forces, Zahedi defeated Ehsanollah Khan's forces within four weeks, although he had superior equipment and was backed by foreigners. After this victory, Zahedi was elevated to the rank of colonel.

In those days, as it is recorded in government files and as all of us remember, there were repeated clashes in the north of the country. In all of the most important and most dangerous of those clashes Zahedi was asked to suppress those revolts. It is amazing that due to his valour, wisdom and good fortune he was always victorious, so much so that he was elevated through the ranks from lieutenant to brigadier-general in only five years of fighting. In other words, he received all his promotions in the course of fighting different wars. Everybody knows that such rapid rise in military ranks is very rare in the world.

2. A short time after the 1299 [1920] coup d'état, the revolt of Esma'il Khan Semitqu, who was one of Iran's most bloodthirsty and most frightful rebels, reached its peak and resulted in a great deal of bloodshed in a number of cities in Azerbaijan. They beheaded so many men and women, they tore apart so many people and threw them into the river that at that time most of us had terrible nightmares in Tehran.

Major-General Sheibani, the governor general of Azerbaijan, who had heard about Zahedi's bravery and who had experienced Semitqu's fighting capabilities in a few battles, welcomed the participation of that young brigadier-general in that battle and gave him the command of the army in Khoi to confront the rebels. Semitqu's forces started their attacks, joined by various Kurdish armed groups in other fronts, and managed to conquer many other cities where they caused a great deal of bloodshed. That critical situation had forced Sardar Sepah to personally issue military orders from Tehran. In a cable he ordered Sheibani to attack the headquarters of Semitqu's forces in Chehriq fortress.

Major-General Sheibani, who was one of the most remarkable and highly educated officers of his time, replied that attacking Chehriq was a very difficult operation and did not seem possible in view of the prevailing situation. As soon as Brigadier-General Zahedi learned of the situation, he sent a cable directly to Sardar Sepah and promised to liberate the formidable Chehriq fortress with his own forces, without any need for additional troops. The courage and bravery exhibited by Brigadier-General Zahedi in that cable had amazed all the military commanders, including Sardar Sepah. However, as he had personally seen Zahedi on different fronts and knew him well he knew that his claims would not be empty boasts. Despite the objection of Major-General Sheibani, Sardar Sepah accepted Zahedi's proposal. Zahedi attacked Chehriq fortress and became victorious in that battle, which military historians rightly regard as one of the most important factors in safeguarding Iran's territorial integrity. It was after that war that the highest military decoration, namely the Zolfaghar Medal (which at that time had been given to only two officers), was awarded to Brigadier-General Zahedi...

3. Brigadier-General Zahedi had not yet recovered from the battle with Semitqu when he was ordered to establish calm and security in the south of the country. He went to Fars province, and after some time, he clashed with Sheikh Khazal, who was known as the un-crowned sultan of Khuzistan. The story of the arrest and detention of Sheikh Khazal is so interesting that it should be narrated in detail, but as it is beyond the scope of this article we leave it for now. Very

briefly, despite his vast amount of equipment and his reliance upon foreigners and the support that he received from influential sheikhs, Zahedi arrested him one evening on his boat and sent him under escort to Tehran. Overnight, he managed to smash the strange and deep-rooted feudal system created by Sheikh Khazal in Khuzistan.

4. After those brilliant victories and establishing calm and security in the south, in the year 1304 [1925] General Zahedi was appointed as the commander of northern forces. At that time, certain reports indicated that Turkmen fighters had created mayhem in Turkmen-Sahra and had killed a large number of men, women and children in a brutal way, as you have all heard.

Reza Shah believed that in order to suppress the Turkmen militia, who had fought and defeated government forces for many centuries and whose brutality had struck fear in the hearts of the people it would be better to attack them from two directions. Consequently, he ordered Mohammad Khan from Khorasan in the east and Brigadier-General Zahedi from Rasht in the west to attack Turkmen-Sahra. After overcoming many dangers that resemble ancient tales, Zahedi gained control of Turkmen-Sahra. Instead of centres of rebellion and mischief, he established public schools, which apparently are still known by his name. As the result of the calm and security that Zahedi established there, the people of the region still refer to Zahedi as "father." However, despite all those services, due to his courage and his bluntness in expressing his views, for a long time he was out of favour with Reza Shah. He was even detained for a few days in the Ministry of War building…

All the stories that are told about General Zahedi's private life confirm his unusual courage. For instance, one of the clerical MPs says, "One day we were travelling on a minor road with General Zahedi and he was driving the car. We reached a very high bridge that was cracked in the middle, and it seemed that the merest weight would make the whole thing collapse and would send everybody on it to the bottom of the river. Brigadier-General Zahedi stopped for a while at the side of the bridge, and I was sure that he would reverse the car and would turn back. He reversed the car for a few meters and in high speed he drove towards the dilapidated bridge. I closed my eyes and said my last prayers. The rear wheels of the car had hardly passed the middle of the bridge when the whole bridge collapsed, and we heard the general roaring with laughter."

Apart from everything that he has done in the past, his behaviour during the past two weeks that we have all witnessed has been the best proof of his unique personality. His recent activities show that Zahedi's courage is extraordinary, but at the same time it is combined with wisdom and knowing the requirements of different times.

Two: General Zahedi's second remarkable characteristic is his "supervisory quality."

All the members of Zahedi's family, both his close and distant relatives, the members of his immediate family, as well as members of his extended family, all his friends and acquaintances and all those who are somehow connected with him look up to him as a guardian, a father figure and the head of the family. Whether they like it or not, they all accept him as the "leader of the clan."

This is why General Zahedi has many faithful and sincere friends, and his sphere of influence (apart from his official positions) is very extensive. As the saying goes, "each man's personality is commensurate with the amount of interest that he shows and responsibility that he feels towards other people's lives." Consequently, a selfish person who has no interest in anyone and who feels no responsibility towards anyone except himself has a zero personality. If he marries and loves another person and shows interest in someone else's well-being his personality would grow to some extent. If he pays greater attention to the well-being of his children, his personality would also grow proportionately. If he shows an interest in something and dedicates himself to his work, again his personality would grow further, until he reaches the status of the philosophers, prophets and great writers who devote all their attention and interest to humanity.

General Zahedi's vast and unlimited character is due to his feeling of guardianship regarding the lives of his relatives and anyone who can somehow attach himself to him and come under the umbrella of his overarching support.

Three: Another remarkable characteristic of General Zahedi is his intense hostility and his easy forgiveness. These two characteristics might seem contradictory—and they are—but the present prime minister clearly possesses both qualities at the same time. If he turns against someone, he would confront him with intense severity and would show no compromise or tolerance towards him, until he submits. However, once he submits and confesses his mistakes, the general immediately becomes very soft towards him and his heart is filled with forgiveness and affection. The story of Dr. Mossadegh's arrest is a good example of his character. Despite the fact that for many months Dr. Mossadegh had made life hell for General Zahedi and his family and during his last days in office had officially announced on radio and television that he would give a prize to anyone who would arrest General Zahedi, when Mossadegh was arrested General Zahedi housed him in the Officers' Club. Had it not been due to his legal and national duty, and his own personal conscience and the pressure of public opinion (to all of which he pays a great deal of attention) he would have even freed him at once.

Four: Another remarkable characteristic of General Zahedi is loyalty towards his friends, without having any expectation of personal benefit or interest. Among General Zahedi's friends are a number of elderly and ill individuals, from whom he does not derive the least benefit or advantage. Nevertheless, the respect and affection that General Zahedi shows to them is truly remarkable and even might be the source of envy to some of those close to him. Were it not for my desire to respect their privacy, I would have mentioned their names and you would clearly see how strong is his feeling of personal loyalty to his friends, associates and colleagues.

Five: His fifth remarkable characteristic concerns the way that he works. Experts in management skills believe that a successful manager must possess the following five characteristics:

The first quality is hard work and perseverance. Continuing his efforts against Dr. Mossadegh's government, despite all the problems and obstacles that he had created for him, will by itself demonstrate General Zahedi's dedication and perseverance.

The second quality is the ability to accept risks. The operations on 28th Mordad [19 August] when the powerful head of the government had turned his house and a few hundred metres around it into a solid military fortress, and despite this he still did not feel secure inside his own house, demonstrated a high level of risk taking. Under the conditions that the government was offering a bounty for General Zahedi's head, he went all alone to the Radio Station, and amidst a vast crowd of people whose intentions were not clear to him, he spoke openly against the government of the day and was not afraid of anything.

The third quality is to act on the basis of a pre-conceived plan. General Zahedi has demonstrated this ability in all his military operations and campaigns, and the future will show whether or not he will be able to demonstrate the same ability regarding national issues.

The fourth quality is to win the support of others. You must have heard that not only Majles deputies from the minority faction, but also some of the retired military officers and some high-ranking political figures, and even the soldiers that were sent by Mossadegh to arrest him, as soon as they confronted him on 28th Mordad and heard his speech, all of them laid down their weapons and joined his ranks. Sincere help provided for General Zahedi throughout his life by different people shows that, just as in the case of the late Davar, everybody volunteered to support him…

The fifth quality is the ability to distribute the work and share the responsibilities with others. His long experience of military command and being in charge of numerous forces had taught him that no one, no matter how clever and capable, will be able to do everything by himself. Therefore, as soon as he trusted an army unit he would relegate power and responsibility to it in keeping with its capabilities and duties.

In any case, these five qualities that include hard work and perseverance, risk taking, acting on the basis of a plan, winning the support of others, and division of labour and responsibilities are clearly manifest in our prime minister. If, in the first instance, international development and, in the second instance, clever cheats and self-seeking hypocrites (who are the most dangerous enemies of any government) allow him, it is very likely that the present head of the government will pass on his "supervisory capabilities" to the entire Iranian nation, and with wisdom and enthusiasm will prepare the necessary means for helping this hard-pressed nation.

The events of 16th Azar 1332 [7 December 1953], according to the account left by Dr. Ali Akbar Siassi, the former president of Tehran University. Quoted from *The Report of a Life*, by Dr. Ali Akbar Siassi, volume 1:

> The coup d'état of 28th Mordad 1332 [19 August 1953] that resulted in the toppling of Dr. Mossadegh and the return of the Shah from Rome to Tehran came about out of the blue. At that time, no one, or at least not many people, knew that the CIA or the American intelligence and counter-intelligence services had been involved in the coup, and had spent four or five million dollars with the help of one of the famous clerics (S. M. B.). They did not know that the coup had been carried out with the collaboration of Ashraf, the Shah's sister, and an American officer called [Herbert Norman] Schwarzkopf (who at one time had founded Iran's gendarmerie).
>
> The Iranian people felt sad at Dr. Mossadegh's overthrow, but they were also happy about the Shah's return (of course they did not know under which conditions he had been brought back). The Shah, who had fled to Rome, had difficulty even to meet his daily expenses and had to turn to certain individuals such as Ariyeh for help. At that time, he was very different from the person that he turned out to be a few years later. The vast majority of Iranians sincerely liked the Shah, because up to that time they had not experienced any wrongdoings by him.
>
> In any case, Dr. Mossadegh and some of his colleagues were arrested and jailed, and the security forces of General Zahedi's powerful government could be seen everywhere. Some of those forces were constantly moving in the streets around the university. On 16th Azar as they were guarding in front of the Faculty of Technology some students mocked them and apparently had used some swear-

words against them, and had immediately run inside the entrance hall of the faculty. The security forces chased them inside. Just at that time, faculty bells began to sound and the students poured out of their classrooms and confronted the soldiers in the entrance hall of the faculty and engaged in clashes with them. There was a great deal of shooting and three students were shot dead.

When I received the reports of those clashes I immediately telephoned General Zahedi and I lodged a strong protest. I said, "In the face of such barbaric activities by your law-enforcement forces I can no longer remain in charge of the university." He replied, "I will be sorry if you do that. It will not be beyond the capabilities of the government to directly run the university, but you must know that in that incident the staff in the Faculty of Technology had been completely at fault. When the soldiers had entered the faculty's foyer they simply intended to talk to the students who had mocked them with their words and actions and to inquire what they had meant by that. They simply wanted to ask them not to repeat such acts again, but all of a sudden the staff in charge of the faculty had dismissed the students from the classrooms and had sent hundreds of students to attack a few soldiers. In order to protect themselves the soldiers had shot in the air. Unfortunately, three of the students who were grappling with the soldiers were shot and killed."

I told him, "So far, it has been the practice that the law enforcement forces never entered the university campus without the permission of the university president. Why did your soldiers enter the faculty? It also seems that the reports that they have submitted to you about the incident have not accurate."

He replied, "They cannot give me inaccurate reports. You also carry out your investigations and we will speak again later."

The next day, in a meeting with the deans of various faculties, I spent two hours speaking about that incident and about what policies we had to adopt. The first reaction was that all of us should resign collectively. Then we came to the conclusion that this mass resignation would only fulfill the wishes of the government. In other words, the despotic and powerful government would directly control the university and would destroy the independence of the university for which we had fought hard for 12 years. The government would appoint a harsh military or civilian president and they would select and appoint the deans of the faculties as they pleased. They would run the university as they had done prior to the year 1321 [1942], under the direct supervision of the Ministry of Education and its affiliated departments. As the result of all the discussions and weighing the options, we decided not to vacate our positions and to continue to resist. I made an appointment with the Shah and I intended to protest about the criminal behaviour of the law-enforcement forces. The Shah did not give me any chance to speak and as soon as he saw me he said, "What is the meaning of this disturbance that your colleagues in the Faculty of Technology have created? They have allowed hundreds of students to attack three or four soldiers and have given rise to that unpleasant incident." I replied, "It seems that some people have reported the incident in a distorted manner and in a way that they have wished to present it." The Shah said, "They have not lied to us. It seems reasonable that the incident has come about as they have reported to me. Otherwise, how can one imagine that the soldiers would shoot at the students without any cause?" I said, "Whatever the truth of the matter, the result is that three families are mourning the death of their children, and the university staff and students are also very upset and are in a state of mourning." The Shah said, "Yes, that is right, and I am also sorry, but what can be done now? I replied, "The least action that should be taken is to arrest those soldiers and to interrogate them in front of some of the students who have witnessed those events. The next thing is that you should issue orders that the families that have lost their children should in some way be consoled." The Shah liked my suggestion and said, "Tomorrow I will ask the Court Minister Ala to contact those families and to express my condolences to them and to make them feel satisfied in any way possible. At the same time, I will ask the government to investigate that important matter and to see whether there has been any conspiracy involved that such clashes have taken place between the students and the law-enforcement forces."

Two days later, the Prime Minister made an appointment for me to go and see him. When I arrived at the Prime Minister's office the cabinet meeting was going on. The head of the Prime Minister's bureau, who was waiting for me, told me that the Prime Minister had asked me to go to the cabinet meeting. I said, "I have nothing to say to the cabinet." He replied, "But apparently the cabinet has something to say to you." Hearing those words reminded me of the saying "The rat has given up its prey, but the prey does not give up the rat." The head of the Prime Minister's bureau went to the cabinet meeting and immediately came out and left the door open and said, "The Prime Minister says please come in." Therefore, reluctantly I entered the room and I saw that all the ministers were seated round a long table. The Prime Minister stood up as a sign of respect to me, and all the ministers followed suit. Then the Prime Minister warmly pressed my hand in his hands and made me sit on an extra seat that they had placed next to his. Then he told the ministers to continue with their discussion. It became clear that they were discussing the events in the university. The minister whose remarks had been interrupted as I had entered the room continued to speak, and then a couple of other ministers also spoke until it was the turn of General Hedayat, the minister of war. He strongly and severely attacked the university, and then concluded, "If a part of a body becomes infected and dies they will cut it off so that the body may remain healthy. If it is necessary to safeguard the country, the university should also be cut off and it should be closed..." The decisive and harsh words of the minister of war were followed by complete silence. It was clear that everybody was waiting to hear my reaction. I tried to remain calm and collected. Then I calmly said, "The words of the general need to be taken seriously. First of all, comparing the university to a limb that may be cut off from the body is not correct. It is a false analogy. If you cut off a limb from a body it will not react and after it is cut off it will become a lifeless object and will be ineffective. However, if the university that is made up of thousands of dynamic and lively professors, lecturers, students and staff is attacked it will resist and will defend itself. Even if it is silenced for a while, it will not always remain so and will continue like a cinder under the ashes and its flames will eventually burn bright. Furthermore, it is not established that there is any corruption or disease in the university. Of course, different people have different views and everybody looks at the issue from his own viewpoint, based on his own emotions, ideas and values. Therefore, first of all we should try to establish whether we are faced with a corruption, or whether we are making false assumptions. Then, even if it was established that we are faced with a corruption, we must try to deal with it with wisdom and maturity, and we should never give in to emotions and engage in some drastic surgery in haste... If our country wishes to make the wheels of its daily activities turn, in the first instance, it requires educated, expert and capable individuals in order to achieve progress. It needs doctors, engineers, teachers, judges, economists, etc. So far, the University of Tehran has taken the lead in training these people, and from now on it should do so even on a larger scale than before. In that case, how can one close down the university? Is it in our interest even to imagine such a thing?"

General Hedayat tried to explain, but the Prime Minister did not give him the chance and said, "The war minister did not mean that the government should close down or dissolve the university. He meant to say what Your Excellency has just said, namely to improve it... Now, we will act in any way that you see fit. The government has full confidence in you. What should the government do? Your Excellency was asked to come here so that we can ask you what the government's duty is towards the university."

I said, "I am most grateful that you are asking my view about this issue. In my view—and this is something that I have always believed and there is nothing new about it—the government must refrain from any interference in the affairs of the university. It should give us the responsibility for maintaining security in the university. Ever since 1321 [1942] we have made this great academic centre independent and autonomous. Throughout that period, by maintaining the policy of the university's impartiality we have not allowed anyone, or any political party or faction to interfere in the affairs of the university. The Tudeh [Communist] Party, at the height of its power when it could arrest a police officer in Ferdowsi Street and take him to the party's headquarters to interrogate him, was not able to engage in propaganda and publicity inside the university. No other party or faction was able to influence the university either. In short, so far we have managed to keep this scientific institution independent of politics, and we have not allowed either the left or the right to be active there. Please believe me that it is in the government's interest to leave us free and not to interfere in our affairs, in the same way that it has acted during the past eleven years."

The Prime Minister thanked me for my remarks and made some general and vague remarks, from which I could gather that he was confirming my views. At the end of his remarks, I got up and said, "I do not wish to take any more of the cabinet's precious time." The Prime Minister got up and warmly shook my hand, and I waved to the rest of the ministers who were all standing up and left the room.

The following day, law-enforcement forces who had been stationed inside the university after Mossadegh's downfall left the university, and so long as I was the president of the university the government did not interfere in it anymore.

Moshfeq Hamedani writes in *The Memoirs of Half a Century of Journalism*:

During the events of 28th Mordad the offices of *Kavian* newspaper were burnt down, the same as was done to the offices of *Bakhtar-e Emruz*. General Zahedi and Dr. Mehdi Pirasteh came to my help. Otherwise, I do not know what my fate would have been. General Zahedi was a patriotic officer, and his fear of the domination of communism over Iran forced him to join the ranks of Mossadegh's opponents.

Selected Bibliography

Asgari, Nour-Mohammad. *The Shah, Mosaddegh, and General Zahedi.* Stockholm, 2000.

Bakhtiary, Princess Soraya Esfandiary. *Palace of Solitude.* London: Quartet Books, 1992.

Douglas, William O. *Strange Lands and Friendly People.* Hicks Press, 2007.

Esfandiary-Bakhtiary, Soraya. *Palace of Solitude.* London: Quartet Books, 1992.

Esfandiary-Bakhtiary, Soraya. *The Autobiography of H.I.H. Princess Soraya.* London: Arthur Barker Limited, 1963.

Hamedani, Moshfeq. *The Memoirs of Half a Century of Journalism.* (Persian language).

Jenson, Janet. *The Many Lives of Franklin S. Harris.* 2nd ed. Bethesda, Md.: Ibex Publishers, 2003.

Matini, Jalal. *Negahi be Karnameh-ye Siasi-ye Doctor Mohammad Mosaddeq* [A Look at the Political Resume of Dr. Mohammad Mosaddeq]. Los Angeles: Ketab Corp., 2006.

Milani, Abbas. *Eminent Persians: The Men and Women Who Made Modern Iran, 1941–1979.* Syracuse, NY: Syracuse University Press, 2009.

Milani, Abbas. *The Shah.* New York: Palgrave Macmillan, 2011.

Millspaugh, Arthur Chester. *Americans in Persia.* Washington, DC: Brookings Institution, 1946.

Millspaugh, Arthur Chester. *The Financial and Economic Situation of Persia, 1926.* London: The Persia Society, 1926.

Millspaugh, Arthur Chester. *The American Task in Persia.* New York: Century, 1925.

Pahlavi, Mohammad-Reza. *Answer to History.* New York: NY: Stein and Day, 1980.

Pahlavi, Mohammad-Reza. *Mission for My Country.* London: Hutchinson, 1961.

Rouhani, Fuad. *Mossadegh: A Political Biography.* 2012.

Shuster, William Morgan. *The Strangling of Persia: A Record of European Diplomacy and Oriental Intrigue.* London: T. Fisher Unwin, 1913.

Siassi, Ali-Akbar. *The Report of a Life* (Persian language).

Warne, William E. *Mission for Peace: Point 4 in Iran.* Bethesda, Md.: Ibex Publishers, 1999.

Zahedi, Ardeshir. *Mémoires d'Ardeshir Zahedi: Témoignage sur l'Iran d'hier Tome I* (French edition). Paris: Éditions Godefroy de Bouillon, 2009.

Zahedi, Ardeshir. *Memoirs of Ardeshir Zahedi, Volume II (1954–1965)* (Persian edition). Bethesda, Md.: Ibex Publishers, 2010.

Zahedi, Ardeshir. *The Memoirs of Ardeshir Zahedi: Volume 1: From Childhood to the End of My Father's Premiership* (Persian edition). Bethesda, Md.: Ibex Publishers, 2006.

Foreword to the French Edition

(translated by Martine Jackson)

The translation into French of the first volume of my memoirs was to be published shortly after the English version. It is just the opposite that is happening with the hazards of publishing. This is why I believed it was my duty to briefly mention certain personalities from European or Mediterranean countries to pay my tribute to them. I will talk about them at more length later on.

In the later years of my life, far from the land of my ancestors, I have decided to entrust Stanford University in the United States with all of my archives, documents as well as photographs and correspondence or notes taken during the decades, so that they would be safe and to enable researchers to have access to them. I have entrusted my friend Dr Abbas Milani, a historian and political scientist and a Professor at Stanford, to oversee this transfer as soon as the writing of the memoirs is over and the classification of the content of these resources which I dedicate to future generations, particularly to my young fellow countrymen.

Throughout my memoirs—especially in the second volume for which the Persian edition was to be published by the end of the spring of 2009; I relate my meetings, conversations and relations with many great figures of this world.

I should like to mention specific personalities for they have left me with indelible memories irrespective of any political consideration which may be of historical value today. I will, of course, mention personalities from the other side of the Atlantic or other continents in the foreword of the English version of the memoirs.

How not to start with Pope Paul VI? During the five years that I was at the head of my country's diplomatic service I was fortunate enough to have the opportunity to have long conversations with Pope Paul VI, a particularly courteous and charismatic personality with a deep and refined knowledge and understanding of international issues. He knew and appreciated the history and culture of Iran and never stopped feeling concerned and worried by the peace problem in the Middle-East. The visions of Iranian diplomacy and of the Vatican were often close on that subject.

As for France, I could never forget my meetings with General de Gaulle. The relations between the General and the Shah revealed a deep friendship and esteem. They started during the hard years of the Second World War. I sometimes heard de Gaulle speak of the Shah in a filial way, as if to a son. The Shah showed an admiration and respect for him which he never did for any other international figure. After de Gaulle's death, the Shah was the only foreign Head of State to meet with Mrs. de Gaulle alone at the Boisserie at his funeral. Unfortunately, there is no account of their conversation which was probably not about politics.

My meetings with the general during the weeks and days before the Six-Day war that opposed Arabs and Israelis (in June 1967) sometimes had a dramatic turn. Both our countries did everything to try to prevent the tragedy or, at least, to circumvent its consequences. We failed. We had made the same analysis of the situation and expressed the same worries.

Before these conversations, I had met de Gaulle during a dinner with a limited number of guests after Winston Churchill's funeral. He was representing France, and I my country as a young ambassador and son-in-law of the Shah of Iran. The dinner party was held at the French Ambassador's Residence in London.

I will refer to these meetings at great length in the second volume of my memoirs.

I wish to also mention three other French statesmen who all worked with de Gaulle: Michel Debré, Georges Pompidou, and Maurice Couve de Murville. They were very different but such endearing characters that I want to pay tribute to them here.

Two great French diplomats are dear to me as well: Ambassador de Courcelles who had been de Gaulle's aide-de-camp and was my counterpart in London, and Ambassador Hervé Alphan who represented France in the United States during my first time as ambassador to Washington. Mrs. Hervé Alphan was a perfect hostess and the essence of courtesy and distinction. It is also well known that Ambassadors de Courcelles and Alphan were General Secretaries at the Quai d'Orsay and played an important part at the lead of French diplomacy.

I must not forget to acknowledge a few Italian personalities whom I knew well among so many others: presidents Amintore Fanfani, Giovanni Gronchi, and Giovanni Leone; Prime Minister Aldo Moro who had a great noble spirit and was to have a tragic fate as we know; as well as Giulio Andreotti and my friend Ambassador Brosio, who has unfortunately passed away.

I was fortunate to know well and have several long meetings with Chancellor Konrad Adenauer to whom Germany and Europe owe so much. The Chancellor was charismatic and showed a great strength of character and a deep knowledge of international issues, which impressed his interlocutors.

As I am talking about German personalities, I must also mention Professor Ludwig Erhardt, who was the father of the economic miracle in his country after the war and who succeeded Konrad Adenauer; Willy Brandt, the legendary mayor of Berlin and then minister of Foreign Affairs and chancellor of the Federal Republic who played an important part in the thaw of East–West relations as everybody knows; Franz-Joseph Strauss, the minister president of Bavaria, a true friend of Iran; and finally the great diplomat Hans-Heinrich Herwarth von Bittenfeld, who came from one of the most prestigious families in his country and always proved to be a faithful friend. I have indelible memories of them all.

The relations between Great Britain, or more exactly the British Empire, and Iran, and our family in particular, have known ups and downs. In this volume, one can read the detailed account of my father's arrest and deportation when he was considered by London to be 'the most dangerous of all the British Empire's enemies in Iran.' My father was not an anti-British simpleton. He respected and appreciated the culture and history of the country but was always opposed to

London's interference in Iranian affairs, which he, rightly so, deemed intolerable. He thus played an important part in the movement that led to the nationalization of the Iranian oil industry in 1951.

When I was appointed ambassador at the Court of St James's, my father reminded me that I was going there to represent Iran and interests, and that I should forget about my personal feelings, memories, and of course, my resentments. He was right and I obviously followed his advice.

I can hardly forget some of the great Englishmen that I knew and not pay them tribute. I will start with HM Queen Elizabeth II and the Queen Mother who was so kind with my wife, Princess Shahnaz, and myself.

Lord Louis Mountbatten was a true friend, a brother to me. He had an exceptional personality and I cannot but pay him a fond tribute.

I met Sir Winston Churchill so many times. I cannot say that I was not aware of his prior stands on Iran and could not forget them. His exceptional personality, historic role during the war, and prophetic view of the cold war were nonetheless fascinating.

I would like to add Princess Alexandra, who is a great lady, as well as Princess Margaret, the Queen's sister, to this list as well as politicians with a stature such as Harold Macmillan, Alec Douglas Hume, James Callaghan, my friend Edward Heath, Michael Stewart, George Brown, the great jurist Lord Shawcross, who was a judge in Nuremberg and then minister of justice, a true friend of Iran, and his wife Lady Jon, and finally my great friend Sir Elton Griffith who was such a fine connoisseur of Iran.

If I am to list other non-communist countries of Europe, I must pay my tribute to His Majesty King Baudouin of Belgium, a friend of the Shah and of my country, just like Queen Fabiola. They both knew Iran well and had a great respect for its civilization and culture that dates back thousands of years. I believe I know that Queen Fabiola continues to follow up on Iranian affairs despite recent health problems. I do not forget them.

Queen Juliana of Holland, a great lady, really impressed me. Her husband, Prince Bernard, was a friend. Together and with some other people, we founded the W.W.F. and worked for the protection of the environment on a global scale. This was at a time when no-one or hardly anyone talked about it.

How can I not mention here His Majesty King Haakon of Norway, the King of Sweden, and his son who was the Crown Prince at the time and is on the throne today, Her Majesty the Queen of Denmark and the Prince Consort, His Majesty King Juan Carlos of Spain and Queen Sophia, and finally, General Franco, a controversial character who gave an impression of strength and sturdiness.

Since I have mentioned Queen Sophia of Spain, I should also mention her brother, King Constantine of Greece, whom I knew and met with on diverse occasions. I always appreciated his courtesy and urbanity.

Mentioning a few personalities from non-European Mediterranean countries can naturally only begin with the great statesman and historical character Anwar Sadat. He was a friend in good and bad times, a generous man with conviction.

The Iranians will never forget his attitude toward the Shah. I pride myself on having initiated the renewal of diplomatic relations between Iran and Egypt when I was at the head of my country's diplomatic service. I am also proud to have, in a way, been at the origin of the solid and unwavering friendship and alliance which brought both of our countries together with my counterpart Mahmoud Riad. The tribute I wish to pay here to President Sadat is not only one from the heart—I will never forget that great man, like so many others. I would also like to add my very dear friend Boutros Boutros Ghali to this tribute. There is no need to introduce him or his charming spouse.

I am also deeply moved to mention here His Majesty King Hussein of Jordan, his brothers Prince Mohammed and my friend Prince Hassan, as well as the present sovereign, King Abdullah.

King Hassan II of Morocco was a great friend of my country, of the King, and of mine. He proved it on numerous occasions. His dignified successor, King Mohammed VI, continues to follow in his footsteps. My warm and sincere tribute to the former is conveyed to the present sovereign and to the task he is to accomplish. Of course, I do not forget Prince Moullay Hafid and the great statesmen Abdeslam Jaïdi and Ahmed Laraki.

I keep an exceptional memory of President Habib Bourgiba, whom I so often met with, of his outlook on Tunisia and on today's world. His son, the Minister of Foreign Affairs, was and still remains a dear friend.

The Algerian President, Houari Boumedienne, a controversial character but someone with deep convictions, played a significant role in the normalization of the relations between Iraq and Iran—a role I will refer to in my next volumes. I must not forget today's President Bouteflika when he was at the head his country's diplomatic service.

During my career, I have had the pleasure of meeting Israeli personalities. I wish to mention Aba Eban here—a fine diplomat, a few non-political memories of whom are referred to in the appendices of this volume.

A very special thought for my Turkish friends and personalities: President Celal Bayar, former Prime Ministers Adnan Menderes, who knew a tragic fate, and Süleyman Demirel, but more particularly and especially for Ihsan Sabri Caglayangil, my friend and brother who was interim Minister of Foreign Affairs, President of the Assembly, Interim Head of State—an endearing character who felt such a strong attachment to Iran.

To end this tour of the Mediterranean, I should mention my Lebanese friends. When I arrived in Beirut as a young student, Bechara El-Khoury, the president of the country, welcomed me with such courtesy, treating me like his son. Then, much later, I was to have privileged relations with President Camille Chamoun and many others that were both political and friendly. These are some examples among many others.

The place of Switzerland in this much too short preliminary acknowledgment is, of course, quite particular.

The relations of such a civilized and hospitable country with Iran go back a long time. Many Iranian personalities who played a determining role in the history of our country did their studies in Switzerland and drew their expertise and knowledge from its excellent universities before applying them for the benefit of their country.

Crown Prince Mohammad Reza Pahlavi, my beloved king and friend for the rest of his life, my father-in-law and thus the grandfather of my only daughter Mahnaz, followed his secondary studies there during the 1930s. He cherished and appreciated Switzerland, just like my father, who stayed there a few times before settling down in the country in the middle of the 1950s when he had to step down from power and preferred to leave Iran.

The Villa des Roses in Montreux, where I still live, was bought by my father and has become our family home for half a century, especially after the Revolution. I cannot forget for an instant the kindness, courtesy, and discretion of the inhabitants and authorities of the city of Montreux, which I consider my own. As I am to mention certain personalities, I would like to name Presidents Max Petitpierre, Pierre Aubert, and Roger Bonvin; my really dear friends Dr. Frantz and Countess Blankart and Dr. Jacobi. There are so many names I could mention. They will be referred to later. I am so grateful to all of them.

Finally, I must thank my friend Professor Aziz Nabavi, who has unfortunately passed, away for encouraging me to write my memoirs, Professor Parviz Amouzegar for his advice and my very dear friend Dr. Houchang Nahavandi, who has followed my work from near of far and given me relevant advice.

My special thanks to Mrs. Elizabeth Santa-Croce for her faithful and accurate translation and to my publisher Richard Haddad, Director of Godefroy de Bouillon Publishing, who carried out this work.

— Ardeshir Zahedi
Montreux, April 5, 2009

Documents relating to Fazlollah Zahedi's Imprisonment in 1942

This all looks to me pretty good. At least someone in authority knows what he wants. BMAH 20/4! *(handwritten note)*

No.13 (329/I/45).   British Vice-Consulate,
                                              Isfahan.
See note attd MAW 20/4 *(handwritten)*   April 8th.,1942.

D.S. Note that p.18 was sent off after this. Re-instated end of the dep. A 22/4 *(handwritten)*

HAM 27/4 (W) *(handwritten)*

          Sir,
                    I have the honour to report hereunder the
gist of a conversation on the Bakhtiari question which I have
just had with Sartip Fazlullah Zahidi,the new General Officer
Commanding,Isfahan,on whom I was paying a formal call:-
2.   General Zahidi was confident that he could
deal with the existing unrest among the Bakhtiari. He had had
wide experience of the tribal areas in Persia,having served in
Fars,Kurdistan,Azerbaijan and Gurgan,and he felt that he knew
his adversary well enough to be able to deal with him. He
considered any bargaining to be a step backwards and he had
therefore strongly opposed the offering of the Bakhtiari
Governorship to Morteza Quli Khan. Tribesmen were,as a rule,a
cowardly lot. They made a good showing against those who were
frightened of them,such as villagers and townspeople,but if
they were to come up against even a much smaller force of
regular troops,well organized and led,they caved in quickly.
He did not think the Bakhtiari had many rifles or much ammunition and the recent defeat that Abul Qasim Khan's band had
suffered near Lurdekan,(see my telegram No.49),in which many
casualties were inflicted on the rebels by a smaller body of
Persian soldiers,had,he thought,cooled many of the hotheads &
reduced the band from over a thousand to a few hundred. Another such encounter would finish them. He had sent out
Shahab-es-Saltaneh from Isfahan to find Abul Qasim Khan and
tell him that if he came in now with his band nothing more
would be said but that if he refused,he,the General,would
start operations against him.
3.   General Zahidi thought that the root of the
trouble had been that,when the strong hand of Reza Shah had
been taken away and lawless bands had begun to move about
again,sufficiently strong action had not been taken against
them by the Persian Government and thus the bands had been
allowed to feel their power and develop their activities. The
reason why the Government had not taken sufficiently strong
action was that at that time,as a result of the "events of
Shahrivar" the morale of the troops,and especially of the
officers,had gone to pieces and rendered the army useless as
a fighting force,even against tribesmen. Now,as he said,that
the army was finding its feet again and had mastered the situation in the other tribal areas he thought it should not be
difficult to settle things here. He also thought that much of
the present trouble in this area was because of the Amir Jang's
policy,when in prison with other tribal leaders,of persuading
or paying them to undertake,when released,to make common
cause with the Bakhtiari against the Government.
4.   The General considered that the tribe most to
be feared was not the Bakhtiari but the Boir Ahmadi and what
he would like to do would be to prevent the Bakhtiaris,Boir
Ahmadis and Qashqais from joining up during the spring migrat-
ion,so as to minimise the risk of concerted action later by
the three confederations. He was hoping to arrange co-operation

But now see p.18, which under the "military" has decision. A 2 *(handwritten margin note)*

His Majesty's Minister,   /to this

          British Legation,

                    Tehran.

to this end with Shiraz and Behbehan. The Boir Ahmadi were
the most dangerous because most of their leaders were with
them whereas all the big Bakhtiari leaders were either in
Isfahan or in Tehran and not really disposed to take to
their hills and raise trouble. This they left for their
young men whom, while telling the Government and the world
in general that of course these young firebrands were acting
entirely without their approval, they privately encouraged.
The Bakhtiari leaders were therefore more vulnerable to
action by the Government and, in addition, the whole confeder-
ation was disunited and thus easy to divide against itself.
5.   No doubt, as a new broom, General Zahidi is
anxious to sweep clean and so declares that his task is
really simple enough. None the less he does give the impression of knowing firstly what he wants to do and secondly how
to do it. This at least is a good sign. His predecessor, perhaps because he had been here longer, had much less confidence
in the power and ability of the central Government to control
the Bakhtiaris. It remains to be seen which of the two sees
the more clearly. One thing, however, must be said - if
General Zahidi is to do his job here properly it is essential
that he be strongly backed by the central Government in Tehran in all his actions. If he begins operations and the
rebels see that he is not being supported by Tehran - and
they will find this out quickly - he can do little here.
6.   I am sending a copy of this despatch to
His Majesty's Consul at Shiraz (No.7).

                  I have the honour to be, Sir,

                        Your most obedient, humble Servant

                              Chevin A Gault.

                        H. M. Vice-Consul.

     Zahidi is an intriguer and womaniser and gambler:
however he is not without ability and is energetic.
He seemed a little less confident on the 12th April
(page 18).   The other complicating factor is
the proposal to appoint Fahim ed Douleh to the
Governorship of Isfahan: if this comes off, and everyone
seems to think it will, Fahim ed Douleh will go as
Ustandar with authority above Zahidi - he told me he would
insist on this.
     The Boir Ahmedis are the main problem, not only in
Zahidi's but also in Genl. Firuz' opinion. The B.A.
are a hopeless lot of robbers and murderers who live
in almost inaccessible mountainous strongholds. The
only way to deal with them that I know of is Zahidi's
Zahidi's way.
     I agree with M.A.'s draft, with two additions, *inserted*.

                        $A \mathcal{Z}$
                        26/4

-319-

ERFAN.   No.1981.   April 21st. 1942.

1.Important.   A declaration made by General Zahedi.

To the noble family of Bakhtiari:-

There is no difference between you and the other people of this country and you are respected just like others.

I can assure you that nobody desires to hurt you and that the Government is trying to support you and help you by all means.You men are born not to be killed by their brothers but to help their country. It is the duty of all of us to serve our country and our king,

You are all Iranians and we should be all united. We should not be excited and deceived by mischievous persons who put out false rumours for their own dirty intentions.

I promise that I will protect and support those who have made a mistake if they repent and surrender to my soldiers. I promise that I will forgive them and I will try to help them within my powers and authority. But those who try to make disturbance and do not listen will be severely punished. I,my officers,and my soldiers have decided to defeat them and crush them.

To-day our country needs security and peace. I am not only addressing to the people of this (Astan); but also to the people of Fars, Luristan and Kuh-Gelui. They should also cooperate with the Government and the Government will also help them, and I promise that they will be safe and in peace,and their rights will not be violated.

(Signed) Sartip Zahedi,

Commander of the 9th.Lashgar.

Isfahan.

-320-

Internal Situation - Isfahan + Bakhtiari.

237/25/42

This seems worth sending to F.O, with a cover, saying what we've done about Abul Qasim. + why — Could you concoct a short covering draft very kindly?

No. I5 (390/I/58).

3 spares

British Vice-Consulate,
Isfahan.
April 25th., I942.

Sir,

I have the honour to transmit to you herewith a copy in translation of a proclamation made by General Zahidi, General Officer Commanding, Isfahan, regarding the Bakhtiaris, which has been published in all the Isfahan papers. There is some hope that Abul Qasim Khan, to whom this proclamation is, in the first place, addressed, as being the only rebel Bakhtiari in the neighbourhood, will come in for his position is steadily weakening owing to defections among his followers and exhaustion of his cash. If he does not come shortly General Zahidi has said he will attack him.

2. According to Sarem-ed-Douleh the flight of Abul Qasim Khan to Semiran last month was the first step in a Bakhtiari plan for a coup de force. Abul Qasim Khan was to start trouble in the Bakhtiari country, then some of the Isfahan Khans, his accomplices, were to arrange for a few days' rioting in Isfahan itself. General Shaqaqi, then General Officer Commanding, Isfahan, was to say that the situation was beyond his control and a few hundred Bakhtiari horsemen would descend from the hills and restore order. Thereupon some of the "honest citizens" of Isfahan would go to the Telegraph Office and announce to the Shah and the Persian Government that Isfahan wanted to have its old friends and protectors the Khans to look after it. Finally Morteza Quli Khan would be appointed Governor of Bakhtiari and Isfahan. The plot failed, and now General Shaqaqi has been replaced by General Zahidi whose intention is to secure a settlement between the Khans and the Persian Government by negotiation but showing the Khans all the time that he had force in reserve and would use it as a last resort.

3. I cannot say yet how true this story is. Sarem-ed-Douleh is an enemy of the Bakhtiaris and would not hesitate to blacken their faces. On the other hand there were a week or two ago rumours in the town that some sort of trouble was soon to break out and since then both Manuchehr Khan and Jahanshah Khan have shown nervousness regarding the intentions towards them of the Persian Government which may point to a guilty conscience. So I think that the story may be regarded as possible. It would explain the sudden subjection of the Khans both here and in Tehran to police surveillance (see my despatch No. I4).

4. General Zahidi on his arrival here let it be known that if trouble did break out in the Bakhtiari country he would have all the Khans now in Tehran brought down to Isfahan and then push them and the Isfahan Khans out into the mountains to restore order or be a prey to the Persian army. This threat, according to Sarem-ed-Douleh, had considerably frightened the Khans and at present they had dropped their "forward policy" and were inclined to wait and see how the Government's attitude developed. From our point of view this is satisfactory.

5. The immediate problem, however, is to bring Abul Qasim Khan to reason. Again according to Sarem-ed-Douleh, General Zahidi, realising that the Pahlevi policy towards rebels had destroyed trust in the Government's word, had had the idea of

/using

His Majesty's Minister,
British Legation,
Tehran.

-321-

using the intended visit of the Minister of War to Isfahan last week to persuade Abul Qasim Khan to come in. The idea was that Abul Qasim Khan should come in to Isfahan when the Minister was here, see him, receive an assurance of forgiveness and be allowed to go where he liked. Unfortunately, General Jahanbani could not leave Tehran because of the budget and this hitch had made Abul Qasim Khan suspicious of a trap. However General Zahidi is now trying to bring General Jahanbani down here for a day or two next week to show Abul Qasim Khan that his original proposal was genuine. If Abul Qasim Khan still refuses to come in General Zahidi proposes to attack him. His arguments in favour of this are reasonable. Abul Qasim Khan is now weak. Many of his original followers have left him and disputes have broken out between him and the Boir Ahmadis. He is also short of cash. Moreover every sign of an approaching settlement between General Firuz in Shiraz and Nasir Qashqai must weaken his position still more. So one form thrust now should finish him and do so without starting trouble elsewhere. The difficulty is not, however, whether General Zahidi would be able to carry out this manoeuvre but in whether his officers on the spot can be ~~relied~~ relied upon not to make a mess of the operation. If the Government embarks on the operation it must not fail. By success it would eliminate one rebel and the other two, Nasir Qashqai and Nadir Quli Khan are already parleying. But if Abul Qasim were not to be broken it would encourage the Bakhtiaris to believe in their own strength which might have disastrous results. Mr. Brenan, whom I took to see General Zahidi, made this point and I emphasised it to Sarem-ed-Douleh. There is alo the important point that if General Zahidi attacks Abul Qasim Khan now and does not succeed the latter will very shortly be able to obtain reinforcements from his own tribesmen who are already moving north and will soon be near him.
6.   I am sending a copy of this despatch to His Majesty's Consul at Shiraz, (No.9).

I have the honour to be, Sir,
Your most obedient, humble
Servant,

Chevli A Crull
H. M. Vice-Consul.

TELEGRAM.

Cypher   XXX

~~Code~~

~~Clear~~

From:—   ISFAHAN   To:—

IMMEDIATE
=========

Despatched 1/6 (1700)   Received 1/6 (2000)

No.   76   of   1/6/42

Addressed to Tehran
repeated   Shiraz No. 11 Saving.

My immediately preceding telegram.
If wheat does not reach Isfahan in time I
consider there will be serious riots.

2.   Governor-General told me this morning
that he thought ZAHIDI had been sent here to form anti-
British nucleus to act against us if Germans reach the
Caucasus. That was wy ZAHIDI wanted SAYYAH made Governor.
I had already formed this opinion myself. Governor-
General also suspected wheat was being deliberately
withheld from Isfahan by subordinates in Ministry of
Finance so that trouble should break out here which would
necessitate ZAHIDI being made military Governor to "restore
order".

3.   Any riots here would certainly be guided
against us and therefore I do not consider Persian police
or troops would do much to protect our interests. Despatch
of British troops would be necessary.

4.   Governor-General told me ZAHIDI now at Tehran
would try to stop activities of Consulate in tribal area.

5.   I suggest that until supply of wheat to Isfahan
is assured, ZAHIDI be prevented from returning from
Tehran. Any concerted action against our interests would
have to be led by him.

6.   I have spoken to HARRIS and JOHNSON who agree
with me. Please show this to UNDERWOOD and SPENCER.

GAULT.

Int. Sit. Isfahan
Food Suppl. Distr.
  MA
  Cslr
  C
  S

See my minit a 143/243/42
+ draft tel sent saying
My of F. have given orders to buy
locally at invariand price. RMHL ≩.

(15768) Wt.23945/050 5.000 8/40 A.& E.W.Ltd. Cp.685

TELEGRAM.

~~Cypher~~

Code

~~Clear~~=

From :—   ISFAHAN   *To :—*

BRITISH LEGATION
– 6 JUN 1942
TEHRAN

Despatched   5/6 (1600)   Received   5/6 (1930)

No.   77   of   5/6/42

Addressed to Tehran
Repeated   Shiraz   No.12 Saying

My Tel.76.
Governor-General has told me more of intended coup.

2.   SAYYAH and ALIZADEH were to make preparations in ISFAHAN under control of ZAHIDI. Unsuccessful effort was also made to win over Chiefs of Police and Telegraphs. FEROUHAR HUSSEIN (?) Governor FERIDAN was to arrange unrest there, while relative of ZAHIDI, LUTFULLAH ZAHIDI, landowner at SEMIRUM, was to make trouble there.   When general trouble started ZAHIDI intended to take in ISFAHAN, if necessary disregarding any orders from TEHRAN.

3.   Fortunately removal of SAYYAH and ALIZADEH has upset plan. Nevertheless, I think ZAHIDI should be removed as soon as possible. Whatever happens now he will be an obstacle here. Governor-General suggests GOC KERMAN as successor.

4.   Another of ZAHIDI's propaganda helpers now here, Colonel SHOUKAT of TEHRAN Police, who is apparently trying to discover our intelligence system here, should also be recalled at once.

5.   Governor-General's story is borne out by much other information in our possession here and I regard it as reliable.

                              GAULT.

Int.Sit.Isfahan
MA
H/C
Cslr
C

Would appreciate obs. M.A.

COPY OF TELEGRAM.

From H.M. MINISTER   *To* ISFAHAN

No. 106 (XXX)   Date 17/6/42

'Desp:

Addressed Isfahan
repeated Shiraz   No. 71
          Foreign Office No. 57 SAVING

(33,36,39)

Your Tels. 76,77,89.
We mistrust ZAHIDI, but evidence against him
does not seem so conclusive as to justify our asking
for his removal, especially as he was chosen by The
Shah. We consider that, if Governor-General has such
strong evidence of an intended coup, he should be
urged to report matter to TEHRAN and have whole matter
investigated.

2.   Question is complicated by fact that ZAHIDI
is thought to be anxious to get himself made Governor-
General also, in same way as FIRUZ, so it is only
to be expected that present Governor-General will
intrigue in opposite direction. But we do not for
that reason place any confidence in ZAHIDI, who
is ambitious, clever, a notorious intriguer and will
probably arrange to be on winning side.
3.   ALIZADEH and SAYYAH will not return to
ISFAHAN.

4.   I mentioned matter of ZAHIDI to Prime
Minister privately today and suggested that he should
look into matter. He replied that he would do so
and ask Governor-General for a report. Prime Minister
regards ZAHIDI as the type of active officer required
in Bakhtiari area.

                              HOLMAN.

File
Cslr
H/C
C

To: C. A. Gault, Esq., *Inl. lit. refm. in Pers. 237/43/42*
H.M.Consul, ISFAHAN.
<u>———————————</u>

IMMEDIATE.
<u>———————————</u>

No.237/43/42.   19th June, 1942.

Many thanks for your various telegrams about General
Zahidi. As stated in my telegram No.106, we have decided not
to ask for his recall at present. If the allegations made
against him by the Governor-General and the Chief of Police
are really to be believed, then it seems to us that it is
certainly the Governor-General's duty to make an official
report to the Prime Minister, and I would in that case insist
on a full enquiry. But if he is not prepared to do this, then
we are not inclined to accept the reports at their face value.

2.   General Zahidi is an ambitious man with many enemies.
I have no doubt that he would like to be Governor-General as
well as G.O.C. - he is jealous of General Firuze - and he is
probably laying his plans to that end. The Governor-General
is probably well aware of this and may be trying to forestall
him. Until things develop more clearly, I am inclined to let
him fight his own battle.

3.   Meanwhile, as regards General Zahidi, I think your
attitude should be to show no suspicion and to treat him as if
you trusted him. Possibly, given a bit of rope, he will give
himself away. We are, as you know, trying to get the cooperation
of the Persian Army as we are dependent on them to maintain the
security of our lines of communications and to keep order in the
country. This implies that we must encourage and support military commanders until we have good reason not to. General Zahidi
was specially selected to deal with the Bakhtiari situation, which
General Shagagi had said was beyond his capacity, and he appears
to have done so with success up to the present.

4.   You should, of course, watch him carefully, and no doubt
you will discuss with him fully all questions connected with his
duties as a military commander. If he is really engaged in the
nefarious plots attributed to him it is not a matter merely of
his recall, but of his internment. Before I can ask for that,
I must have good evidence.

5.   The general opinion here seems to be that General Zahidi
is too clever a man to commit himself to any definite action
against us in present circumstances and that he will play his

                                                        cards /

cards so that he can eventually prove that he was always on
the side of the winner of the war. This is, I admit, not a
very satisfactory attitude, but it is perhaps the best we can
hope for from a good many Persians.

6.   We shall, however, always be ready to support your
request for the recall of an unsatisfactory official, if we
think we can find you a better.

7.   To mention another matter:- I hope it was wise to
telegraph as you did to Nadir Quli. We are inclined to wonder
whether it does not giev him more importance than he really
merits; further, if he creates trouble, notwithstanding our
telegram, it will be rather damaging to our prestige. But you
are the man on the spot and I am quite ready to rely on your
judgement over this. We fully realize the difficulties you
have to contend with locally.

(Sgd.) Adrian Holman

No.24 (569/I).

27 JUN 1942
TIME ......

British Consulate,
Isfahan.
June 25th., 1942.

2 spares

Sir,

      I have the honour to inform you that towards the
end of last week General Zahidi, Commander of the Isfahan Division, met Khosro Khan Qashqai and his mother near Semirun. As
the result of long discussion during which the mother of
Khosro Khan seems to have done most of the talking for the
Qashqai side and General Zahidi, according to himself, took up
an attitude of reasonableness, Khosro Khan undertook to see
that the proceeds of recent robberies by Qashqais round Semirun were returned to their owners and then to come to Abadeh
and either go down to Shiraz to see Prince Firuz and return to
Isfahan to see General Zahidi or come straight to Isfahan.
General Zahidi declared that he had strong hopes that Khosro
would in fact do as he had said he would do, and from what the
General said it does look as though Khosro and his mother
would not make difficulties about coming in for very much
longer. Khosro's excuse for still remaining out was the usual
one of mistrust of the Persian Government and of its officials.
No doubt the surrender of Abul Qasim Khan some time ago and
of Nadir Quli Khan a few days ago (see my telegram No.95) will
encourage him.

2.   The General mentioned that he had questioned
Khosro and his mother about the European now with Nasir and
also about the two brothers, Malik Mansur and Hussein, believed
to be consumptive, now in Germany. For the first the reply was
that this man was a White Russian who had fled from Tehran when
the Soviet forces were approaching the capital last year and
was at present employed by Nasir as a mechanic. For the two
brothers in Germany no news had been received from them. I had
heard elsewhere that recently Nasir had received a message
from Malik Mansur saying that he must hold out as Malik Mansur
and the Germans would be with him soon! Khosro evidently has
quite a useful body of men with him for the General put their
numbers at about 400 good rifles-i.e., not including muzzle-
loaders and blunderbusses and he thought Nasir had about the
same. I think the General has wholesome respect for Khosro's
force for since his return from Tehran he has told me that he
does not want to have to fight the tribes if he can possibly
secure peace by negotiation.

Sons of Aqay Kerim

3.   Zaki and Ziad Darehshuri are also in the Semirun
district and, it seems, are contriving to keep just on the right
side of the line dividing the lawful citizenry from the bandits
General Zahidi gave them some rifles some time ago to help the
Government to keep order. Last week some Darehshuri were involved in a hold-up between Semirun and Shahreza and also in
looting near Kuhpa on the Isfahan-Yezd road and were said to
have had Government arms. General Zahidi however said that these
were not really Darehshuri of the Zaki and Ziad faction but of
another closely related tribal division.

4.   General Zahidi confirmed to me that Nadir Quli
Khan had surrendered. The General had seen him on June 23rd. &
was sending him out to Chahar Mahal again today to bring in
his arms and disband his men. I told the General that Nadir
Quli had asked to see me but that I had put him off until I had
been able to see the General. The latter said that he had no
objection to my seeing him and asked me to impress upon Nadir
Quli the fact that Persia and Britain were allies and working
in close co-operation and wanted peace in the tribal areas. I
expect to see Nadir Quli when he returns to Isfahan.

        /4.   The

His Majesty's Chargé d'Affaires,
    British Legation,
      Tehran.

4.   The General expressed the hope that things would
now become quiet in the Bakhtiari country and remain so and
talked of the desirability of initiating schemes for developing communications by repairing roads and bridges and sending
doctors out among the tribes. Such plans would open up great
possibilities for us to co-operate both with the tribes and
with the Persian Government but I did not say so to the
General.
5.   I am sending a copy of this despatch to His Majesty's Consul at Shiraz.

                    I have the honour to be, Sir,
                        Your most obedient humble servant

                              Charles Alcraft.
                              H.M. Consul.

بتاریخ ۱۰ تیر ماه ۱ ۱۳۲

شماره ۷۰۱۶۸

پیوست

1   JUL Recd

نخست وزیر

کاردار عزیزم

نامه شماره ۱۱۴۲ مورخ ۲۱/۳/۱۴ متضمن رونوشت گزارش کنسول لیا را انگلیس
در اصفهان واصل گردید . نسبت به مطالب اظهار شده ، در گزارش تعلیمـــــات لازم
بمامورین مربوطه داده شد .

دوست صمیمی

آقای آدریان هولمان
کاردار دولت اعلیحضرت پادشاه انگلستان
تهــــران

-330-

237/64/42

S E C R E T.

Reference:
CICI/TN/166/1

Security Office,
British Legation,
T e h r a n.

To:- H.M.M. through M.A.   30th August, 1942.

SARTIP ZAHEDI.

Before the problem of taking proceedings against SARTIP
ZAHEDI became actual, it is perhaps interesting to recall
that we received a report in early April that he was
hiding a German in one or another of his properties,
though it was not certain which.   The information came
from a member of the SARTIP's own household.

Zahedi's name was included in the report of those who
attended the meetings with the members of the Swiss
Legation and about the same time the first reports came
in on his support of Qasim Sayyah as ~~Governor the~~
successor of Ardelan as Governor of Isfahan.   Sayyah
was known to have the closest connections with the
Germans in Isfahan and was the head of the HUNERISTAN
School, which is regarded as a pro-German propaganda
centre.

He was teacher of German in the Huneristan [handwritten margin note]

On the 1st June Zahedi was reported as saying that it
would be a good thing if "the British Agent" were killed
in the Bakhtiari country, obviously referring to Harris,
and about that time he expressed both verbally and in
writing his annoyance at British agents going to Fereidan
without his permission, not, be it noted, tribal country
or country particularly known for its insecurity.

In conversation with both Gault and D'Aeth he has
expressed his contempt for our sources of information
saying that we are fed with lies, whereas only his
information was true.

and to me [handwritten margin note]

His action in connection with the wheat problem, through
his two nominees, FEROUHAR and ABUL QASIM KHAN is being
turned successfully against the British.   Numerous
independent and reliable sources say that the wheat is
being extorted from the villages with a good deal of
oppression and the blame laid at the door of the British.
Nevertheless, the wheat is not reaching the city and we
are blamed for this too.

Mr Squire might bear this out [handwritten margin note]

Just before our former A.L.O's departure, he (Johnson)
attempted to search a house for hidden arms and Zahedi
said complaints had been made to him about it.   When
taxed on why police matters should be referred to him,
Zahedi replied that there were only 75 police in Isfahan
and they could do nothing without the military, and
added that all the functions of Government would collapse
without the Army.   This is by no means the only time
he has spoken in this strain.

True [handwritten margin note]

Contd/......2

His action during the recent factory strike, which was
well outside the province of the Army, has according to
the last reports left the trouble in such a state that it
may break out afresh.   It is thought that he may well
have interferred in order to create first the disturbances
and then on this excuse to take over control with the
military.   The same suspicions rest with regard to the
wheat situation.

The government of the city is at the moment seriously
impaired by the enmity existing between Zahedi and the
Governor-General, Fahim-ed-Dauleh.   When one is strongly
suspected of plotting against us secretly and everything
points to the other being on our side, it is surely better
to back our friend.

The Governor-General has gone so far as to hint that
Zahedi was himself behind the strike and also behind a
recent demonstration of municipal street waterers outside
the British Consulate saying that they had received no
pay.

There is abundant evidence of an indirect nature pointing
to Zahedi being at the head of a dangerous Fifth Fifth
Column organisation.

He was extremely friendly with Col. Shaukat during his
recent brief tenure of office in Isfahan.   Shaukat,
who was in Germany during the last war and was believed
to have been on Von Mackensen's staff is now head of the
uniformed Police in Tehran.   According to Moezzi, who
was at one time head of the Personnel Department of the
Police, Shaukat has an extremely bad reputation even for
the Police, and he even hinted at his pro-German
activities.

Zahedi, through Qasim Sayyah, tried to get Mukhtari, the
hitherto co-operative Chief of Police in Isfahan, to join
his fifth column organisation.

At the time of the crisis involving the fall of Soheily's
cabinet, Zahedi was reported, not only from Isfahan but
from reliable sources here, to be one of the principal
supporters of YAZDANPANAH and his group in their plans
for a military coup.   Moezzi himself was convinced of
his complicity and sent a report through Ardelan Radsar
to the cabinet, urging the strongest action against all
concerned.   Such action would obviously not have been
taken in view of the fact that the Shah was to be placed
at the head of the movement once it had been successful.

There have been suggestions that Zahedi intended after
the coup to put a Qajar on the throne, but he may only
be pretending to have this in view in order to attract
such men as the Governor-General of Shiraz to his side.
Moezzi, who has confessed privately not only his preference for a restoration of the Qajar dynasty but also his
aversion to the present Shah and his family, thinks
however that Zahedi and his clique would put the present
Shah at the head of any military dictatorship.

Contd/....3

-3-

Finally, as in the case of Ferouhar, a very strong
suspicion exists in the minds of almost everyone who
has been investigating the murder of Harris, Griffiths
and his son that Zahedi is at any rate indirectly involved.

Whatever is decided in taking action against Zahedi, we
feel like the British Authorities in Isfahan, both
Consular and Security, that his departure from the area
will be a hard blow to our enemies there.

*But possibly
again to
our enemies
elsewhere.
true!*

                                        Major,
                                        S.O. Tehran.

Copies. Minister 93.
Baghdad 79.
India 139.
10th Army 41.
Isfahan 25.

No.390 (257/52/42).

British Legation,
TEHRAN,
1st September, 1942.

Sir,

I have the honour to transmit herewith a copy of a despatch from His Majesty's Consul, Isfahan, reporting the nomination by General SAHIDI of two Bakhtiari Chiefs, Manuchar Assad and Abul Qasim (until recently a rebel) to be the unofficial representatives of the Persian army of Mamur-i-Intizamat in Chahar Mahal.

2.   As you are aware, efforts have been made by the Persian Army and Military Authorities since last spring to settle tribal questions and arrange relations with the tribes on a more settled basis. No serious rising took place in the Bakhtiari country, though Abul Qasim was for a time in a state of dissidence together with some of his followers, but the Persian Government seem now to have decided upon a new departure, viz., that some of the more forward elements in the tribes themselves should be used by the Persian Authorities to conduct their relations with the tribes.

3.   Although neither of the Khans now appointed enjoys any great reputation among the tribes, it would appear from some information which I have received from secret sources, that a meeting of less important Bakhtiari Chiefs was held at CHAGHAKHUR, the HAFT LANG summer quarters, at the end of July, at the instigation of the Persian Military Authorities and that the present appointments arose out of that meeting. Many influential Khans however refused to attend the meeting.

4.   On the other hand it would appear that General SAHIDI, in proceeding thus, has acted with the approval of the Shah, but without the approval of either the Ministry of War or of the Ministry of the Interior, who seem unaware of what has happened and also do not seem to agree with these appointments. I understand from Mr.Trott, Oriental Secretary to this Legation, that if the Persian Government really wished to hand over the affairs of the Bakhtiari area to one of the influential Khans, the natural choice at the present moment would be Morteza Quli Khan Samsam-Bakhtiari, who not only has great prestige with all sections of the tribe, but is rich and has so much property in the vicinity of the capital that he would not be likely to countenance any policy likely to lead to a breach with Tehran. In fact he was offered the post about six months ago, but he then made various conditions which were unacceptable.

5.   Much the same policy is now being pursued in Kurdistan, where the Kurdish rebel Hama Rashid's brother and other dissident persons have been appointed to minor administrative posts in the Baneh district.

6.   This policy is very much less strong than that of the late Shah, who visited any signs of dissidence among the tribes with immediate military retribution. Nevertheless, it seems to accord well with our policy of securing justice for the tribes and will, I hope, if successfully pursued, result at any rate in temporary quiet.

7.   It is true, I am afraid, that the Bakhtiari Khans are disappointed with the attitude of the British towards them. It has not been possible to arrange for the re-purchase of the Khans'

oil /

The Rt. Hon. Anthony Eden,
P.C., M.C., M.P., etc.,
THE FOREIGN OFFICE.

oil-shares (see my telegram No.486 and your telegram No.757)
and we have felt more than doubtful about the desirability of
appointing a Bakhtiari Governor and giving this troublous area
virtual autonomy, which was another point in the desiderata of
the Khans. They are also anxious to get the Persian Army out
of Chahar Mahal but I am unwilling to hamper the efforts of the
local Persian G.O.C. to maintain internal security in his area
unless real abuses on a large scale come to light. We are,
however, doing what we can to hasten a settlement of the claims
of certain Khans to lands of which they were dispossessed under
the régime of the last Shah. I understand that their claims are
now under consideration and I have asked Mr.Gault to report
separately on the local position, which can then be taken up
here by Colonel Galloway if this seems necessary.

8.   Meanwhile, the late Mr.Vice-Consul Harris' tours in
Bakhtiari country seemed to show that tribesmen are still favourable to the British cause. There is a proposal, originating
from Mr.Harris himself, that the bridge at DOPULAN be repaired
and that another similar one should be put up at an important
river crossing over the AB-I-BAZUFT in tribal country in memory
of Mr.Harris and I have asked Col.Underwood's department to proceed with this scheme.

9.   Mr.Gault describes the feeling of local mistrust which
exists as regards the real intentions of General ZAHIDI. As you
are aware, we have been watching General ZAHIDI carefully for
some time and it may well be that we shall shortly ask for his
removal. In order to do this we shall have to have a strong
case, as he is an exceedingly clever man and enjoys the special
confidence of the Shah. So far as purely tribal affairs are
concerned, he seems to have handled the situation with skill
and considerable success.

        I am sending copies of this despatch and its enclosure
to His Majesty's Minister of State at Cairo, to H.Q., Tenth Army,
to His Majesty's Ambassador at Baghdad, the Government of India
and to His Majesty's Consul at Isfahan.

        I have the honour to be with the highest respect,

                Sir,

        Your most obedient, humble Servant,

                (Sgd.) R. W. BULLARD

COPY OF TELEGRAM

To be PARAPHRASED before
Communicated to any outside Office

From H.M. MINISTER   To   ISRAHAN

No. 166 (XXX)   Date   10/9/42

(632

DECYPHER YOURSELF

Your Tel. 146

SECRET.

We are considering this with other problems concerning ZAHIDI. We should like to get him out, but have not so far quite got adequate grounds. Meanwhile we suggest you encourage RAHIM and DOWLEH to take a firmer line and to play a more active part. If you can get anything conclusive against ZAHIDI, please let us know. He is inconveniently clever and has powerful backing here, and we shall need a first class case against him.

2.   As regards Tudeh party, we want to avoid being drawn into party politics. Our policy here is to remain in friendly contact, but not identify ourselves with any one party.

BULLARD.

File
Cair
H/C
C

-336-

Internal Stn. Bakhtiari + Isfahan   237/7?/42

I must say I'd like to see Zahidi go. I wonder what the P.M. thinks of him ?! I
entirely agree the Shah's views should not protect him, but there isn't   **RMAH.** 17
much of a —— see in all this ? Fatim ed Douleh locks himself up in his   ?
country —— estate & just blames us !
Persian

cc
MA ? for obs (—— ——)   *Dear Barclay,*

  British Consulate,
  Isfahan,
  September 18th., 1942.

  Legation telegram No. 160 of September 10th. to me
about Zahidi.

    As you do not feel you have sufficiently strong
evidence of his political colour to have him removed on those
grounds would it not be possible to unseat him on the grounds
that his activity here is at variance with the declared policy of the Persian Government?

    For instance-his handling of the Bakhtiaris. There
is evidence here-see my letter to you No. 785/X of September
14th,-that he has won some of the Khans to his side by pro-
mising them his support in obtaining their lands back and
that, under the cover of confiscation of the produce of these
lands pending a settlement of the case by the Commissions, he
has really allowed his two Khans in Chahar Mahal to take the
produce for themselves or at least enough of it to keep them
sweet. This no doubt makes for the greater glory of the name
of Zahidi, since he can tell the world and Tehran what a fine
job he is doing in keeping the tribes quiet and can tell the
Bakhtiaris how much he is helping them. But this does nothing
practical towards reaching a settlement of tribal troubles &
moreover has had the result of stopping the work of the Lands
Commission here in reaching a legal settlement. If, too, the
Khans decide eventually that Zahidi is unable or unwilling
really to help them are they not more likely to make trouble
than before? You have evidence that the Persian Government, as
represented by the Ministries of War and the Interior, do not
really approve of Zahidi's activities in this line. Have we
not then got a case against him? The fact that the Shah is
supposed to approve should not stand in the way for, on paper
at least, he is a constitutional monarch and should therefore
not be encouraged by us or by anyone else to disregard the
advice of his ministers.

    There is also Zahidi's continual interference in the
civil administration of Isfahan and the province, and his
scheming to obtain control as Military Governor. You know of
the 'plot' of a few months back. The tale of this plot eventually became common bazar talk down here. There are many
other small instances of his complete disregard for the civil
administration here and even for the central Government. His
attitude is that if he wants something he is entitled to
have it whatever others including the Persian Government in
Tehran may think. This has all been reported to Tehran by the

The shah was wobbled into approving the ———— of this —— very unwilling (at least I mean in its application)   RMAH.

The Hon. R.M.A. Hankey, British Legation, Tehran   /Governor-

-337-

Governor-General and I myself consider that his complaints
are fully justified and well-founded. There is no doubt
that the lack of harmony between Zahidi and Fahim-ed-Douleh
is having a bad effect both on the public in general here
and on the running of the administrative machine. Zahidi
gives instructions to civil departments and if they are
impracticable because of departmental regulations he says
'take no notice of Tehran.' It seems to be accepted by the
Legation that Zahidi is an undesirable and that Fahim-ed-
Douleh is on our side. Why do we not back Fahim-ed-Douleh
more effectively, then, and try and get him out on purely
civil grounds? It seems to me clearly in our interest to
have a man as senior Government official here who is from
our point of view reasonably reliable, the more so as this
is now on the supply line from India. Why do we risk having
Zahidi here for we are taking a big risk which we down here
may be able to prove to you shortly. As regards encouraging
Fahim-ed-Douleh to take a stronger line, that is more easily
said than done. Rightly or wrongly, Fahim-ed-Douleh came
back from Tehran with the impression that we, the British,
were not prepared to back him right through against Zahidi
and now he is discouraged, disappointed in our lack of interest in what seems to him, rightly, I think, a definite danger to the British war effort, and talks of throwing his
hand in so that someone can be sent here who will work
with Zahidi, which would mean against us. If the Legation
won't give Fahim-ed-Douleh encouragement in Tehran what can
I, a junior official, do here?

Zahidi's latest efforts are his part in the strike
of factory workers. There is evidence to show that he secretly
encouraged them to strike so as to be able to show the disturbed state of Isfahan and he took charge of the settlement
which it was not his job to do. Now he has had sent down from
Tehran a colonel, Aftassi, who I am told was had out of Kermanshah by us, to do the purely military work here, so as to leave
him (the General) more time to devote to his non-military
interests. A few days ago he took by force the car of one of
the factory owners here, who had refused to sell it to him (the
car has now been given back, I hear).

No doubt Zahidi has 'powerful backing' from the
Shah but it seems to me that we can go too far in throwing
dust on our heads at the feet of the King of Kings and that we
run the risk of allowing the Imperial shadow to appear more
formidable than the reality. Zahidi would not have behaved in
the way he does now under the father—why should we have to
suffer him under the son, with his ~~amangtata~~ democratic education and views?

Yours sincerely, Charles A Gault.

secure the return of the arms lost by the Persian Army as
a result of the occupation on 1941. Encouraged by the
possession of arms and by money which they were said to be
getting from General Zahidi, the Bakhtiari Khans were, so
Miss Lambton found, already penetrating into the settled
districts where the robbery and plunder of flocks was becoming frequent. The Khans were also seizing the produce
of the land and had blocked the roads out of the district
in order to prevent any products being exported from it except by themselves. This ran directly counter to our policy
of making Persia, so far as possible, independent in cereals,

The Rt. Hon.,
Anthony Eden, P.C., M.C., M.P.,   237/405/42   especially//

THE In my Despatch No.290 of the 1st September I reported
the nomination by General Zahidi at Isfahan of two Bakht-
iari Khans to be the unofficial representatives of the
Persian Army in the Bakhtiari Areas of Chahar Mahal, and
I drew attention to the new departure in the Persian
Governments tribal policy which these nominations involved.

2.   I regret to report that General Zahidi's policy has
not been a success. When Miss Lambton, Press Attaché to
this Legation, visited the Isfahan area in September, she
found that security had deteriorated considerably towards
the end of September. The tribes were to some extent re-
armed and the sources of their arms were not only those
taken from the Persian Army when the Allies entered Persia
(including light machine-guns, Bren-guns and rifles) and
arms which had been hidden when Reza Shah disarmed the
tribes, but also arms given by General Zahidi to Manuchehr
Khan and Abul Qasim Khan and distributed by them among
the tribes. No attempt had been made by General Zahidi to
secure the return of the arms lost by the Persian Army as
a result of the occupation on 1941. Encouraged by the
possession of arms and by money which they were said to be
getting from General Zahidi, the Bakhtiari Khans were, so
Miss Lambton found, already penetrating into the settled
districts where the robbery and plunder of flocks was becoming frequent. The Khans were also seizing the produce
of the land and had blocked the roads out of the district
in order to prevent any products being exported from it except by themselves. This ran directly counter to our policy
of making Persia, so far as possible, independent in cereals,

The Rt. Hon.,   especially//
Anthony Eden, P.C., M.C., M.P.,
THE FOREIGN OFFICE.

especially as the produce from Chahar Mahal, when
sent out of the districts by the Khans, was
mostly sold on the black market and was not officially available for the feeding of Isfahan.
I enclose a copy of a Minute by H.M.Consul,
Isfahan, dated October 8th, on the local situation in Chahar Mahal, together with a copy of his Saving-
ram No.17 of the 22nd November, showing how the situation
has further deteriorated.

+ previous

3. The removal of General Zahidi now raises the question
of the Persian Government's future policy towards the
Bakhtiaris. We are ourselves most anxious, as I said in
my despatch, to remain on good terms with them, but we
cannot afford to allow the situation to deteriorate in an
area which is near one of our main L of C with the South
and from which an important surplus of agricultural produce
for the feeding of Isfahan is to be expected. Mr. Gault
considers, and I agree, that Manuchehr Khan and Abul Qassim
Khan should be recalled from Chahar Mahal and a carefully
chosen Military Governor appointed. Mr. Gault states that
a Military Governor would be acceptable to the Khans and
that in his opinion, with which I fully agree, the district
is best with no Khans in official positions, though there
is no harm in their going there as private persons to look
after their lands. The Military Attaché is discussing with
the Ministry for War the question of the appointment of a
suitable military Governor.

4. We understand that Manuchehr Khan is ready to remain in
Isfahan, but is anxious to have his family lands back. I
believe the claim is a very complicated one, but as soon as
a new Minister of Justice has been appointed, the Oriental
Secretary will take the case up and see whether a just
settlement can be obtained for him. As regards Abul Qassim
Khan, it has been suggested that he should be offered some
minor Governorship elsewhere in order to prevent him from
making trouble. I understand he did well formerly as Governor of Kashan and Mr.Trott will see what can be done for
him also when the new Government is firmly established.

5. I am sending copies of this despatch to H.M.Minister of
State, to Minbranch and PAIC, Baghdad, the Government of
India, 10th Army and to H.B.M.Consulate at Isfahan.
I have the honour to be with the highest respect, Sir,
Your most obedient, humble Servant,

(Sgd.) R.W.BULLARD.

No. 861/3.   [stamp: BRITISH LEGATION 18 OCT 1942 TIME........ TEHRAN]   British Consulate,
Isfahan.
October 16th., 1942.

Dear Sir Reader.

Thank you for your letter No. 237/80/42 of 5th.
October about Zahidi.

I agree that there is now little likelihood of
any coup d'état by him. I think there was a risk before we
got rid of certain officials here and if the Germans had
come through the Caucasus. I still feel however that Zahidi
does not want a settled and contented Isfahan.

The evidence against Zahidi which I hoped would
damn him was the matter of the W/T transmitter which he is
said to have and which is now being dealt with by CICI,
Tehran.

I agree that, for the Bakhtiaris, it is arguable
that he were better left here until the tribes have gone
south. I agree also that, for the reasons given in the third
sentence of your third paragraph, it will not be easy to
replace him.

But there are two other points which, I feel, need
positive and not negative action.

First, the Bakhtiaris. The longer he is left to
do what he likes in Chahar Mahal and, through Ferouhar, who
is still with us, in Feridan too, by means of backing the
local Khans and allowing them to take all they want from
the villages, the more uneasy will the populations there become. One result of this has been that the wheat surplus of
these two areas is not coming into Isfahan properly, where
it is badly needed, because the local Khans are taking it
all for themselves. This is directly due to Zahidi's encouraging them to take back properties which they once
owned. The longer, too, he is allowed to back his Khans the
more powerful will they become. I don't mean to say that
they are now very strong but their nuisance value to the
Persian Government and consequently to us is undoubtedly
increasing. In fact Zahidi is now doing what we decided
not to do-backing the Khans, or more correctly, some of them.

Second, and most important, is the food situation
/in

Sir R. W. Bullard, K. C. M. G., C. I. E.,
British Legation,
Tehran.

/in

I spoke /to

to the Ministry of Food the other
day: they said the Rais for Isfahan was here at
the moment receiving instructions: his name was
Iskandari, a brother of the head of the Tudeh party:
he would return to Isfahan by the end of this week or sooner
if possible.   I said how urgent and necessary it was that he
should return quickly.

Draft RMH 28/10.   Aug 28/10

in Isfahan. I have already spoken in my telegram No. 161 and
in my diary for the second half of September of the lack of
co-operation between the civil and the military power here
and of the harm it has done. The Prime Minister's effort to
do away with this friction, which you mention, has failed and
the position is now much worse because, after having insulted
the Head of the Economic Department here it is hard to see
how any other Head will be able to work here with Zahidi. And
as a result of this row we have been without a head of the
department here for the last fortnight just at the time when
a responsible official is most necessary. Since his arrival
Zahidi has worked against the civil departments and the Governor-General and will, I am sure, continue to do so in spite
of any orders he may receive from Tehran. In this he is egged
on by Sarem-ed-Douleh who ought to know better. Consequently
nothing is done, especially in the matter of wheat collection.
Fahim-ed-Douleh will not do anything that requires the General's help because he knows he will not get it and he does
not want to risk a snub. As a result there is only a very
small stock of wheat in the Government stores which only
does for current requirements. There is considerable discontent in the town over this among the poorer part of the population which realizes that if an adequate stock is not laid
in very soon there will be no bread next year, towards the end
of this winter. This I hold to be entirely Zahidi's fault for
with mutual co-operation the Governor-General and the General
could by now have collected quite a lot of wheat and that
would have restored public confidence. Fahim-ed-Douleh may be
lacking in energy but from his own point of view he is, I feel,
justified since neither his own Government nor we appear to
give him any active encouragement so why should he run his
neck into a noose when he can blame it all on Zahidi? It is a
pity that we cannot back those who are genuinely friendly to
us more strongly for that would surely require less energy
than fighting our many enemies.
          In short the longer Zahidi stays here the greater
the risk of a famine later on. It will be an artificial famine, but that will not help the 100,000 or so of the town's
poorer inhabitants who will do the starving. With proper co-
operation I do not think it would be difficult to get in
enough wheat now, especially with the new high price, but as
long as Zahidi remains I don't hope for much.

P.S. I am sending a copy of
this to Brennan.

Yours sincerely,
Charles A. Gault

-342-

From:- C. in C. Persia/Iraq.   Desp. 1405 7 Nov 42.

To:-   War Office.   Recd. 0020 8 Nov 42.
        rptd: Tenth Army.
            C. in C. Middle East (for
                Minister of State AMD S.I.M.E.).

IMMEDIATE.

CS/10680 cipher 7 Nov.   MOST SECRET.

From Gen. Wilson.

Further to my CS/9882 of four Nov.

First. Investigations have produced conclusive evidence incriminating following Persians beyond doubt. One cabinet minister, three members of Parliament eleven generals twelve colonels eighteen other officers Chief of Gendarmerie number of tribal chiefs and over fifty other persons. The German organiser Franz Mayeq has fled Efom Ispahan believed to Qashgai country but may now have returned. No definite information as to locations other Germans but this followed up.

Second. Persian suspects being classified. A. For immediate internment. B. For dismissal from their posts. C. To be bound over or cautioned. D. No action. Minister Teheran agrees that arrest of Persians would have to be carried out by us.

Third. Arrest of generals and important Persians must entail military occupation of Teheran which would inevitably cause fall of Cabinet. Minister Teheran therefore considers it would be of advantage if currency question could be settled before arrests. I agree with this as it is most unlikely that any of the highly placed
Persians/

-343-

Persians will take flight as they consider themselves
secure against action by us.

Fourth. As currency problem may take anything
up to three weeks to settle I propose making military
plans for arrests and occupation of Teheran which if
Cabinet fell on currency question would in any case be
necessary for taking over banks.

Fifth. Other centres where arrests will be
necessary are Kermanshah Hamadan and Ispahan. For
arrests Ispahan despatch of a column will be necessary.

Sixth. Request early reply to my CS/9882 four
Nov. asking approval my proposal to take action independent of Persian authorities. Evidence confirms previous
conclusion that organisation is widespread and would be a
serious menace to us if Germans approach Persian frontier.
Essential therefore that organisation should be completely
broken up.   T.O.O. nil.

C.6.(Tels.)

        To:- M.O.5 (for action).

Copies to:-

S.of S.   Foreign Office (Mr. Pink).
C.I.G.S.   India Office (Brig. McCay).
V.C.I.G.S.   Brig. Jacob (War Cabinet Offices).
D.M.O.   C.A.S. (Air Ministry).
D.D.M.O.(O).   A.M.C.S. (Air Ministry).
M.O.1.5;12.
D.M.I.
D.D.M.I.(I)(S).
M.I.2,2a,5,6,14,17.
S.of S. Foreign
   Affairs.

[This telegram is of particular secrecy and should be
retained by the authorised recipient and net passed on].

[CYPHER]   DEPARTMENTAL (SECRET).

FROM TEHRAN TO FOREIGN OFFICE.

Sir R. Bullard.   D. 5.20 p.m., 11th November, 1942.
No. 1424.
11th November, 1942.   R. 7.20 p.m., 11th November, 1942.

Repeated to Bagdad for Minbranch and P.A.I.C.,
              Minister of State, Caire.

                        3 5 5

MOST IMMEDIATE.
MOST SECRET.

My telegram No. 1407.   E 6516/6515/9

     Documents were seized from the house of German agent
Franz Mayer in Isfahan where he had for some time been
suspected of operating by our Security Authorities. As a
result, however, of quarrel between Mayer and his Armenian
confederate which led to a culminating affray, the latter
immediately went round to the British Consulate with
information as to what had happened. British Security
representative therefore went and searched Mayer's house
and took away with him all documents, maps and codes which
he could find. Mayer had in the meantime fled. In view
of the nature of the documents which I have carefully
examined with Counseller and the Military Attaché, and of
the manner in which they were obtained, it is impossible
to suspect their authenticity.

     From evidence in documents it is quite clear that there
is in existence in Persia wide organisation composed of
German agents assisted by large number of Persians who are
preparing a coup against us when the moment appears favourable.
One important document shews that a plan had been prepared
for execution on July 25th which was the date fixed by the
Germans for the capture of Stalingrad and also coincided
with our retreat in Egypt. Arrangements for seizing
aerodromes, blocking reads and adequately dealing with our
forces with German assistance and setting up a military
government were all worked out in detail. Many prominent
Persians, mostly army and tribal leaders, including
Chief of General Staff, Generals Kupal Shabakti and Zahidi
and Nasir Khan etc. are apparently implicated. The Shah
does not seem to be directly involved. From later documents
dated October 15th it is estimated that the Axis organisation
here is still operating actively and has plans for the
employment of secret aerodromes. This has since been
confirmed by the recent discovery by Royal Air Force
aeroplane of secret landing ground at Farreshband which
actually puts out signs on the landing ground exactly as
provided for in the seized documents. Further, much of
the contents of the documents confirms information already
in the hands of our security authorities.

                                              The/

The existence of this organisation and the plot
involving high army officers etc. must expose our position
here to serious and perpetual danger. It is impossible
to expect the Persian police force which is notoriously
corrupt and wholly unreliable to effect arrests, so that
if arrests are to be made they can only be effected by
British army without any previous warning. This would
presumably entail the entry of British troops into Tehran
and possibly other places. Present moment for such action
is of course particularly favourable owing to our military
successes elsewhere. Further, as our action would
principally be directed against the army and tribes, it
might give some satisfaction to the Government and civilian
elements. The fact, too, that we mean business would I
think have steadying effect and in the long run might be
appreciated by the masses. On the other hand our action
would most probably entail the fall of the government and
create more extensive commitments for us from the military
and civil point of view. There might even be some dislocation
of supplies to Russia. Any organised opposition from the
Persian army is not to be expected.

In conclusion, the effect of action would be the
removal of many hostile elements and the complete dislocation
of the Axis organisation here, thus affording us considerable
measure of security for some time to come. The names of
these selected for arrest would need most careful consideration
as it cannot be assumed that every person whose name appears
must ipso facto be regarded as implicated. As stated in my
telegram under reference any measures taken must be closely
co-ordinated with our general policy here.

I have just given the Soviet Ambassador the general
outline of the plot with some details relating to the area
occupied by Soviet troops. He agrees personally that the
leaders will have to be arrested. I assume that the Soviet
Government will wish to participate in the arrests and in
the precautionary movements of troops.

[Copies sent to Mr. Armstrong]

(OTP)

083021.

From:- C. in C. Persia/Iraq.   Desp. NIL.

To:-   The War Office.   Recd. 1900, 13 Nov. 42.
       British Miss: Teheran.
       Rptd. C. in C. Middle East.
           (For Min: of State and S.I.M.E.)
           C. in C. India.

IMMEDIATE.

CS/12542. cipher 13 Nov. Most Secret.

FIRST CIPHER PART.

Ref. my CS/10680 of Nov. 7 to Troopers and HBM
Teheran number 1424 of Nov. 11 to F.O.

From Gen. Wilson.

Documents Persian Fifth Column plot now reached me.
Plot evidently laid in anticipation of German successes
early September, and discloses intention of raising army
and tribes against us in conjunction with arrival
paratroops and German forces in North Persia. Organisation
is therefore not immediate danger unless in event unlikely
decision to use it for diversionary action. No direct
evidence at the moment against prominent persons and
production of evidence to justify arrest is certain to be
met with usual contention that plot is a frame up and did
not exist. If organisation is broken up immediately, with
Germans still loose in country, scope for recasting same
before Spring is created. Recommend therefore no action
against Persians implicated be taken at the moment but kept
in cold storage and further evidence built up until
favourable political opportunity presents itself, unless
our hand is forced over currency crisis causing fall of
Govt. arrests without ref. to Persians by our forces will
be carried out when locations traced of Germans and certain
Persians, whose arrests have been demanded of Persian
Govt. without result and whose Axis activities borne out by
documents. Evidence also refers to use for subversive
purposes of landing ground at Firuzabad whose existence
previously denied by Persian officers in Shiraz and Nazer
                                                   /Khan,

Khan, but now confirmed by air recce, and photos. Reference
found also to alleged landing arms and ammunition from Axis
submarines in Persian Gulf between Jask and Lingeh in
response to wireless request to Germany from Franz Mayer,
concerning which information received recently from other
sources. A.O.C. has undertaken to control and check
movements Persian Air Force. Further investigations
proceeding. Conclusive evidence Nazer Khan and Qashgais
deeply implicated in plot as well as sheltering Germans and
alleged gun running. Russian air route Bushire Shiraz
Isfahan now seriously threatened thereby.

SECOND AND LAST CIPHER PART.

Persian forces sent Shiraz for internal security have
proved themselves singularly ineffective and from association
with German agents unlikely to act vigorously. Now
necessary take action in this area. Possible courses (A)
contact Nazer Khan with offer of subsidy to win him to
our side or neutrality, accompanied by strengthening our
political and intelligence services in South Persia. (B) to
take military action against Nazer Khan and Qashgasi. This
course likely entail providing permanent garrison. Consider (A)
should prove more effective and less costly in end, but
Legation Teheran have hitherto forbidden any contacts with
tribal leaders. In view present situation request agreement
with my suggestion. T.O.O. 0930/13 G.M.T.

C.6. (Telegrams)   To :- M.O.5. (for action).

Copies To :-
S. of S.
C.I.G.S.
V.C.I.G.S.
D.M.O.
D.D.M.O.(O).
M.O.1.5.12.
D.M.I.
D.D.M.I.(I).(S).
M.I.2.2a.5.6.14.17.

Foreign Office. (Mr. Pink).
S. of S. Foreign Affairs.
India Office. Brig. Mc.Cay).
Brigadier Jacob. (War Cabinet
                    Offices).
C.A.S. (Air Ministry).
A.M.C.S. (Air Ministry).

Ballard must be the judge.

Internal Stn. Isfahan   237/97/یر

Sheridan told me y'day that he had
complained to Ahmedi that Zahidi was interfering
with the collection of wheat at Isfahan and ought
to be moved, and that Ahmedi promised to speak to
the Shah abt it. It is possible then that Zahidi
may be withdrawn.

27th Nov., 1942.

084398.

From: C. in C. Persia-Iraq.   Desp.2125 20 Nov)
) 42.
To: British Minister Teheran   Recd.0630 21 Nov)
rptd. C. in C. Middle East.
     (for Minister of State and SIME).
     War Office.
     C. in C. India.

IMPORTANT.

CS/14985 cipher 20 Nov. MOST SECRET.

     From: General Wilson.

     Ref. My CS/(? 12)542 of Nov. 13th (repeat 13th) and
H.B.M. Tehran Number 1449 to Foreign Office of 17th repeat
17th Nov. thereon.   Agree that 4 (repeat 4) individuals
quoted should be arrested by British forces other than those
engaged in (? security) services (? .).   C.G.S. will arrive
Tehran 23rd (repeat 23rd) Nov. to discuss method.   Consider
plan should be concentrated on arrest of Z (repeat Z) as
first priority and others simultaneously or subsequently.

     Will send my views on your suggestion re NAZ(? I)R
KHAN and QASHGAIS separately.

                            T.0.0. 2035/20.

C.6.Telegrams.   TO: M.O. 5 (for action).

Copies to:- S. of S.   M.I. 2.2.a.5.6.14.17.
           C.I.G.S.   Foreign Office (Mr. Pink).
           V.C.I.G.S.   S. of S. Foreign Affairs.
           D.M.O.   India Office (Brig. McCay).
           D.D.M.O. (O)   Brig. Jacob (War Cabinet
           M.O. 1. 5. 12.   Offices).
           D.M.I.   C.A.S.
           D.D.M.I. (I)(S).   A.M.C.S.

Eastern [?]

P.M./42/270.

<u>PRIME MINISTER.</u>

My minute of November 6th (P.M./42/261) about the
plot which has been unearthed in Persia. It is clear from
Bullard's telegram No. 1434 of November 11th (copy attached)
that this plot is a serious matter. The Chiefs of Staff and
I agree that we cannot afford to leave a widespread German-
Persian organisation free to carry out a coup if events
should turn against us in this area.

I therefore propose the following actions:

1. Foreign Office and War Office to inform Bullard and
General Wilson respectively that we agree that the
conspirators should be arrested by British troops. This may
entail the occupation of Tehran and possibly other places and
may well bring about the fall of the Government. The timing
of our action must be concerted between Bullard and General
Wilson, but operations must in any case not begin before a
reasonable time (as judged by the men on the spot) has been
allowed for the settlement of the present currency crisis in
Tehran. General Wilson has himself recognised the necessity

for/

for this. We must also try to bring our Russian and
American allies into line, and time must be given for
this. I do not want to act without Russia and the United
States.

    2. In order to save the Shah's face and if possible
to prevent the Government from resigning and ourselves from
being confronted with a situation in which we might have to
take over the administration of the whole country, I propose
to instruct Bullard to tell the Shah at the last moment
before action is taken that we have been obliged for security
reasons to proceed to these arrests and that we hope he will
understand and approve our action. His Majesty's approval
ought if possible to be made public, e.g. by means of a
Firman in which His Majesty would state that he had learned
of the plot with indignation and had sanctioned the taking
of the necessary measures by his Allies. This approach can
only be made at the last moment: otherwise the conspirators
might be warned of our intentions. And should the Shah
refuse to act as we suggest, our plan would nevertheless
be put into effect.

                                3. 1/

3. I will inform Maisky of the plot and ask if the Soviet Government wish to participate in the arrests and in precautionary troop movements. I will also instruct Clark Kerr to approach Molotov.

4. I will also explain the position to Winant. The Americans have emphasised the need for caution in this matter, but we must explain that our security needs make action essential.

5. War Office and Air Ministry have been consulted. Chiefs of Staff have seen this minute and agreed.

(Sd.) ANTHONY EDEN.

13th November, 1942,

13   Flag C

In my minute of November 13th (P.M./42/270),
I suggested, with the concurrence of the Chiefs
of Staff, that military action should be taken
against those concerned in the widespread plot
against us in Persia.

From his telegram C.S./12542, of November
13th, you will see that General Wilson now
recommends that no action should be taken for
the moment against the prominent Persians
involved in the conspiracy, unless our hand
is forced by failure to reach agreement over the
currency question.   General Wilson proposes,
without reference to the Persian Government,
to arrest all Germans he can find, together with
certain Persians whom the Government have
failed to arrest and whose activities on behalf
of the Axis are proved.

The action now proposed by General Wilson
will not involve asking the Shah to issue a
Firman nor should it entail the occupation of
Tehran by British troops.

In approving it I propose to comment on
General Wilson's final paragraph in the sense
that the suggestion of subsidising the Qashgai,
or any other tribe, does not seem likely to
yield results.   I am willing to consider
General Wilson's alternative proposal of
military action against the Qashgai.   But this
matter must be regarded as falling within the
political sphere and I should require the
comments of the Legation at Tehran before
endorsing it.

It is a little disconcerting to find such
rapid changes of opinion as to the validity
of the evidence secured by the raid on Meyer's
hide-out in Isfahan.   I shall see that the
examination of this evidence and the presentation
of a final report is not delayed.

ab.
Nov. 15/42.

AE Nov 17

From:- C.in C. Persia/Iraq.

Desp:- 0755 1 Dec.42.
Recd:- 1330 1 Dec.42.

To:- The War Office.
Rptd. C.in C. Middle East (For Minstate).
S.I.M.E. H.B.M. Teheran.

IMMEDIATE

CC/60 cipher 1 Dec.   MOST SECRET

        To Chiefs of Staff.

        From Gen.Wilson.

        Officer decipher. Reference W2034
COS (Pl)4 of 27 Nov.discussions with H.B.M. Teheran
proceeding on following lines.

        One. First essential arrest of
General Zahidi at Isfahan to which Foreign Office
demmuring, for which request you press for agreement.
Telegrams F.O. to Teheran No.1520 of 20 Nov. and reply
thereto from HBM 1497 of 25 Nov. refer.

        Two. Kosrow brother of Nazir Khan has
come in with desire to negotiate. Persian Government to
be pressed to give safety guarantee and possibly offer
to make Nazir Khan a deputy as enticement.

        Three. Scheme being examined to give
assistance to tribes in kind in return for employment on
road repair and extension, dependent on no incidents
occurring on each tribal sector.

        Four. Persian Army to place garrisons in
certain villages and to patrol road.

        Five. Increase of British contacts with
tribes dependent on our ability to produce suitable Persian
speaking Officers.   T.O.O. 1030/30.

C.6.Tels.

                Distribution over/

To:- M.O.5.(for action)

Copies to:- S. of S.
C.I.G.S.
V.C.I.G.S.
D.M.O.
D.D.M.O.(O)
M.O.1.5.12.
D.M.I.
D.D.M.I.(I)(S)
M.I.2.2a.5.6.14.17a.
S. of S. Foreign Affairs
Foreign Office (Mr. Pink)
India Office (Brig. McCay)
Brig. Jacob.
C.A.S. (Air Ministry)
A.M.C.S. (Air Ministry)
Secretary C.N.S. (Admiralty)

E

Enter from
Green

E7130

086945.   21

From:- C. in C. Persia/Iraq.
                    Desp.0950 5 Dec 42.
                    Recd.1410 5 Dec 42.

To:- British Minister Teheran.
      The War Office.
Rptd. C. in C. Middle East (for Minstate and Lime).

IMMEDIATE.

CS/19529 cipher 5 Dec. MOST SECRET.

        From General Wilson. Ref. telegram F.O. to

E4913   Tehran No.1560 of 30 Nov. and H.B.M. Tehran to PAIC.
6515   E7070/G
                Rptd. F.O. No.454 of one Dec. Orders have been sent
G
          to Tenth Army and Three Corps to carry out arrest

          Zahidi. Consider that reasons for arrest should include
A
          in addition to other charges mentioned in your telegram
E6795
          1449 of 17 Nov. to F.O. that of harbouring and
G
          contacting German agents. Urge most strongly no

          reference to our seizure of documents exposing plot

          and names of any individuals implicated therein. It

          will thereby be possible to keep these individuals

          in suspense as to extent of our information and not

          prejudice their arrest at a future date. Also

          recommend strongly that Russians be asked to arrest

          Kupal. T.O.O. 1025/5.

C.6.(Tels).   To :- M.O.5. (for action).

Copies To :-
S. of S.   D.M.I.
C.I.G.S.   D.D.M.I.(I)(S).
V.C.I.G.S.   M.I.2.2(a).5.6.14.17(a).
D.M.O.   S. of S. Foreign Affairs.
D.D.M.O.   Foreign Office. (Mr. Pink).
M.O.1. 5. 12.   India Office. (Brig. McCay).
                   Brig. Jacob. (War Cab. Offices).
                   C.A.S. (Air Ministry).
                   A.M.C.S. (Air Ministry)
                   Secretary C.N.S. (Admiralty).

Enter soon green

087516

E7193

43

From:- C. in C. Persia/Iraq. Desp. 1420 8 Dec 42.
                                Recd. 2255 8 Dec 42.

To:-   The War Office.
        Reptd: C. in C. Middle East.
                        (For Minister of State)

IMMEDIATE

SIME CS/20546 cipher 8 Dec MOST SECRET
        Ref CS/19529 of fifth Dec.
        Zahidi arrested at Isfahan without recourse to
force. Now accommodated Sultanabad awaiting air
passage to Palestine delayed by weather.

                        T.O.O. 1210 G.M.T.

C.6.Tels.
            To:- M.O.5 (for action)

            Copies to:- S. of S.   D.Plans (2)
                        C.I.G.S.   M.O.1,5.
                        V.C.I.G.S.   D.M.I.
                        D.M.O.   D.D.M.I.(I)
                        D.D.M.O.(O)   M.I.2,5,6,14,17a.
                        S. of S. Foreign Office.
                        Foreign Office (Mr. Pink)
                        India Office (Brig. McCay)
                        Brig. Jacob.
                        C.A.S. (Air Ministry)
                        A.M.C.S. (Air Ministry)
                        Secretary C.N.S.

[This telegram is of particular secrecy and should be retained by the authorised recipient and not passed on.]

27

[Cypher]   DEPARTMENTAL (SECRET)

                                                    E7161

FROM TEHRAN TO FOREIGN OFFICE

Sir R. Bullard   D. 2.36 p.m. 8th December, 1942.
No.1542.   R. 5.45 p.m. 8th December, 1942.
8th December, 1942.

Repeated to Minister of State, Cairo No.543
            Bagdad No.466. (for P.A.I.C.). and
            Minbranch
            Government of India No.590 (Foreign Office please
                                                    pass)
            All Consuls No.91 Circular.

                        [ ] [ ] [ ]

IMMEDIATE.

MOST SECRET.

        After the arrest of Zahidi it is most important that we
all adopt similar line with Persian authorities, and I propose
speaking to the Shah and Prime Minister in the following terms:-

        Zahidi has consistently interfered in various ways with
grain situation in Isfahan area and his continued presence there
as General Officer Commanding constitutes serious danger to
Persian economic life and his influence has made orderly
government impossible. On my recommendation to the Prime
Minister Zahidi was recently recalled to Tehran but was allowed
to return to carry on his nefarious activities without any
action being taken against him by Persian authorities. Zahidi
is a born intriguer and is notorious for his anti-Allied attitude.
In particular he failed to co-operate in tracing the murderers
of Harris and Griffiths. More recently he is known to have
harboured German agents and to have been encouraging Nasir in
his seditious activities and supplying him with arms. His past
record gives no grounds for any confidence in his integrity.
In 1929 when Commander of detachment of guards, he was arrested
and degraded for neglect of duty. After pardon and re-instatement
he was made Chief of Police in 1931 but relieved of this post
after a few months and dismissed from the army. His removal
from his present post even if it does not lead Nasir to submit
to Persian Government, will certainly eliminate one of the
greatest dangers to our most important line of communications,
particularly in so far as it concerns our aid to Russia.

        Zahidi's recall to Tehran or transfer elsewhere would merely
leave him to continue his intrigues to our detriment. It would
have been quite futile to have asked the Persian Government to
effect his arrest as they would have been powerless to do so.
His Majesty's Government therefore considered it desirable to
take the required action themselves and thus relieve the Persian

                                            Government ..

-360-

2.

Government of a grave responsibility. Our action
does not in any way imply a change of policy towards the
Persian or Qavam Governments but has been taken in the best
interests of Persia in her position as an ally of United
Nations.

I propose to take the same line with the press and shall
impose a strict censorship on all outgoing press messages
and newspapers. It will be better if the B.B.C. do not
refer to the arrest unless their hand is forced.

[Copies sent to Mr. Armstrong and Telegraph Branch
India Office for repetition to Government of India].

-361-

TELEGRAM.

CYPHER

Cypher
Code
Clear

From — ISFAHAN

BRITISH LEGATION
13 DEC 1942
TIME
TEHRAN

To. 237

| Despatched | 11/12(1700) | Received | 12/12(0800) |

No. 204 of 11/12/42

(36)

My telegram No. 202.

Arrest of ZAHIDI has had good effect.
Town is relieved at his going.   Prices have fallen.
Some resentment amongst army officers with whom ZAHIDI
was popular, but acting Commander Colonel SHAQAQI took
prompt steps to calm disturbances and situation is quite
normal.

2.   In case there is difficulty
in choosing suitable successor I think SHAQAQI could
well be left in cha.... for the present.

3.   MANUCHEHR KHAN is in Isfahan.
ABDUL QASIM is said to be at Ardal in Bakhtiari.   I
propose to ask local authorities to call him in.

File
CLSR
H/C
C

Ch. 1212(1245)   GAULT

I have just passed to you a detailed
tel from Mr Gault about policy in Chahar
Mahal. After considering that phase state
whether we can agree to last sentence by
telegraph. I think myself we can, but if
we can at the same time approve his
suggestions for an alternative to Abul Qasim
& Manuchehr so much the better.

I suggest you consult Col Underwood.
I don't know if he's interested in them.

RMH 13/12

I presume Dr Gault
has considered the
effect on Abul Qasim's
followers of his recall.
If he must approve
he knows what he is
doing. Telegram does
not seem to require
reply. [initials] 14/12

See separate
minute. RMH 14/12

I said in my previous minute that I could
ask the Miny. of the Interior to get a job for
Abul Qasim.   He did well at Kashan and we could
say that. I think he should NOT be employed
in Bakhtiari however.
I am all for his being recalled by the local
authorities : I presume that Mr. Gault thinks that
the local authorities are strong enough to get him
to obey their summons.
[initials] 14/12

-362-

[CYPHER]   DEPARTMENTAL (SECRET)

FROM TEHRAN TO FOREIGN OFFICE

Sir R. Bullard
No. 1550   D. 1.00 a.m. 9th December, 1942.
8th December, 1942.   R. 1.25 a.m. 9th December, 1942.

Repeated to Minister of State Cairo No. 547
            Bagdad for P.A.I.C. and
            Minbranch No. 468   E.7167
            Government of India No. 595
            Kuibyshev No. 328

                      ddddddd

IMMEDIATE

        Foreign Office please pass to Government of India.

        Demonstration outside Majlis this morning arising on account
of food situation developed into fairly serious looting and
rioting.   The Prime Minister's house has been denuded and set
on fire.   Persian army and police though out all day made
little attempt to restore order until evening when some shooting
occurred and a few looters were arrested.

        2.   I called on the Prime Minister this morning to inform
him of the arrest of Zahidi (on which I will report separately)
and found him more concerned about the situation and the
extreme hostility of Majlis and the Shah.   The food situation
is admittedly the cause for popular discontent (there is almost
no bread in Tehran to-day) but there are good grounds for
attributing much of the agitation to elements in Majlis and
outside who want office or do not wish measures against hoarders
and speculators, which have just been announced, to be carried
into effect.   I cannot acquit the Shah of a share in the
responsibility.   Yesterday he said to some deputies whom he had
summoned that unless something drastic was done there would be
a revolution from below and suggested that a revolution from
above would be better.   At this interview he complained
several times that he had no authority.

        3.   After discussing the situation with my Soviet
colleague and my United States colleague I had audience with
the Shah previously arranged for Lord Moyne (whose visit has
been delayed by bad weather).   I found His Majesty quite on the
side of the Majlis though he admitted that he had the greatest
contempt for the deputies.   I urged strongly on my colleagues'
behalf and my own that it would be most dangerous to yield to

                                                    the/

-363-

the agitation of certain deputies and part of our venal press and that to have yet another change of government at this moment was highly undesirable. The Shah suggested change of government to satisfy "public opinion" and declared that if Majlis again refused to co-operate he would dissolve it. He proposed the Minister for Foreign Affairs Saed as Prime Minister. This I know is the plan of the Chief of Staff who is far too much with the Shah. I objected that Saed, though friendly and honest, was quite incapable of running the administration (he is quite futile at any ordinary business). When I left the Shah the position was that Qawwam should change some members of his Cabinet and that steps should be taken to remove some of the worst of the officials he has appointed but that he himself should stay. An hour later, however, the Shah pressed Qawwam very strongly to resign. His determined hostility to Qawwam in face of the advice of British, Soviet and American representatives and the fact that the demonstrations were engineered and were allowed to reach such dimensions are disturbing features of the situation.

4.   After taking the opinion of the Soviet Ambassador and United States Minister I advised Qawwam in our joint names not to resign now but to wait until we can talk to him to-morrow.

5.   In the midst of these events the disappearance of Zahidi has so far attracted little notice.

[Copies sent to Mr. Armstrong
       "   "   " Telegraph Branch India Office for
   repetition to Government of India].

[This document must be paraphrased if communicated to
any person outside Government service].

[Cypher]   DEPARTMENTAL (SECRET)

    FROM TEHRAN TO FOREIGN OFFICE NO.1554.
                    INDIA NO.597.
                    MINISTER OF STATE CAIRO NO.284 SAVING
                    BAGDAD FOR MINBRANCH
                    P.A.I.C. NO.209 SAVING.

Sir R. Bullard.   D. 11.00 p.m. 9th December, 1942.
                         R. 11.35 a.m. 10th December, 1942.
9th December, 1942.
                                        E.7216
                         c c c
IMMEDIATE.

    My telegram No.1543.

        The Prime Minister expressed no surprise that
Zahidi had given cause for arrest but asked whether we
could not have informed him first.   I said that it would
have been very awkward for him and that it was thought
better that British military authorities should take
full responsibility.

        2. The Shah asked the same question and received
the same reply. He said that if we had asked him he
would have removed Zahidi at once.   He thought it
desirable that such persons should be tried and punished.
He showed no incredulity when I said that Zahidi had
been dealing with and harbouring German agents and
encouraging Nasir/Kahn and even supplying him with arms.

        3. As I have reported, elsewhere arrest of Zahidi
has passed almost unnoticed amidst crisis at Tehran.

[Copies sent to Mr. Armstrong].

/Khan

[This telegram is of particular secrecy and should be
 retained by the authorised recipient and not passed on].

[This document must be paraphrased if communicated
 to any person outside Government service].

[Cypher]

<u>WAR CABINET DISTRIBUTION</u>

<u>FROM PERSIA</u>

<u>FROM TEHRAN TO FOREIGN OFFICE</u>

Sir R. Bullard
No. 1553   D. 11.00 p.m. 9th December, 1942.
9th December, 1942.   R. 1.50 p.m. 10th December, 1942.

Repeated to Government of India No. 596

Copy to Minister of State Cairo
        Minbranch (for P.A.I.C.)

:-:-:-:-:-:-:

<u>IMMEDIATE</u>

        My telegram No. 1550.

        Unless the Shah again breaks his promise, Qawam will
remain in office. He is ready to take into the Cabinet two or
three men acceptable to the Shah (e.g. Muhsin Rais, No. 172
and/Mutamddi No. 137). He also wishes to secure support of
Sipahbod/Aheedi (Military Governor of Tehran since yesterday)
by making him Minister of War. The Shah was eventually
persuaded to accept this solution on my urging that to change
the Prime Minister immediately after disturbances of
8th December would be fatal to security and stability in future.

        2. Solution was not secured without difficulty. Shah
seems to have sounded Soviet Ambassador yesterday about the
possibility of forming Cabinet with considerable military
elements and to have received discouraging reply. I followed
this up with an interview to-day in which I spoke to the
following effect.

        3. I was shocked to learn that after promising me
yesterday that Qawam could stay in office on certain conditions,
the Shah had repeatedly telephoned to him insisting on his
resignation. In other circles this was called bad faith. I
assumed that Chief of Police would be discharged for criminal
inactivity and that a strict enquiry into the matter would be
made (Prime Minister had already undertaken to do both these
things). It was essential to discover why the police and
troops did nothing until the evening and why the crowd was

                                              allowed/

-366-

allowed to loot the Prime Minister's house. It is known that
certain deputies had encouraged the demonstrations and unfortunately
many persons attributed the inactivity of policy and army to orders from
above and even to the Palace. Although there was undoubtedly
dissatisfaction at the food shortage, there was very good reason
to believe that circles hostile to the Allies were trying to get
at us through Qawam who had only just concluded with us various
important agreements to the advantage of both countries. It was
curious that there should be this attack on Qawam when he had
just secured the promise of Great Britain and America to supply
Persia with wheat. I greatly feared that Shah's encouragement of
Parliament was partly responsible for the disorders. I deplored the
tendency I noticed in the Shah to rely on the army against the
Government. I thought it dangerous for the country and even for
his dynasty. He did not realise how intensely unpopular the Army
was. He had urged removal of persons alleged to be corrupt
whom the Prime Minister had appointed and I was strongly in favour
of the elimination of the corrupt, but there was no more corrupt
element in Persia than the Army and I was sure that if the people
came to believe the Shah hoped to rule by means of the Army with
a puppet cabinet and parliament, as was done in his father's time,
their fear and indignation would be great.

4. I cannot say that the Shah enjoyed this talk but he
evidently had a bad conscience about the disorders. He threw the
blame on the Prime Minister for not keeping order though police
were evasive until the evening and then demanded written
instructions before dealing with the crowds. He even suggested that
Qawam himself promoted the demonstrations though he admitted
the Prime Minister was unlikely to have plundered his own house.
He disclaimed any intention to rely on the army (I expressed my
satisfaction but not my disbelief) and claimed to be ultra-
constitutional. He declared that his oath to preserve the
constitution had prevented his approving Prime Minister's proposal to
dissolve parliament but immediately afterwards he maintained that
if he got a government to suit him and deputies still gave trouble,
he would dissolve parliament.

5. We have not solved all our difficulties but Qawam seems to
be encouraged by the support of the three allied representatives.
For our part we must try (1) to eliminate bad elements in higher
ranks of officials (2) spur the Prime Minister to greater activity
in matters affecting general public and (3) [grp. undc. ? supply]
some wheat or flour as soon as possible as material proof of
soundness of [grp. undc.]'s foreign policy.

Foreign Office please retransmit to Kuibyshev as telegram
No. 329.

[Repeated to Kuibyshev under No. 1668. Copies sent to
Mr. Armstrong].

163

E

46

Registry Number } E 7217/14/34

TELEGRAM FROM
Sir R.Bullard (Tehran)

No. 1557

Dated 10th Dec.,
Received } 11th Dec.,
in Registry } 1942.

E : Persia.

Situation in Persia; Tehran riots.

Refers to Tehran telegram No.1553 of 9th December (E 7215/14/34). New Military Governor has situation in hand. Town is quiet and shops re-opening. Battalion of British troops arrived during night of 9th December, two British soldiers were killed and two injured. An 8 p.m. curfew has been introduced and press not allowed to appear. Majlis has been closed for the moment. Ahmedi hoped for support for himself and the Prime Minister and agreed the Army must be purged. Soviet Ambassador does not object to reconstitution of Cabinet.

Repeated Minister of State 549, Bagdad 469, Kuibyshev 330 and India 598.

Last Paper.

L 7215

References.

(Print.)

(How disposed of.)

Egred H/Armstrong
& I.O. Mr Hausnum
FS. India.

Mr Waley
Mr N.E. Young } Try
Mr Peel LO
Mr Somerlaw Nos
Mr Arkell mwi
7) Tehran 1602
8) (8) Y-State 3581
Kuibyshev 1679
India 13 Dec
8) India 14 (Index).
(Action completed.)

Next Paper.

E 7228

(Minutes.)

↑SE within Amended Copy

Please see also E 7215. Sir R. Bullard appears to have spoken to the Shah on much the same lines as those authorised in our telegram No. 1590 (E 7167). I submit that we should approve his language. The Shah has been opposed to Qawam for some time and it now seems clear that he hoped to get rid of him and to set up some sort of a military Government over which he would exercise considerable control.

The appearance on the scene of Field-Marshal Ahmadi is interesting. He is of Caucasian rather than Persian origin and, though he may be dishonest, is an energetic man who should be able to restore order. He appears to have the right views about the Majlis and it would, I submit, be in our interests to support him as well as the Prime Minister. The post of Minister of War is of course that occupied by Reza Shah before he made himself head of the State. The other proposed changes in the Cabinet seem quite suitable from our point of view. I submit a tentative draft. News Dept. have been primed about the arrival of a battalion of British troops ...

JM.B.

11th December, 1942.

11/12

Then were British military casualties in the rioting.

11. xii

als
Dec. 11.1942.

Tel. approved by
Sept. despatched
22910 9/41 F.O.P. 2
13/xii

[This telegram is of particular secrecy and should be retained
by the authorised recipient and not passed on.]

[This document must be paraphrased if communicated to any
person outside Government service].

[Cypher]   WAR CABINET DISTRIBUTION

                       FROM: PERSIA

              FROM TEHRAN TO FOREIGN OFFICE

Sir R. Bullard   D. 7.40 p.m. 10th December, 1942.
No.1557.   R. 11.25 p.m. 10th December, 1942.
10th December, 1942.

Repeated to Minister of State's Office Cairo No.549
            Bagdad for P.A.I.C. Minbranch No.469
            Kuibyshev No.330
            Government of India No.598 (Foreign Office please
                                                      pass).

                      [ ] [ ] [ ]

IMMEDIATE.

        My telegram No.1553. E 7215

        New Military Governor seems to have the situation well in
hand. The town is now quiet and shops are re-opening.
Battalion of British troops arrived in Tehran night of December
9th as a precautionary measure for the protection of military
supply dumps, oil installations, etc. Casualties during the
rioting appear to have been comparatively light. Unfortunately
two British soldiers were killed and two injured. The matter is
being taken up with Ministry of War by Military Attaché. 8 p.m.
curfew introduced and press has not yet been allowed to appear.

        In conversation with Oriental Secretary on December 9th,
Ahmedi stated that he was determined to restore order with vigour
and to arrest and shoot all instigators of disorders. He had
for the time being closed [group undec.] as its immediate opening
might only lead to confusion and embarrassment for the Government.
He hoped we on our side would give Qawam and himself our fullest
support and do everything possible regarding the bread supply.
Ahmedi realises the defects of the army and agreed it must be
drastically purged. In interview [2 groups omitted] Zahidi
whom he called a dangerous traitor.

/Mejlis

        Oriental Secretary informed Ahmedi that we would back him
and not let him down.

        Soviet Ambassador raises no objection to reconstitution of
the Cabinet on lines of my telegram No.1553 with the addition
of Bahrami (No.46) who may be offered Ministry of the Interior.

        [Copies sent to Mr. Armstrong.]
        [Copies sent to Telegraph Branch India Office for repetition
                        to Government of India].

(E.7167/14/34)   WAR CABINET DISTRIBUTION.

[CYPHER]   TO: PERSIA.

                   FROM FOREIGN OFFICE TO TEHRAN.

No. 1590.   D. 2.35 a.m. 10th December 1942.
9th December, 1942.

Repeated to Minister of State, Cairo No. 3057;
            Bagdad (for Minbranch and P.A.I.C) No. 1122;
            Government of India;
            Kuibyshev No. 1664;
            Washington No. 7767.

                        q   q   q

IMMEDIATE.

        Your telegram No. 1550 [of 9th December: rioting in
Tehran].

        Attitude of Shah is most disappointing and you should,
unless you see objection, seek further audience of His Majesty
at the earliest moment. Subject to your discretion, you should
speak on following lines:

        (1) His Majesty's Government have learned with great regret
of the attitude taken up by His Majesty during the recent
disturbances.

        (2) His Majesty cannot sincerely imagine that it is either
the desire of the Allied Governments or in their interest to
change a Persian Government with which they have just concluded
the recent Agreements over currency and food.

        (3) Both present Prime Minister and the Allied Governments
have done their best to meet Persian requirements in this latter
respect and it ought to have been possible, and still is possible,
for His Majesty to make known his consciousness of this. It
ought to have been equally possible for His Majesty to remind his
people that their privations, serious as they are, are infinitely
less than those which are being undergone by all countries which
are under Axis domination, as well as by many which are not. The

                                        /alliance .....

-370-

alliance has so far secured Persia from much greater
hardships than anything she has yet endured and it will
continue to do so.

(4) As regards the Majlis, it is most disconcerting
to His Majesty's Government to find His Majesty apparently
encouraging the most irresponsible elements of that unsatisfactory assembly. Should disorders continue, enforced dissolution would certainly be among the measures
which would impose themselves.

(5) His Majesty has complained that he has no
authority. It is now for him to assert himself in support
of a Prime Minister who has the confidence of his Allies.

[Copies sent to Mr. Armstrong].

1 copy

London, December 10, 1942.

M 10 —

Dear Baxter,

We have just received a further telegram from the
State Department concerning the economic and political
conditions prevailing in Iran. The Department tells
us in this telegram that according to a report reaching
it from Tehran the political situation in Iran has, due
largely to the obstruction of the Majlis, deteriorated.
A new crisis, brought on by the intensified shortage of
food, threatens to bring about the fall of the Qavam
Cabinet or the dissolution of the Majlis. On December 8
widespread rioting took place in Tehran.

With reference to these most recent developments
the Department reminds us that, as so often stated by
it, it is in favor of the present cabinet remaining in
power, unsatisfactory as this may be in some respects.
It prefers this to a change bringing into power a group
which might turn out to be even more unsatisfactory and
which would enjoy an even lesser measure of popular
support.

Any/

Mr. C. W. Baxter, C.M.G., M.C.,
     Foreign Office,
          London.

Any comments which the Foreign Office may care to make on the foregoing information and observations would be appreciated by the Department.

We have also been asked by the Department to advise the Foreign Office that the Department's reports indicate that the food situation in Iran continues to deteriorate. In this connection the Department expresses the hope that the British authorities will make every possible effort to expedite the transportation of wheat from ports in North Africa and everything possible to effect advances of grain from neighboring areas in the Middle East.

Yours sincerely,

H. Freeman Matthews

E   7267

                               1942

                               140

Arrest of Zahidi: United States attitude.

Registry
Number E 7267/122/34.

FROM Mr. Freeman
Matthews (United States
Embassy) to Mr. Baxter.

Dated 11th Dec. 1942.
Received
in Registry 13th Dec. 1942.
E: Persia.

Has been informed by the State Department that
the United States Minister in Tehran has reported
that General Zahidi the Governor-General of
Isfahan, was arrested and interned on 8th December
by the British Army at Sultan Abadan. The Shah and
Prime Minister are much disturbed by this action.
The State Department wish to express their concern
over this turn of events, having understood that
His Majesty's Government felt as they did, that
caution should be observed in the matter of arrests
and they are surprised that such drastic action was
taken without the concurrence of the Persian
authorities.

Last Paper.

Ł 7265

References.

(Minutes.)

Mr. Gallman, of the United States Embassy, brought
me this morning this letter regarding instructions
received from the State Department to express to us
their concern and surprise at our arrest of General
Zahidi.

X   Mr. Gallman said that there was a further extremely
long telegram in from Washington. It had not yet been
fully decoded, but it appeared to deal with the general
question of our policy towards Persia. The United
States Embassy would probably communicate with us on
Monday as a result of this further telegram.

(Print.)

I explained that it had been found necessary for
us to arrest General Zahidi as he was implicated in the
Persian plot and had been harbouring Axis agents. We
had also many other serious charges against him. It
was true that the Persian Government were not consulted
in advance, because this would have put them in a very
difficult position. Our information, moreover, was
that very little notice had been taken of the arrest;
and it was certainly not the cause of the serious riots
in Tehran, which were due to the food shortage and
other causes.

(How disposed of.)

As regards the desire of the State Department and
of ourselves that caution should be observed in the
matter of arrests, I pointed out that we had not thought
it necessary so far to arrest the other Persians who
were implicated in the plot.

We shall evidently receive on Monday further
representations from the State Department about our
policy in Persia.

(Action
completed.)   (Index.)

Next Paper.

≃ 7268

23238 12 41 F.O.P.

12th December, 1942.

13. XII

AE Dec 14

141

London, December 11, 1942.

Dear Baxter,

The State Department informs us that our Minister at
Tehran reported that on December 8 General Zahidi, Governor
General of Isfahan, was arrested and interned at Sultanabad
Bagdon by the British Army. The Shah and the Prime
Minister, according to the report of our Minister at Tehran,
are very much disturbed by this action and they take the
view that the action is both unfair and arbitrary. They
say it is unfair because the Government of Iran was not
consulted, and arbitrary because the British authorities do
not have the right to make arrests. A personal representative of the Shah called on our Minister at Tehran to
register a protest.

According to our Minister, the arrest of General
Zahidi has intensified the already critical situation. As
evidence of this, widespread and serious rioting in Tehran
is cited.

We have been asked to express to the Foreign Office
the State Department's concern over this turn of events.
The State Department, having understood that the British
Government felt as we did; that caution should be observed

in/

Mr. C. W. Baxter, C.M.G., M.C.,
      Foreign Office, London.

-2-

in the matter of arrests, was surprised that action
along such apparently drastic lines was taken, and
apparently without the concurrence of the Iranian
authorities.

Yours sincerely,

H. Freeman Matthews

[CYPHER].   WAR CABINET DISTRIBUTION.

                                From PERSIA.

                    FROM TEHRAN TO FOREIGN OFFICE.

Sir R. Bullard   D. 11.20 p.m. 11th December, 1942.
No. 1563   R. 3.30 a.m. 12th December, 1942.
11th December, 1942.

Repeated to Minister of State Cairo No. 553,
             Bagdad (for P.A.I.C. and Minbranch) No. 470
             Government of India No. 599
             Kuibyshev No. 332.
                         rrrrrr

IMPORTANT.

        Foreign Office please repeat to Kuibyshev.

        Your telegram No. 1590 evidently crossed my telegram No. 1553
recording my last interview with the Shah. The Shah seems
chastened and it seems unnecessary to add at present to what I have
already said. I will keep in reserve comments in your telegram
under reply insofar as they go beyond those I have already used.
If I said little about food supplies it was because I thought
(as I still think) that this question was not the main cause of
the disturbances.

        2. The Shah has not shown up well during this crisis.
Yesterday he sent to me to say that he could not understand how I
had gained the impression that he wished to rely on the army, but
having questioned General Jahanbani who had called on the Soviet
Ambassador [grp. undec. ?semi-officially] (paragraph 2 of my
telegram No. 1553) he had found that the General after conveying the
Shah's message had chattered on and omitted some general ideas of his
own which might perhaps have been taken for the Shah's. As after
seeing the General the Soviet Ambassador had a two-hour talk with
the Shah this excuse seems thin besides being unworthy of a crowned
head.

        3. I think the Shah means well by his country and imagines
himself as the philosopher king bringing justice and prosperity to
all. He is, however, too young and inexperienced to play this rôle
and had he succeeded in his scheme to secure power over the Cabinet
by means of the army with noisier section of the Majlis as a screen,
he would have been in the hands of his generals who are not

                                                    interested/

2.

interested in justice or in prosperity of anyone but themselves.

To the messenger from the Shah whom I met yesterday I gave warning (which he said he agreed with) that if the Shah's throne was ever in danger it would be due not to any civilian but to some ambitious general.

[Copies sent to Mr. Armstrong.   Repeated to Kuibyshev under telegram No. 1673].

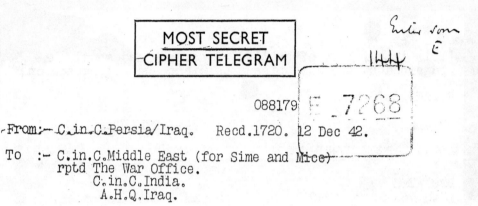

Enter son
E

144

088179 F 7268

From:- C.in.C.Persia/Iraq.   Recd.1720. 12 Dec 42.

To   :- C.in.C.Middle East (for Sime and Mice)
         rptd The War Office.
         C.in.C.India.
         A.H.Q.Iraq.

IMMEDIATE.

ED/76 cipher 12 Dec...

    From C.I.C.I.Baghdad.

    Isfahan reports reaction to General Zaḥidi's
arrest good. News evidently spread slowly and chief
reaction was surprise. Army quiet though displeased
and Colonel Sheqaqi present Acting C.O. Outwardly
cooperative.

               T.O.O.0720/12.

C.6.(Telegrams)   To:- M.O.5 (for action).

Copies to:-

S.of S.	M.I.2,2a,5,6,14,17,17a.
C.I.G.S.	S.of S. Foreign Affairs.
V.C.I.G.S.	Foreign Office (Mr.Pink).
D.M.O.	India Office (Brig.McCay).
D.D.M.O.(O).	Brig.Jacob.
D.Plans (2).	C.A.S.
M.O.I. 5.	Soc. C.N.S.
D.M.I.	A.M.C.S.Air Ministry.
D.D.M.I.(I).	

[This telegram is of particular secrecy and should be
retained by the authorised recipient and not passed on]

E.7263/6515/G.

[CYPHER]   DEPARTMENTAL (SECRET)

FROM FOREIGN OFFICE TO TEHRAN

No. 1603
13th December, 1942   D. 7.15 p.m.   13th December, 1942

Repeated to Minister of State's Office Cairo No. 3103
            Bagdad No. 1131 (for P.A.I.C. and Minbranch)
            Government of India

                        g g g g g

IMMEDIATE

MOST SECRET

    Your telegram No. 472 to Bagdad [of 12th December:
proposal to arrest Colonel Ferouhar and Nowbakht].

    State Department have expressed deep concern about
situation in Persia and in particular about arrest of
General Z[ahidi].

    Our case against F[erouhar] and N[owbakht] is not very
strong and to arrest them now might cause more trouble
than they are worth.   You should therefore defer action
against them for the present and until matters have been
discussed with United States Ambassador here.

            [Copies sent to Mr. Armstrong]

OTP.

Combined Intelligence Centre 'Iraq,
BAGHDAD.

CICI/H/62
Ext. 426.
12 Dec 42

Dear *Colonel*

Reference your D/O No. 500/GSI(b) dated 8th December '42.

2.   I attach 2 copies of a brief note on what we consider to
be the root causes of our present troubles in Persia. I am
sure you will agree that it is not easy to be brief on such a
subject and at the same time give a clear picture, but we have
done our best.

3.   The real difficult question to answer is the remedy.
Are we looking for a remedy which will suit us or suit the
Persians ? What we both want is Security and a cheap and even
distribution of food. We can't help but admit that these
existed under the late Shah but that didn't suit us. Everyone
knows of the late Shah's greed for money, etc., but he did
rule Persia; officials may have been corrupt but this was
controlled in that all bribery, etc., was from the Shah down-
wards - now this is not so - it's a case of every man for
himself. Therefore, to remedy this one must either clean the
whole administration or once again have a dictatorship rule.
If you are to clean the administration it means employing many
European advisers with full executive powers - in short -
taking over the control of the country. To my way of thinking
there are no other alternatives - anything else will not be
a cure and it will only mean drifting as we are now and the
chaos will become worse and worse. I know that this is dead
against our declared policy but, in my opinion, it's time we
faced facts.

Yours *sincerely*

E.K.

Colonel C.D. Quilliam,
    D.D.M.I.,
        G.H.Q.,
            Paiforce.

The Root Causes of our present troubles in Persia.

The main causes of disaffection and unrest in Persia are, in brief,

(1)   An oppressive, corrupt and inefficient administration.
(2)   Economics.
(3)   Government inability to enforce its authority, outside town areas.
(4)   Enemy agents.

A comment on these headings is as follows :-

(1)   The reign of Reza Shah saw the opening up of the country by road and rail development. This was financed entirely by onerous taxation and was accompanied by the Shah's unequalled personal rapacity. The greater part of the revenue was derived from Government monopolies of essentials and, particularly towards the end of his reign, its collection and the Shah's confiscation of private properties, resulted in a nation-wide hatred of a tyrannical ruler and his puppet Government. On his abdication, and released from his control, Persian Government officials seized the opportunity to indulge in unlimited extortion and bribe-taking, a state of affairs which still exists. It is not surprising then that the populace is resentful and rebellious or that British prestige is as low as it is when our declared policy is to back the Qavam es Sultaneh and his inefficient Government and at the same time to refuse responsibility for the ensurance of effective administration. The Qavam is possibly not blameless and his many political opponents, when advertising his deficiences and those of his Government, take care to apportion to his British backers a large part of their complaints of maladministration.

(2)   Chaos reigns in the economic field. Reliable reports indicate that the autumn harvest was sufficient for the country's total requirements yet, even from areas where exceptional harvests were gathered, come reports of famine conditions and prices. The official explanation for these conditions is lack of transport to move grain supplies, and foreign interference. The truth is that here again is official maladministration and corruption and private hoarding and speculation; there is no wheat shortage for those who are prepared to pay the profiteers' prices. The fate of the poorer classes, particularly the town-dwellers, is undoubtedly hard and the recent riots in Tehran are an indication of the temper of the people.
        The incompetence of Persian administration is to a great extent responsible for present conditions but it must not be forgotten that war conditions, our invasion of Persia and Allied local financial requirements set the ball of inflation and rising prices rolling.

(3)   In town areas Persian forces can, if they wish, maintain a semblance of order but in almost every case the Persian military and gendarmerie commanders in tribal areas protest that lack of men, material and transport renders them incapable of asserting Government authority. It is not denied that these deficiencies exist but there appears also to be a lack of desire to take action against naturally unruly tribal raiders and there are good grounds for belief that in some cases there is collusion between Persian military leaders and tribal representatives and that this collusion is fostered to our detriment by enemy agents. Anti-British or pro-Axis sentiments are not alone the reasons

for this inaction. Persian military leaders, usually unpaid or
under-paid, like their administrators look upon bribes as legitimate income and from their point of view it would be foolish
to eliminate their sources of supply.

(4)   Enemy agents are widespread throughout the country and
in this category are included many Persian officials of high and
low degree as well as foreign nationals. For reasons of policy
the Persians, in most cases, are being temporarily left at large
but under observation. The foreign nationals are receiving
Persian and tribal protection and although every effort is being
made to round them up the difficulty of this task is considerable.

Effects.

          The effect of the foregoing is seen in continued reports
of public demonstrations and protests against a deplorable
economic situation where an artifical bread shortage is allowed
and where soaring prices of other essential commodities are
uncontrolled. There is also general insecurity in the country
and while it is admitted that interruptions on British lines of
communication and supply routes to Russia have not been serious
so far, there is no guarantee that the situation might not deteriorate as opposition to the present form of Government increases.
In an effort to combat these effects American advisers have been
appointed to Persia's essential services but unless they are
entrusted with some administrative or executive power it is
unlikely that Persian officials will give much effect to their
recommendations.

Conclusion.

          When considering a remedy for the situation in Persia
our policy towards that country has to be considered. Our policy
at present consists of support for the Central Government and
non-interference in Persia's internal affairs. The support is
given to a very shaky structure and the non-interference, which
is belied in practice, has been construed as an evasion of
responsibility. Whatever the result of the policy it rules out
any suggestion of Allied administration of the country and any
possibility that the root causes of Persia's ills might be
speedily and effectively removed. There remains the problem of
ensuring security in our military areas and on our lines of
communication. Since time is a consideration it appears that
finer political feelings should be disregarded and the issue
decided by Allied force or by British or Allied negotiation
with those elements which are the causes of insecurity.

C.I.C.I. BAGHDAD.
12.   12. 1942.

E.7371

17 DEC 1942

[CYPHER].   WAR CABINET DISTRIBUTION.

                          FROM   PERSIA.

                 FROM TEHRAN TO FOREIGN OFFICE.

Sir R. Bullard.   D. 9.50 p.m. December 16th 1942.
No.1586.   R. 7.50 a.m. December 17th 1942.
December 16th 1942.

          Repeated to Minister of State's Office Cairo No.566,
                     Minbranch Bagdad No.109,
                     Government of India No.608.

                    ~~~~~~~~~~~~~~~~~~~~~~~~~

IMPORTANT.

          Your telegram No.1602. E 7217 | 14 | 34

          Majlis is to meet December 20th. I gather that the
Prime Minister has consented to this under constant pressure
from the Shah. Both of them are aware of our views but if
they are agreed on re-opening there is nothing to be done
for the present. The Prime Minister considers the deputies
are rather frightened and will behave well, at least at
first. To save their faces he will not announce changes
in the Cabinet until after December 20th so that they may
appear to have been consulted. Whether they will respond to
this gentle treatment is extremely doubtful especially if the
Shah is going to continue to encourage them. So long
however as British, Soviet and American representatives
continue to support Qavam I hope the Shah will not again
try to get rid of him.

          Foreign Office please repeat to Kuibyshev as my
telegram No.340.

          [Repeated to Kuibyshev under Foreign Office No.1695].

          [Copies sent to Mr. Armstrong].

-384-

E   64

[Cypher].   WAR CABINET DISTRIBUTION   F.7533

                          FROM PERSIA

                 FROM TEHRAN TO FOREIGN OFFICE

Sir R. Bullard.   D. 8.00 p.m. 15th December, 1942.
No. 1578
15th December, 1942.   R. 2.50 a.m. 16th December, 1942.

Repeated to Minister of State's Office Cairo No. 563,
              Bagdad for P.A.I.C and Minbranch,
              Government of India,
              Kuibyshev Saving.

                         111

IMMEDIATE.   E7215/14/34
    My telegram No. 1553.

    Following is substance of two hour private conversation which
the Counsellor had on December 14th with the Shah on the present
political situation.

    The Shah was incensed that it should be alleged that he had
instigated demonstrations.   I calmed him down by saying that this
was eminently a country of rumours and intrigues and that I myself
had been rather surprised that His Majesty's Legation had not yet
been accused of engineering the plot.   The Shah then admitted he
had committed an error of judgement in changing his mind shortly
after he had agreed with Sir R. Bullard to the retention of Qawam
with a reconstructed cabinet.   The fact was rioting was rapidly
getting worse and from all sides he was receiving telephone calls to
the effect that the only way of restoring order was the resignation
of Qawam.   In the stress of the moment he had failed to understand
the situation as clearly as he should have done, particularly as he
had no candidate immediately in mind who could suitably replace
Qawam.   However he had now accepted Ahmedi as Minister of War and
was fully ready to support Qawam Government, reconstruction of which
would very shortly be completed.

    The Shah was deeply pre-occupied with the future of the Majlis.
Speaking personally I expressed the view that it seemed to be in
the best interest of the country that if possible it should remain
closed for the present to enable Qawam to reconstruct the cabinet
and get into the saddle.   Although inclined to agree, the Shah
felt that if the Majlis was kept closed it would be unconstitutional
and might be used against him later as a convenient precedent.   At
the same time he obviously feared that without the Majlis he might
find himself unable to impose any restraint on Qawam.   I pointed
out that if Qawam ran amok or failed to co-operate, I did not
imagine the Allied Powers would continue to give him their support.

                                                    /The....

DEC

                         -385-

The Shah was not fully convinced.   He felt that recent events might have had a chastening effect on the deputies and that if warned in addition they might behave properly in future.   I replied that deputies were like a school of children and that the effect of such warning would wear off in 24 hours.   If the deputies could be induced to vote for themselves a holiday or to recommend that they should be dissolved for the purpose of holding election the position would be easier.   I much feared however that once the Majlis was re-opened there would be slashing attacks on Qawam and possibly a vote of no confidence.   In that event the Shah would find himself compelled to choose between the retention of Qawam or the dissolution of the Majlis.   If he adopted the latter alternative he would have to make it clear that the dissolution was only preliminary to new election, the date of which might have to be advanced.   This would give him and the Government useful respite, but of course there was no guarantee that the new deputies would be any improvement on their predecessors.   The Shah said he would reflect on the issues involved and discuss it again.

The Shah again complained of our arrest of Zahidi saying that if he had been consulted he would have arranged everything.   I replied that Zahidi was a clever and dangerous intriguer and that with the examples of Vaziri, whose arrest we had patiently awaited for 8 months, and of four outstanding suspects of whom one at least was in the army, we felt it unfair to impose a task on the Persian authorities which they might be incapable of fulfilling.   The Shah admitted that the police were a poor body.   I then told the Shah that he must have no illusions about the infallibility of his army.   How could he expect junior officers whose pay was less than that of his cook to be honest and free from political intrigue.   He agreed and hoped to arrange for increases in pay.   I suggested that to keep down the expenditure involved he might at the same time comb out some of the worst offenders.   I warned him not to trust too implicitly senior officers who, once they found themselves in a position of power, might well put their personal ambitions before the throne.   The Shah seemed to appreciate this aspect.

I asked the Shah why he did not broadcast some declaration to the effect that he had his people's welfare at heart, was opposed to any repetition of recent disorders and that the present Government had his full confidence in the work of reconstruction.   Such a declaration, coupled possibly with reference to Persian solidarity with the Allies, might have calming effect as showing united front against intrigue and subversive activities.   He promised to think over the idea.

In conclusion I suggested that when the political situation cleared he might like to inspect recently arrived battalion of British troops.   The idea seemed to appeal to him.

[Copies sent to Mr. Armstrong].

GENERAL ISMAY, FOR C.O.S. COMMITTEE.

Now that it seems that the Persian opposition
is not very serious, I wish to know what are the plans
for pushing on and joining hands with the Russians, and
making sure we have the railway in working order in our
hands. We do not simply want to squat on the oilfields,
but to get through communication with Russia. We have
made certain proposals to the Shah, but these may be rejected or the Russians may not agree to them. What therefore are the plans to join hands with the Russians, and
what are the troop movements foreseen in the next week
by our different forces?

W.S.C.

2...

153

PERSIA.   December 16, 1942.

CONFIDENTIAL.   SECTION 1.

ARCHIVES

[E 7330/122/34]   Copy No.   8

(1)

Memorandum from the United States Embassy in London.

THE embassy has been asked urgently to bring to the attention of the Foreign Office the following observations of the State Department on recent developments in Persia :—

The Government of the United States has, in the course of the past year, felt that it had an increasingly direct interest in Persian conditions. It is primarily because of the importance of Persia in the United Nations' war effort, an importance which, it is felt, is given full recognition by the British Government, that the Government of the United States has been led to adopt this position. In common with all of the United Nations, the United States Government has a general interest in the successful conduct of the war in all theatres, but, in addition to this, it has, for the reasons given immediately below, felt a special responsibility so far as Persia is concerned :—

(1) It is believed that American prestige in Persia is such that it makes it possible for the United States Government to bring considerable influence to bear on the interests of the United Nations, and it is felt that an asset of such importance ought to be conserved and used.

(2) With a view to strengthening the internal administration of Persia, the Government of Persia has asked for a considerable number of American advisers. The Government of the United States naturally feels obliged to see to it that these advisers can begin and carry on their work under conditions favourable to the success of their efforts. The British Government, it is understood, has been whole-heartedly in favour of the sending of these advisory missions to Persia. As a matter of fact, the British Government has on several occasions been the first to urge that such missions be organised. Obviously, such advisers are in a position to exert on behalf of the common cause a most effective influence.

(3) Heavy commitments in connexion with furnishing the Soviet Union with supplies have been made by the Government of the United States, and, consequently, the United States Government is concerned in a direct way in maintaining the route over which, necessarily, a large part of these supplies must be carried. Furthermore, an agreement was recently reached under which the military authorities of the United States undertake the physical operation of the ports, railroads and highways of Persia by which supplies for the Soviet Union are handled and transported across Persia.

On a number of occasions the Government of the United States has been given to understand that the interest in Persian affairs shown by the United States was welcomed by the British Government, and that it was desired that the United States actively co-operate in settling the questions arising from time to time. The Government of the United States feels certain that it is understood by the British Government that considerations of self-interest in no way motivate the policy of the United States, but that this policy is concerned only with the furtherance of the war effort of the United Nations and with the laying of the basis in Persia, as well as in the rest of the world, for satisfactory and lasting peace-time conditions.

The Government of the United States has, with this in mind, as the British Government is aware, taken an active part in the negotiations and exchanges of view on the acute economic and political situation that has prevailed in Persia. The State Department has consistently maintained that the problem could be satisfactorily solved only if, in one way or another, adequate provision were made for the minimum economic requirements for the people of Persia and Persian authority and responsibility in the internal affairs of Persia were maintained to the maximum possible extent. It has been the view

[37—14]   B

-388-

of the State Department, quite apart from the obvious moral principles involved, principles to which the United Nations are pledged and to which the British Government subscribes without reservation, that considerations of a purely practical kind, in any event, would dictate that the civil responsibilities and the military forces of the Governments of the United Nations concerned ought to be held to a minimum in that country, so that the civilian personnel and these military forces could be employed in areas where, in the prosecution of the war, their services would be of the greatest immediate value.

The State Department accordingly, in communications to the British Government and to the American Minister at Tehran concerning the crisis which started in October, expressed its wish repeatedly that adequate early arrangements be made for transporting supplies of wheat to Persia, which would serve to prevent famine from arising in those areas which were deficient in stocks of grain. The State Department, in taking this position, has recognised that the Government of Persia might be at fault in part at failing to take the steps necessary to ensure the best use of the food supplies that were available within Persia. It was felt, however, that the matter was so urgent that there was no time for prolonged discussions or for a reorganisation of those Persian agencies which were concerned. Moreover, it was felt that resort to coercion on the authorities of Persia would not only lead to many undesirable repercussions but probably also to failure to achieve the desired objective. The State Department gathered, from the exchange of communications which has taken place between London and Washington, that the Foreign Office took substantially the same view.

It will be recalled by the Foreign Office that the State Department on more than one occasion expressed the view that the occupation of Tehran by military forces, or the setting up of a puppet Government, would be undesirable. The State Department believed, in the light of views expressed by the Foreign Office to the American Embassy in London, and to the Department by the British Embassy at Washington, that the British Government was in agreement with this. Likewise, on a number of occasions the fear of the State Department was expressed that, unless handled with great care, action by the British authorities in Persia against subjects of Persia alleged to be implicated in activities inimical to the United Nations, would have unfortunate and serious repercussions. The State Department urged particularly that such matters be handled by the Persian authorities themselves. The American Embassy at London, it appears, understood that the Foreign Office also felt that caution should be employed, and that, in fact, the British Minister at Tehran had been telegraphed to that effect. It appears also to have been the understanding of the embassy that the Foreign Office hoped that it would not be necessary to proceed in this matter against the wishes of the Government of Persia.

As the Foreign Office and the State Department were apparently in agreement with respect to the principal questions involved, the State Department notes regretfully that events which have taken place in recent weeks in Persia do not appear to have been entirely in keeping with the policies of the two Governments. The events in question, as reported to the State Department, are briefly :—

(1) The signature and publication of the Anglo-American-Persian Agreement for Wheat for Persia, although recognised by all three Governments as urgent, was held up for a period of several weeks, largely, it appears, because the British authorities in Persia wanted successively to impose on the Government of Persia, before proceeding with the signing, more difficult conditions. It was only on the 4th December that the agreement, whatever the reason, was concluded, and by that time it failed to have the reassuring effect anticipated because popular dissatisfaction in Persia had become so great.

(2) In spite of what was thought to be the view of the Foreign Office that caution should be exercised with reference to the contemplated arrests of prominent Persians, the Governor-General of Isfahan was interned by the British authorities in Persia on the 8th December. The State Department understands that this was done without first consulting the Government of Persia and that a most unfortunate effect was produced.

(3) On the 9th December the British Minister at Tehran informed the American Minister that on that same afternoon a battalion of British troops would enter Tehran.

(4) On the 9th December the American Minister at Tehran reported that for some reason the British authorities in Persia had failed to arrange the transportation to Tehran of the 1,500 tons of flour and 3,500 tons

154

of barley earmarked at Basra for Persia. The British Minister, likewise on the 9th December, advised the Shah that, unless the Government of Persia were favourable to the Allies, the importation of wheat into Persia would not be viewed favourably. The same statement, it is understood, was made by the British Minister to the Prime Minister of Persia. This attitude, of course, conflicts with the action which it was understood was previously taken by the Foreign Office when it instructed the British Minister at Tehran and the Minister of State at Cairo to try to arrange the prompt shipment to Persia of wheat and barley from neighbouring sources, including Iraq. It is also in contrast with what was understood to be the view of the Foreign Office, that the extreme shortage of wheat, particularly in Tehran, was causing unrest and disorder.

The foregoing, the State Department points out, is placed before the Foreign Office solely for the purpose of effecting closer co-ordination of action between the Governments of Great Britain and the United States and in the hope that whatever is done in Persia will be entirely in keeping with the views maintained London, and Washington.

December 14, 1942.

(2)

Memorandum to the United States Embassy in London.

THE United States Embassy's memorandum of the 14th December, communicating the observations of the State Department on recent developments in Persia, has been considered in the Foreign Office with the greatest care and sympathy. It is believed that the policy of His Majesty's Government towards Persia corresponds very closely with that of the United States Government. At the same time, it is felt that a full and frank exchange of views on this subject will be of great value, lest misunderstanding should arise on points such as those enumerated in the latter part of the memorandum under reply.

2. In the first place, the Foreign Office wish to confirm their entire agreement with the views expressed in the embassy's memorandum as regards the increasing importance of the United States Government's interests in Persia. Indeed, the growing interest which the United States Government have shown in Persian affairs has been very welcome to His Majesty's Government, who, as the State Department point out, took the lead in suggesting that United States advisers should be sent to Persia to strengthen the internal administration of the country. His Majesty's Government therefore fully understand and share the anxiety of the United States Government that these advisers should be enabled to carry out their work under favourable conditions, and are confident that their work will prove of the greatest value in reorganising the finances of Persia and in putting the administration on a sound and efficient basis. His Majesty's Government also recognise that the arrangement whereby the military authorities of the United States are to take over the operation of Persian ports, railways and roads greatly increases the interest of the United States Government in the maintenance of law and order throughout the country.

3. His Majesty's Government also confirm that it has for long been their desire that the United States Government and the United States authorities in Persia should co-operate more actively in settling the questions arising from time to time. Until recently the task of maintaining the interests of the United Nations at Tehran has fallen almost exclusively on the British Legation. It is hoped that it may henceforward be possible for the United States representative at Tehran to take an equally active part in helping to solve important problems of common concern to the Allied Governments; and it is believed that the task of the two legations may be greatly eased by the steadying influence which will be exercised on the Persian authorities through the United States advisers.

4. As the State Department are aware, it has been the policy of His Majesty's Government not to occupy Tehran by military forces, but to allow the Persian Government to continue to administer the country with as little interference as possible. In order to encourage a spirit of collaboration in the Persian authorities, His Majesty's Government took the initiative in the negotiations which culminated last January in the signature of the Anglo-Soviet-Persian Treaty of Alliance. By this treaty Persia acquired the status of a non-belligerent ally. This policy has on the whole been successful hitherto; the degree of

[37—14]

B 2

collaboration afforded by the Persian authorities has in general proved sufficient; but on three problems of major importance it has been necessary, in the interests of the United Nations' war effort, to bring strong pressure to bear upon the Persian Government and to contemplate measures which have, as it appears, led the Persian Government to put forward complaints to the Government of the United States.

5. These three problems are:—

(1) The provision of local currency for the United Nations' forces in Persia;
(2) The wheat problem; and
(3) Security measures against Axis agents in Persia.

6. In the United States Embassy's memorandum under reply, it is stated that considerations of self-interest in no way motivate the policy of the United States, but that this policy is concerned only with the furtherance of the war effort of the United Nations and with the laying of a basis for satisfactory and lasting peace-time conditions in Persia, as well as in the rest of the world. His Majesty's Government readily accept this assurance, and they must request the United States Government in return to accept a corresponding assurance on their behalf. In dealing with the three problems mentioned above, and in all their dealings with the Persian authorities, His Majesty's Government have not been moved in any way by considerations of self-interest, but have been concerned with the furtherance of the war effort of the United Nations.

7. The difficulties raised by the Persian Government in connexion with the supply of rials to the British forces in Persia were, in fact, difficulties which had to be surmounted by some means or other in the interests of the war effort. Without rials it would have been impossible for the Allied forces in Persia to pay for local purchases and local labour. It was absolutely essential that rials should be forthcoming. Otherwise, the Trans-Persian lines of communication for supplies of war material to the Soviet Union would have broken down. After difficult negotiations a solution appeared to have been reached through the conclusion of an Anglo-Persian Financial Agreement on the 26th May; and it was therefore all the more deplorable that the Persian authorities, despite the clear terms of this agreement, should again have sought only a few months later to withhold the necessary currency from the Allied forces. The State Department are aware how, mainly as the result of the common front displayed on this occasion by the Allied representatives at Tehran, it proved possible to solve these difficulties without having recourse to forcible measures; and it may be hoped that, with the forthcoming arrival at Tehran of the United States Financial Mission, a further Persian threat to withhold the currency essential to the United Nations need no longer be apprehended.

8. Again, as regards the wheat problem, the policy of His Majesty's Government has been directed solely towards furthering the essential war interests of the United Nations, with due regard also to the minimum requirements of the Persian people. It has been based upon two governing considerations. The first is that, quite apart from the shortage of shipping, the clearance capacity of Persian ports and transport routes is strictly limited, so that every ton of wheat imported into Persia for Persian consumption involves a reduction in the quantity of vital war-supplies sent to the Soviet Union by the Trans-Persian routes. The second point is that Persia in normal times grows sufficient cereals for her own use, and the 1942 harvest is believed to have fallen very little short of a normal harvest, so that there must exist in the country sufficient stocks of cereals to last nearly until the harvest of 1943. It will be recalled that, during the period between the military operations in August 1941 and the summer of 1942, some 50,000 tons of wheat were imported from British and United States sources to satisfy in the exceptional circumstances then existing the needs of the Persian civil population. But the Persian Government, almost immediately after the harvest of 1942, complained that there was already a serious shortage and requested that further wheat should be imported for their use. It was evident that they were reluctant to take drastic and unpopular measures against hoarders, speculators and profiteers, and thought it easier to appeal to the Allies to solve their difficulties for them by arranging further imports. This attitude was clearly inadmissible. It would have meant a reduction in the supplies sent across Persia to the Soviet Union, for reasons which could not have been justified to the Soviet Government. His Majesty's Government agree that it is in itself desirable that steps should be taken to save the Persian people from want, but it is clearly necessary to insist upon the Persian authorities making the best use of the food supplies available within Persia, and the only wheat imports

5

155

to which His Majesty's Government have hitherto agreed during the present season are the 25,000 tons of wheat which are being imported to replace the Persian-grown cereals required by the Soviet occupying forces.

9. Security measures against Axis agents have also been the cause of serious difficulties with the Persian Government. For many years past German influence in Persia has been very extensive, and it was largely owing to the presence of Germans and German agents in key positions throughout the country that it became necessary for British and Soviet forces to undertake the military occupation of certain areas in August 1941. At the present moment there are still some Germans in hiding in the unoccupied districts of Persia, there are still German agents who are active throughout the country, and there is still a considerable amount of pro-German sympathy in influential Persian circles. His Majesty's Government regard it as absolutely essential to take such steps against German agents as may be required to safeguard the Allied troops and communications in Persia. Some Germans and some German agents have already been arrested; others have been allowed to escape by the Persian police or are said to be untraceable. But proof has been obtained of a widespread conspiracy organised by the Germans with the help of a number of influential Persians, involving definite plans for sabotage against Allied communications, and risings against the Allies in the event of a German invasion of Persia. It is clear that drastic action is justifiable and necessary against those implicated in such matters, though such action has hitherto been confined to a minimum.

10. The foregoing general observations are intended to cover the main aspects of British and United States policy in Persia, and although emphasis has naturally been laid upon these points which have caused most difficulty, and on which differences of outlook are most likely to arise, the Foreign Office believe that on the whole the views of the two Governments are very closely in agreement as regards the major issues. There remain the four questions referred to at the end of the United States Embassy's memorandum under reply.

(1) It is true that the signature of the Anglo-United States-Persian agreement for wheat was delayed because it was desired to ensure, in connexion with the Wheat Agreement, a satisfactory long-term settlement of the currency dispute. As stated above, rials are absolutely essential for the United Nations' forces in Persia. His Majesty's Government felt therefore that it was essential to insist on some new currency arrangement, whereby the Majlis would no longer create difficulties on every occasion when they were asked to provide the necessary rials. As soon as a satisfactory solution on these lines was reached there was, so far as His Majesty's Government are aware, no further question of delaying the signature of the Wheat Agreement in order to impose on the Persian Government more difficult conditions. And, as distinct from the agreement, His Majesty's Government have at all times, and irrespective of their disputes with the Persian Government, sought to accelerate the despatch of the wheat which was urgently needed owing, primarily, to the Soviet requisitions in Northern Persia.

(2) General Zahidi, the Governor-General of Isfahan, was arrested because he was implicated in the serious conspiracy referred to above. Careful consideration was first given to the question whether the Persian Government should be consulted in advance, but it was decided that to adopt this course would involve the risk of leakage, and would, in addition, be most embarrassing to the Persian Government themselves. The information at the disposal of His Majesty's Government indicates that the effect locally of General Zahidi's arrest has been very salutary.

(3) The sole reason for the despatch of a battalion of British troops to Tehran during the recent rioting was to protect Allied property and military stores.

(4) The Foreign Office were surprised by these reports from the United States Minister at Tehran, which implied that the despatch of certain consignments of food-stuffs to Tehran was being delayed by the British authorities for political reasons. This, as in the case of the wheat shipments, would certainly have been opposed to the views and intentions of His Majesty's Government. They therefore telegraphed to Sir Reader Bullard, who has explained that there is, of course, no foundation whatever for any suggestion that the despatch of this flour and barley to Persia had been deliberately delayed in order to put pressure on the Persian Government. On the contrary, the British Legation had done everything possible to hasten its despatch. (Such delay as occurred seems, in fact, to have been due partly to an unexpected fall in the level of the

-392-

Karun river while the barges conveying the grain were on their way to Ahwaz, but mainly to the physical difficulty of moving it from Shaiba to Margil, thence by water to Ahwaz, and thence by rail to Tehran.) Nor did Sir Reader Bullard speak to the Shah or the Persian Prime Minister on the lines mentioned, or threaten them in any way with the possibility that supplies already arranged might be withheld. It is hoped that it may be made clear to the United States Minister at Tehran that he has been misinformed on these points.

Foreign Office, January 4, 1943.

E 7561/65/15/6   14/34

Sir R. Bullard,
Tehran

Tel: No. 1630
Dated: 28 Dec.
Received: 29 Dec.

Persian Plot

Refers to F.O tel. 1603 regarding the arrest of certain other Persians connected with the plot. Thinks it would be safer to arrest all persons mentioned in papers relating to plot.

Last Paper.

E 7486

References.

(Print.)

'd. T.O.E. (signed) Palmer
April 6
Copies: Col. Price W.O.
At. Calthorpe M.o.S.
Major Shaw M.E.A.
W/Cdr Sadler Air M.
Mr. Peel L.O.
+ Mr. Palmer I.O on
Mr. Gram Law M.o.I.

Tehran 1631   30/12

Draft to Major Cowan
from Mr. Peile 31/1
Tel. 14 to Tehran 4/1
reptd 42 to H/S Cairo
Copied as for ref. 5/1

(Action completed.)   (Index.)

EC 5/1

Next Paper.

(Minutes.)

Please see also Tehran tel. 1631 attached (within)

Sir R. Bullard suggests that we should do nothing about General Kupal, that we should ask the Persians to arrest Colonel Ferouhar and that we should arrest the deputy Naubakht ourselves. He here reverts to his suggestion in E 7263/G.
Sir R. Bullard's reasons for taking no action against General Kupal (paragraph 2) seem to me convincing. As for Colonel Ferouhar, I think it would be a mistake for us to arrest him ourselves when we know that the United States Government would dislike the idea and that General Ridley (American adviser in the Persian Ministry of War) considers that the arrest of Persian officers by us might lower the morale of the Army. If we ask the Persians to arrest Ferouhar and they fail to do so, we shall have a perfectly good case for effecting his arrest ourselves. The only weakness I can see is that our grounds of complaint against Ferouhar do not seem to us very convincing. But Sir R. Bullard states (paragraph 2) that he can produce good reasons without referring to the plot and I submit that we should authorise him to act as he suggests, making it clear that he must make out an adequate case. A further argument in favour of asking the Persians to arrest Ferouhar is that the Russians recently asked the Persians to arrest two officers and to interrogate them. I doubt if the Russians would be able to put up a better case against these two officers than we could against Ferouhar.

The proposal to arrest the deputy Naubakht seems to me much more dangerous. As he enjoys Parliamentary immunity, the Prime Minister cannot arrest him. To arrest a deputy ourselves would provoke a considerable outcry and I doubt if we have any very convincing evidence against him.✱ It seems best for the moment to confine ourselves to asking the Persians to arrest Colonel Ferouhar. If they fail to do so, we could then arrest him and perhaps Naubakht as well. But it seems illogical to ask them to arrest one man and at the same time to arrest another ourselves, which is the one thing that both the Americans and the Persians dislike our doing.

✱ Tehran tel. 1631 strengthens our case slightly but would the deputy confirm this before a Board?
21107 1/41 F.O.P.   Query/

Query. Reply that we agree that no action should be
taken against General Kupal and that the Persian Government
should be asked to arrest Colonel Ferouhar, but that
we consider Naubakht should be left alone for the present.

*I submit a Dft. for consideration, which will
need the concurrence of the
W.O.*

I.M.Pink.

30th December, 1942.

The case against Colonel Ferouhar, apart from his
share in the plot, is given in Tehran telegrams Nos.
1449 and 1507. It boils down to the fact that he displayed an attitude of complete indifference as regards
the Harris murder, and did not help the search party,
or take any other useful step as the result of the
murder. He has already been removed from his command
for this apparent neglect of duty. As regards his share
in the plot, we have no information whatever. He may
have been more deeply involved than some of the others,
or he may not. Sir R. Bullard has told us nothing on
this point. But it has been decided to take no action
for the present against others implicated (except
General Zahidi). On the other hand, one of those implicated, General Shahbakhti, has just been recommended by
Sir R. Bullard for the Governor General of Shiraz.

Altogether, our case against Colonel Ferouhar, so
far as we know it, is a very weak one indeed. And if
the Persians are to be asked to arrest him, for detention and interrogation at Sultanabad by a joint Anglo-
Persian Commission, it will become evident to the Persians
how weak our case is.

Moreover, it does not appear that the British
Military authorities in Persia are urging his arrest on
security grounds. It seems to be on the political
gounds that Sir R. Bullard recommends the arrest. He
thinks it would have a good effect on the political
situation generally if we followed up our arrest of
General Zahidi by further arrests of those implicated in
the plot. Personally, I doubt whether a series of
arrests would in the long run improve the political
situation, or would cause other ill-disposed Persian
officials to refrain from anti-Allied activities.

I think therefore that, as regards Colonel Ferouhar,
Sir R. Bullard should be asked to reconsider his recommendation in the light of the foregoing observations;
but we might say that we remain open to conviction.

Revised draft on these lines submitted herewith.

December 31st, 1942.

Please see General Wilson's telegram of Dec 30
~~now attached~~
in E 38/G.

Tel. approved & sent

-395-

No. E 7330/128/34.

Dear Freeman Matthews

     I enclose a memorandum regarding our policy in Persia, which has been prepared as a reply to the memorandum communicated to the Foreign Office by Mr. Gallman on the 18th December.

     I hope that this memorandum will clear up any minor misunderstandings which may have arisen between our two governments on Persian problems. I believe that on the main issues we are both in substantial agreement.

     There is one further point, not dealt with in the memorandum, which I should like to bring to your personal notice. It is implied in the State Department's comments that, although our two governments see more or less eye to eye, nevertheless Sir Reader Bullard is carrying out a policy of his own, which is not in accordance with our views, but creates unnecessary difficulties with the Persians. I hope that the State Department will dismiss this possibility completely from their minds. I am convinced that Bullard is loyally carrying out the policy of His Majesty's Government to the best of his ability, and I have the fullest confidence in him. It is true that he has sometimes had to take action of a nature displeasing to the Persians, who thereupon are apt to run round to Mr. Dreyfus to complain.
     But

Mr. H. Freeman Matthews.

-396-

But on these occasions he has acted with the full
approval of His Majesty's Government and as I believe
in the interests of the United Nations. If, as I hope,
the United States representative in Persia is able to
co-operate more actively in future in maintaining the
interests of the United Nations, I think we shall
encounter far less difficulty than hitherto in our
dealings with the Persian authorities.

Yours sincerely

(S) Anthony Eden

From: H.M.MINISTER, TEHRAN   **To:** FOREIGN OFFICE, LONDON

No. 432 (CYPHER)   Despatched: 17/4/43

ated to:

STATE No.112
(ing)
OAD for MIN-
ANCH & PAIC
,52(Saving)
IA No.82
(ing)

My tel. No. 426.

I fear that SOHEILY Administration, in spite of the fact that it contains good elements, is proving complete failure and may not last much longer. This "futility" Prime Minister utters fine words and makes fair promises but achieves nothing. In fact Government business seems to have come to a standstill, through lack of driving power and leadership. Important issue of inflation and high prices which Dr. MILLSPAUGH is prepared to tackle is held up through delay of Majlis even to debate grant of required powers. A programme of general reform has been proclaimed but no concrete proposals put forward. Prime Minister is proud of having remained on good terms with the Deputies, and does not see that this success has been achieved by his permitting them to remain idle when much urgent work is waiting to be done. His hobby of political tight-rope walking may involve his down-fall. Further his failure to use means at his disposal or if necessary to devise fresh means for dealing with recalcitrant newspapers has not added to his prestige and press attacks on the Americans and especially on ourselves continue unpunished and undiminished. Manoeuvres between Prime Minister and the Military Governor about the press are reproduced in regard to the Qashgai question where Prime Minister and SHAHBAKHTI accuse each other of being unwilling to deal with NASIR and to establish order in his country.

2. If SOHEILY falls the only candidates for his place who are likely to meet with much support are ZAYYID ZIA and ALI MANSUR (former Prime Minister and at present Governor-General at MESHID). The Russians are still against the former officially, though as I have reported before, there are signs that they are in touch with him in secret. The Minister of Supply, TADAYYUN, who is vigorous and ambitious, is said to be trying to conciliate the Russians with a view to succeeding SOHEILY.

3. Meantime the population continue to suffer from privation and neglect, and successful efforts are being made by many newspapers and doubtless by other means to make them believe that the British are responsible. No newspaper thanked us handsomely for the gift of the typhus hospital, while one said that we ought to do more and another said it would have been better if the Allies had not caused the typhus epidemic. It is at this moment that salvation comes in the form of 25,000 tons of wheat from RUSSIA. The Prime Minister who thanks them, and the journalists who write fulsome articles about the offer, all know that the Russians are taking away twice as much grain as they now offer to send in, but no one dares to utter still less to print the facts. Recent disappearance apparently by kidnapping of four Caucasians of whom at least one was a Persian subject has increased the respect in which the Russians are held and a well-educated newspaper proprietor recently gave this quite seriously as the reason why he often attacked the British and never the Russians.

4. Persians are longsuffering and cowardly, but if conditions become much worse it would not be surprising if general unrest xxxxxxxxxx ensued and if that unrest took some form which would be satisfactory to the Russians. A firm Government which would cooperate with the Americans and the British in an attempt to master the economic crisis might be able to arrest this tendency, but can such a Government be found in time, if it is to be found at all?

MA   1
CGS   1
DMO & I   1
Minbranch 1   (MOST SECRET
           & OFFICER ONLY)

BULLARD

SMC 230845 c

Documents relating to 28th of Mordad

P E R S I A

Mr. Palmer of the United States Embassy called on me
this afternoon, having previously telephoned to say that he
had information of some importance to give me.

Emphasising that what he would say was of the greatest
delicacy and on the ~~/~~basis of strict "need to know", he gave me
the following information.

Mr. Henderson had just reported that the last meeting
between the Shah and Dr. Musaddiq had not really been concerned
with the relatively minor topics which had been advertised in
the Press, but that Dr. Musaddiq had, in fact, suggested that
the Shah should leave Persia.   The Shah had been delighted
and had asked how soon he could go.   He suggested leaving
today for Iraq from /where, after visiting some of the Holy places, he
would proceed to Europe.   Later it had been agreed that any
definite plan should be postponed until Saturday.   In the
meantime the Spanish Chargé d'Affaires at Tehran had been
asked to inform his Government that an invitation to the Shah
to visit Spain would be appreciated.

Mr. Henderson had taken no action.   Much as he
regretted having to remain a spectator in view of the support
which the United States had given the Shah in the past, he felt
that there was really nothing he could do, more particularly
now that General Zahedi had tamely allowed himself to be
arrested.

Mr. Palmer said that the State Department would
probably be asking for our views.

I told Mr. Palmer that in my personal opinion it was an
illusion to think that we could influence events in Persia.   I

/ wondered

wondered what the United States Government thought about it? We had not been favoured with their views, though we had given them our estimate two days ago on the spur of the moment.   At that time we thought that the worst of all possibilities would be that the Shah should go and leave Dr. Musaddiq in power.   However, if you had a weak Shah and a strong Prime Minister, it was probably inevitable that the strong Prime Minister would win. Mr. Palmer assented and added "particularly as there is no alternative leader."

Mr. Palmer again emphasised that the matter was of great secrecy.   The Spanish Chargé d'Affaires did not know any of the background.

He added that so far there had been no mention of abdication.

Mr. Palmer subsequently telephoned to say that he hoped he had made it clear thatDr. Musaddiq had not suggested that the Shah should leave permanently.   What he had apparently said was that the Shah should leave until the situation became more settled.

Rom Ross

(A.D.M. Ross.)
26th February, 1953.

c.c. Sir Pierson Dixon.) On board ship.
Private Secretary.)

I do not think there is much to add to what Mr. Ross said

6

-401-

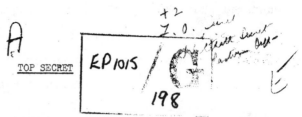

TOP SECRET

I have discussed briefly with Middleton the points raised by the Department in the suggested joint appraisal.

(a) This will be covered in a separate telegram.

(b) Both of us are of the opinion that it does not appear likely that any alternatives to Mossadeq could be brought into power at the present time except perhaps by a coup d'état by the military; that we do not know of any outstanding military leaders of ability who have the required strength, standing or intelligence to assure the success of a coup d'état and to govern Iran in the event that such a coup d'état should be successful; that Generals Zahedi and Hedjazi seem to be best fitted for leadership in bringing about a coup d'état; that these two Generals differ in their political views, since Zahedi sympathizes with the National Front moderates whereas Hedjazi's primary interest would probably be in setting up a strong government which would exterminate the Communists and strengthen the Shah's hand. (The US has the impression that Zahedi's character is rather weak, while the British have a somewhat more favorable impression.)

(c) In order to be successful, the coup d'état would have to be carried out and executed entirely by the military in the Shah's name, but without the Shah's knowledge as the Shah probably would not have the stamina to see it through and, at a certain stage, might weaken and denounce the leaders; probably it would be necessary at least for the Commander of the army division stationed in Tehran to be a fellow conspirator and, at some point, probably the Commander of the Shah's bodyguard; if the army could attain complete control of Tehran and if the conspirators, in the Shah's name, could appoint a new Chief of Staff, it is believed that most of the Provinces, with the possible exception of Khuzistan, would recognize the new Government. Difficulty might be caused by the Qashqai tribes. (From such information as had come to us, we believe that there might be more trouble from the Qashqais than the British seem to believe).

(d) Middleton and I both agreed that neither the US nor UK Governments should undertake to encourage or to support a coup d'état and that the two Embassies should avoid becoming involved in any manner.

It should be borne in mind as well that a successful coup d'état would almost certainly result in the Tudeh gaining control of the National movement. The military dictatorship therefore might encounter increasing difficulties in carrying out a constructive program and in controlling the country.

END

TOP SECRET

B.

-402-

INWARD SAVING TELEGRAM

$P\ 10345$

FROM WASHINGTON TO FOREIGN OFFICE

$E\ P\ 10345$

By Bag

DEPARTMENTAL
DISTRIBUTION

Sir R. Makins
No. 386 Saving
May 7, 1953.

R. May 9, 1953.

TOP SECRET

Addressed to Foreign Office telegram No. 386 Saving
Repeated for information Saving to B.M.E.O.

Persia

The State Department have informed us as follows:-

"On May 3 in the presence of Khosre Qashqai,
a discussion was held between an attaché of the United
States Embassy at Tehran and Abol Qasem Amini, Acting
Minister of Court. Amini stated that the differences
between the Shah and Musaddiq, which were of benefit
only to Tudeh, should be settled as soon as possible, and
that before advising the Shah regarding the terms of settlement he would like answers to certain questions.

Following are the questions put by Amini and the
answers which Ambassador Henderson proposed be made by
the Embassy attaché: (The Ambassador's proposed answers
have been approved by the Department).

(i) Q - What is United States policy regarding Iran
and in particular regarding Musaddiq?

A - The fixed policy of the United States
Government is not to intervene in Iranian internal
affairs by giving political support to any
particular Iranian political leaders or groups.
The United States Government would like to maintain
friendly relations and cooperate with the Iranian
Government headed by Musaddiq just as with a
constitutional government headed by another Iranian
political leader who had indicated by public word
and action a desire to maintain friendly relations
with the United States. There are no assurances
that the United States will extend financial or
substantial economic aid to Iran since it would be
difficult, because of United States public opinion,
to extend this kind of aid in view of the present
status of the oil dispute.

/(ii)

-403-

(ii) Q - If the Shah should go abroad, would
the United States Embassy assist in arranging an
invitation?

A - The United States Government, while not
intervening in Iranian domestic affairs, is of the
opinion that the institution of the Shah is a
[mutilated word ? stabilizing] and unifying factor
and that any substantial weakening of this institution
might result in events which would undermine Iranian
independence. Therefore, the United States
Government would not be willing to become involved
in facilitating the Shah's departure from Iran.

(iii) Q - What would be the United States position
if the advisability of a change of régime should be
raised (shift from the system of monarchy or
replacement of Mohammed by another Shah)?

A - The United States would not favour an
attempt to effect a change in régime.   In view of
Iran's geographic position and internal political
pressures, a change of regime would be a hazardous
advanture which might seriously jeopardize Iranian
independence and social stability".

2.   In giving us the above information the State Department
explained that the initial approach was made in an atmosphere of
secrecy and the attaché when he accepted Khosro Qashqai's
invitation had no idea he was going to have questions of this
kind put to him.

3.   The United States Embassy in London are being informed
by the State Department, who added that reply to Amini was
probably given on May 5 or 6.

[Copy sent to the Prime Minister].

DISTRIBUTED TO:

Eastern Department
Economic Relations Department
News Department

Green

EP1948/

EP

FROM BAGDAD TO FOREIGN OFFICE

Cypher/OTP   DEPARTMENTAL DISTRIBUTION

EP

Mr. Bromley
No. 488   D: 5.27 p.m.   August 17, 1953
August 17, 1953   R: 6.50 p.m.   August 17, 1953

IMMEDIATE   EP 105/205
SECRET

Addressed to Foreign Office telegram No. 488 of August 17,
Repeated for information to B.M.E.O.   Washington.

My telegram No. 483: Persia.

Yesterday evening the Iraqi authorities arranged clandestine
meeting between the United States Ambassador and the Shah at the
latter's request.

2.   The United States Ambassador told me this morning that the
Shah was tired and perplexed. The Shah's account of events was as
follows. Some time ago it had been suggested to him that coup
against Musaddiq was desirable. He had agreed in view of Musaddiq's
increasingly unconstitutional actions and insane jealousy. On
reconsideration the Shah had, however, felt that he must act as
constitutional monarch and had decided to issue letters dismissing
Musaddiq and appointing General Zahedi Prime Minister. Only
sufficient forces would be on hand to ensure peaceful change over.
The Shah had so informed those in his confidence.

3.   On August 13 the Shah, who had gone to the Caspian to avoid
suspicion, had accordingly sent trusted [grp. undec. ? emissary]
to Zahedi bearing letters and messages that the latter should act
when he saw fit. He had learnt by code wireless message that the
letters had reached their destination. He had expected immediate
[? grp. omitted], but for two days nothing happened. He had received
code message explaining the delay. Then came the astonishing news
of failure. It appeared that the officer who had taken the letter
of dismissal to Musaddiq's house had been arrested, and that the same
had happened to the other plotters, who had just begun to act. The
Shah, who had been assured that the plan was foolproof, assumed either
that he had been betrayed or that the code had been broken. He had
then decided that as the constitutional ruler he should not resort
to force as that would lead to bloodshed, chaos and Soviet infiltration. He had therefore come to Bagdad.

/ 4. The Shah ......

SECRET

4.   The Shah had then asked the United States Ambassador's
advice whether he should take public stand against Musaddiq,
and what he should now do. He thought of going to Europe soon
and wanted urgent guidance. The latter had said he would refer
the matter to Washington and has done so. The Shah had
emphasized that he had not abdicated and would return to Persia
if he were wanted.

5.   Doctor Jamali asked me to call this morning. He had just
seen the Shah. The latter had said that he did not want to
complicate matters by meeting me, but wanted Jamali to ask me
to find out whether you thought he should now speak openly
against Musaddiq or not, and what you thought he should do.
I said I would pass this on. I will also inform the United
States Ambassador.

6.   I should be grateful for very early guidance.

      Foreign Office pass Immediate to B.M.E.O., Washington as
my telegrams Nos. 88 and 7 respectively.

      [Repeated to B.M.E.O. and Washington].

DISTRIBUTED TO: ADVANCE COPIES TO:

Eastern Department   Sir P. Dixon
                                 Private Secretary
                                 Sir J. Bowker
                                 Head Eastern Department

44444

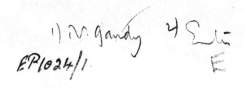
SECRET

SITUATION IN PERSIA

Thinking over our rather inconclusive discussion in the Persia Committee yesterday, I wonder whether it would not be wise to give the State Department an indication of our first impressions of the policy ~~that we and the Americans ought to pursue.~~ problems facing us.

The discussion in the Committee yesterday showed that there is a general feeling that

(a) we ought to wait for the dust to settle before reaching any definite conclusions,

(b) we have no reason to expect that a Zahedi Government would be non-nationalist and pro-British, and

(c) however friendly a new Government might be, there is really no practicable alternative to impartial arbitration as a method of settling the Anglo-Persian oil dispute.

On the face of it we need be in no hurry to communicate such discouraging conclusions to the Americans. But if we do not sound a word of warning I am afraid that we may be faced by an American decision to make Zahedi a large financial gift not tied to oil, coupled probably with pressure on us to devise some new way of settling the oil dispute. There is in fact a dilemma here. On the one hand it may be very desirable to help Zahedi to maintain law and order and deal with the Communists by giving him money to pay the troops, civil service, etc. On the other hand, if he can get money out of the Americans that way (not tied to oil), he will be less inclined to come to a reasonable settlement of the oil dispute.

Our reports suggest that the danger from the Communist side should not be underrated, and I do not think we should be on very comfortable ground in opposing the Americans if they wish to subsidise Zahedi in order to ensure the stability of his regime.

All this leads me to think that it would be wise to get into contact with the Americans about the situation. We could confine ourselves at this stage to saying that we have been considering what our policy should be on the assumption that General Zahedi gets into the saddle and the Shah is re-established.

Our preliminary view, on that assumption, is that H.M.G. should work for a resumption of relations and a settlement of the oil dispute. We are not optimistic about the prospects of being able to work out a

/"new

"new deal" for a settlement of the oil dispute, but should be glad to exchange views with the Americans as soon as it is certain that Zahedi is firmly in the saddle and we have been able to get our own ideas clearer. Meanwhile we feel sure that it has occurred to the State Department that American aid on any considerable scale might have a very repressive effect on Persia's readiness to settle the oil dispute on reasonable terms. At the same time we recognise that it may be very desirable to give Zahedi all possible support, and we should be glad to concert with the U.S. on ways and means of doing this.

P. Dixon.

August 21, 1953

Eastern Dept.

Copies: Lord Reading
         Sir J. Bowker
         Mr. Belgrave
         Private Secretary

EP 114/5

Dear Mr. President,

I wish to express to you and through you to the American people the appreciation of the Iranian Government and people for the aid which the US has extended Iran during recent years. This aid has contributed much to the security of the country and to the raising of its technical efficiency. The assistance which the US is already rendering Iran, helpful as it is, is unfortunately not sufficient in amount and character to tide Iran over the financial and economic crisis which I find it to be facing. The treasury is empty; foreign exchange resources are exhausted; the national economy is deteriorated. Iran needs immediate financial aid to enable it to emerge from a state of economic and financial chaos.

Iran also requires aid of an economic character to enable it to carry out programs which the government is preparing for developing its agriculture and industry, for exploiting its rich mineral resources, for improving its transport and communications, for strengthening its internal and foreign trade, and for raising the health, education and technical levels of the Iranian people.

The people of Iran are anxious to have a prosperous, orderly country in which they can enjoy higher standards of living and make greater use of their talents and resources. They are willing, if given an opportunity, to work hard in order to obtain these objectives, but the realization of their aspirations may be delayed for some time unless they receive technical, financial and economic aid from abroad. I hope that the US will find it possible at this critical moment in Iranian history to come to my country's assistance as it has done on occasions in the past.

In conclusion, I would like to emphasize that it is the intention of the new Government of Iran not only to strengthen the country internally but also to improve its international position. The government desires to maintain friendly relations with the other members of the family of nations on a basis of mutual respect. It will pursue a policy of eliminating such differences as may exist or which may develop between other countries and itself in a spirit of friendliness and in accordance with accepted principles of international intercourse. I am sure that I voice the feelings of the great majority of the people of Iran when I state that Iran desires to contribute its share to the maintenance of peace and to the promotion of international goodwill.

Please accept, Mr. President, the assurance of my highest consideration.

EP 1114/5

Letter from President Eisenhower to Prime Minister Zahedi

Dear Mr. Prime Minister,

    I have received your letter of August 26 regarding the problems which you face in Iran. The American people continue to be deeply interested in the independence of Iran and the well-being of the Iranian people. We have followed policies in Iran, as in other countries of the free world, designed to assist peoples of those countries to bring about economic development which will lead to higher standards of living and wider horizons in knowledge and opportunity. I am gratified that the aid which we have extended has contributed to the security of Iran and to the raising of the technical efficiency of the Iranian people. I am also pleased to have your assurance that your Government desires to maintain friendly relations with other members of the family of nations and that it will pursue a policy of eliminating such differences as may exist or which may develop with other countries in a spirit of friendliness and in accordance with accepted principles of international intercourse.

    In an effort to assist you in dealing with your immediate problems, I have authorized my Ambassador to Iran to consult with you regarding the development of our aid programs there. I recognize that your needs are pressing. Your request will receive our sympathetic consideration and I can assure you that we stand ready to assist you in achieving the aspirations for your country which you have outlined.

    Please accept, Mr. Prime Minister, the assurances of my highest consideration.

/s/ Dwight D. Eisenhower

Top Secret

In handing over the attached memorandum regarding Mr. Henderson's second audience with the Shah on August 25, Mr. Houghton, of the United States Embassy, also gave us the gist of Mr. Henderson's subsequent report on his interview with General Zahidi on August 26.

2.   It appears that the conversation covered four principal topics:-

(a) United States aid.

Mr. Henderson explained that the funds available to the State Department were limited and could only be made available within existing legislation (which I gathered might preclude an outright grant). He declined to name a definite figure and said that any help given would be for the purpose of tiding Persia over her present crisis and not for financing sudden and grandiose capital projects. (As will be seen the Shah is still thinking of an immediate erection of cheap housing for homeless families).

(b) Relations with the Soviet Union.

General Zahidi reported that the Soviet Ambassador had already complained to him about anti-Soviet demonstrations, particularly one directed against the Soviet Embassy's Information Office. The Prime Minister had replied that Persia wished to be on friendly terms with all her neighbours, including USSR. He commented to Mr. Henderson that he would not on this account weaken his drive to suppress the Tudeh Party.

(c) Relations with the United Kingdom.

Mr. Henderson said that he thought it imperative that Persia should now establish diplomatic relations of a friendly character with the United Kingdom. ~~And~~ General Zahidi agreed.

(d) Oil.

General Zahidi said he did really want a settlement and was considering preparing the public mind for one by revealing to the Persian people the extreme seriousness of the economic position in which Musaddiq's policy had landed them. Thus he hoped that pressure would be put on him to conclude an oil settlement in order to solve these difficulties.

/ 3. Mr.

-411-

3.   Mr. Henderson had a better
impression /of General Zahidi than
previously, whom he now considers capable
of doing a great deal for Persia, provided
that he is given good guidance.

/ than previously

Christopher Gandy

(C. T. Gandy)
August 27, 1953.

Reference last para. of the
attached memorandum: it
is to be hoped that dr.
Musaddiq could be tried
in secret, perhaps under
his own emergency laws.

P.W. A) U.S. Embassy - 27/8
(Conversation: U.S. Ambassador - Zahidi) 28

A summary of Mr. Henderson's
conversation with Gen. Zahidi is now attached.
Flag B.

28/8

Sir W. Strang

Mr. Nutting

Encouraging a
start.

W. Strang
28/8

Sir J. Bowker

MEMORANDUM

August 27, 1953

Ambassador Henderson (presumably yesterday) met with Prime Minister Zahedi for approximately an hour. After the Ambassador had extended his congratulations and wished the Prime Minister success, the Prime Minister expressed appreciation for the moral support of the United States. Zahedi went on to say that unless the Iranian people could be convinced that the new government had something to offer them, success in keeping Iran from Cummunism would be only temporary. Something must be done. For example, he hoped within a week to employ 100,000 people on the roads which were in extremely poor condition. It was also necessary to commence the construction of thousands of houses for homeless people in Tehran and elsewhere. People no longer had any confidence in government promises. It was necessary to do something. Unfortunately, his government was not only bankrupt but indebted. Consequently, he needed United States financial aid. Dr. Mossadeq had been expending money which people had entrusted to insurance companies, banks, etc. He found it difficult to understand what Mossadeq had in mind as the latter must have known he was leading the country into financial chaos. Zahedi hoped that United States financial assistance would not be a question of too little-too late.

In reply, Ambassador Henderson expressed the opinion that the United States Government would extend aid, but that it would have to be done in an orderly fashion and in accordance with United States law. The Government of the United States did not possess enormous sums of money which could be spent freely. Consequently, the quantity and the form of the aid must be within the framework of existing legislation. The Ambassador said he could not give any idea as to the amount but he thought that it would probably be enough to meet Iran's present crisis. He doubted if it would be sufficient to pay for projects for the employment of workers on a mass scale. The Prime Minister mentioned that he was planning to enact certain radical reforms concerning taxes, etc. but the benefits from such reforms would, of course, not be immediate. He mentioned in passing the oil problem. He said he was considering explaining Iran's bankrupt condition to the country and hoped that the reaction might be requests from the people themselves to try to settle this problem. Much, however, depended on Britain's attitude. Ambassador Henderson felt the occasion was not appropriate to press the Prime Minister on this problem.

The Prime Minister also mentioned that the Soviet Ambassador had protested against the anti-Soviet demonstrations on August 15 and the

attacks/

attacks on the Information Center of the Soviet Union. He was endeavoring to smooth the matter over by assuring the new Soviet Ambassador of his government's desire to maintain friendly relations with all its neighbors, including the Soviet Union. Zahedi, however, explained to the Ambassador that he would not alter his campaign to root out Communists in Iran merely to placate the Soviet Union. Ambassador Henderson expressed his pleasure that Zahedi desired to improve his relations with his neighbors and thought it particularly important that Iran strengthen its relations with Pakistan, Iraq, Turkey and Afghanistan. The Prime Minister agreed. He also told Zahedi that it was imperative that in due course friendly diplomatic relations be re-established with the United Kingdom. Zahedi agreed. Ambassador Henderson also said that he thought it time for Iran to play a role in international affairs commensurate with Iran's national importance. This did not mean Iran's taking a provocative attitude toward the Soviet bloc. Nevertheless, the international prestige of Iran would be greatly enhanced if it came out definitely but unostentatiously in support of efforts to promote collective security and discourage aggression. Zahedi commented that he agreed with this and that he hoped to be able to clarify Iran's foreign policies. He had asked Meftah and Entezam to discuss with him during the day foreign policy problems facing the Iranian Government. He said that he intended to make use of Entezam's diplomatic experience on an informal basis until a Minister of Foreign Affairs was appointed.

The Ambassador found Zahedi clearly a man of action who, if given wise guidance and not frustrated by the Shah, could contribute greatly to the extrication of Iran from its present economic and political morass. Considering Zahedi's limited background, the Ambassador was surprised at his sensitivity regarding foreign and internal political matters.

EP1015/231

August 27, 1953

At a meeting Ambassador Henderson had with the Shah on the evening of August 25, the Shah again expressed unhappiness regarding the composition of the present Iranian Cabinet. The Shah felt that the Cabinet had made a poor impression and that it might be necessary to have changes made fairly soon. Ambassador Henderson pointed out that if the remaining vacancies in the Cabinet were filled wisely, the Cabinet would be substantially strengthened. He added that the Shah would undoubtedly be deluged with dissatisfied politicians who would be critical of the policies of Zahedi's Government. The Ambassador hoped that the Shah would in no way convey to these people any lack of confidence in his Prime Minister. He thought all Iranians, including Zahedi, must have the impression that the latter has the complete support of the Shah. The Prime Minister might well be the type of man who could be decisive if he was confident of the Shah's backing, but who would otherwise become ineffectual. The Shah appeared to agree with the Ambassador's remarks and said he would endeavor to build up Zahedi. In this connection, he pointed out that during the course of the day he had given Zahedi active army status, had promoted him to Lieutenant-General and had bestowed on him the highest Iranian decoration. The Prime Minister had conducted himself with courage and wisdom during the crisis. As a result of the Shah's estimate, Zahedi had risen. Nonetheless, it must be clear to everyone, including Zahedi, that no one can come between the Shah and the army. A vigorous effort must be made to strengthen the solidarity of the army and no favoritism must be shown as that would result in rifts. High positions in the army should go only to men of proven loyalty, ability and of the highest character. The Shah also said that certain additional military aid from the United States would be necessary but that he would discuss this matter at a later date.

On another subject, the Shah maintained that internal programs which would appeal to the country's youth should be devised rapidly. Communists must be fought: (1) by constituting programs which would undercut Communist propaganda; and (2) by ruthlessly ferreting out Communist leaders who had lost themselves in a number of United Front organizations. The Shah thought that Iran should be moving more towards Socialism and that there should be a more equitable disposition of the country's wealth. He emphasized that effective measures must be taken in the near future to convince the poorer classes that their interests were being looked after by the Government. In this regard he was hopeful of re-launching his program for distributing crown lands on a wide scale and wondered if the Bank for Reconstruction which he had organized might not have been endeavoring to obtain an Export-Import Bank loan for the purpose of constructing workers houses in Tehran and other large towns. He thought it would have a highly salutary effect if cheap but healthy living quarters could be

built/

built immediately for perhaps 10,000 homeless families in Tehran and
a thousand or more in each of the large Iranian cities. As to whether
the Export-Import Bank could extend a loan to the Reconstruction Bank
without the Majlis approval, Ambassador Henderson said he was not
qualified to discuss the problem. In referring to the Majlis, the Shah
said he still thought the Majlis should be dissolved, although Zahedi
considered it would be politically wise to permit the functioning of a
rump Majlis while elections were held to fill vacancies. The Shah
feared that any kind of a Majlis would be of considerable handicap to
the Prime Minister. Ambassador Henderson said that it was his opinion
that if Iran was to receive substantial aid from the United States,
particularly for road building, etc., it would probably have to be in the
form of loans.

As to Mossadeq's fate, the Shah said he was not sure what should be
done. The Shah thought that Mossadeq should be tried for treason but
was afraid that a trial might result in the former Prime Minister's
becoming a martyr. On the other hand, how could the Government justify
the trial of army officers acting under the orders of Mossadeq without
trying Mossadeq himself. An impression might be created that the Government was afraid to try Mossadeq. He had been toying with the idea of
permitting Mossadeq to go abroad for medical treatment but thought if
such happened, Mossadeq should go to some distant place like the
United States and also give an undertaking not to engage in the future
in Iranian political activities. On being asked his advice, the Ambassador
replied that the matter was far too complicated for him to venture an
off-hand opinion, but he did think that if Mossadeq were publicly tried,
he might succeed, with his histrionic ability, in making it appear that
his accusers, rather than he, were being tried.

FOREIGN OFFICE AND WHITEHALL
DISTRIBUTION

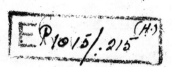

TEHRAN SITUATION REPORT

(6 p.m., August 27, 1953)

Internal

Fears of an immediate Communist attempt at a counter-coup have receded. The police have raided some Communist headquarters and claim to have found large quantities of arms and ammunition, subversive literature and duplicating equipment. They have also made some arrests. A drive seems in progress to clear certain government departments of Communists and sympathisers who have been infiltrated gradually over the past seven years. At a memorial service held on August 27 for those killed during the rising of August 19, the celebrated preacher Falsafi delivered a spirited attack against the agents of "Red Colonialism" and the Musaddiq régime which had allowed them to operate so openly.

2.   There is no further news of the rising in the Qashqai tribal country which was reported last weekend.

3.   Dr. Musaddiq has been transferred to a prison from his more comfortable quarters at the Officers' Club. Mr. Fatimi, the former Foreign Minister, is still at large.

4.   Tehran radio claims that the number of telegrams and messages of support for the Shah and the new régime is unprecedented. Burujirdi, the most eminent of the Shia divines, has sent a message of congratulation and support to the Shah.

5.   There is so far little sign of the new régime being subject to the expected pressure from former Nationalist supporters of Dr. Musaddiq, who had quarrelled with him before his collapse. It is reported that Kashani intends to go into non-political retirement.

6.   The Shah has expressed more than once to the United States Ambassador his dissatisfaction that General Zahidi had included in his Cabinet too many of the traditional Persian politicians. His reason was, apparently that he had had to form this Cabinet in a great hurry before the Shah's return.

/ Foreign Relations. ....

Foreign Relations.

7.   The Persian Minister for Foreign Affairs has invited
telegrams of congratulations from all Heads of States and many
have sent messages.   But diplomatic representatives of Iron
Curtain, Arab and Asian countries looked glum during their
first meeting with the new Prime Minister, except for the Iraqi
Ambassador, whose Government had already been for sometime
strongly and openly opposed to Musaddiq.

8.   General Zahidi has announced that he will resume the
economic and political negotiations begun under the previous
régime with the Soviet Government.   When the Soviet Ambassador
complained of anti-Soviet demonstrations, which have included
an attack on the Soviet Embassy Information Office, General
Zahidi assured him that he would aim to maintain friendly
relations with all Persia's neighbours.   But he has made it
clear on other occasions that this will not prevent him from
waging an-all-out campaign against the Persian Communist (Tudeh)
Party.

9.   He had also said that he will "go slow" in re-establishing
diplomatic relations with the United Kingdom, but has privately
agreed with the United States Ambassador that Persia must
re-establish these relations and on a basis of real friendship.
Meanwhile the British correspondents who "gate-crashed" into
Tehran recently are under notice to quit..

Economic.

10.   The new Government appears to be pursuing a policy of
frankly explaining its economic difficulties to the Persian people.
Tehran radio broadcast on August 27 a government communiqué
stating that Musaddiq had left a debt of over 17 billion rials.
This may represent something like £80 million and is approximately
twice the normal annual budget.   Nevertheless exchange rates in
the Tehran Bazaar have moved in favour of the rial since the
change of régime.

to offer, but the United States Ambassador has told General Zahidi
that only limited funds are available for such aid; it will have
to be extended under existing legislation and could not in any
case do more than tide over the immediate crisis, nor could it
be used to finance grandiose capital projects to impress the people,
of which the Shah and the Prime Minister are talking.

Oil.

12.   The Prime Minister has announced that he will not renew
Musaddiq's offer of Persian oil at 50% discount on world market
prices which was made on April 27, to last for six months. It is
not yet clear what effect this will have on contracts, (particularly
those for the exchange of Persian oil against Italian industrial
products) which have been concluded but not yet executed.

13.   There is no sign either in Tehran or in Washington of undue
haste for an oil settlement with the United Kingdom.

Eastern Department,
Foreign Office.

August 27, 1953.

44444

MEMORANDUM

September 1, 1953

In a talk Ambassador Henderson had with Zahedi yesterday, the Ambassador told the Prime Minister that he questioned whether any emergency assistance which the United States might be able to extend to Iran would be enough to carry Iran further than about April 1* if it could carry Iran that long. Consequently, the Ambassador thought that as soon as possible consideration should be given to some sort of an oil settlement with the United Kingdom in order that there might be available to Iran for her rehabilitation programs income from her oil. After pointing out that he was without instructions in this regard and had no specific suggestions in mind, the Ambassador said that he thought it might be helpful to both the United Kingdom and Iran if some secret explorations could take place in order to determine whether one might at least be able to find agreement in principle as to the manner in which one could settle the oil problem. The United States Government would find it difficult to continue to defend to the people and the Congress of the United States the extension of economic and financial aid to Iran except on an emergency basis unless the Iranian Government could show itself prepared to reach an agreement with the British on the oil problem along the lines of accepted principles of international intercourse.

Zahedi expressed understanding of the above and stated that he hoped to be able to find a settlement of the oil problem which would be mutually fair to the United Kingdom and Iran. He pointed out, however, that to move too rapidly on this problem would be suicidal. It was his opinion that under conditions of secrecy it might be valuable for both sides to learn something about each other's views concerning a resolution of the oil dispute. He said that he understood that the British possessed an innate sense of fairness. Should they be willing to accept a solution which in their own hearts they judged fair to Iran and which would not involve an undue burden on the Iranian people, the British would find him receptive. It was a different matter, however, if they tried to drive a hard bargain with him. He hoped that both the United States and the United Kingdom would appreciate that a resentful Iranian public would overthrow his government immediately if he should conclude an agreement which they considered betrayed the interests of Iran. Should by some chance his government survive for a time after such an agreement some future government would surely disavow it.

In reply Ambassador Henderson told Zahedi that he thought that an attempt to reach an agreement should be made just as soon as public opinion could be prepared even if there were no Majlis in session to ratify it for several months. He pointed out that the early conclusion of an agreement might result in tension between the United Kingdom and Iran being relaxed and that it might even make possible taking the necessary steps to prepare the refinery for immediate production. In this

connection/

*Assumed text   SECRET

connection the Ambassador stated that he hoped that the necessary
measures to stop anti-British propaganda over the radio and in the
Iranian press would be taken immediately. The continuation of such
propaganda was not only embarrassing to the United Kingdom but also
to the United States Government and the public of the United States
would not be receptive regarding extending financial assistance to a
government which was countenancing propaganda against an ally of the
United States.

Zahedi said that orders forbidding such propaganda against any
foreign government, including the Soviet Union, had already been
issued. He said such propaganda was stupid. He hoped that the
Ambassador would not think he was personally anti-British. Although
he had worked against the British in the early part of the second
World War and had been imprisoned by them, he harbored no hard feelings.
He worked against the British because they were associates and allies
of the Soviet Union, Iran's most dangerous and implacable enemy, and
not because they were British. An ally of the Soviet Union he considered
to be ipso facto an enemy of Iran and a foe of the Soviet Union a friend
of Iran. He ceased to regard the British as enemies when the United
Kingdom ceased to be an ally of the Soviet Union. It was his desire
that relations between the United Kingdom and Iran should be friendly
and in due course he was willing to do what he could to make this
possible.

SECRET

MEMORANDUM

September 2, 1953

In his talk with Ambassador Henderson on August 31, Prime Minister Zahedi also mentioned some developments concerning relations between Iran and the Soviet Union. Zahedi stated that in reply to a recent inquiry from the Soviet Embassy, he had stated that Iran desired normal friendly relations with the Soviet Union. He further replied to the Soviet Embassy that such relations were possible provided: (1) the Soviet Union treated Iran as an equal and refrained from making open or impolite threats; (2) the Soviet Union did not meddle in the internal affairs of Iran and especially with reference to providing moral or material support to the Tudeh and other organizations of a subversive nature; and (3) relations between the two countries were maintained on a basis of mutual advantage.

Continuing his talk with Ambassador Henderson, General Zahedi pointed out that Razmara and Mossadeq when Prime Ministers had been too flamboyant in their negotiations with the Soviet Union on various relatively unimportant matters. He thought that it was necessary for Iran to maintain correct relations with its largest neighbor with whom Iran had a common border of more than 1200 miles in length. Consequently, he had ordered the continuance of the trade negotiations with the Soviet Union at "appropriate levels" which meant between officials in the various interested ministries and the representatives of the Soviet Union. If these negotiations, which were proceeding, were successful, Iran would trade with the Soviet Union but not with strategic materials. He did not think it was to Iran's interest to trade in commodities which would increase the military power of the Soviet Union.

Ambassador Henderson replied that he was sure the United States Government would understand the Prime Minister's position as outlined above and respect it. The Government of the United States certainly did not desire Iran to pursue a policy which could justifiably be considered provocative or unfriendly by the Soviet Union. The Ambassador did remark that he thought that previous Iranian Governments had erred in thinking it was to the advantage of Iran to endeavor to "play off the United States and the Soviet Union against each other". Such attempts were too obvious and resulted only in decreasing the respect of both the Soviet Union and the United States for Iranian sincerity. Such tactics were also resented in the United States

because/

SECRET

-422-

because it conveyed the impression that Iran considered that the
United States and the Soviet Union had like ambitions of an
aggressive or at least a selfish nature regarding Iran. Intelligent
Iranians must know that the United States wanted nothing from Iran
except that Iran should maintain its independence and improve its
economic position. The Prime Minister replied that the Ambassador
could be assured that his government would not indulge in any such
childish game.

ЕР1051/10

MESSAGE FROM GENERAL ZAHIDI.

a

message which General Zahidi wishes transmitted
secretly to the Prime Minister. The text is as
follows:

"Everything I suffered at British hands
is forgotten. The centuries old friendship
between Britain and Iran, which was
temporarily broken by mischief makers,
must be restored.
I want Iran to be one family with Britain
and America, to stand firmly hand-in-hand
against Soviet communism. To survive, we
must act as one. I pledge my hand.
Because of Iran's present condition, she
is in need of friendship. She will accept
friendly gestures as only proud and
dignified people can do, recognising at
same time dignity and nobility which
prompts friends to give her assistance.
This is spoken to you from a soldier's
heart, withholding nothing from greater
soldier whom I greatly admire and respect".

2.　　Any reply would presumably have to be sent
through the same channel, but I imagine that
the Prime Minister will not in any case wish to
send one before Monday.　I submit that before
sending a reply, it would be best to ascertain

/from

from Mr. Henderson what "friendly gesture"
General Zahidi is hinting at in the penultimate
sentence.

Christopher Gandy

(C.T. Gandy)
September 5, 1953.

Advance Copies to:
~~Lord Salisbury~~
~~Private Secretary~~
Private Secretary,
   No. 10 Downing Street.
Sir William Strang.

Mr. Anthony Nutting

The Private Secretary at No. 10
has been asked to see that only the
message itself is given to the Prime
Minister and not the whole of
Mr. Gandy's minute.

I have ~~discussed~~ with Mr. Gandy
and agree with him that the best
way of dealing with this message
would be to ~~ask~~ convey, through the
same channels, a message to
Mr. Henderson on the lines of the
attached draft.

The message recently received
through the Swiss from the Shah
contained a similar vague appeal for
a gesture and we have asked the
Swiss Govt. to ask their minister if
he has any idea of what the Shah
~~had~~ had

-425-

Secret

EP1015/237

(113)

Mr. Houghton of the United States Embassy told me this afternoon of the conversation between Mr Henderson and Shah, who insists that he must be Commander in Chief of the Persian Armed Forces in effect as well as in name. If he did not retain effective control of the armed forces he would sink into insignificance and eventually be forced to abdicate.

2. The Shah spoke with such vehemence that Mr Henderson asked him whether there were differences between him and General Zahidi on this matter, stressing the vital importance of complete understanding and confidence between the two of them. The Shah replied that General Zahidi could be sure of his support provided he did not interfere in the control of the armed forces and rooted out corruption. . He had not apparently specifically stated this to General Zahidi, and Mr Henderson urged him to do so.

3. The Shah went on to say that he lacked confidence in some of Zahidi's colleagues particularly the Deputy Prime Minister and the Ministers of Defence and Interior. He had not told General Zahidi of these misgivings but had insisted on immediate action.

4. The Shah repeatedly expressed his resentment at allegations in the United States Press (Time and News Week) that he was a weak monarch.
"I will not" he said, "have the impression created that I am a puppet of General Zahidi's

(C.T. Gandy.)

September 14. 1953.

News Opt qua 4. Copy

Sent to Mr Campbell

DNGreenhill
15/9.

15.9.53 (LACFRY)

We have been taking the line that recent events in Persia have tended to suggest that /the

-426-

Communicated by U.S. Embassy

September 17, 1953

M E M O R A N D U M

On the evening of September 14th, Ambassador Henderson had a brief conversation with Prime Minister Zahedi concerning the oil problem. According to the Ambassador, it was apparent from the conversation that Zahedi had not had a chance as yet to give serious consideration to this problem. Although he seemed to appreciate the fact that the demand for oil now was not what it was in 1951, he seemed quite uninformed as far as details were concerned. The Prime Minister stated that he had discontinued oil sales at a discount as such sales represented a financial loss especially when at the same time a certain percentage of the sales was being set aside for compensation. Furthermore, a continuance of the practice might make more difficult the marketing of Iranian oil at world prices in the future. He asked the Ambassador if the latter had any information as to: (1) the channels through which the United Kingdom would like to negotiate; and (2) the type of settlement acceptable to the United Kingdom. He wondered if Anglo Iranian as a goodwill gesture would be willing to advance the £49 million which he understood Anglo Iranian admitted as owing to Iran. Ambassador Henderson replied that such a payment was out of the question – the Prime Minister's information was based on the deceptive propaganda of the Mossadeq Government and that it would be most unfortunate if his Government should raise issues as unrealistic as those developed by Mossadeq. The Ambassador explained to Zahedi the spurious reasoning by which the Mossadeq Government had concluded that Iran was owed £49 million by Anglo Iranian. The Ambassador went on to say that as yet he had no idea as to the type of settlement which the United Kingdom would accept. He thought that the British were currently studying the question in the light of the new situation. The Ambassador then mentioned the February 20 proposals, pointing out that they were based on the situation prevailing at the time. He did not know whether the proposals still held good or whether they were still considered by the United Kingdom and the United States as the best method of reaching a settlement under present conditions. The Ambassador explained United States Government involvement in the proposals as resulting from the U.S. Government's offer to purchase, under certain conditions, quantities of oil and to make an advance payment should the United Kingdom's offer re. compensation be agreed to. In reply to a question by the Ambassador, Prime Minister Zahedi said he had not had time to study the February proposals yet. It had been difficult to compile the documents as apparently the originals had been burned in Mossadeq's house. He wondered if Ambassador Henderson might sometime explain the proposals to him in detail. The Ambassador replied that he would be quite happy to do so provided the Prime Ministed appreciated

that/

that he was not negotiating but only explaining what had taken place in
order to enrich the Prime Minister's background. It was quite possible
that from the point of view of the Iranian Government, which he knew was
most anxious to sell its oil, that the proposals might be deficient in
that they did not provide a definitive plan for resuming immediately the
sales of Iranian oil in substantial amounts. The proposals were primarily
aimed at settling the compensation issue. This the Ambassador thought
was because Mossadeq apparently was anxious to separate the question of
compensation from that of future sales. The Ambassador said that although
he did not know as yet what channels the United Kingdom would prefer to
use in the negotiations, he had the impression that in the past the British
had considered direct negotiations the most effective way. This was quite
natural as direct negotiations might well result in a speedier settlement
than those handled by intermediaries. The Prime Minister voiced the
personal opinion that the channels which had been employed in the past
might be easier but nonetheless he would like to utilize channels acceptable to the British. He said he assumed that it was understood that it
would be difficult for his Government to negotiate outside the framework
of the Iranian 9-Point Nationalization Law. The Ambassador told Zahedi
that in any event the latter should lose no time in studying the oil
problem preparatory to the commencement of negotiation and voiced the
hope that as advisers Zahedi would use realistic technicians rather than
theoretic dreamers and politicians. The Ambassador also pointed out that
although the settlement of the compensation issue was primarily political
in scope, any settlement which involved substantial sales of Iranian oil
would have to be on a commercial basis. The oil companies who were in
a position to distribute Iranian oil in large quantities could not be expected to pay more for it than oil obtainable in plentiful quantities
elsewhere. Zahedi replied that although he understood this situation,
he felt it would not be easy to make the Iranian people understand in
view of the propaganda in Iran over the past two years.

The subject of the resumption of diplomatic relations with the
United Kingdom was not raised by the Prime Minister during the conversation
and the Ambassador considered it inopportune to bring it up himself. The
Ambassador did, however, mention it to the Prime Minister's son when the
latter was escorting him to the car. The son thought that his father
still considered that it would be preferable to wait until it was apparent
from conversations or feelers that an oil settlement could speedily be
reached. He did not think, however, his father held firm views on the
problem and probably would be influenced by British thinking concerning
the problem.

FROM WASHINGTON TO FOREIGN OFFICE

EP1051/13 G EP

Cypher/OTP

DEPARTMENTAL
DISTRIBUTION   EP105

Sir R. Makins
No.1987   D.9. 3 p.m. September 17, 1953.
September 17, 1953.   R.6.27 a.m. September 18, 1953.

IMMEDIATE
DEDIP
SECRET   / EP1051/10 G

Fl.. A

Your telegram No.3515: Persia.

Mr. Henderson has commented as follows:

[Begins].

I desired discreetly probe situation here before undertaking
reply. I do not believe that General Zahedi's friendly message
was prompted by any motive other than one of general character of
letting recipient know he had friendly feelings and was anxious,
just as soon as atmosphere could be prepared, to establish really
friendly relations. Since assuming office he has been working at
least fifteen hours daily in an effort to meet the desperate
economic situation which he has inherited and strengthen internal
political foundation of his Government. He tells me that he has
not yet found a breathing spell which would enable him to give
serious attention to the delicate foreign problems including oil
settlement and timing and method of resumption of relations. I
understand that two days ago for the first time these two problems
were openly raised in secret Cabinet meeting and that three members
of the Cabinet openly advocated that they be grappled with immediately.
Other members were silent although practically all friendly to
West and United Kingdom. Some uncertainty among friends West
whether preferable establish relations first and then try to
solve the oil problem or vice versa. General Zahedi, I believe,
has no firm idea this regard. From remarks made by him to me I
think he would like to exploit any kind of friendly gesture which
United Kingdom might make in promoting more friendly attitude on
part Iranian public towards United Kingdom. If, for instance,
United Kingdom could relax restrictions which would permit certain
urgently needed equipment ordered by Iran before nationalisation to

/proceed to

-429-

proceed to destination, such gestures I believe would immediately
be given friendly publicity in Iran. If Her Majesty's Government
has views as to whether it preferable establish relations before
negotiation or settlement of oil problem or ideas as to methods for
breaking ice and would let me have them I might try to steer
Iranian Government in direction indicated.

[Ends].

2. State Department said that in referring to equipment
Mr. Henderson probably had in mind the rails, bolts, spikes etc.,
for the Persian State Railways referred to in your despatch No.959.

DISTRIBUTED TO

Eastern Department

ADVANCES TO

Sir P. Dixon
Private Secretary
Sir J. Bowker
Head Eastern Department

Flag B
EP 1151/24

B B B

SECRET

MEMORANDUM

September 22, 1953

1. Ambassador Henderson had a ninety minute talk with the Shah on the morning of September 18. The Shah said he was concerned at the growing number of complaints concerning the new government. The complaints seemed to center for the most part on the weakness of various members of the Cabinet and the appointment in key posts of men who had previously proved themselves incapable or dishonest. The most recent complaints were that incompetent and dishonest people were being retained and even introduced into the Ministry of Justice. The army had also been weakened by Zahedi's bring/back into active service retired, corrupt and incompetent officers. He had warned Zahedi on several occasions concerning this but the latter apparently had paid no heed to his warnings.

2. The Ambassador replied that he found the Shah's remarks disheartening as he was convinced that both the Shah and the Prime Minister were well-intentioned and desired to work together. He was worried that they were not being frank with one another. He considered Zahedi the type of man with whom the Shah could and should speak openly and thought that the Shah should encourage Zahedi to express his views frankly as otherwise, because of his deep respect for the Shah, Zahedi would almost be sure to hesitate to disagree with the Shah.

3. The Ambassador informed the Shah that there were various rumors in Tehran that the Shah and Zahedi were not in agreement concerning the army. Some people were saying that Zahedi was taking actions with regard to the army without consulting the Shah, while other people were saying that the Shah was issuing instructions direct to the Chief of Staff without consulting Zahedi. This sort of situation was one which the Tudeh and other enemies of both the Shah and Zahedi would delight. The Shah said that if the Prime Minister would realize that he had nothing to do with the army there would be no differences. Zahedi apparently found it difficult to remember that as a Prime Minister he was a civilian and not an army officer. The Shah was quite prepared to listen to anything Zahedi might say personally and confidentially concerning the army, but was not willing to permit the Prime Minister to give advice openly.

4. The Ambassador pointed out that in the present delicate situation, the political stability of the country might well be effected by changes in the army's high-ranking personnel or organization. The Shah consequently should make no such changes without at least informing the Prime Minister in advance. The Shah replied he was willing to do this but was not prepared to promise to refrain from any action with regard to the military simply because the Prime Minister objected. As Commander in Chief of the Army he could give orders to the Chief of Staff without going through the Prime Minister. The Prime Minister on

the other/

the other hand could not give orders to the Chief of Staff without
going through the Minister of Defense who would have the opportunity
of consulting the Shah before conveying such orders. The Ambassador
suggested that in general orders of importance from the Shah should
be channeled through the Prime Minister and Minister of Defense to
the Chief of Staff, as otherwise the Prime Minister and Minister of
Defense might have no knowledge of certain developments for which they
should be prepared. The Shah repeated that he intended to inform the
Prime Minister in advance of any important instructions he intended
to give to the Chief of Staff, but he did not indicate willingness to
send his instructions through the Prime Minister.

5. According to the Shah, another criticism of Zahedi's government was that it was doing nothing to reduce unemployment or to develop
the country economically. The Ambassador said he though such criticism
unfair and then explained some of the financial difficulties which the
government had to face. The government had not only inherited bankruptcy, but an inflexible fiscal system which hampered its activity.
The Shah said he realized the criticism was unfair but nonetheless he
was concerned about it. He considered the government partly to blame
in that it had been very ineffective in making known to the Iranian
public its difficulties.

6. In reply to a question from the Shah, the Ambassador said he
had not been pressing for early elections but had pointed out to the
Prime Minister difficulties which Iran might encounter should there be
no Majlis by March 1. The Shah said he thought it might be dangerous
to hold elections before the government had undertaken a development
program of wide impact to convince the people it intended to assist
them, not by promises but by acts. The Ambassador replied that the
government was not in possession of sufficient funds to implement such
a program and probably would not have such funds until an oil settlement
was reached and there were a Majlis to ratify it and to approve any
loans.

7. The Shah replied that if the United States were more interested
in saving Iran from communism than in achieving a settlement of the oil
controversy he could see no reason why additional credits could not be
granted by the United States Congress in January in order that a public
works program could be undertaken in Iran before elections were held.
He wondered if the United States wanted an oil settlement at the expense
of Iran's independence. The Ambassador replied that he thought if there
were no oil settlement, Iran would probably lose its independence anyway.
It seemed to him quite beyond the realm of possibility that Congress

would/

SECRET

would grant more credits to Iran unless an oil settlement were reached or at least in prospect. The American public would not permit Congress to take such action. In addition, British public opinion would be incensed and would bring pressure to bear on the government of the United Kingdom. The Shah knew as well as he that should the United States and the United Kingdom work at cross purposes in Iran, the Russians would have a clear field. The Shah agreed but expressed the fear that free elections without an economic development program would bring back to the Majlis many rabble-rousers and irresponsibles would bring the operation of the government to a standstill. The Shah thought that in the circumstances it might be safer to have "supervised" elections. The Ambassador said that the Shah and the government were in a better position to judge in this respect than he was. He did venture the remark, however, that if the Shah felt elections should be supervised, the aim should be to fill the Majlis with intelligent, loyal and patriotic Iranians who possessed qualities of leadership rather than second raters. The Shah said he fully agreed but before elections could be held on this basis it was necessary for Zahedi to weed out doubtful members from his Cabinet and advisers in several ministries. The most important step, however, was to strengthen immediately the morale and equipment of the army.

8. Then with great earnestness the Shah pointed out the needs of the army. He said that the financial situation of army personnel, particularly non-commissioned officers and commissioned officers up to the rank of captain was unbearable and consequently he had been forced to promise them better housing conditions and increases in salary. He could not be sure of army morale until this had been done. With army morale intact, he thought the government would be safe even if it were impossible to institute the economic programs he desired. With a loyal army he would not hesitate, in the event that supervised elections should fail to produce a "good Majlis", to disapprove the Majlis and exercise a dictatorship until impact programs would prepare an atmosphere conducive to a second round of elections. He hoped the government of the United States appreciated the importance of a loyal army to Iran in the present difficult circumstances.

9. In a general discussion on Iran's economic situation, Ambassador Henderson told the Shah that he thought Iran's best financial brains should be used in working out Iran's financial difficulties. In response to a question by the Ambassador, the Shah said he had urged Zahedi to bring Ebtehaj back but the Prime Minister had apparently done nothing to effect Ebtehaj's return as yet. He thought Ebtehaj a much more capable and trustworthy man than the present Minister of Finance.

10. In returning to the Majlis problem, the Ambassador said that

it seemed/

it seemed to him that in the near future it would be necessary to
pass legislation concerning the oil settlement, concerning the reform
of the fiscal and taxation system, concerning possible loans, etc.
With regard to loans, the Shah replied that several European countries
had indicated willingness to advance substantial sums to Iran on a
loan basis. Credits to the extent of even $200 million had been
mentioned by German bankers and industrialists. Interest had also
been shown by Japan in furnishing credit in return for future oil
deliveries.

11. The Ambassador replied he was sure that any credits which
Japan and European countries were prepared to offer Iran were based
on an assumption that an oil settlement would be reached. Iran should
not build up any false hopes as it was inconceivable that any responsible
group of foreign businessmen would make loans or make substantial
investments in Iran as long as the present abnormal situation persisted.
Iran's international credit was worthless in the absence of an oil
settlement. It would be a great tragedy if Iran should erroneously
decide that it could play one group of businessmen in the free world
against another in the absence of an oil settlement. Consequently,
he should bring all his influence to bear to effect at the earliest
possible moment a settlement of an oil agreement.

12. In reply to a question from the Shah, the Ambassador said
he did not have any ideas as yet as to what would be necessary to effect
a settlement of the oil problem. He was sure that Iran would find the
United Kingdom full of good will and anxious to reach a settlement that
was fair to both countries. It could not be expected, however, that
the United Kingdom would sacrifice principles on which international
intercourse must be based in order to reach a settlement. The Shah
wondered whether it would be preferable to reestablish diplomatic
relations with the United Kingdom before reaching an oil settlement.
It was his personal opinion that the oil settlement should come first.
The Ambassador said he did not know what the British attitude on this
point was but he thought diplomatic relations should be resumed and an
oil settlement effected without delay.

AMEMBASSY TEHRAN   185

September 25, 1953

The ZAHEDI Cabinet

Among the immediate problems with which the ZAHEDI Government was faced upon coming to power on August 19, 1953, were those of establishing security in Iran, of purging Government departments and agencies of pro-Communist elements, and of placing in office men capable of carrying out the Zahedi program successfully. The tasks of checking the overt activities of the Tudeh and of trying to root out and arrest the leaders of the party and their agents in Government have been tackled, but because of the nature of the problem are far from finished. The problem of Governmental reorganization through new appointments is more difficult, and thereby further from solution.

The first steps toward providing effective state administration have, of course, been taken. New heads have been appointed to all ministries, most important Government departments, key military posts, and the like. In some sectors, attempts have been made to rid the Government of pro-Tudeh small fry. The difficulties of administering such wholesale housecleaning require that the man in charge be endowed with perseverance and integrity to an extent seldom found in Iranian officials under previous regimes. So far, General Zahedi has drawn mainly upon the droves of ever-available former Government employees to fill most of the important positions.

As a result, disappointment in many of his selections has inevitably been expressed, not only by such newspapers as Mozaffar BAQAI's Shahed, which appears to be moving into opposition to the Government, but also by papers which seem sincerely convinced for the moment that the Prime Minister is a good man for the job. These newspapers often editorialize on the necessity for making sweeping changes in Government administration, and warn the Prime Minister that failure to make such changes will result in disaster for his Government.

It has become obvious to the Embassy that General Zahedi is quite aware of the problem he faces in seeking men to implement his program. In the civilian field he does not have the familiarity regarding personal capacities of appointees that he naturally has acquired with regard to professional colleagues through his years of military service. He no doubt feels that his own position is not secure enough

HRMalone:JHCunningham:
lms

CONFIDENTIAL
SECURITY INFORMATION

P/051/27.

SECRET

RESUMPTION OF DIPLOMATIC RELATIONS
WITH PERSIA

Mr. Houghton of the U.S. Embassy today gave me the following information of talks which Mr. Henderson, U.S. Ambassador in Tehran had had with members of the Persian Government on this subject.

2. Learning that General Zahidi was to lunch with the Shah on October 7, Mr. Henderson saw General Zahidi himself, the Minister for Foreign Affairs, and Mr. Ala, the Minister of Court and discussed this subject with them.

3. Mr. Henderson told General Zahidi that he knew that the Shah and his Prime Minister thought that the resumption of diplomatic relations should be simultaneous with the settlement of the oil question but he himself was fully convinced that relations should be resumed as soon as possible and that they should not be linked with an oil settlement. Such a resumption would, he considered, strengthen Persia's position internationally and also internally, since there were influential groups of pro-Western people who would not give the new Government their full confidence and support until it was in relations with H.M.G. If General Zahidi did not soon resume relations with the U.K. his Government would lose some sympathy in the U.K. and in the United States. Finally, Mr. Henderson pointed out there was no logical connexion between diplomatic relations and an oil settlement. He had told General Zahidi that as Persia had broken diplomatic relations with Britain it was for her to resume.

4. General Zahidi replied that he was unprepared to resume diplomatic relations before an oil settlement had been reached or, at least, concrete steps had been taken in that direction. He feared that the British Embassy when re-established without an oil settlement, would be a target for Nationalist attacks which would impair relations between Persia and the U.K. His Government would also appear to be a puppet of the United States and United Kingdom Governments. He entirely agreed that Persian public opinion would need to be prepared before it could accept a resumption of relations, but he did not think this preparation would be difficult or need take much time.

Mr Henderson

5. The Minister for Foreign Affairs thought it would be suicidal to resume diplomatic relations at this moment and said that the Prime Minister and the Shah were convinced that they should not be resumed until at least some principles for a settlement had been agreed, either in private unofficial conversations or by the use of mediation.

6. Mr. Ala, the Minister of Court, doubted whether the Shah would think it wise to resume diplomatic relations before an oil settlement.

7. Mr. Henderson has also advised the State Department that in his view it would be unwise for Mr. Hoover to talk to the Persian Government about the resumption of diplomatic relations. He points out that as there is no logical connexion between the two subjects they should not be treated together by Mr. Hoover, who had much better confine his activities to discussion of oil problems.

8. In passing on this information to me Mr. Houghton emphasised that we should regard invocation of advice given by Mr. Henderson to the State Department as being highly confidential.

C. T. Gandy.

October 13, 1953.

Advance copies sent to Sir W. Strang and Mr Allen

DW Greenhill
13/10.

Once again, Mr. Henderson seems to have spoken on the right lines (para. 3 of Mr. Gandy's minute). The Persian opinions that he quotes in favour of oil talks before a resumption of relations were /

19/10

-437-

FOREIGN MINISTERS CONFERENCE   EP1024/12

Second Tripartite Meeting

Saturday, October 17

PERSIA

Mr. Eden explained that he intended to make a short statement
in Parliament on October 20 about Persia.   He wished to say
something friendly to the Persians.   He could not do so earlier,
for fear of embarrassing the Persian Government.   (Mr. Eden
then read his proposed statement to the American delegates who
approved of it.)   Mr. Eden went on to say that we had received
the message from the Shah through the intermediary of the Swiss.
The Shah had asked for our views on the order in which we should
resume discussions on oil and diplomatic relations.   We had a
preference for resuming diplomatic relations at once in order
to make discussions on oil more easy.   He understood that the
Persians were timid of making the first step and we were making
it easy for them.   He then enquired from Mr. Dulles about the
prospects of Zahedi's Government.   Mr. Dulles replied that he
considered that Zahedi's Government could not last long unless
further sources of income were found.   The United States
Government had made available something over forty million dollars
which would carry him on for a few months but there was no money
currently appropriated in the United States which would permit
these gifts to continue indefinitely.   Mr. Hoover was in Tehran
exploring the situation.   Mr. Dulles said that increased oil
production elsewhere would make it difficult to market Persian oil.
There was some slackening of demand and there were also complications
due to American anti-trust laws.

Mr. Eden said that we did not want the oil but we considered
an oil settlement of great political importance.

/Mr. Dulles

-438-

Mr. Dulles agreed and said that if Zahedi collapsed we should not be given a second chance. He considered there was little hope of a better regime than the present one.

Mr. Allen explained that we were considering making available a certain number of locomotives, urgently needed in Persia, on very easy credit terms. There would be nothing to pay for two years and the Persians could suggest the rate of payment thereafter. It was impossible, for Parliamentary reasons, to make a gift of the locomotives.

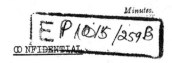
TRIAL OF DR. MUSADDIQ

Mr. Wilson of the U.S. Embassy has given us a most useful assessment of the trial so far, as reported by Mr. Henderson.

2.   Although at the outset the Prosecutor had maintained a high standard in his initial address and the President of the Court had handled Musaddiq with wit and tact during the first two days, the proceedings had degenerated after November 10 when it appeared that there had been a decision to allow Musaddiq to hold the floor almost indefinitely whether or not his remarks had any relevance to the proceedings. Musaddiq's tactics had thus given him a large measure of control over the character of the trial and no effective steps had been taken to counter the effect of his declaration that this was a political trial in which he must be allowed to discuss political subjects. The Court officials, who had started by trying to construct serious cases had tended increasingly to rely on demagoguery. Little order is apparently being kept in the Court, photographers move about constantly and in the pauses journalists and other observers are allowed to talk with members of the Court, the Prosecution and the Defence.

3.   The U.S. Embassy in Tehran consider that Musaddiq's trial with all the publicity could be a serious blunder. The extensive press coverage with photographs is capable of arousing public opinion in his favour. The trial they think is allowing him to assume the status of a fully-fledged opponent of the Government and may rebound greatly to his advantage.

4.   It appears that General Zahidi is conscious of this and told Mr. Henderson on November 11 that he had no control over the trial, which is being held under military auspices and thus is the responsibility of the Chief-of-Staff and in the last analysis the Shah. One of the Shah's Private Secretaries has told a member of the U.S. Embassy that he had argued unsuccessfully with the Shah to persuade him to change his mind and adopt a secret and speedy court martial procedure.

Christopher Gandy

C. T. Gandy.

November 13, 1953.

FROM TEHRAN TO FOREIGN OFFICE

Cypher/OTP

Mr. Wright

No. 6

December 23, 1953

P 1051/94.

D: 6.58 p.m. December 23, 1953

R: 7.54 p.m. December 23, 1953

CONFIDENTIAL

       Before my arrival the Shah, through his sinister [sic] secretary Perron, had asked the Swiss Minister to arrange an immediate mealtime meeting between me and Bahram Shahrukh (1951 personality number 174). After discussing with the United States Ambassador I felt I could not well refuse this rather embarrassing invitation, and accordingly I met Shahrukh and Perron alone at dinner last night with the Swiss Minister.

       2.   Shahrukh did all the talking. He said that the Shah was very pleased that diplomatic relations had been resumed and was most anxious to help me in my mission; I could at any time send him a message through Shahrukh or Perron. Shahrukh's main theme was that there was much latent good will toward us and that he thought my first objective should be to sound this out by making suitable gestures e.g. by early delivery of rails stored at Basra, by friendly references by the B.B.C. to Persia and by developing contact with the Persian press. I agreed with this objective. I pointed out that the rails were no longer in Basra but that you were personally interested in seeing that speedy action was taken over the rails now in the United Kingdom.

       3.   Shahrukh talked rather woolily about the oil problem. I stressed that we were as anxious as the Persian Government to reach a speedy settlement and that we should do all we could to this end which I believed possible provided question of fair compensation formed part of it. I stressed that this was a principle to which we were as firmly attached as the Persians were to that of nationalization. Shahrukh mentioned last week's talks between the A.I.O.C. and the American Oil Company and appeared to believe that some firm arrangement on marketing had been agreed upon. I explained the hypothetical nature [grp. undec] and sounded him out on the possibility of direct negotiation between A.I.O.C. and the Persian Government pointing out that this would be the most practical way to reach a quick solution. His view was that because of very strong feelings

/against .. ...

against the company in Persia such negotiation would be
impossible, but he did not exclude the representative of the
A.I.O.C. being included in any negotiating team that might be
sent here.

4.   At one stage Sharukh whispered that the Shah was
thinking of dismissing Ala but would not wish to do so if this
might be taken by us as an anti-British move.   I said that
neither I nor the members of my staff had any intention of
interfering in Persian domestic affairs, and that it was for
the Shah and his Prime Minister to decide what actions were for
the good of the country.   I also took the opportunity, when he
started criticizing General Zahedi's adviser, of stressing my
admiration for the Prime Minister's achievements since August,
and mentioned that you had expressed sympathy for his efforts
in the House of Commons on December 17.

5.   Although the Swiss Minister was anxious I should keep
this meeting secret (presumably at the request of Perron) I
decided after discussion with Henderson to tell the Minister for
Foreign Affairs of it when I called on him this morning.

6.   I have not yet been able to discover how important
Sharukh is in the present scheme of things here.

vvvvv

FROM TEHRAN TO FOREIGN OFFICE

Cypher/OTP.

E P10.51/93

FOREIGN OFFICE AND
WHITEHALL DISTRIBUTION

Mr. Wright
No: 15
December 26, 1953.

D: 4.14 p.m. December 26, 1953.
R: 4.37 p.m. December 26, 1953.

PRIORITY
CONFIDENTIAL

My immediately preceding telegram.

Following is text of message handed to me yesterday by Shahrukh.

Begins:

All matters of diplomatic routine including the oil matter should be discussed by you with Minister for Foreign Affairs (Mr. Entezam).

All matters of high policy i.e. matters above or outside diplomatic routine should be presented to His Majesty through Mr. Peron and myself jointly. Since however the oil matter is of preliminary [sic] importance in relations with the two countries, His Majesty wishes that after you have made your study and reported to your Government, and have received suggestions on the manner the oil matter should be or could be settled, that you inform through this channel (Peron and myself) His Majesty in advance and before you present them to the Minister for Foreign Affairs you await His Majesty's approval or counter proposal. Thus His Majesty wishes to avoid any serious difficulties arising during negotiations.

His Majesty accepts principles suggested by your Government

(i) that principle of compensation to the Anglo-Iranian Oil Company should stand firm subject to a generous treatment by your Government

and

(ii) that profits of Persia in oil should not be higher than in other countries of the Middle East though formula must be face-saving for the Persian Government.

With regard to the nomination of your Ambassador, His Majesty is not opposed to your approaching Mr. Entezam for an agrément but His Majesty emphatically wishes that

(i) this.....

(i)   this should be done without much publicity
                        and

(ii) that the Ambassador comes when oil negotiations have
reached their final stages near a settlement.

His Majesty states as reasons the following

(a) Persian public opinion has already got used to Wright
and regard him already with certain sympathy.   Thus it would
be much easier to conduct negotiations with Wright without a new
embarrassment.   The Persians would thus keep favourably quiet
until the results of the negotiations are known.

(b) His Majesty wishes to make the best use of the day when
the new British Ambassador presents his credentials to His Majesty.
His Majesty intends to speak very friendly words which would
subsequently switch over Persian public opinion to a friendly spirit
vis-à-vis Britain.

His Majesty wishes to add to this morning's statement that,
in his conversation with Mr. Nixon, His Majesty did not only strongly
suggest non-interference in the internal affairs of Persia, but
His Majesty also emphatically asked Mr. Nixon, i.e. United States
Government, to co-ordinate her policy in and for Persia with the
United Kingdom, for otherwise it would be only the Russians who
would profit.   His Majesty wishes to have real view of your Governme
on this point and would appreciate any suggestions your Government
might have.

On Sunday, December 27, His Majesty will leave, for a holiday
of 10 to 12 days, for Ramsar on the Caspian.   However an aircraft
will stand ready for any message you may wish to convey to His
Majesty through this channel.

                        Ends.

JJJJJ

FROM TEHRAN TO FOREIGN OFFICE

Cypher/OTP

EP.051/90

FOREIGN OFFICE AND
WHITEHALL DISTRIBUTION

Mr. Wright
No. 12
December 26, 1953

D. 1.01 p.m. December 26, 1953
R. 1.28 p.m. December 26, 1953

PRIORITY
CONFIDENTIAL

My telegram No. 6. N/π

The Shah's Friends.

I was called upon twice on Christmas Day by Messrs. Peron and Shahrukh allegedly at the urgent request of the Shah who is leaving for the Caspian on December 27.

2. At the first meeting Shahrukh again did all the talking, this time from typewritten notes which he said embodied the Shah's views. Briefly these were:

(a) The Shah was a firm believer in Anglo-Persian friendship as a basis for a strong, independent and prosperous Persia.

(b) The Shah's strong personal position as Head of the State was such that we would be able more easily to reach a settlement of our problems by agreeing things first with him, rather than through other persons; in other words we should clear our lines with the Shah first.

(c) The Shah was willing to act as strongly in Persian internal affairs but, in order to do so, he needed a clear understanding of our aims and an assurance that we would not interfere with "various groups" in Persia. The Shah had recently made a similar request to the United States Government through Mr. Nixon and the United States Ambassador. If I could give such an assurance it would help the Shah to avoid interference either from the Americans or from the Russians.

(d) The Shah wanted a quick settlement of the oil question and therefore wanted me to inform him in confidence how we proposed to settle it.

/(e) With

(e) With reference to what I had said in my earlier conversation with Shahrukh about direct negotiations with A.I.O.C., the Shah's view was that the appearance in Persia of an A.I.O.C. Mission "would greatly provoke Persian public opinion and thus handicap the negotiations but he believes that A.I.O.C. experts could participate later in the negotiations under the cover of the compensation question, and preferential rights they have by law for purchase of Persian oil." The Shah's view was therefore that the oil negotiations should be started on a governmental basis.

(f) The appointment of Ambassador should wait until a the way had been cleared for a settlement of the oil problem.

3. In reply I made the following points:

(a) Her Majesty's Government were equally anxious to develop Anglo-Persian friendship and see a strong independent and prosperous Persia.

(b) While I welcomed the Shah's willingness to help me by direct contact to settle our problems, I could not be put in a position where I should be negotiating secretly with the Shah without the knowledge of his Prime Minister and Minister for Foreign Affairs. Anything I said to the Shah I should also wish to be able to say to his Ministers, and I hoped they would be aware of the messages the Shah was sending me.

(c) I could give a solemn assurance that neither I nor my Government had any intention of interfering in Persian internal affairs. If such rumours came to the Shah's ears I should be glad if he would discuss them with me immediately.

(d) Her Majesty's Government was equally anxious for a speedy settlement of the oil problem. My first task was exploratory and I had no solution in my pocket which I could show to the Shah. We would, however, welcome any realistic proposals that the Persian Government might care to let me have. In submitting such proposals the Shah

/should know

-446-

should know that there was no real demand in the
world for Persian oil at the moment, and that any
acceptable settlement would have to safeguard two basic
principles viz., payment for fair compensation and that
Persia should not do better out of it than her
neighbours.

(e) I had only a few hours previously been instructed
by you to request agrément of an Ambassador and I
proposed to do so when I saw the Minister for Foreign
Affairs early next week. The question of when the
Ambassador should arrive could, I thought, be mutually
agreed but I hoped the Shah would not dissent from my
request of agrément.

4. Please see my immediately following telegram.

7777777777

Cypher/OTP

E P1051/92

Mr. Wright
No. 14
December 26, 1953

D. 2.34 p.m. December 26, 1953
R. 3.11 p.m. December 26, 1953

PRIORITY
CONFIDENTIAL

My telegram No. 12 ~~NOT~~ ~~EP105~~

Some 5 hours after our first talk Messrs. Peron and
Shahrukh returned with a piece of paper allegedly setting out the
Shah's comments on our morning's discussion.

2. After reading it I said that I was still not happy about
the Shah's view that I should deal with him exclusively, even
on certain oil matters. I felt that, since this was a matter
so closely affecting Persian public opinion, I must be able to
discuss it freely with his Minister for Foreign Affairs. I
considered it imperative that I should retain his Ministers'
confidence and I could only do this if I knew they were being
kept informed of what the Shah was saying to me and vice versa.
I suggested therefore that in order to clarify the position
I should see the Shah.

3. Peron and Shahrukh said they were willing to arrange
a secret meeting with the Shah though, in view of certain
changes which the Shah was contemplating in the Government, it
might be better if I saw him after his return from the Caspian,
otherwise I might be accused of interference in internal affairs.
I agreed that it would be better to wait, adding that I should
not want to see the Shah without the knowledge of the Minister
for Foreign Affairs; subject to this (which they clearly disliked)
I had no objection to the meeting being kept secret.

4. Shahrukh asked me what were the views of Her Majesty's
Government regarding the participation of the International Bank
in our oil settlement. I replied along the lines of my brief
and Shahrukh promised to let me have the Shah's views on this
in due course.

/5. I assured

5. I assured Shahrukh that Her Majesty's Government were determined to work hand in hand with the United States Government in Persia. I told him I was already in the closest contact with Mr. Henderson and that I had no objection to him telling the United States Ambassador of his conversation with me. Shahrukh looked a little shifty at this saying that the Shah used other channels for his dealings with the Americans.

6. The United States Ambassador has not hitherto come across Shahrukh and is inclined to think that this is a personal intrigue of Peron and Shahrukh. Until I have seen the Shah it will be difficult to confirm this. Another possibility of course is that the Shah, hopeful of an early oil settlement is anxious to get all the credit for it by keeping the strings in his own hands. In any case I think it most important that I should not start off on the wrong foot with Entzam and unless you dissent, I propose when I see him next week, to give an account of this discussion with Peron and Shahrukh.

7. Please see my immediately following telegram.

7777777

PERSIA: SHAH'S INTERMEDIARIES

The Department have submitted the attached draft telegram, which is self-explanatory.   If the Shah really did send Perron and Shahrukh to Mr. Wright, the sooner it is made clear to him that we do not like such emissaries, the better. If however by any chance the emissaries were self-appointed, the sooner they are exposed, the better, and I do not think we need be afraid of arousing their hostility.

2.   I therefore think on the whole that it would be a good thing to send a telegram on the lines of the draft.

Sir I. Kirkpatrick.

Roger Allen
(R. Allen)
December 30, 1953.

I. Kirkpatrick
30. xii

FROM FOREIGN OFFICE TO TEHRAN

Cypher/OTP and
By Bag

DEPARTMENTAL DISTRIBUTION

No. 1
January 1, 1954

D:1.55 p.m. January 1, 1954

Addressed to Tehran telegram No. 1 of January 1, 1954
Repeated for information saving to :　Washington No. 2
　　　　　　　　　　　　　　　　　　　　B.M.E.O. No. 2

My telegram No. 7 [of December 28: Mr. Wright's relations with the Shah].

I should see advantage in your making clear to the Shah himself at the earliest convenient moment that you would prefer any messages he may wish to send you to come either through the Minister for Foreign Affairs or the Minister of Court. If meanwhile you are again approached by unofficial intermediaries, I suggest that you might see the Minister of Court and give the message to him. You would of course not convey the impression that messages from the Shah were in any way unwelcome. It is solely the channel through which they pass that you wish to be clear about.

DISTRIBUTED TO:

Eastern Department

22

Mr. Fry.

Mr. Maitland, M.P., told Mr. Turton this afternoon that he would be seeing Mr. Hamzavi, Press Counsellor at the Iranian Embassy, on Thursday afternoon, March 10. Mr. Hamzavi, who is being recalled to Tehran, had put three questions to Mr. Maitland, who would be grateful for any advice which we could give him about answering them.

The questions are:-

(a) Why did we not press the Shah when he was in London to join the Turko-Iraq Pact?   It would appear that H.I.M. is a bit discouraged that we did not.

(b) Do we consider Zahedi to be the best available Prime Minister of Persia?

(c) Did the Shah put a foot wrong during his London visit?

The answers to these questions are due - so Mr. Maitland understands - to be retailed to the Shah by Mr. Hamzavi.

Mr. Turton's views on these questions are as follows:-

(a) He told Mr. Maitland, in a preliminary way, that Iran should be internally strong before she undertook any external commitments.   He feels that if we can brief Mr. Maitland fairly fully on the answer to this question, it might be useful.

(b) This sounds as though the Shah is intriguing behind Zahedi's back and trying to involve us as well.   Mr. Turton thinks we should be very cagey indeed about suggesting an answer; it might even be better to say nothing at all.

(c) Mr. Turton ~~says there is~~ sees no reason why we should not return a straight "No".

I should be grateful if you could let me have, by Wednesday ~~Morning to morrow evening~~, a brief note on your views about these questions, which Mr. Turton could use orally with Mr. Maitland

(C. R. A. Rae)

March 7, 1955

Mr. Rae's minute of March 7, ~~attached~~ above, records

three/

R.F. Wel.

three questions put to Mr. Maitland, M.P. by Mr. Hamzavi, Press
Counsellor at the Persian Embassy.

2.   The full answers to these questions are:-

(a) For months past we have consistently taken the
    line that, while we should wish to see Persia
    associated in defence arrangements with her
    neighbours, we leave the timing entirely to her.
    It is not for us to judge whether Persian opinion
    is ready for such a step.   The Secretary of
    State repeated this advice to the Shah when he
    was in London.

(b) We do not know.   General Zahedi has his faults,
    but any of the possible successors might well
    prove to have as many or more.   In any case we
    have no intention of giving Persians advice on
    this purely internal affair, or even discussing
    it with them.

(c) So far as we know, the Shah did not put a foot
    wrong.

3.   The Department hope, however, that it will not be
necessary to authorise Mr. Maitland to give detailed answers to
Mr. Hamzavi.   Mr. Hamzavi, who of course is well known to us,
is almost certainly more interested in Persian politics than in
his job;   and we have none too high an opinion of his reliability
as a reporter of our views.   He has already caused one
misunderstanding, and there is danger of further and worse misunderstanding if he puts questions to H.M.G. through the intermediary of private Members of Parliament.   The Shah had a long
talk with the Secretary of State, and that should be enough for
Mr. Hamzavi.

4.   Mr. Turton may wish to give Mr. Maitland a full
explanation in confidence, but the Department suggest that the
latter should be invited to keep his answers to Mr. Hamzavi as
short as possible.   They might be:

(a) he is not able to speak for H.M.G.;

(b) he knows only that H.M.G. have no intention
    whatever of interfering in Persian internal
    politics;

(c) he is sure that the answer is No.

(L.A.C. Fry).
March 8, 1955.

Mr. Rose (I have not submitted this through
Mr. Shuckburgh since he is so preoccupied with discussions at the moment).
Mr. Turton warned Mr. Maitland about Mr. Hamzavi,
and suggested to him that he should speak
guardedly (and without, of course, quoting F.O.) on
the lines of para 2 above.   C. Rose 9/3

No. 308

788.11/2-2853: Telegram

The Ambassador in Iran (Henderson) to the Department of State[1]

TOP SECRET   NIACT   TEHRAN, February 28, 1953—5 p. m.

3449. Early this morning stories regarding imminent departure Shah pouring in from many sources. These stories had conflicting details. Altho some reflected confusion and bewilderment, there seemed be general impression that Shah's decision depart was in some way connected with friction between him and Prime Minister. Most common version was that Shah had decided leave because Mosadeq was threatening if Shah did not do so he would issue proclamation to country criticizing Shah and asking people to choose between Shah and himself.

2. Embassy Attaché reported that at dinner yesterday evening attended by Bazaar merchants, Qashqai Chieftain Khosro, and others, rumors of Shah's departure in immediate future was chief source conversation. Practically all guests present, with exception Khosro, who privately expressed gratification that Shah was leaving, indicated in their opinion Shah's departure would be detrimental to interests country. Similarly at dinner attended by myself last evening editor of largest newspaper in country and chief protocol Foreign Office told me of rumors expressing their concern at ultimate effects on country.

3. I decided this morning that since news was now out I was more free than hitherto to try to effect cancellation or at least postponement Shah's plans leave country. Unable obtain appointment with Foreign Minister I was able arrange see Ala, Minister Court, at 11:15. Ala had just returned from audience with Shah. He told me he had done utmost persuade Shah at last moment not to leave. Shah however was determined insisting that if he did not depart Mosadeq would issue proclamation attacking him and members his family; it would be difficult for him without necessary facilities effectively to answer charges which would be made against him. He preferred leave country to becoming involved in one-sided squabble. Ala said that while he was with Shah word had been received that at instance Kashani, President Majlis, who claimed to have heard news of Shah's departure only this morning, informal closed meeting of some 57 members Majlis was taking place to discuss situation. When Shah received this news he had become excited and insisted on leaving at once before lunch because he was

---

[1] Transmitted in four sections; also sent to London, Baghdad, Ankara, and Dhahran.

afraid that if he did not get away so much pressure would be brought upon him that he would have difficulty leaving without incident. . . .

. . . .

5. . . . At that moment messenger informed Ala that Bureau of Majlis had arrived with request that Ala arrange for it deliver urgent message to Shah. I returned to Embassy.

6. On my arrival I learned that members Majlis in secret session had decided send message to Shah to effect that his departure from country at this time would be inadvisable. I was also told by acting Air Attaché that Chief Air Staff had just informed him that General Baharmast Chief of Staff was en route Palace to inform Shah that whole General Staff had decided to resign in case Shah should leave country. Thus far unable to obtain confirmation firmness of resolve General Staff in this respect.

Baharmast not strong character and he might well wilt in delivering General Staff message to Shah. General Zimmerman thinks Baharmast rather weak character.

7. I decided make endeavor see Prime Minister at once and asked Saleh Embassy Iranian Adviser seek appointment. Saleh learned from Mosadeq Secretary that Prime Minister in Palace with Shah. At Saleh's request Secretary left at once for Palace to tell Mosadeq I wished see him urgently. I called on Mosadeq at 1:15.

8. Mosadeq back in bed apparently suffering from severe headache. He received me in friendly though guarded manner. I told him I coming without awaiting instructions from Washington in view of what seem to me urgency of situation. Widespread rumors throughout city that Shah was leaving Iran at once because if he did not do so Prime Minister would issue proclamation denouncing him and family. As friend of Iran and as his personal friend I considered it my duty tell him that departure Shah just now would tend confirm these rumors. Support of Iran independence was basic policy re Iran. In my opinion and I sure my opinion represented that of US Government Shah's hasty departure in these circumstances would weaken security country and I therefore, had come to him in hope that he could take some last minute measure to prevail on Shah not to leave or at least to postpone his departure. Mosadeq replied Shah preferred to leave country. He did not request him do so and was not in position order him not to do so. At this very moment groups of persons including representatives British agents were in Palace trying persuade Shah not leave. Some of these people had entered Palace while he was telling Shah farewell and had made unnecessary scenes. Shah was receiving these people

freely and could decide for himself what to do. I asked Prime Minister why it was necessary for him to issue proclamation which clearly would be critical of Shah unless Shah left. Prime Minister replied he could not institute necessary reforms or obtain solution oil problem so long as court served as basis of operations of British agents who were trying stir up dissension in country. Unity was necessary if Iran was successfully to emerge from present crisis. I told Prime Minister had myself some knowledge of Shah's attitude and I convinced Shah not engaging in or countenancing participation of court in activities against interest Iran.

Prime Minister maintained that people around Shah were causing great injury to country. After some discussion it became clear it quite useless endeavor prevail on Prime Minister alter his attitude. I told Prime Minister regretted having troubled him personally at time when I knew he harassed with many worries. I had hoped discuss matter in preliminary way with Foreign Minister but had been unable to obtain appointment today. I had therefore called on Ala who clearly was not in position deny Shah was leaving almost immediately. My call on Prime Minister had been prompted by hope that latter would cooperate in preventing developments which might ultimately if not almost immediately have consequences unfavorable to Iran. Prime Minister said it would be better for me if I did not make call on Ala or anyone else connected with court at this critical time. . . . Prime Minister altered his attitude and in more friendly manner repeated that he was not insisting that Shah leave country. If Shah did not do so he had no choice other than to issue proclamation to Iran people. I said that in his political career he had undoubtedly on previous occasions found it possible to prevent differences from developing into open conflict which would be harmful to country. Was he sure that he had no alternative other than to issue proclamation critical of Shah and court unless Shah should leave country? Prime Minister said he had given this matter much thought and he considered that he was following proper course.

9. Before departing I gave Prime Minister note amending alternative text of original Compensation Agreement as suggested in London telegram 194, Feb. 27, repeated Department 4838.[2] We agreed that in case of press inquiries both he and I should merely state that during course my visit I had corrected minor omission in one of documents which I had handed him on February 20.

10. On my way to Prime Minister's residence I found all neigboring streets blocked with soldiers. On my departure 50 minutes later observed still more soldiers. Groups of persons in surly mood ap-

---

[2]Not printed. (888.2553/2-2753)

parently ready for demonstrations of some kind were observed gathering in vicinity.[3]

HENDERSON

---

[3]Jernegan and Richards informed Henderson on Feb. 28 that they concurred completely with Henderson's decision to take the measures, which he had reported in telegram 3449 from Tehran, to discourage the Shah's departure. (Telegram 2254; 788.11/2–2853)

No. 309

788.00/2-2853: Telegram

The Ambassador in Iran (Henderson) to the Department of State[1]

TOP SECRET   NIACT   TEHRAN, February 28, 1953—7 p. m.

3454. 1. Thousands of people demonstrated for Shah and blocking Kakh Street in vicinity royal palaces and Mosadeq residence. As I was leaving Mosadeq's house General Mohanna, Department Ministry Defense and General Afshartus entered his room. As I was leaving, compound jeep with Iranian soldiers swung out of curb towards gate compound. I have since been informed that this jeep crashed gate breaking it and served as signal for rioting. Guards resisted firing in air but throng coming up street from Shah's palace some 200 yards distant gradually overwhelmed guards and demonstrated against Mosadeq. Mosadeq in pajamas appeared on balcony in effort quiet throng. He was booed down. He then telephoned Ala demanding additional guards from palace charging that rioting was instigated by British agents of court. As rioting increased in violence Mosadeq escaped over rear wall in pajamas accompanied by Fatemi Foreign Minister. They entered auto and proceeded some unknown destination. 30 minutes later woman identified as Mosadeq's daughter-in-law and another woman climbed wall and left in waiting auto. About same time brigadier-general, probably chief police, scaled wall, commandeered Point Four jeep and went with it to police station.

2. At 5 p. m. thousands of people continued block vicinity royal palaces and Mosadeq's residence. Loud-speakers are calling on people if they are for Shah, now is time to demonstrate that fact.

3. I have talked with Ala by phone at 4:30 p. m. He confirmed massive throng still are in vicinity of palace. Shah in order quiet people appeared personally on balcony to inform them that he had decided not to go away at least for time being. My impression is

---

[1]Also sent to London, Baghdad, Ankara, and Dhahran.

that demonstrations are organized. So far as I can ascertain, however, there is not as yet any definite plan, at least as far as court is concerned, for future. Unless Zahedi or some other figure with backing of military takes control of situation immediately either security likely deteriorate or Mosadeq from some new base with backing various elements including Nationalist Movement in Tehran and in country and possibly certain military groups will reassert his power. If Mosadeq successful as is quite possible, he will probably take extremely vindictive measures. Latest news is that certain groups now in street shouting "long live Shah and Mosadeq". This might be indication that Mosadeq backers trying to prevent pro-Shah supporters from demonstrating against Prime Minister. They may succeed thus in changing attitude of streets which originally were against Prime Minister. Pan Iranists also appearing on street. Tudehs not likely also fail to enter scene in opposition to Shah. Most of Tehran still undisturbed.

HENDERSON

No. 310

S/P-NSC files, lot 61 D 167, "Iran, US Policy Regarding the Present Situation, NSC 117, 136, 136/1"

Memorandum Prepared in the Office of National Estimates, Central Intelligence Agency, for the President

SECRET   WASHINGTON, 1 March 1953.

Subject: The Iranian Situation

Ever since the assassination of General Razmara in March, 1951, and the subsequent impasse and diplomatic break with Britain over the oil negotiations, the Iranian situation has been slowly disintegrating. The result has been a steady decrease in the power and influence of the Western democracies and the building up of a situation where a Communist takeover is becoming more and more of a possibility. However, even the present crisis is likely to be unsatisfactorily compromised without a Communist Tudeh victory. . . . The events of the past 48 hours have brought a few surprises. The fanatical Moslem leader, Kashani, who is also President of the Majlis, has shown more power than expected both in influencing the Majlis and in quickly marshaling for mob action his fanatical followers. The institution of the Crown may have more popular backing than was expected.

Today the situation in Tehran remains tense and unresolved. Some street demonstrations have occurred today, but the curfew is still in effect and general order is apparently being preserved.

would have a much narrower basis of support than Mossadeq enjoyed before the current crisis and would, therefore, be likely to resort to ruthlessness to destroy opposition. In his struggle to do so Tudeh influence and opportunities for gaining control would increase rapidly.

Retired General Zahedi, currently imprisoned by Mossadeq, also wishes to become Prime Minister, and his adherents are active in the Majlis. It is unlikely that he will succeed.

The present situation offers the Shah an opportunity which he has not as yet seized. His past record does not suggest that he will act.

No. 311

788.00/3-253: Telegram

The Secretary of State to the Embassy in Iran[1]

TOP SECRET   NIACT   WASHINGTON, March 2, 1953—7:38 p. m.

2266. While situation obviously still confused, your latest reports seem to us to bring out or confirm following points:

1. Immediate Tudeh objective is to eliminate Shah and for this purpose it is making common cause with Mosadeq. Presumably if Shah were eliminated Tudeh would then turn once again and work to eliminate Mosadeq, following which its chances of coming to power would be greatly increased.

2. Mosadeq is determined either to eliminate Shah or to reduce him to utter figurehead. Although he may not openly seek or welcome Tudeh support, he cannot disassociate himself from it and if he wins present struggle is likely to find himself unable vigorously to defend himself against Tudeh. This will be especially true if disorders take increasingly anti-western tone and Mosadeq victory is based on anti-western appeal to masses.

3. On other side, there appears to be substantial and relatively courageous opposition group both within and outside Majlis. We gather Army Chiefs and many civilians still loyal to Shah and would act if he gave them positive leadership or even if he merely acquiesced in move to install new government.

4. Shah, however, seems to be maintaining policy of complete inaction, with result that Mosadeq opponents, both civilian and military, are afraid to act positively.

On basis foregoing it seems likely Mosadeq will retain power and that this will mean early disappearance of Shah from Iranian political scene, rapid deterioration in relations between Iran and West

[1]Drafted and signed by Jernegan; cleared in draft with the Secretary of State, Under Secretary of State, Deputy Under Secretary of State, and Nitze.

and greatly increased possibilities of communist takeover. Would appreciate your comments on this analysis.

It is of course quite possible that we can do nothing in this situation and we shall be guided by your judgment in this regard.[2] . . .

•   •   •   •   •   •   •

DULLES

---

[2]Henderson responded in telegram 3543 from Tehran, Mar. 4, that there was no evidence yet that Mosadeq had made arrangements with the Tudeh, but he was capable of doing so in order to retain power. Henderson added that no reconciliation between Mosadeq and the Shah appeared possible except on terms of the latter's capitulation. (888.00/3-453)

No. 312

Eisenhower Library, Eisenhower papers, Whitman file

Memorandum of Discussion at the 135th Meeting of the National Security Council, Washington, March 4, 1953[1]

TOP SECRET   EYES ONLY

Present at the 135th meeting of the Council were the President of the United States, presiding, the Vice President of the United States, the Secretary of State, the Secretary of Defense, and the Director for Mutual Security. Also present were the Secretary of the Treasury, the Director, Bureau of the Budget, General Vandenberg for the Chairman, Joint Chiefs of Staff, the Director of Central Intelligence, the Administrative Assistant to the President for National Security Matters, the Special Assistant to the President for Cold War Operations, the Military Liaison Officer, the Executive Secretary, NSC, and the Deputy Executive Secretary, NSC.

There follows a general account of the main positions taken and the chief points made at this meeting.

[Here follows discussion of item 1 concerning the question of Stalin's illness and the United States Government's program for exploiting psychologically Stalin's passing.]

2. Developments in Iran Affecting U.S. Security (NSC 136/1)[2]

When the Council turned to this item on the agenda Mr. Cutler sketched briefly current United States policy on Iran as set forth in NSC 136/1. He further informed the Council that the Senior NSC Staff had discussed this policy and the situation in Iran at its meet-

---

[1]Drafted by Gleason, on Mar. 5.
[2]Document 240.

ing on the previous Monday.[3] At that time the Staff had requested that the Director of Central Intelligence and the Secretaries of State and Defense be prepared to answer certain questions and to set forth the situation when the Council met on Wednesday.

Mr. Dulles then proceeded to brief the Council on the developments of the past two or three days in Iran. Mr. Dulles said that there was little doubt that the Shah had once more missed an opportunity to take control of the situation, and that the present prospects were that Mossadegh would remain in control for the immediate future though with diminished power and prestige. It could be predicted that he would set about destroying what remained of the Shah's position and would attempt also to "get" Kashani. It was also explained that, for reasons of its own, the Tudeh Party was at the moment supporting Mossadegh. Nevertheless, the true Communist position, said Mr. Dulles, could be deduced from a broadcast of the secret Communist radio in northern Iran. Its report on recent events was violently anti-Shah, but, unlike the position taken by the Tudeh Party officially, this radio also attacked Mossadegh as a vile servant of the Shah and warned him that if he were to survive he must join with the people of Iran and act with and for them against the Shah.

The probable consequences of the events of the last few days, concluded Mr. Dulles, would be a dictatorship in Iran under Mossadegh. As long as the latter lives there was but little danger, but if he were to be assassinated or otherwise to disappear from power, a political vacuum would occur in Iran and the Communists might easily take over. The consequences of such a take-over were then outlined in all their seriousness by Mr. Dulles. Not only would the free world be deprived of the enormous assets represented by Iranian oil production and reserves, but the Russians would secure these assets and thus henceforth be free of any anxiety about their petroleum situation. Worse still, Mr. Dulles pointed out, if Iran succumbed to the Communists there was little doubt that in short order the other areas of the Middle East, with some 60% of the world's oil reserves, would fall into Communist control.

The President then asked the members of the Council what they could suggest as to what the United States might do now to avert the crisis. Was there any feasible course of action to save the situation in Iran?

In reply, Secretary Dulles said that for a long time now he had been unable to perceive any serious obstacle to the loss of Iran to the free world if the Soviets were really determined to take it. We

---

[3]The Record of Meeting of the Senior NSC Staff on Mar. 2 is not printed. (S/P-NSC files, lot 62 D 1, "1953—Record of Planning Board Meetings NSC files")

do not have sufficient troops to put into the area in order to prevent a Communist take-over, and the Soviets had played their
game in Iran very cleverly and with a good sense of timing. Nevertheless, continued Secretary Dulles, he believed it was possible to
gain time if we followed certain courses of action. The real problem, it seemed to him, was what to do with the time thus gained,
in view of the apparent hopelessness of Iran's ultimate fate. Perhaps, he suggested, the Joint Chiefs of Staff might provide some
answer as to what we could do with the time we could save.

In commencing his outline of these courses of action, Secretary
Dulles noted that all three courses were hazardous and all of them
subject to change in case Mossadegh was assassinated. The first
course of action suggested by Secretary Dulles was to recall Ambassador Henderson before he was dismissed by Mossadegh. . . . the
Ambassador's influence with Mossadegh was probably now hope-
lessly impaired, and it might therefore be best to recall him before
he was kicked out.

The second course of action proposed by the Secretary of State
was for the United States to disassociate itself, regarding Iran,
from the British in an effort to regain popularity on the merits of a
policy of our own. This subject, he added, he desired to discuss with
the President and Foreign Secretary Eden.[4] But, he said, it was
known that our unpopularity in Iran is largely a derivation of British unpopularity and our previous association in the minds of Iranians with unpopular British policies. The trouble with such a
course of action as this was whether we should not lose more by
going it alone, in the face of British opposition in many other areas
of the world, than we should gain in Iran itself.

At this point the President interrupted Secretary Dulles' outline
to state his firm belief that in such countries as Syria and Iraq,
America was hated even more than Britain, because of the policy
which we had been pursuing toward Israel. Had anyone ever
thought, continued the President, of saying to these other Middle
Eastern states that they ought to make a coalition with us as a
means of withstanding an assault by the Russians on them across
the mountain ranges which separated them from the Soviets?

Secretary Dulles then asked if, before answering the President's
question, he could go on to make his third and last point on courses
of action to gain time in Iran.

---

[4]British Foreign Secretary Eden and Chancellor of the Exchequer R. A. Butler
were scheduled to arrive in Washington on Mar. 4 for a series of political and economic talks with their American counterparts that continued through Mar. 7. For a
summary of the discussions that pertained to Iran, see Document 314.

settlement. The only thing which would produce a settlement would be a complete British capitulation.

Secretary Humphrey inquired whether he was to understand that Secretary Dulles was already convinced that Russia would ultimately secure Iran in any event, or, in other words, that we are going to lose that country.

Secretary Dulles replied in the affirmative, and Mr. Cutler pointed out that this, of course, meant that with the loss of Iran we would lose the neighboring countries of the Middle East and that the loss would be terribly serious.

The President commented that we could not move forces of our own into Iran, but this did not imply to him the necessity of sacrificing the other Middle Eastern states, because it was possible to get United States troops into some of these countries. The difficulty in trying to do this in Iran was the probability that an attempt on our part to do so would result in Soviet invocation of its treaty of friendship and non-aggression with Iran.[5] We would then find ourselves at war with Russia.

Mr. Cutler again pleaded the wisdom of American policy in Iran independent of the British, and suggested that it might even be wise for the United States to buy out the British oil company.

The President replied that he had long believed that this should be done, but he could see no way of convincing Congress that it was the part of wisdom for the United States Government or any American oil company to buy the bankrupt Anglo-Iranian.

Mr. Stassen noted that it might well be possible for the United States to get its money back once Iranian oil began to flow again.

But the President observed that at the moment at least there was no market for Iranian oil, and that to obtain one would require cutbacks in production in other oil-producing areas.

Reverting to the President's worries about the attitude of Congress, Mr. Cutler inquired how Congress would like it if the United States stood idly by and let Iran fall into the hands of the Soviet Union.

It was generally agreed that Congress would take a poor view of this eventuality.

At this point, Mr. Jackson said he believed that another possibility existed for saving the situation in Iran. He thought that if the

[5]The Soviet Union and Iran had concluded this treaty on Feb. 26, 1921. The provision to which the President was referring was Article VI. It states that if a third party attempted armed intervention in Iran or tried to use Iranian territory as a base against the Soviet Union, and if the Iranian Government was unable to stop this menace after being asked once to do so by the Soviet Government, the Soviets had the right to send troops into Iran to conduct military operations necessary to the defense of the Soviet Union.

United States could manage to secure a peace between Egypt and Israel, and that if the Roman Catholic Church, as seemed likely, would agree to the internationalization of the Holy Places in Jerusalem, and finally, if the British could be persuaded to go along, the Arab powers would fall in line and the United States would be able to create a position of reasonable strength in the whole Middle East area, including Iran.

The President said that Mr. Jackson was absolutely right, but, unhappily, what he proposed would take a long time, and we are in the midst of a crisis. "I'd pay a lot", said the President, "for this peace between Egypt and Israel."

Secretary Dulles added that this case was on the agenda for his forthcoming talks with Anthony Eden.

The President then reverted to Secretary Dulles' third course of action, which involved giving material and financial support to Mossadegh.

That, said Secretary Dulles, would certainly give us time, but he would like to hear now from the Joint Chiefs of Staff as to the value of gaining time.

General Vandenberg responded by a statement that the only real reason for gaining time was to get the Middle East Defense Organization started.[6] If the MEDO begins to function it might very well provide the stability that we so desperately needed in the Middle East. General Vandenberg, however, confirmed the President's opinion that it would take a very long time to get US or UN troops in position in Iran. . . .

General Vandenberg warned, however, that there was now more serious question as to the loyalty of the Iranian armed forces to the Shah. The latter had had several opportunities to assure himself of the loyalty of his armed forces, but, as in other cases, had lost his opportunity. There was now a new Chief of Staff of the Army who was one of Mossadegh's own choice.

Secretary Humphrey expressed himself as shocked to think that we were contemplating the loss of Iran in this fashion, and Mr. Cutler again inquired of the Secretary of State whether it would not be possible, in the forthcoming conversations with the British, to induce them to waive their claims and let the United States proceed to negotiate unilaterally with Iran. The British had lost their investment in Iran in any case, and a unilateral course of action by the United States was about the only thing which had not been tried.

---

[6] For documentation regarding the interest of the United States in developing a regional security organization in the Middle East, see vol. IX, Part 1, pp. 1 ff.

The President was impressed with this argument, and informed Secretary Dulles that he ought to try to work out a position with the British that would save their face but actually give the United States control of the situation and freedom to act along the lines suggested by Mr. Cutler.

Secretary Dulles answered that he had already talked about this to Mr. Eden in the course of his recent visit to London.[7] He had found that the British did not anticipate any real crisis in Iran for a long time to come.

Secretary Humphrey interposed with the statement that the British always said that you could perfectly well take your time, and cited instances where their estimate had been wrong.

The President said that the latest illustration of their wrongness was in Egypt.

The Vice President said that there was yet another factor to be considered in discussing this problem with Mr. Eden. It was the Vice President's opinion that greater rather than less hostility was to be expected from the Russians after Stalin's death. It was quite likely, therefore, that they would increase their pressure in Iran to secure its control as rapidly as possible by a *coup d' état*. Such a course of action might constitute the miscalculation, which we all dreaded which would cause the beginning of World War III. Could not the British be made to see this dangerous potentiality? We, not the Russians, insisted the Vice President, must make the next move.

Secretary Dulles complained that we are constantly slowed up by the British, French, and other of our allies, in actions which we feel it is vital to take in many parts of the world. They slow us up, we can't move in time to avert the consequences of our tardiness. Perhaps something like Supreme War Council is the only solution for this situation. At any rate, some mechanism should be found which would enable us to act in time at the critical moment.

The Vice President rejoined that if the next move on the world scene could be ours and not Russia's the whole situation in the world might change for the better.

The President said that if a real Soviet move against Iran actually comes, we shall have to face at this council table the question of going to full mobilization. If we did not move at time and in that eventuality, he feared that the United States would descend to the status of a second-rate power. "If", said the President, "I had $500,000,000 of money to spend in secret, I would get $100,000,000 of it to Iran right now."

---

[7]See footnotes 5 and 7, Document 295.

The President then inquired of Secretary Dulles how soon it would be possible for the President and Secretary Dulles to sit down with Mr. Eden. Would it be possible this evening? We must find out immediately how the British really feel—whether they are ready to concede to us on this situation, or whether they are going to be stiff-necked. The question of unilateral action by the United States was clearly posed.

Secretary Humphrey interjected several times his conviction that this was the propitious moment to strike a bargain with the British, who were in need of assistance from us, and Mr. Stassen added that we ought also to try to indicate that it is not an objective of United States policy to liquidate the British Empire. If the British and, for that matter, the French could be induced to believe this, they might prove more amenable to leadership by the Secretary of State.

Secretary Wilson said that there seemed to him to be two great things in the world to which the United States did not have an answer. One was the obvious collapse of colonialism; the other was Communism's new tactics in exploiting nationalism and colonialism for its own purposes. In the old days, when dictatorships changed it was usually a matter of one faction of the right against another, and we had only to wait until the situation subsided. Nowadays, however, when a dictatorship of the right was replaced by a dictatorship of the left, a state would presently slide into Communism and was irrevocably lost to us.

Mr. Stassen had already stated, in reply to the President's wish that he had money, that the Mutual Security Administration had available funds.

The President therefore turned to Mr. Stassen and asked him how much he could actually dig up.

Mr. Stassen replied that he could probably find as much as the situation required—five million, ten million, forty million—if Secretary Dulles decided that he could make headway by the use of such funds.

Apropos of a statement by the President, that he also wished that for a change he could read about mobs in these Middle Eastern states rioting and waving American flags, Mr. Jackson said that if the President wanted the mobs he was sure he could produce them.

The President said in any case it was a matter of great distress to him that we seemed unable to get some of the people in these down-trodden countries to like us instead of hating us.

At this point in the discussion Mr. Cutler interposed to read a four-point record of possible action by the Council on this particular item, which included an attempt to explore with the British the possibility of unilateral United States action in Iran.

The President replied that it certainly seemed to him about time for the British to allow us to try our hand.

Mr. Jackson then said he had another point which he felt would contribute to an improvement of our position in the Middle East and about which he felt it was possible to do something. This was American action to remove the festering sore in the Middle East represented by the 800,000 Arab displaced persons in Israel.

Secretary Dulles agreed that this was indeed a festering sore, but pointed out that the Arab countries themselves were unwilling to absorb these 800,000 unfortunate people, since to do so would deprive them of a bargaining point in their dealings with the Israelis. Accordingly, said Secretary Dulles, he did not see what could be done about them.

Mr. Jackson replied that it would certainly be possible to resettle 200,000 of these refugees, and that all 800,000 could at least be fed.

The President added that it was not enough to feed them, but that he would be awfully glad if we could get some one of the Arab countries to take these people if we would pay a subsidy for each head.

After General Vandenberg had informed the Council that there was one point relevant to the military aspects of the Iranian problem, namely, the existence of a fair-sized British force in Iraq, Mr. Stassen inquired whether it was indeed the President's view that some funds should be expended at once in Iran if the Secretary of State agreed.

The President replied that of course this was a gamble, but if upon examination it seemed a good gamble, he was prepared to take it.

The National Security Council:[8]

a. Discussed the subject in the light of an oral briefing by the Director of Central Intelligence.

b. Agreed that the following possible courses of action should be explored in anticipation of further Council action at the next regular or special meeting:

> (1) Persuading the British to permit the United States to put the Iranian oil industry in operation, without prejudice to an ultimate settlement of the Anglo-Iranian controversy.
>
> (2) The military feasibility of holding a line through the Zagros Mountain range.
>
> (3) Replacement of Ambassador Henderson.

---

[8] Paragraphs a–b constitute NSC Action No. 729. (S/S–NSC (Miscellaneous) files, lot 66 D 95, "Record of Actions by the NSC, 1953")

(4) Provision of limited economic aid to strengthen Mossadegh's position.

[Here follows discussion of basic national security policies.]

S. EVERETT GLEASON

No. 313

788.00/3-653: Telegram

The Ambassador in Iran (Henderson) to the Department of State[1]

TOP SECRET   PRIORITY   TEHRAN, March 6, 1953—5 p. m.

3576. 1. Arrests or removal from key positions of officers armed forces considered as more loyal to Shah than to Prime Minister are sharpening dissatisfaction in military circles with course events and at same time are rendering it progressively more difficult for this dissatisfaction to be expressed through direct action. Nevertheless possibility and advisability of attempting military *coup d' état* continues be surreptitiously discussed. Whether these discussions will result in recourse violence or merely in further arrests not fully clear. Tendency of most educated Iranians to prefer talk to action combined with incapacity organize causes us to have considerable doubt ability groups loyal to Shah stage successful coup at this time.

2. According Palace sources Shah has not totally abandoned struggle despite statements ascribed to him to effect he supporting Mosadeq. These sources insist he has sent secret messages to opposition in Majlis and to other civilian and military groups loyal to him asking for continued support and indicating that he has been passive thus far merely because of his belief that he not yet in position openly to resist Mosadeq. These sources say Shah still has hope Mosadeq government will be overthrown by peaceful means in not distant future.

3. Difficult for us believe Shah really would have courage or resolution to take part in movement to effect either by force or peacefully downfall Mosadeq government. He would undoubtedly be frightened at thought of military coup being attempted in his name and if given opportunity would probably try discourage it. Miscarriage of attempted coup would be likely to complete ruin of Shah and dynasty, to result in increase of arrests of persons suspect-

---

[1] Also sent to London.

ed of pro-British sympathies, and to strengthen forces antipathetic to west.

HENDERSON

No. 314

788.00/3–753: Telegram

The Secretary of State to the Embassy in the United Kingdom[1]

TOP SECRET   WASHINGTON, March 7, 1953—3:58 p. m.

5959. Secy in Mar 6 mtg with Eden[2] gave following evaluation present Iranian political situation. While picture still obscure authority Shah has probably largely and permanently disappeared. Mosadeq will probably come through present situation remaining in power. As a result, however, loss authority and prestige by Shah and Army risk of Iran going Communist greater and possibility of transition to an orderly govt when Mosadeq does fall diminished. End evaluation.

Secy indicated if Mosadeq rejects present oil proposal we do not intend to make another believing under this contingency oil question shld be held in suspense. Under such situation large scale US financing Mosadeq Govt not contemplated. Mosadeq shld not receive a premium for acting as he has. There shld be no large US purchases oil. However, we shld be tolerant of minor measures sufficient to keep Mosadeq barely afloat and thus attempt avoid disastrous possibility of Communists replacing him. Illustrative minor steps might include such items as arranging small sales of oil or letting Jones technicians go to Iran.[3]

Eden made strongest kind of plea that we not permit Jones technicians go stating effect thereof in UK would be very serious. He made plea that we render assistance in ways not directly related to oil. Secy felt certain aspects problem wld have to be played by ear

---

[1] Also sent to Tehran. Drafted by Raynor, approved by Jernegan, and cleared with Bonbright.

[2] See footnote 4, Document 312.

[3] According to a memorandum to the Secretary of State from Byroade, Mar. 4, Alton Jones, President of Cities Service, when leaving Iran in late summer of 1952, indicated that his company might supply technicians to the Iranian oil industry if requested. Since that time the Iranians pressed him to furnish these technicians, but Jones refused because he thought it would cause the administration embarrassment. The British also felt that the dispatch of these people would have adverse effects on British public opinion. Despite this fact, however, Byroade recommended that Secretary of State Dulles inform Foreign Secretary Eden that the U.S. Government could no longer discourage Jones from sending technicians to Iran. (888.2553/3–453)

of Iran" (OARMA, Tehran M–175, August 10),[4] while Embassy believes for near future schismatic factors within regime may lack sufficient strength manifest themselves. Any tactic of potential opposition in boring from within regime would take some time. On this point, however, it should be emphasized that Tudeh has consistently followed this tactic with increasing success among Mosadeq's entourage.

5. Mosadeq has tried through suppression opposition to make reality of his theme to West that it must choose between him and Tudeh. It believed that deterioration of country, Tudeh infiltration state administration, and growth discontent at all levels population make this rationale untenable today. Embassy thinks under current conditions so long as security forces remain substantially unaffected by Tudeh infiltration, despite latter's program designed capture civil authority, that these forces, together with non-Communist elements in Iran, still could offer alternative to Mosadeq other than Tudeh Party.

MATTISON

---

[4]Not found in Department of State files.

No. 342

788.00/8-1653: Telegram

The Chargé in Iran (Mattison) to the Department of State[1]

RESTRICTED   NIACT   TEHRAN, August 16, 1953—9 a. m.

331. At early hour this morning Embassy received reports of confusing nature to effect that Shah had issued decree removing Mosadeq as Prime Minister and that resultant activity had involved various troop movements and arrests in Tehran. At 7 a. m. Radio Tehran announced *coup d'état* against Mosadeq government had been attempted last night and had been successfully thwarted by government. Information received by Embassy at about same time tended confirm fact government had situation under control.

ARMISH has been informed General Riahi, Chief of Staff, under orders Prime Minister has arrested three of five brigade commanders Tehran garrison and General Kiani, Assistant Chief of Staff. Meeting at Iranian officers club now in progress presided by General Riahi attended by general officers.

MATTISON

---

[1]Repeated to London and Beirut for Ambassador Henderson.

No. 343

788.00/8-1653: Telegram

The Chargé in Iran (Mattison) to the Department of State[1]

RESTRICTED   NIACT   TEHRAN, August 16, 1953—10 a. m.

333. Embassy received unconfirmed report from good source Shah in dismissing Mosadeq issued royal decree appointing General Zahedi Prime Minister. Reports also received Acting Minister Court Amini and other court officials arrested this morning.

Up to 9:30 a. m. city appears calm, extra police on duty, with tanks and truck loads security forces around royal palaces and Prime Minister's residence. Embassy eyewitness reports seeing orderly crowd approximately 200 proceeding toward Baharestan Square waving Iranian flags.

Prime Minister's office phoned Embassy 8:45 a. m. advising Embassy and Point IV close as trouble expected. Appropriate instructions issued.

Rumors now prevalent and received by varied Embassy sources to effect alleged coup inspired by government. Reasoning behind this general impression is this action necessary give Mosadeq excuse move against Shah.

MATTISON

[1]Repeated to London and Beirut for Ambassador Henderson.

No. 344

788.00/8-1653: Telegram

The Chargé in Iran (Mattison) to the Department of State[1]

RESTRICTED   NIACT   TEHRAN, August 16, 1953—3 p. m.

342. Late morning August 16, correspondents Donald Schwind, Associated Press, and Kenneth Love, *New York Times*, went to hills north of Tehran at request son of General Zahedi for conference. Zahedi not present, but son showed signed decree from Shah and gave photostats of it to newsmen.

Decree, signed by Shah, dated Thursday, August 13, 1953, said:

"View of fact situation of nation necessitates appointment of an informed and experienced man who can grasp affairs of country readily, I therefore, with knowledge I have of your ability and

[1]Repeated to London and Beirut for Ambassador Henderson.

merit, appoint you with this letter Prime Minister. We give into your hands duty to improve affairs of the nation and remove present crisis and raise living standard of people."

Zahedi's son said father naturally in hiding; that coup not intended; that Colonel Nasari went to Prime Minister's home this morning with soldiers to present this decree to Mosadeq and was arrested by guards.

Translator US Embassy, well acquainted with Shah's signature because previous employment, saw photostat and declared belief Shah's signature genuine.

MATTISON

No. 345

788.00/8–1753: Telegram

The Ambassador in Iraq (Berry) to the Department of State[1]

TOP SECRET   PRIORITY   BAGHDAD, August 17, 1953—7 a. m.

92. For Under Secretary—no distribution. Shah of Iran expressed to Iraqi Government desire to meet me.[2] In order to provide Department with first hand account of recent Iranian events as Shah sees them, and recalling his basic pro-western attitude and Department's policy of supporting him, I called quietly at 9:30 last evening at Iraqi official guest house where he is staying. I found Shah worn from three sleepless nights, puzzled by turn of events, but with no bitterness toward Americans . . . .

Shah stated that in recent weeks he had felt increasingly that he would have to take action against Mosadeq as the latter became bolder in flouting Iranian Constitution. Therefore, when a fortnight ago it was suggested that he sponsor a military coup he accepted the idea. However, in giving it more thought he decided that such action as he took must be within the framework of his constitutional power, hence, not a coup. Thus, . . . decided to appoint General Zahedi as Prime Minister in place of Mosadeq. After being assured that everything was arranged and that there was no possibility of failure, he left Tehran for his Caspian Palace in order to put Mosadeq off guard and from there three days ago sent letter of appointment of General Zahedi to Tehran with a trusted Iranian Colonel. The letter was delivered to General Zahedi and he was to choose

---

[1] Repeated to Tehran.

[2] According to telegram 90 from Baghdad, Aug. 16, the Shah and Queen arrived in Baghdad that morning following the apparent failure of an army *coup d'état* against the Mosadeq government. (788.11/8–1653)

the timing and method for informing Mosadeq. The Shah expected action would take place that very day. But no action took place, apparently because message arrived too late in day, and no action took place the following day, apparently because it was a holiday. On the third day Mosadeq by some means had been alerted and had had the time to take successful countermeasures so that when the Colonel arrived at Mosadeq's house he was himself arrested.

This morning the Shah left his Caspian Palace in a Beechcraft with a pilot, one Palace official and his Queen and landed in Baghdad at 10:15. King Faisal returned from Jordan at 11:00. This afternoon the Shah called upon King Faisal and King Faisal returned the call, offering hospitality, but, lacking the supporting presence of his uncle who is in Cairo, seeming somewhat overpowered by events.

The Shah said that he will have to issue a statement very soon and possibly tomorrow. He needs, however, to be informed of the situation in Tehran . . . . He will try to hold off giving out a statement until he gets advice, but the pressure to issue is great and mounting. He is thinking of saying in his statement that three days ago he dismissed Prime Minister Mosadeq and appointed General Zahedi as Prime Minister, taking his action because Mosadeq had continually violated the constitution. As he himself had sworn, upon ascending the throne, to respect and uphold the constitution, he had no choice, but to remove the Prime Minister of a government acting unconstitutionally. When it was apparent that his orders were not being followed, he left the country to prevent bloodshed and further damage. He is ready to return when he can serve the Iranian people and in the meantime prays for the independence and safety of Iran and that all true Iranians will never allow their country to fall under the control of the illegal Tudeh Party.

The Shah said that he is utterly at loss to understand why the plan failed. Trusted Palace officials were completely sure of its succeeding. . . . Now he needs information and advice upon his next move. He said that he thought that he should not stay here more than a few days, but would then go to Europe and he hoped eventually to America. He added he would be looking for work shortly as he has a large family and very small means outside of Iran. I tried to boost his morale by saying that I hoped that soon he would return to reign over his people for whom he had done so much, but he replied that Mosadeq was absolutely mad and insanely jealous, like a tiger who springs upon any living thing that it sees moving above him. Shah believes Mosadeq thinks he can form a partnership with the Tudeh Party and then outwit it, but in so doing Mosadeq will become the Dr. Benes of Iran.

BERRY

No. 346

788.00/8-1853

Memorandum by the Under Secretary of State (Smith) to the President

TOP SECRET   [WASHINGTON,] August 18, 1953.

The attached message[1] is self-explanatory and will give you the Iranian situation in a nutshell. The move failed because of three days of delay and vacillation by the Iranian generals concerned, during which time Mosadeq apparently found out all that was happening. Actually it was a *counter*-coup, as the Shah acted within his constitutional power in signing the firman replacing Mosadeq. The old boy wouldn't accept this and arrested the messenger and everybody else involved that he could get his hands on. We now have to take a whole new look at the Iranian situation and probably have to snuggle up to Mosadeq if we're going to save anything there. I daresay this means a little added difficulty with the British.

WBS

[1] According to information on the source text, the message attached for the President's consideration was telegram 92, *supra*.

No. 347

788.00/8-1853: Telegram

The Ambassador in Iran (Henderson) to the Department of State[1]

SECRET   NIACT   TEHRAN, August 18, 1953—10 p. m.

384. 1. My talk with Mosadeq this evening lasted one hour. He received me fully dressed (not pajama clad) as though for ceremonial occasion. He was as usual courteous but I could detect in his attitude certain amount smoldering resentment. Usual exchange amenities after which I expressed sorrow at chain events since my departure over two months ago, adding I sorry see Iran apparently

[1] Transmitted in three sections; repeated to London. Ambassador Henderson returned to Tehran on Aug. 17.

even worse off politically and economically than it was then. He acknowledged my statement with sarcastic smile and there lull in conversation.

2. I remarked I particularly concerned increasing number attacks on American citizens. After Shiraz incident he had issued instructions to law enforcement agencies which had afforded high degree protection to American nationals. Unfortunately law enforcement agencies appeared again to be becoming lax. Every hour or two I receiving additional reports attacks on American citizens not only in Tehran but also other localities.

3. He said these attacks almost inevitable. Iranian people thought Americans were disagreeing with them and, therefore, were attacking Americans. I said disagreements no reason for attacks. He replied Iran in throes revolution and in revolutionary stress and strain it would require three times as many police as exist to afford full protection to American citizens. I should remember that in American Revolutionary times when Americans wanted British out, many Britishers in US were attacked. I said if Iranians wanted Americans out individual attacks not necessary. We would go en masse. He said Iranian Government did not want Americans leave but some individual Iranians did and, therefore, were attacking them. I replied Chiefs of American military mission, American *gendarmérie* mission, and TCI had informed me today that Iranian officials with whom they dealt had assured them they were anxious that these missions continue to function in Iran. These missions could be assured of maximum cooperation from Iranian authorities. These chiefs had also told me that at no time had they been receiving more full and effective cooperation from Iranian authorities than at present. I had refrained from informing Washington of this situation until I could talk with him. I wanted to know what his present attitude was re these American aid missions and also re giving adequate protection to members these missions. It did not make sense for certain Iranian authorities to insist that these missions remain in Iran while members of these missions were subject to insults and attacks from gangs of hoodlums.

4. Prime Minister said he sure law enforcement agencies doing all possible give protection. I disagreed and read to him excerpts various memoranda which I had received from members American aid missions during course of day, some of which indicated that police were passive while they were being attacked. He said he wished assure me that he desired aid missions to stay. He thought they were performing valuable services and would look further into matter protection of their members.

5. After another lull I told him I would be grateful if he would tell me confidentially for use my government, just what had hap-

pened during recent days. US Government interested with respect both events and legal situation. He chose interpret my remarks as reference to President's letter to him last July. He reminded me that we had had agreement to effect existence these letters would be confidential and exchange would not be published unless US reply would be favorable. He maintained American officials either in Washington or in Tehran had directly or indirectly deliberately leaked information to pro-British Iranian press re this exchange and against his will US had insisted on publishing notes. He said he had actually never consented to their publication and was astonished to receive letter from Embassy expressing appreciation his willingness that exchange be published. When he saw US Government was determined to publish, he had finally insisted previous messages exchanged last January between him and President-elect be also published. I told him it had been my understanding leak had occurred in his office and in view distorted public version of President's letter unfavorable to US, US Government had thereupon insisted exchange be published. He denied heatedly Iranians had been guilty of leaks. No Iranian except himself and Saleh, US Embassy Iranian assistant and interpreter, had been aware of existence these letters. He had kept them among his own private papers, not in office files. I intimated I not sure his private papers were kept in manner which would prevent clever agents having access to them. I also pointed out there were certain modern hearing devices which might result in knowledge this kind falling into possession of agents parties hostile both to Iran and US. He continued insist certain Americans had deliberately leaked in order that public knowledge of contents of President's letter might weaken his government. I told him that I knew that exchange had been handled in US and Tehran in most discreet manner by trusted officials and I sure no US leak.

6. Mosadeq then outlined events which led to dissolution Majlis. His narrative in general line with information already furnished Department by Embassy. He maintained however that 30 members Majlis had been bought outright by British. Only 40 votes had not been bought. Ten of these 40 votes could easily have been purchased for 100,000 tomans and when he learned that negotiations were in progress to complete such purchasing operation he decided that British-purchased Majlis was unworthy of Iranian people and should be eliminated. He asked me if I had any comments to make regarding his dissolution Majlis.

7. I reminded him he inviting me comment on Iran internal affairs. I realized it not usual for comments of this kind to be offered by foreign diplomat. Nevertheless he would recall that during some of our past conversations I had overcome my scruples in this re-

spect. I said only comment which I wished to offer at this point was that it seemed to me unfortunate for Iran and no compliment Iranian people that Government of Iran apparently could not be based on a Parliament. Iran was in most dangerous international position and I thought it would be more secure if all organs provided for in Iranian constitution could be functioning with at least certain degree of harmony.

8. I told him I particularly interested in events recent days. I would like to know more about effort replace him by General Zahedi. He said on evening of 15th Col. Nasiri had approached his house apparently to arrest him. Col. Nasiri himself, however, had been arrested and number other arrests followed. He had taken oath not try to oust Shah and would have lived up this oath if Shah had not engaged in venture this kind. Clear Nasiri had been sent by Shah arrest him and Shah had been prompted by British.

9. I asked Mosadeq if he had reason believe it true Shah had issued firman (decree) removing him as Prime Minister and appointing Zahedi in his place. Mosadeq said he had never seen such decree and if he had it would have made no difference. His position for some time had been that Shah's powers were only of ceremonial character; that Shah had no right on his personal responsibility issue firman calling for change in government. I said I particularly interested in this point, and I would like to report it carefully to United States Government. Was I to understand (a) he had no official knowledge that Shah had issued firman removing him as Prime Minister, and (b) even if he should find that Shah had issued such firman in present circumstances he would consider it to be invalid? He replied "precisely".

10. Before departing I told Mosadeq that during 24 hours since my return Tehran, members American official family here had received intimations from various Iranian authorities which caused me believe some Iranian officials suspected Embassy harboring Iranian political refugees. I would like tell him point blank this untrue. My present policy in this respect was as follows: (a) if political refugees should endeavor to enter Embassy, efforts would be made to stop them; (b) if they should succeed in entering compound, efforts would be made to persuade them to leave voluntarily; (c) if they should refuse to leave voluntarily, it my intention to notify Iranian authorities that persons had taken refuge in Embassy and that I was telegraphing my government for instructions.

11. Mosadeq thanked me for my statement and said he would like add statement of his own. In case any Iranian political fugitives would take refuge in Embassy, he would like Embassy keep them there. I asked if in such event Iranian Government prepared defray expenses for lodging and food or whether he would expect

this to come out of Point IV funds. He said Iranian Government would be glad, despite limited budget, pay expenses these refugees.

12. Mosadeq seemed to be in much better frame of mind when I left him. Nevertheless, from his unusual reserve I inclined believe that he suspicious United States Government or at least United States officials either implicated in effort oust him or sympathetically aware of such effort in advance. His remarks to me were interspersed with number little jibes which, although semi-jocular in character, were, nevertheless, barbed. These jibes in general hinted that United States was conniving with British in effort remove him as Prime Minister. For instance, he remarked at one point national movement was determined remain in power in Iran and it would continue to hold on to last man, even though all its members would be run over by British and American tanks. When I raised my eyebrows at this remark, he laughed heartily.

13. Hope special care be taken prevent leaks contents this message.

HENDERSON

No. 348

788.00/8-2053: Telegram

The Ambassador in Iran (Henderson) to the Department of State[1]

CONFIDENTIAL   NIACT   TEHRAN, August 20, 1953—noon.

419. 1. Too early as yet to furnish precise detailed report of events last 36 hours. Nevertheless we shall attempt herein give preliminary outline assessing flow of events in light such knowledge at present available to us.

2. Evening August 18 break appeared to take place between Communist-controlled Tudeh and Mosadeq regime. Apparently Tudeh partisans began demonstrating on streets without having obtained usual appropriate clearance from Mosadeq and engaged in acts violence. Mosadeq ordered streets cleared and cessation of demonstrations. For first time in several months serious fighting took place between security forces and Tudeh.

3. Morning August 19 supporters Shah had arranged pro-Shah demonstration for purpose of showing sentiment continued exist in country for him. This demonstration began in small way in bazaar area but initial small flame found amazingly large amount combustible material and was soon roaring blaze which during course of

---

[1] Transmitted in three sections; repeated to London, Rome, Dhahran, and Baghdad.

day swept through entire city. Security forces sent to put down demonstration refused to resort to violence against crowd some joining demonstrators and others remaining passive. As crowds increased in volume in various parts city they destroyed offices of those newspapers which during recent days had been most scurrilous in their attacks on Shah including most violently pro-government and pro-Communist organs. One of first strategic points seized was Office of Posts and Telegrams which was used in sending messages to stir up whole country. From center city huge crowds commandeered vehicles of all kinds and rushed northward engulfing Tehran Radio Station. Members of Embassy had good opportunity observing character these crowds at this time. They were primarily civilians interspersed with members Security Forces some of whom bore arms. Crowds however appeared to be led and directed by civilians rather than military. Participants not of hoodlum type customarily predominant in recent demonstrations in Tehran. They seemed to come from all classes of people including workers, clerks, shopkeepers, students, et cetera. Crowds seemed to be imbued with strange mixture resolution and gaiety. Holiday mood which seemed to prevail did not prevent execution of grim missions which on at least two occasions resulted in loss life. Defenders radio station failed to put it out commission. By early afternoon it was effective means of maintaining high morale of demonstrators and of transforming their enthusiasm.

4. In early part of day attacks made by demonstrators against House Prime Minister and against General Staff were repulsed with some loss life. Later in day, however, despite resistance defenders Prime Minister's house overrun and gutted. Apparently he had in meantime, escaped and gone into hiding. Shortly before night-fall General Staff offices fell into possession Zahedi Government[2] and General Batmanqilich assumed his duties as Chief of Staff. Almost simultaneously General Zahedi occupied desk in Prime Minister's office which had not been used by Mosadeq.

5. Considerable concern up to night-fall regarding what attitude commanders of military units in suburbs Tehran might take. Some fear lest under orders General Riahi Mosadeq's Chief of Staff they would descend on city during night and retake it on behalf Mosadeq. Also rumors afloat that Tudeh was preparing "show its hand" after public enthusiasm pro-Shah crowds had worn itself out and they had dispersed. When, however, Batmanqilich assumed duties Chief of Staff it would seem all army units in vicinity Tehran automatically began taking orders from him. It then became possible for orders to be issued clearing streets and proclamation 8 o'clock

---

[2]The Zahedi government came to power the previous day, Aug. 19.

curfew. Since 8 p.m. last evening strict law and order has prevailed. Plans to arrest prominent members Tudeh party early this morning seem to have failed as result of inefficiency of police. Tudeh reputed to be gathering for counterattack this morning. Security forces being assembled to thwart this counter move. Outcome this struggle extremely important for security city and future Iran.

6. At this moment no reliable news from provinces. Unconfirmed reports, however, would indicate most of Iran is at present under control of forces new government. According one report some resistance Isfahan. More information this respect will be included in subsequent factual telegrams.

7. Not only members Mosadeq regime but also pro-Shah supporters amazed at latter's comparatively speedy and easy initial victory which was achieved with high degree spontaneity. Among factors believed responsible for this are following:

a. Iranian people of all classes were disgusted at bad taste exhibited by anti-Shah elements supporting Mosadeq. For instance, they were outraged when gangs of hooligans bearing red flags and chanting Commie songs began tearing down statues of Shah and father, breaking into houses and shops for purpose destroying Shah's pictures, etc. They were repelled by vituperative language employed by Foreign Minister Fatemi and by Iranian newspaper editors in attacking Shah.

b. Iranian people of all classes in general also worried by what seemed to be at least temporary alliance between Mosadeq and Tudeh. They were alarmed at seeing thousands of Tudeh demonstrators whom they regard as agents Soviet Union marching openly arm-in-arm through streets denouncing Shah and Western countries particularly US. Tudeh clearly overplayed hand by causing Iranian people believe latter had to choose between Mosadeq and Soviet Union on one hand and Shah and Western world on other.

c. Iranian people had become thoroughly tired of stresses and strains of last two years. They yearned for period of quietness which would give them chance to improve their economic and social status. Many had lost hope of improving their conditions under Mosadeq.

d. Rupture which had taken place between Mosadeq regime and Tudeh on evening August 18 prevented effective cooperation on morning August 19 between these two anti-Shah forces in facing pro-Shah demonstrators. Tudeh was conspicuously absent all day. It possible that Tudeh leaders were sure that during course of day they would be called upon by Mosadeq regime come to its assistance. However, once demonstrations got underway Mosadeq regime not in position ask for such help.

e. Most armed forces and great numbers Iranian civilians inherently loyal to Shah whom they have been taught to believe is symbol of national unity as well as of stability of country. Army in particular extremely friendly US partly as result fear of strong

No. 351

788.00/8–2153: Telegram

The Ambassador in Iran (Henderson) to the Department of State[1]

SECRET   NIACT   TEHRAN, August 21, 1953—2 p. m.

436. 1. Unfortunately impression becoming rather widespread that in some way or other this Embassy or at least US Government has contributed with funds and technical assistance to overthrow Mosadeq and establish Zahedi Government. Iranians unable believe any important political development can take place in country without foreigners being involved. Intensive propaganda in Tudeh newspapers prior to their disappearance and over Soviet Radio that US Embassy working for Shah and Zahedi against Mosadeq has helped create this impression. Public, therefore, in general, inclined interpret various incidents or remarks as evidence American intervention. For instance, fact member American Embassy staff happened to be living in same compound in which Zahedi understood to have taken refuge has been interpreted to mean that this American was harboring Zahedi even though Iranian landlord who also resides in this compound is also being given the credit for protecting Zahedi. Remarks by associates of Zahedi to effect Iran deeply indebted to Americans for success their efforts also being given deeper meaning than intended. Undoubtedly during struggle between forces Shah and Mosadeq considerable sums were expended by both sides. Iranians living up to their old traditions have tendency credit foreigners with financing side which they supposed to be favoring.

2. For moment at least more praise than criticism heard from those who believe US involved in shift of government. Nevertheless we doing utmost discreetly to remove this impression because (a) it not in US interest over long run to be given credit for internal political developments in Iran even if those developments might be to Iran's advantage; (b) Zahedi's Government will be somewhat handicapped if impression continues that it creature foreigners; (c) Zahedi's Government like all governments of Iran eventually will become unpopular and at that time US might be blamed for its existence. We do not believe, however, that it would serve any good purpose for Embassy to make formal denials.

3. We do not believe it would serve any useful purpose as far as Iran is concerned for Department to deny US intervention unless it receives inquiries of character which would render such denial de-

---

[1] Repeated to London.

sirable. It might be useful, however, if spokesman for Department could find suitable occasion stress in factual way spontaneity of movement in Iran in favor of new Government, touching upon some factors which according to reports received from various sources responsible for what has happened. In making these suggestions I realize perhaps charges already made over Soviet Radio are of character which cannot be ignored. Denial these charges would of course give Department one such occasion. We sincerely hope means can be found either through US Government channels or through private American news dissemination channels for American and world publics to understand that victory of Shah was result will Iranian people. Such comments in this respect as are made by Department or private news agencies could be immediately useful here if disseminated by means USIA news bulletin and over VOA.

HENDERSON

No. 352

S/P-NSC files, lot 61 D 167, "Iran, US Policy Regarding the Present Situation, NSC 117, 136. 136/1"

Memorandum by the Assistant Secretary of State for Near Eastern, South Asian, and African Affairs (Byroade) to the Director of the Policy Planning Staff (Bowie)[1]

[Extracts]

SECRET   WASHINGTON, August 21, 1953.

Subject: Iran

Problem

A. How will the Iranian situation be affected by the recent change of government?

B. What attitude should the United States take toward the Zahedi government?

Discussion

A revolution is in progress in Iran. It has deep-rooted origins in the wave of nationalism sweeping Asia. The old pattern of rule has been irrevocably shattered and any leader must shape his program on the basis of nationalist aspirations.

The replacement of Dr. Mosadeq by General Zahedi is not a reversal of this trend. It is still too early accurately to appraise the

---

[1] Drafted by Stutesman and approved by Richards.

No. 353

788.11/8-2353: Telegram

The Ambassador in Iran (Henderson) to the Department of State[1]

TOP SECRET   NIACT   TEHRAN, August 23, 1953—10 p. m.

466. At Shah's request that I visit him privately without publicity, I saw him six o'clock this evening. Pirnia, master of ceremonies, who met me rear entrance Palace, said I would find Shah changed man. He was right. Shah showed vigor, decisiveness and certain amount clear thinking which I had not found in him before. Only time will determine whether this change merely temporary result discovery that people of country had deeper sense of loyalty him than he had realized. In any event, I did not find hesitation, brooding, discouragement and air "what can I do" which I had noticed practically all previous conversations.

2. He greeted me warmly and expressed deep appreciation of friendship which US had shown him and Iran during period. I read oral message from President to which I had taken liberty of adding introductory paragraph as follows: "I congratulate you for the great moral courage which you displayed at a critical time in your country's history. I am convinced that by your action you contributed much to the preservation of the independence and to the future prosperity of Iran."[2] The Shah wept as I read this message and asked me in reply to tell the President how grateful he was for interest which President and Government of US had shown in Iran. He would always feel deeply indebted for this proof of genuine friendship. Miracle of saving Iran which had just been wrought was due to friendship West, to patriotism Iranian people and to intermediation God. It impossible for him believe so many factors could have contributed simultaneously to this salvation his country unless Providence had so willed.

3. Shah dwelt for some time on part which "common people of Iran" had played. People of poorest classes who were ill-clad and hungry had been willing sacrifice their lives on his behalf. He could never forget this and he would never be satisfied until hunger had been eliminated from his country. Iran had been saved

---

[1]Transmitted in two sections; repeated to London.

[2]No copy of this oral message from the President has been found in Department of State files. According to telegram 922 to London, however, Henderson was authorized on Aug. 22 to give the Shah a short oral message from the President. (788.11/8-2353) Henderson also suggested in telegram 462, Aug. 23, that, in addition to the President issuing a public message of congratulation, he, Henderson, should be authorized to convey privately and orally a message from the President to the Shah on his recent success. (788.11/8-2353)

but victory would be short-lived unless substantial aid came from US immediately. No time could be lost. This was Iran's last chance to survive as an independent country. I said I agreed that if present government should fail, Communism seemed to be only alternative. He said "if I fail, no alternative but Communism. People have shown their trust in me and it rests upon me prove their trust merited. I must help new government live up to expectations and I cannot do that without quick aid from the US. How soon can this aid come and in what quantities and form?"

4. I replied US prepared extend aid but it must be given in orderly way and in circumstances which would be acceptable US public as well as Iranian public. I had been endeavoring all day to get in touch with financial and economic experts new government in order begin conversations. If he wished quick aid, he should take steps see that conversations begin immediately. He promised talk to Zahedi this evening in effort accelerate.

5. Shah said he not completely happy re Cabinet which Zahedi had presented him on his arrival. Same old faces which had been rotating in office for years. He had hoped for Cabinet which would stimulate country particularly youth. He had been told Americans had insisted Amini be included as Minister Finance and that Cabinet be selected before his arrival and presented to him as *fait accompli*. I told him information incorrect.

I do not know who had selected Amini. Certainly not Americans. There had been feeling in Embassy that Cabinet should be formed quickly so Government could begin to function earliest possible moment, no idea endeavoring have members selected without consultation with him. He said he relieved hear me say this. He sure Americans would not begin trying interfere in personnel matters of Government. They should know from experience this would be surest way change friendship into suspicion. Particularly important no interference in future in his control armed forces. Neither foreigners nor Iranians should come between him and army. Razmara had been unsuccessful in trying to separate army from Shah. Mosadeq had been able to break down army unity. It was his task and it would be difficult and delicate one to rebuild army as solid block loyal to him. Otherwise there would be no stability in country.

6. I asked if I to infer he dissatisfied with way Zahedi had been conducting affairs or if he under impression Zahedi attempting exert authority which should be vested in him. He replied negative insisting he had complete confidence in Zahedi. He did not believe Zahedi had ambitions other than serve Iran and its Shah, nevertheless he thought that certain advisers around Zahedi were pressing latter to take actions without proper consultation with him. He

had had several discussions with Zahedi and was sure that he had achieved understanding with him re extent consultation in future.

I said Zahedi and many other army officers had risked their lives for Shah and country. I hoped Shah would show in some way his appreciation. He said he intended to do so but he must disappoint many retired army officers expecting resume active service. Most of them outmoded, some corrupt. He could give them decorations and other awards but not jobs.

7. In discussing failure of plans on night of August 15 he said someone must have betrayed them. Could it have been British agents?

I expressed surprise. I pointed out on various previous conversations he had said if Iran to be saved necessary for British and Americans to have common policy re Iran and work with mutual confidence. This situation had been achieved and I hoped he would never again make either to British or Americans remarks which might tend undermine that mutual confidence. I knew for fact that British were dealing honestly with him and he should get out of his head once for all idea they engaging in double dealing. He said he relieved hear this and believed me. I told him Communists espionage facilities well developed. They had many dangerous hearing devices. He said perhaps they had broken down code telegrams exchanged between Tehran and Ramsar. I agreed this quite possible.

8. I said if Iran wanted British and US pursue common policy re Iran Government should not expect receive substantial aid from US while it was making British whipping boy. I worried lest when Majlis reassembled there would again take place long tirades against British. I also concerned re Tudeh press in this respect. He said he would endeavor arrange for those members Majlis who had not resigned to meet and vote dissolution Majlis. Elections would then be held in spring so Government could accomplish much without interference Majlis. It was his intention also not to convene Senate until new Majlis elected. He intended taking steps also to reward in some way although not with Cabinet positions small band Majlis members who had at risk lives refused resign. It also his intention completely root out subversive press. He determined completely wreck Tudeh organization while at same time maintaining as correct relations as possible with USSR.[3]

9. In terminating conversation he again urged me impress on US Government importance receiving substantial and immediate fi-

---

[3]The Embassy in London informed the Department and Tehran on Aug. 26 that Lord Salisbury, Acting Foreign Secretary in Eden's absence, requested the Embassy to express to the Department and Ambassador Henderson its appreciation for the position that the Ambassador had taken in paragraphs 7 and 8. (Telegram 816; 788.11/8-2653)

nancial and economic aid. In absence Majlis it would be difficult arrange for loan. Therefore most of this aid must be in form grant. I said if this true we might be severely hampered in our efforts. For instance it might be easier quickly to obtain funds for road building and similar programs through loans rather than grants. He promised look into legal aspects this problem but said he feared it might be impossible for Iranian Government to accept loans without consent Majlis.

HENDERSON

No. 354

788.00/8–2453

Memorandum by the Assistant Secretary of State for Near Eastern, South Asian, and African Affairs (Byroade) to the Acting Secretary of State[1]

SECRET   WASHINGTON, August 24, 1953.

Subject: Message from President to Shah of Iran

Discussion:

Tehran's telegram 461, August 23,[2] informs the Department that has been suggested by the Iranian Chief of Protocol that it would be appropriate for heads of state to send public congratulatory messages to the Shah of Iran. Ambassador Henderson agrees that such a message should be sent. Other diplomatic representatives in Tehran are advising their governments accordingly.

Recommendation:

It is recommended that the President's approval of a public congratulatory message be obtained. A draft of such a message along the lines suggested by Ambassador Henderson is attached.

---

[1] Drafted by Richards.
[2] Not printed. (788.00/8–2353)

But the people were restive. I suggested that some of our
friends quietly persuade members of the committee to disperse.
We did not want to alarm them.

Ardeshir and I remained at the airport until midnight. He
had rustled me a curfew pass. No word came from Baghdad,
Basra or Abadan, where alternate landings might have been
made. Driving past the embassy on the way home, I was flagged
down by a Marine guard. He had just learned from the airport
that the plane had arrived safely at Baghdad. I went to bed relieved and happy. I had been sure we were waiting for news of
disaster.

The morning of December 23, 1951, was startlingly, crystalline
clear. A heavy mantle of snow covered the mountains, the hills
and even the plain. At the Darband I heard a small plane circling over the foothills but paid no attention. At the office an
hour later I learned that a search plane had located the wreckage
of Dr. Bennett's airliner. My shock was even deeper because of
my trust in the false information of the previous night. No satisfactory explanation of that telephone call was ever made.

Ardeshir, son of a prominent Iranian general who later became prime minister, somehow hurriedly obtained a jeep for the
trip into the Elburz foothills. We drove through rutted snow as
far as roads went, then broke trail. Soon the ground became too
rough even for a jeep. At the steep edge of a canyon we began a
slow trek toward the reported site of the wreck. On a hilltop we
saw a shattered propeller standing like a cross. We rounded a
shoulder. In the bottom of the canyon we saw the little that remained of the plane. All but the wings and tail had burned. The
impact had thrown Dr. and Mrs. Bennett forward, clear of the
wreckage. They had died instantly. They were still side by side,
strapped in their seats. Between them lay a Bible which Mrs.
Bennett must have been reading. Most of the twenty-one victims
were in the burned wreckage. One of these was Benjamin Hill
Hardy, chief of public affairs for the Technical Cooperation Ad-

ministration, whom President Truman praised as "a convinced idealist" who made "important contributions" to the Point 4 idea. James Thomas Mitchell, a staff photographer, and Albert Cyril Crilley, a foreign service assistant to Dr. Bennett, had also been on the plane.

As we drove back to town Ardeshir and I took some comfort in the fact that I had not been able to persuade Si Fryer to return. It was impossible not to talk about Dr. Bennett. Ardeshir listened with a friend's indulgent silence.

"I went to say good-by to Dr. Bennett the day before I left Washington," I said. "It was only about five weeks ago. He said that we had a hard job ahead. An easy job, I told him, would not have attracted me any more than such a task would have drawn him. He said he had absolute confidence in the success of Point 4 because it was right for the great United States to help her neighbors as our pioneer forefathers had co-operated with each other on the frontiers. He added that talk of atom bombs did not frighten him. Then he said, 'I think you are like me in that we do not scare easily.' I am sure Dr. Bennett did not scare even at the end."

Ardeshir was one to understand. A tall, handsome young man, he is among the very few I have known whom I believe to be without any sense of fear. He was not reckless beyond reason, but he would and did risk his skin fearlessly when he thought it was important and right to do so. "Right," to him, meant "in the interests of Iran."

Dr. Harris had brought Ardeshir into Point 4. This was not their first contact. On an earlier advisory mission to Iran Dr. Harris had met his father, General Fazlollah Zahedi, and his family and had persuaded Ardeshir, then only a boy, to follow him to USAC to complete his education.

Persian to the very core, Ardeshir was a generous and considerate friend. One must know something of his country's history to understand how he has been molded. His father was a distinguished military commander. He had reached army field grade at an earlier age than any other in Iran's recent history. He had stopped invading rabble in a mountain valley in 1921 and had pacified rebellious tribes in the 1930s without open warfare. He had been interned by the British during the Second World War, and his son, then just a lad, had not known his father's fate for months. Rugged and independent, the general had continued to serve his country where and when he could, though his health had been undermined by some of his experiences. He carried several bullets in him. Ardeshir and his father were deeply attached.

"When you believe in a thing deeply, Bill," Ardeshir explained, "you just have to go ahead whether it's dangerous or not."

In the United States today not many are called on to live dangerously. But peril is not unusual in Iran. Dr. Bennett would have understood Ardeshir. He had died on a gravel bank by an Iranian mountain stream for something he believed in strongly.

Late on the afternoon of Christmas Day we finally completed the last identification of the victims. I returned to the hotel weary and sick at heart. The manager mentioned the forgotten Christmas tree.

"You may take it down," I told him.

"I am sorry, Mr. Warne," he said. "Our little orchestra had learned some of your Christmas carols. Everyone grieves."

During these bad days new technicians kept arriving. Recruiting in the United States was in full swing. Our growth in numbers alarmed some, who doubted our chances of signing a country agreement. A few, more experienced than I in international negotiations, repeatedly urged stopping recruitment. If, as seemed possible, no mission at all were needed in Iran, the cost of assembling one would be wasted. Dispirited one evening shortly after Christmas, I drafted a message that would have had the effect of suspending all further action until an agreement had

"That is past," he reminded Ardeshir, who might have told me more. "Let us turn to the work ahead."

General Zahedi had a hundred things in mind—agricultural advancement, improvement of transportation and roads, resumption of the Shah's land distribution, a program similar to His Majesty's for the peasants of the government-owned villages, an extension of rural education.

I thought as I listened to him that in the optimism of the moment the new prime minister was underestimating the seriousness of some of the problems ahead. He was above all a soldier. And although he had served at various posts in the government he had not had much opportunity to deal with fiscal management. At that moment everyone underestimated the difficulty of Iran's financial predicament.

"I want particularly to complete the railroad," General Zahedi said. "It is disgraceful to have its two main arms outstretched toward Meshed and Tabriz but, after all these years, not reaching them."

On August 26, 1953, the day preceding my call, Prime Minister Zahedi had written to President Eisenhower. His message as printed in the Persian Press expressed gratitude for the assistance already given and for the contribution the American programs had made to raising the standard of technical knowledge in Iran. But the letter went on:

The United States aid being now contributed to Iran, although useful, is unfortunately inadequate in amount and nature to relieve Iran of financial and economic crises facing us. The treasury is empty, there is no foreign exchange available, and the national economy is deteriorated. In order to save Iran from such economic and financial chaos, we need urgent aids.

The prime minister promised that Iran would endeavor to use her wealth and resources to strengthen her economic position and would also strive "to improve Iran's international position."

He said that Iran wished to contribute "her share in the maintenance of world peace and the furtherance of good will in international relations."

President Eisenhower responded in a letter which appeared in the Iranian papers on the same day. The President wrote that the people of the United States continued to have "a deep interest in the independence of Iran and the prosperity and happiness of her people." After reviewing the Prime Minister's proposed program he said, "I can assure you that we stand ready to help you. . . ."

Events moved at such a pace in September 1953 as to sweep me, for the time being, completely loose from my moorings in the technical co-operation program. An exchange of letters between Ambassador Henderson and the prime minister on September 1 placed the Point 4 program on its firmest footing. The letters acknowledged all the previous agreements, beginning with the one signed on October 19, 1950, by Prime Minister Ali Razmara and Ambassador Henry F. Grady. The notes that I had exchanged with Dr. Mossadegh on January 19 and 20, 1952, were also recognized, as was the December 1952 correspondence relating to all of the project and program agreements. This action by the general and the ambassador removed once and for all the cloud cast by Dr. Mossadegh's refusal to acknowledge the commitment of his predecessor.

When the Joint Commission met on September 2 Dr. Adl assumed its chairmanship.

But a new task now fell to my lot. I had to delegate to other members of the staff more of the responsibility for the basic technical program and spend more and more of my time wrestling with the job of resuscitating the almost completely moribund economy of Iran.

The letters of August 26 between President Eisenhower and the prime minister brought very quick action.

On September 5, 1953, the President announced that in response to her request for urgent aid $45,000,000 had been made available on an emergency basis for immediate economic assistance to Iran. The announcement added that this allotment was in addition to the regular technical assistance and military programs.

The President's message said:

There is great need of immediate assistance to restore a measure of stability and establish a foundation for greater economic development and improvement in the living standards of all the people of Iran. It is hoped that, with our assistance, there will be an increase in the internal stability of Iran which will allow the development of a healthy economy to which an early effective use of Iran's rich resources will contribute.

On the same day General Zahedi expressed his thanks for "much-needed quick action in helping to overcome the financial and economic crisis." He continued:

My government will make every effort to alleviate the existing financial crisis of the country and will be enabled for a limited period of time to take urgent steps to put into effect programs designed to improve the living standards of the Iranian people. In the near future, if we carefully apply ourselves to these programs, we should also be able to make maximum use of our national resources.

Two days later I wrote a note to Dr. Ali Amini, minister of finance, who later was to engender an international reputation as the negotiator of the oil settlement. This note set the pattern for the use of the first of the emergency aid. It contained essential details of how the aid money was to be handled and used. In countersigning it, Dr. Amini made of it an agreement.

The next morning bright and early I called on Dr. Amini in his office. Since we had estimated what the first month's requirement would be I handed him a check drawn on the United States

Treasury for $5,400,000. This he took to the Bank Melli, the state bank of Iran. Immediately 508,000,000 *rials* were deposited to the Ministry's account.

Thus were three achievements recorded at once. The Government of Iran was able for the first time in many months to meet its current obligations. The Bank Melli had foreign exchange to supply to importers. And the black market which had seen dollars selling in July for as much as 132 *rials*, thirty-two above the highest official commercial rate, was immediately eliminated. With these achievements behind us we settled down to the hard work of making use of the time we had bought. Never have I worked more arduously than I did in the next three months. And never have I felt more heavily the weight of the responsibility of any assignment.

The Iranian officials were as green at their internal financing as I was. And we had time neither to assemble a staff nor to deal with any problem except as it cropped up. There were times when success seemed impossible. I almost felt that the patient was so sick that even the shock of applying medicine might kill him.

The exhaustion of the *rials* available in the Bank Melli presented a nightmarish problem. I was caught between the unassailably correct positions of each of two diametrically opposed agencies. The Iranians said that $10,000,000 of the aid should be deposited with the Currency Control Board as backing for an issue of additional *rials*. Washington felt, on the other hand, that this would sterilize the money and would not be constructive use. Mr. A. A. Nasser, governor of Bank Melli, said that the new government's precarious political position ruled out trying to solve the problem in any other way. The two governments finally worked out a compromise, barely in the nick of time, I felt, to forestall a complete collapse, for the bank was having difficulty cashing government checks.

The $10,000,000 was deposited with the Control Board, and

کلیشهٔ چند فراز از نامهٔ رضا کی‌نژاد

۱

برادر عزیزم مهربانم لرد لستر برادر دعایی تو در رنجیرین بدرود گودیک
وس از تندوع در ثرنو کنگو اکان گرد ندیده مرهم میکردند
بسمت کمی دید که زرحمت میخواهم بنویسم وبدرخط سذرت بنویاۀ
در زنو لطورکه بدانی هرروز مرحومی بدرست بوس بام بودم واز بیرد رگل
معت میگردم بنگا از زمان رضا ثمه و دکتور گرفیس خرجل در جهنم
و جنگها کک با برکمس ۶ و در رسال یا روسیا و منده هرروز
رامیم مهر صوری بیبر داخنم - بهم باخبر بجلی کمتر از رامم
درست ودباری دیگر در زندگی خود دستم گذاری بیادم تا چدنی کرداهم
بدادنی سیاسی ابران هراز راضی رضاثه و عملیات دوکده رئیس
و استکه سیع دقت بهس مخاست بودجه برجلکت را بکه جا بصور
کند دهبسه بایک دولدیم بدرد جنید لنو نتولی مجیدرپربدولت
مانع خدربت و پیشرفت دور اقتصادروعر میکردند تاکید کردم
دلت هریم نصدی کردند - تاز باسکه مرحم تراییراسی سیاسوری
انتهاب کردید و علایم علاال شدند - مهم برینی به ابرانبرگیم
وصادرنده در زنو بودند وابادس که در تهران بودم بعتر نوس
دلیرنال بدرعزیزت بودم ولدبردرصحب میگردید وستیر بارزا
نگنید جدردا برگریم بیکردم باکدست زبان مرحم تراییاریاس
بهی بای بصوب گردندانده - واینها بات تهران محمدوس ویراای
بگدید (یسی) بات اقدام بهبر آباد -

۲

۶۱/۱۰/۹
30/12/82

سرور معظم جناب آقای اشرف خان زاهدی

قریب به دو ماه دستخط شریف مورخ ۱۲/۸۲/... چند روز قبل از مراجعت به وصول آن رسید و بنده طبل
تشکر و از شان گهبدص، بعدم آمادگی و دم رستن و صدوقت خون آن رزیشن جواب عرضه بنده
و مرده امیه و لاحمت سه سر و هه محتم پینیر از هر جزو نیل است برای خود و ممد مبتلا بک اخضاء و
و ضعف عصاب و عوارض ناشی از آن که کلأ مربوط بهمین اوضاع نابب آن ایران عزیز و آواره گی
و عدم نظم و ترتیب در منذ نی و آب تیرو مداد ا مینه در مرد ا دیبلمات انگلیسی که نفس را آورد یشی
کرده ام مرار جاب لی العتا بنبیه شده بود وحی سرفته فرمیم بعد که منه نوشته ام اوله
م بت شاه را دعوت کنید و الا ... این مطلب کلأ رستبة ا نیر اولا حی فطع جو د منه
این نکته را احفظ کهم و جوبه در خاطر دارم که ظرفیا بودم و ار ز فرودگا مهرا بادهفوی آن تلقت
کرکیکی پهوایی بدون اطلاع و ظط رفتع ابه بزه فرود پاگوا بزه و مرجع یی راهب زه صادر فرمیعد
با قسم بنفها هی و بمدهم فرمضر بینیم که این انگلیسه هیچو ابزه بعد اشتفی بلا نات کرد و
منه که تهر آن در طلان ت با بد حضور سید کم ادب هم بوجد که عقت نملانات را برم ولی
نیس خودمان سراببه فرمهدآمده بوجد که نیکفت که ما در دعوت ارش محمد نکیم
یا سر فرصت بصمیم گرفته شوم من باد جواب بنی دادم ولی درا واظ انفذا راه کرشا؟
دوست ا نیب را نمی با دادن بلغ مخصر و نفیی انده نشبه کر محمتی معظم پهرا سپز نشم
دیمن گوجب کدوست خا طرشان نش بود خدا مهما را اشفی بریس ما نونت بهواردگی

در مورد اصلاحات ارضی و با یک بندار هم خودش خوب ... طرفدار کرده رسمی که آن تاریخ
سودل ملت عادد و املاک مالکین بزرگ بود ... ۷۰ سال تاریخ که باید بین ایران و ملت بیه منا ... که دوربه
در روزش بین املاک و وصول آن ملائان رنگ خوردن دید جهت نامه

یک بندار هم خودش و ضرورتشان ایران و من بیت که در دنیا در و عراق پنج ملیون و در زحمت بیشم
اگر قرارداد لازم باشد با بند او آخود دار امریکا نیا مسئول با ما عهد باشد و این قرار داد
بطور صحیح و مشروع و قبل اعتبار در مسائل روس شفید بود و له مذکور انش را با کند
در باب ، از هول حلم فردیکی افتاد و حضرت نادر مبارک تصرف و مداخله میشیم در حکومت
وعزل سمیه زاده با امریکا نترسید بود و قبول میکرد که بیدون دام خودم دوام اصلاحات
ارضی کند و باید بعدار اداهم مماکند مشروط را کم بیدو شرایط آن را کار رانگذارد
در گذاریم را که نفر سلطنت و مملک بود دهها هزار رنز خورده ، الکینگنه ، گر او گذشت
شبند ، الکن بزرگم کم بیش سرکت شد ، این جبهه مکل و مدافین بر حسب سلطانی این قسم
سیا آمد ، و چوندیدکنند گلان از امریکا و فرزن قسمت در زان نفردش و ازل ملت
و از زان خود بن گذر که او بندان املاک را تخلیه و ها ۴ را مورد جهوم فوع بلا
و با حسن لا خطره از داران انل انل رفع ا و جهانی ، و د بینه رو رکشی
کروز چها ۴ شیخ وکی رسیده دیمه و خوالطرابهان و الامطرست
اشرف مملکت و ثقل جهه بهار باز ایران عنرر را با بند داد و مذر هنوز هم
طغاوات ناخامیز ، قرا رو در ان نیشه خودآمدم بفک گت مردم از آزار کنم
خط ۲ ی شداست و له با نیه با ایران فکر کنند آ آبردشه لحه دیم دوام و سهار
خیانت انطلیس روس امریکا فی این املگ و زرانه و عن س و مویت
و براز و سردنه خان ، ۱ هم ممترده دیم و انل امنو از مه دا بحر با نیم
و امروز ایوت خالی و کبیر و بسیار رخت ترین املام عمرا مکذ رایم و له دلار ؟
سجاب آمزم مطبه با بگ بره جمع مکله و غازگان هم مشغول عیش کیشدت
از طول مذ ی نخواهم قصد مشغول کردن نیا و سرگرمی تا در ان بر هار رز را
امیدوار م خداوند خودی فرحی برای این ملت سبت برگنده کنه و دوان سیه براهم

۸

تیمسار سپهبد زاهدی نخست وزیر

بنابت روز تاریخی ۲۳ مرداد که فرمان تصدی نخست وزیری معنوان نخست وزیر صادر گردید

و اختیار اجرا بید امحوله که وظیفه حقائرا بانیت تام ملت ایران انجام دهید بوری

برقراری مجدد اصول قانون اساسی دوران کشور را از حکتل مهیب ترین خطرات

توفیق مصدر شد انشاء خداوند موجب این خطط قدر دانا خود را اعلام دارم

۱۳۳۲
۲۳ مرداد

The Zahedis, Father and Son

E. REESEMAN FRYER

To AN AMERICAN who knows the current Iranian Premier, General Fazlollah Zahedi, the most interesting question is how much his twenty-eight-year-old son, Ardeshir, will influence his thinking. The two are constant companions. Now that the father is Premier, the son is his private secretary and official interpreter in meetings with American officials.

General Zahedi has never been in the United States, but Ardeshir Zahedi is one of many young Iranians who have been sent to the Utah State Agricultural College. When the young Shah came to the United States in 1949 Ardeshir accompanied him.

Dr. Franklin S. Harris, the president of the college, had been an adviser to the Iranian government. When the Point Four program was started and Dr. Harris was sent to

19

Iran in 1950 to organize it, the Iranian he selected for his special assistant was Ardeshir Zahedi.

As one of his unofficial duties, young Zahedi took upon himself the job of being host to incoming American technicians and their families. General Zahedi—soldier, landlord, and Senator—entered freely into discussions with them, often expressing skepticism about the quick results the Americans seemed to expect, while his son carried the optimistic side of the argument.

One day General Zahedi invited Dr. Harris and me to stop off at one of his villages. Both of us were impressed. The land was well tilled and the houses in good order. We found the only hospital I have seen in an Iranian village. It was clean and well equipped. The doctor in charge was a well-trained German refugee. We were told that the expense of the hospital was borne entirely by General Zahedi, and that medical services were given free to all peasants. Young Zahedi called it "my father's own Point Four program." Paternalism? Yes, but in Iran a landlord-financed hospital is progress.

In NOVEMBER, 1951, I was invited by General Zahedi and his son to accompany them to Isfahan and from there into the desert country of the Bakhtiari tribes. For four days on the long, dusty ride from Teheran to Isfahan and from Isfahan into the desert I came to know General Zahedi as one man can only get to know another on a camping trip.

He was not then a member of the Cabinet, having resigned a few weeks before as Minister of the Interior. He was still friendly with Mossadegh and supported him, but during our conversations General Zahedi said he believed that Mossadegh was making a great mistake by not moving vigorously to stamp out the Tudeh Party. He said the party was led by Russian-trained Communist agents and unless it was suppressed would become so powerful as to take Iran down the same road as Czechoslovakia.

I pointed out that the promise of land to the peasants was one of the appeals used by the Communists everywhere in the East and asked

how he would propose to counter it. "Land reform," he said. "Some kind of land reform is necessary in Iran. But it must be done in a gradual way. A way must be found to give landlords fair compensation for their land, and the peasants must be trained to assume the responsibilities of landownership and to take the initiative that goes with it." He went on to explain that in Iran capital had always been invested in land;

General Fazlollah Zahedi

that new capital investment opportunities had to be found for the landlords and new values created because, in Iran, prestige and social position were associated with the ownership of land, as contrasted with America and Europe, where business and industry were the goals of investment capital. "Any other approach to land reform," he said, "would lead to chaos and perhaps even to civil war.

"About oil," he said, "we should

find an honorable way to reach a settlement with the British. We cannot keep these resources locked up without losing our markets. But nationalization is an accomplished fact which must be recognized." General Zahedi went on to say that he had perhaps stronger reasons than any other Iranian to dislike the British, but this didn't influence his thinking about the need for a settlement of the oil question.

THE GENERAL's own version of his abduction by the British during the Second World War was somewhat different from the news accounts I had read. He said that it happened at a party in Isfahan. Fitzroy Maclean, the British captain who had orders to kidnap him, was there as a guest and asked to speak to him privately. As they walked outside together, Maclean rammed a pistol in his back and commanded him to enter a sedan in which there were two other British officers. He said that he was handcuffed and driven to a place in the desert where a small airplane was waiting. He was flown to Palestine—to a concentration camp near Bethlehem. The General's eyes flashed and his jaw set as he told how for fourteen months he was held in that camp before being permitted any communication with his family. "I am a soldier," he said, "and can understand some of the things that must be done in wartime, but I will not easily forgive the British for holding me without trial or for keeping my family in suspense. But most of all, I shall never forgive them for stealing my family treasures."

He described how for more than seven hundred years the most treasured heirlooms of the Zahedi family —the medals won by his ancestors, the jewels and special mementos of achievement—had been handed down from father to son; how they were kept in his house in a heavy iron chest. He charged that the British, in his absence, had almost ripped his house apart searching for evidence that would convict him of conspiring with the Nazis (which he heatedly denied doing). He said that he might have forgiven a decent search of his house, "but stealing the ancient heirlooms of my family was something else."

Index